Queer Gothic

Edinburgh Companions to the Gothic

Series Editors
Andrew Smith, University of Sheffield
William Hughes, Bath Spa University

This series provides a comprehensive overview of the Gothic from the eighteenth century to the present day. Each volume takes either a period, place, or theme and explores their diverse attributes, contexts and texts via completely original essays. The volumes provide an authoritative critical tool for both scholars and students of the Gothic.

Volumes in the series are edited by leading scholars in their field and make a cutting-edge contribution to the field of Gothic studies.

Each volume:
- Presents an innovative and critically challenging exploration of the historical, thematic and theoretical understandings of the Gothic from the eighteenth century to the present day
- Provides a critical forum in which ideas about Gothic history and established Gothic themes are challenged
- Supports the teaching of the Gothic at an advanced undergraduate level and at masters level
- Helps readers to rethink ideas concerning periodisation and to question the critical approaches which have been taken to the Gothic

Published Titles

The Victorian Gothic: An Edinburgh Companion
  Andrew Smith and William Hughes

Romantic Gothic: An Edinburgh Companion
  Angela Wright and Dale Townshend

American Gothic Culture: An Edinburgh Companion
  Joel Faflak and Jason Haslam

Women and the Gothic: An Edinburgh Companion
  Avril Horner and Sue Zlosnik

Scottish Gothic: An Edinburgh Companion
  Carol Margaret Davison and Monica Germanà

The Gothic and Theory: An Edinburgh Companion
  Jerrold E. Hogle and Robert Miles

Twenty-First-Century Gothic: An Edinburgh Companion
  Maisha Wester and Xavier Aldana Reyes

Gothic Film: An Edinburgh Companion
  Richard J. Hand and Jay McRoy

Twentieth-Century Gothic: An Edinburgh Companion
  Sorcha Ní Fhlainn and Bernice M. Murphy

Italian Gothic: An Edinburgh Companion
  Marco Malvestio and Stefano Serafini

Irish Gothic: An Edinburgh Companion
  Jarlath Killeen and Christina Morin

Queer Gothic: An Edinburgh Companion
  Ardel Haefele-Thomas

Visit the Edinburgh Companions to the Gothic website at:
www.edinburghuniversitypress.com/series/EDCG

Queer Gothic

An Edinburgh Companion

Edited by
Ardel Haefele-Thomas

EDINBURGH
University Press

Edinburgh University Press is one of the leading university presses in the UK. We publish academic books and journals in our selected subject areas across the humanities and social sciences, combining cutting-edge scholarship with high editorial and production values to produce academic works of lasting importance. For more information visit our website: edinburghuniversitypress.com

© editorial matter and organisation Ardel Haefele-Thomas 2023, 2025
© the chapters their several authors 2023, 2025

Edinburgh University Press Ltd
13 Infirmary Street,
Edinburgh, EH1 1LT

First published in hardback by Edinburgh University Press 2023

Typeset in 10.5/13 Sabon by
by Cheshire Typesetting Ltd, Cuddington, Cheshire

A CIP record for this book is available from the British Library

ISBN 978 1 4744 9438 0 (hardback)
ISBN 978 1 3995 5415 2 (paperback)
ISBN 978 1 4744 9439 7 (webready PDF)
ISBN 978 1 4744 9440 3 (epub)

The right of Ardel Haefele-Thomas to be identified as the editor of this work has been asserted in accordance with the Copyright, Designs and Patents Act 1988, and the Copyright and Related Rights Regulations 2003 (SI No. 2498).

Contents

List of Figures vii
Acknowledgements viii

Introduction to Queer Gothic: 'I would like, if I may, to take you on a strange journey' 1
Ardel Haefele-Thomas

PART I QUEER TIMES

1. Desiring Deformity in the Romantic Gothic 17
   Jeremy Chow

2. Queer Gothic: Romantic Origins and Victorian Innovations 38
   Jolene Zigarovich

3. Strange Cases of the Queer *fin de siècle*: Law, Medicine and the Gothic Imaginative Mode 58
   Jamil Mustafa

4. Gothic Cinema and Sexology in the Weimar Republic: Towards a Queer Gothic Aesthetic on Screen 78
   Dennis Wegner

5. 'Tarting up ideas in costume jewellery': Contemporary Gothic Camp 97
   Thomas Brassington

PART II QUEER MONSTERS

6. Queer Vampires: What We Want is in the Shadows 117
   S. Brooke Cameron

7. Queer Zombies 136
   Xavier Aldana Reyes

8. 'Queer-Wolves and Wolf-Boyz and Were-Bears, Oh My!':
   Queering the Wolf in New Queer Horror Film and TV 154
   Darren Elliott-Smith

9. 'Spectrality is in part a mode of historicity': Representations
   of Spectrality in Queer Historiography and Contemporary
   Fiction 174
   Paulina Palmer

10. Witchcraft, Gender and Queerness in Contemporary
    British Literature 189
    Silvia Antosa

PART III QUEER FORMS

11. Queer Gothic Poetry 209
    Clayton Carlyle Tarr

12. Queer Gothic Visual Art: A Twisted Path from the
    Eighteenth Century to the Twenty-First 226
    Laura Westengard

13. Queering Gothic Slash Fandoms: Harry Potter, Ginger
    Snaps and Worldbuilding 244
    Gregory Luke Chwala

14. Solidarity is More than a Slogan: Queer Representation
    in the Virtual World 262
    Dawn Stobbart

15. 'Y'all ain't from around these parts': Queer Displacement
    in American Folk Horror 279
    Amanda Cruz

16. This is What Queer Resistance Looks Like: AIDS Gothic
    Art 295
    Ardel Haefele-Thomas

Bibliography 313
Filmography 337
Notes on Contributors 339
Index 343

Figures

1 Henry Fuseli, *The Nightmare* (1781). Courtesy of Detroit Institute of Arts — 227
2 William Blake, *The Ghost of a Flea* (1819–20). Courtesy of Tate Images — 228
3 Jordan Eagles, *Illuminations*, installation view, High Line, New York, NY. Photographer David Meanix (2016). Courtesy of the artist — 231
4 Jordan Eagles, *Bloody Nick* (2009). Courtesy of the artist — 232
5 Vaginal Davis, *Fountain of Salmacis* (2015). Courtesy of INVISIBLE-EXPORTS/New Discretions — 235
6 Kiyan Williams, *Dirt Eater* (2019). Courtesy of the artist — 237
7 M. Lamar, *Mapplethorpe's Whip III* (2014). Courtesy of the artist — 239
8 M. Lamar, *Legacies*, video still. Courtesy of the artist — 240
9 M. Lamar, *Negro Antichrist*, video still. Courtesy of the artist — 240

Acknowledgements

To say that this volume took a village is a massive understatement. When I was first asked to edit *Queer Gothic: An Edinburgh Companion*, it was prior to COVID-19. Little did any of us know how much the world and the publishing landscape were going to change. I want to thank Edinburgh University Press for believing in this project, believing in me as the editor, and most importantly over the course of the past few years, being patient and flexible with due dates. EUP are truly a kind and humane lot!

I want to thank Andrew Smith and William Hughes for years of collegiality and friendship. They both have always been incredibly supportive of me and my various Queer Gothic projects. When they approached me to edit this special volume, I did not need to think twice; I am indebted to them and want to give a hearty 'thank you' for asking me to take on this project.

More generally, I would like to thank all of the people at the International Gothic Association Conferences over the years – this is such a supportive academic environment and has truly been my intellectual home for three decades now. Goths tend to be open to all sorts of intellectual inquiries and ideas, and all of the panels and people I have encountered at this welcoming conference have given me such happiness and support.

At Edinburgh University Press, which is always wonderfully supportive, I would like to especially thank Susannah Butler, Fiona Conn, Ersev Ersoy and Elizabeth Fraser for all of their help and guidance at various stages of this process.

I have had two reviewers on this volume, and I would like to thank both of them. Dr Milton W. Wendland at the University of South Florida and I have never met in person; however, he and I have shared teaching tips with regard to our LGBTQ+ studies courses online. The fact that he teaches LGBTQ+ studies in Florida is no small feat given the long history of homophobic and transphobic laws in that state. My other reviewer was Dr Catherine Spooner, Professor of Literature and Culture at Lancaster University. I still remember us riding on a train in London (we were geeky grad students just finishing up the International Gothic Association Conference at Strawberry Hill) in 1997. Now Catherine is one of the leading experts in Gothic Studies, and I am so humbled and grateful that she reviewed this volume. Both reviewers gave me great feedback for improvements.

My fifteen authors! I need to thank them (I am the sixteenth – and am thankful it is finally done). In all seriousness, the authors in this volume have gone through COVID surges, mpox, and all sorts of personal trials, tribulations and uncertainties, and yet they appear before you here in *Queer Gothic: An Edinburgh Companion*. Thank you all for sticking with this project: Jeremy Chow, Jolene Zigarovich, Jamil Mustafa, Dennis Wegner, Thomas Brassington, S. Brooke Cameron, Xavier Aldana Reyes, Darren Elliott-Smith, Paulina Palmer, Silvia Antosa, Clayton Carlyle Tarr, Laura Westengard, Gregory Luke Chwala, Dawn Stobbart and Amanda Cruz. I would like to give a special 'shout out' to Darren Elliott-Smith and Xavier Aldana Reyes because they stepped in when two of the original authors for this book were unable to move forward with contributions.

Finally, I want to thank my family – my spouse, Lisa, and my son, Jalen. I am so thankful every single day to have them in my life.

Dedicated to Paulina Palmer
In Memory of Justin D. Edwards

Introduction to Queer Gothic: 'I would like, if I may, to take you on a strange journey'
Ardel Haefele-Thomas

Queer?

Like this invitation from the beginning of *The Rocky Horror Picture Show*, the journey into the term queer is certainly strange – it is a treacherous path littered with political and theoretical pockets of quicksand. What I mean by this is that the slipperiness of the word and its uses can trick you into a eureka (!) moment while you simultaneously lose your footing and slide down into unbreathable muck. There is no single definition. Kadij Amin and José Esteban Muñoz are two theorists who wrestle with defining 'queer'. As Amin notes, 'Queer theory has long celebrated *queer* as an almost infinitely mobile and mutable theoretical term that . . . need not remain bound to any particular identity, historical context, politics, or object of study and, for that very reason, promises a cutting-edge political intervention.'[1] And, as José Esteban Muñoz argues, 'Queerness is a structuring and educated mode of desiring that allows us to see and feel beyond the quagmire of the present. The here and now is a prison house.'[2] Both Amin's point that queer has been posited to be so vast that it signifies anything – which is part of what purportedly makes it 'cutting-edge' (which Amin actually argues against) – and what appears to be Muñoz's contrary position that queer in the specificity of the present signifies confinement represent the trouble with defining the term. When and where should I start the exploration (but most surely not the definition) of the term queer? Is it vast? Is it confined? The answer must be yes.

'We're Here! We're Queer! Get Used To It!' In 1990, as we were shouting this sentiment out into every public space imaginable in the United States, those of us in Queer Nation were meaning to be disruptive. Slightly two decades beyond the Stonewall Rebellion of 1969 and just a decade into the AIDS pandemic, with no remedy in sight, we were fed up, and the reclaimed term 'queer' was meant to fly in the face of normativity. As a grassroots political term of empowerment for all of those marginalised because of their sexual orientation and/or gender identity, the term queer also became a new theoretical lens through which to view literature, art, culture and history. Queer became an umbrella term for people outside of heteronormativity and cisnormativity. Queer also became another tool for exploring intersectional identities – the ways that race, ethnicity, socio-economic status, age, disability, sexual orientation, gender identity and gender expression could function together. Truly, it began to look as though queer could be all-encompassing. As a new umbrella term, queer was meant to be liberating; queer theory became a way not only to study actual marginalised lives but also to approach literature past, present and future, through a new and nuanced lens – a lens that did not rely on actual, physically embodied sexuality or gender identity. To read something as queer could be to read it as transgressive or different.

Amin rightly problematises queer as a one-size-fits-all model when he notes that 'The use of *queer* as a false umbrella term that, in practice, most often refers to gay white men has often been exposed and critiqued.'[3] Amin is correct with this assertion because the broken umbrella does not truly encompass diversity. Historically, this is nothing new; it is completely reminiscent of the utterly sanitised and normativised retellings of some of the most famous moments of queer resistance – specifically the Stonewall Rebellion of 1969 which is credited as the inception of the modern day LGBTQI2+ rights movement.[4] Here in the twenty-first century, there is an entire mythos surrounding the night a bar room brawl broke out between the New York City Police and the patrons of the Stonewall Inn in New York's Greenwich Village. Anyone wanting to own a piece of history and a piece of queer pride can buy T-shirts, handbags and mugs, or guzzle down a special Stonewall Inn IPA. We are numbed into a sense that current capitalist enterprise can somehow connect us to what were surely tense and terrifying moments in the wee hours of Sunday 28 June 1969 in a run-down bar, when queer patrons – comprised mainly of sex workers of all genders, most of whom were people of colour – decided to fight back against cops raiding the bar to enforce anti-masquerading laws. The police forcefully stripped and beat every gender non-conforming person and their (mostly male) clientele with batons. Who threw the first punch (or the first high heel) is still up for debate, but what is clear is that disenfranchised queer and trans people, collectively, led the rebellion that would herald the beginning of our current LGBTQI2+ rights movement. *But cisnormative and homonormative white gays and lesbians have claimed the actions of that night as specifically theirs*. And, worse, many of the trans women of colour who were in the bar and who *did* start this movement – Sylvia Rivera, Marsha P. Johnson and Miss Major Griffin-Gracy – were shunned by 'gay' community activists almost immediately. They were forsaken by the same community they helped construct and *liberate*.[5]

Amin is correct in his assessment that queer all too often signifies white cisgender gay men and, on occasion, white cisgender lesbians. This is not necessarily what was meant to evolve from a radical political reclamation of a derogatory term, but this is where we find ourselves. We are at the point where there are emerging distinctions between queer *and* trans theories and queer *and* trans studies. Some of the most brilliant and radical work being done in the early twenty-first century is via intersectional trans work.[6] For myself, as a trans and queer person, but also a trans and queer theorist, when I was first approached to edit this volume, I wrestled with the broken umbrella of queer – and I still do. The loaded question for me reflects one of Amin's main points, that queer is 'a term *sticky* with history, one that bears the impression, in its characteristic gestures, dispositions, and orientations, of its travels in time and space'.[7] According to Amin, queer is stuck in 1990s nostalgia, and this 'stuckness' should force us to ask if queer, as a term, can still serve us.

I think if we hold to the past, the answer is no. However, I also take great hope from Muñoz's argument that 'Queer is not yet here. Queerness is an ideality ... the future is queerness's domain.'[8] We need to push beyond this current moment of queer being subsumed by the pressure to sanitise and normativise. In the first two decades of the twenty-first century, we seem to have forgotten our origins. Queer has had all of the sex bled out of it in order for LGBTQI2+ people to be 'presentable' for prime time. AIDS is something over and done with (it is not, actually). Love is Love. We run to the next rally when a baker in Colorado refuses to make a wedding cake for a gay male couple because it was her religious right to deny them. Of course, I understand the problem with her refusal – and it smacks of other rejections of people and communities historically marginalised and denied civil rights. But that wedding cake is a first world problem. In 2022 there were over seventy countries that still criminalised queer and trans people – and many of these impose the death penalty for any type of queer and/or non-gender-normative activity.[9] With the mad dash down the marriage equality aisle specifically (not just in the United States, but globally), we need to ask ourselves – normativisation at what cost? Who and what has been cast aside as less important – discarded as detritus on our way to play happy families? We never should have let ourselves be seduced by the idea of a single-issue movement.

Gothic?

Gothic may be more elusive than queer; I say this only because endeavours to define Gothic have been underway far longer than attempts to define queer. Do we just know something is Gothic when its uncanny clammy hand touches us? (Or is it a long red fingernail scraping our cheek that sends terrifying and anticipatory chills?) As Frankenfurter tells the lost and hapless Brad and Janet, 'I see you shiver with anticipation.' In his Introduction to *The Edinburgh Companion to Gothic and the Arts*, David Punter asks 'What is the Gothic?'[10] As it turns out, Punter's question is rhetorical; he explains that neither he nor the book 'aim to answer'.[11] In his *Key Concepts in the Gothic*, William Hughes explains that the term Gothic comes from a strange imbrication of the Goths – 'warlike Germanic people whose destructive activities' ushered in the Dark Ages – and 'northern European architecture that flourished from the twelfth century CE'.[12] Hughes acknowledges this complex origin: 'Herein lies the paradox of the term, for if the tribal name of the Goths carries a negative cultural charge . . . Gothic *architecture* is frequently positivised.'[13] From its inception as a literary (and then also as an art and cinematic) form, Gothic arrived confused. Or, if not confused, certainly difficult to clearly define – not at all unlike queer.

Punter further elaborates that

> Gothic, it has often been said, is that which is opposed to the classical; it deals in opposition to rules, resistance to regulation. And this, like most things said about the Gothic, is a partial truth – but only partial, because Gothic also has its own rules . . . Gothic plays by *different* rules . . . when confronted by the limitations of the law, Gothic frequently chooses the side of the outlaw, the exile . . .[14]

In my own previous work on queer Victorian Gothic, I have argued that the 'strength of Gothic rests upon its being a liminal genre'.[15] As a genre, Gothic thrives on liminal spaces, marginalised situations, non-normative characters and taboo practices. Gothic is all about defying the norm (even as it sets up, as Punter suggests, its own norms). These understandings that Gothic is a term rife with 'paradox', a form that plays by 'its own rules', and a genre that has thrived in liminal spaces – indeed, a genre that aligns with outlaws and exiles – renders it a rich site to cultivate queer themes, and to produce Queer Gothic.

Queer Gothic?

In his groundbreaking book *Queer Gothic* (2006), George Haggerty explains that queer and Gothic consort well together because, as a genre, 'gothic fiction reached its apex at the very moment when gender and sexuality were beginning to be codified for modern culture'.[16] Gothic fiction itself was a bit of an outlaw, because it employs situations well beyond 'proper' sexual or gendered norms. Haggerty places queer Gothic fiction within a very specific historical context and offers queer Gothic modes up as experimental and transgressive. Three years after Haggerty's work, William Hughes and Andrew Smith edited *Queering the Gothic* (2009), a compilation of essays exploring diverse applications of the term queer to Gothic works. As Hughes and Smith argue in their introduction, 'Gothic has, in a sense, always been "queer." The genre ... has been characteristically perceived in criticism as being poised astride the uneasy cultural boundary that separates the acceptable and familiar from the troubling and different.'[17] They also problematise 'queer' as a term similar to Gothic in that

> it will exist in a tense space between referential associations with the normative and absolute separation from its morals and aesthetics. To be queer is to be different, yet it is also to be unavoidably associated with the non-queer, the normative which, though it implicitly represses through mechanisms of conformist culture, may yet serve as the catalyst to liberation.[18]

Queer frameworks could clearly be used to explore Gothic stories that relied on the 'troubling and different' to create the Gothic tension – the Gothic horror. Richard Marsh's *The Beetle* (1897) provides a perfect example of this: a pansexual, gender-shifting and species-shifting Egyptian scarab wreaks havoc on the streets of London as it assaults (with heavy sexual innuendo) respectable Anglo-British men and women. In Marsh's *fin-de-siècle* piece, the Beetle's race, fluctuating gender and overall queerness are the horror.

However, queer theory and queer possibilities have also allowed us to read other Gothic texts as subversive and empowering. As I argue in *Queer Others in Victorian Gothic: Transgressing Monstrosity* (2012), Elizabeth Gaskell often turned to Gothic as a genre for some of her more feminist and socially progressive ideas. In 'The Grey Woman' (1861), for example, the reader mourns the death of the servant-class trans and queer character at the hands of the heteronormative and cisnormative killer. One would think that normative Victorian society would have readers applauding the murder; however, our Mrs Gaskell cleverly had these Victorian readers mourn the death of Amante, the queer and trans figure.

As early as the mid-1990s at the International Gothic Association Conference, scholars were utilising queer theoretical frameworks to explore Gothic. Even before this, writers such as Paulina Palmer (who has an essay in this volume) were already exploring the ways that Gothic, as a rebellious literary genre, could embrace those marginalised by their sexual orientation and/or their gender identity/presentation. Gothic is inherently queer and Gothic forms can certainly lend themselves to being read as queer. Earlier works in queer Gothic set about proving the ways that various texts *could* be read as queer. Haggerty's *Queer Gothic*, Hughes and Smith's edited collection *Queering the Gothic* and my own *Queer Others in Victorian Gothic* were necessary in exploring a new field and setting the groundwork – because in the 'early days', proving that various queer readings could be done with Gothic texts was critical. The starting point of acknowledging that something can exist is always essential; however, not to move beyond this point is to become stuck. Fortunately, it may be that the Gothic's longevity and constant evolution can shine a light on the path that the term queer must also take. It is the Gothic impetus in queer Gothic that motivates a constant reinvention; of particular note are *Transgothic in Literature and Culture* (2018), edited by Jolene Zigarovich, and Laura Westengard's *Queer Gothic Culture: Marginalized Communities and the Ghosts of Insidious Trauma* (2019). Both Zigarovich and Westengard appear in this volume.

To engage in Queer Gothic is to constantly call the phrase as well as the two terms individually into question. What is Queer Gothic? What does it mean to queer Gothic? Or, for that matter, what does it mean to gothic Queer? What do queer and Gothic get us heuristically and pragmatically as modes of analysis? Each of the authors in this volume engage with these questions as this book attempts to move towards Muñoz's notion of a queer futurity – in this case, a Queer Gothic future that I hope reinvigorates the field of study. With all of these questions about the fluidity of Queer Gothic in mind, I would like to turn now to *Queer Gothic* and the diverse range of essays from the authors. This book is divided into three sections: Queer Times, Queer Monsters and Queer Forms.

The five chapters that comprise 'Queer Times' range from the Romantic Gothic through the second decade of the twenty-first century. Although each of these chapters is rooted in a specific time frame, the issues that each chapter covers weave together past, present and future. The first is Jeremy Chow's 'Desiring Deformity in the Romantic Gothic', in which he explores Queer Gothic via Queer Disability theories as he considers canonical texts such as Horace Walpole's *The Castle of Otranto* (1764) and M. G. Lewis's *The Monk* (1796). However, the main text that serves as Chow's lens is Donatien Alphonse François, Marquis de Sade's *The 120 Days of Sodom* (*Les 120 Journées de Sodome*), which was written in 1785 (while Sade was imprisoned), but not published until 1901. As Chow notes, 'this chapter elucidates the literary and material realms by which representations of deformity, womanhood and sexuality cohere in the Romantic Gothic ... I am thus interested in frameworks of queer disability studies.' Chow's unflinching look at the ways that queer disability and, for Sade, queer filth are embraced in the text sets a new tone in Queer Gothic – one unafraid to embrace graphic, 'taboo' sexual encounters. More to the point, however, Chow, via Sade, sheds new light on two staples of queer Romantic Gothic inquiry – Walpole and Lewis. Sade's tome began to rot over decades hidden in the dank prison walls; however, it was still written very much within that Romantic Gothic time period, although it was not delivered to readers until the twentieth century. In this case, queer time and space à la Jack Halberstam truly is fluid.[19]

In the second chapter, 'Queer Gothic: Romantic Origins and Victorian Innovations', Jolene Zigarovich outlines queer Romantic Gothic in Charlotte Dacre's *Zafloya, or, The Moor* (1806) from the beginning of the 'long' nineteenth century. Zigarovich writes, 'Pleasurable and monstrous, violent and homophobic, Romantic Gothic challenges what later will be "immoral" sexualities. Instituting a "monstrous sexuality" in the face of a growing sexual binary culture, these texts also provocatively explore queerness before modern moral panics and anxieties are formalised in the Victorian era.' After considering *Zafloya* and Mary Shelley's *Frankenstein: or, The Modern Prometheus* (1818), Zigarovich begins her Victorian study with a look at the queer figure of Bertha in Charlotte Brontë's *Jane Eyre* (1847), and the very problematic ways in which Jane describes Bertha with a blend of erotic and imperial language *as well as* a 'queer voyeurism and desire'. (So much for any argument focusing on the purported purity of Miss Jane Eyre!) From Brontë, Zigarovich moves to Wilkie Collins's *The Woman in White* (which has, historically, given queer theorists hours of pleasure – especially in the form of the queer and gender-fluid Marian Halcombe) and *The Law and the Lady* with a focus on the non-binary disabled character of Miserrimus Dexter. The chapter concludes with an exploration of the Queer Gothic bonds between Lizzie Hexam and Jenny Wren in Charles Dickens's last complete novel, *Our Mutual Friend* (1865).

Jamil Mustafa's 'Strange Cases of the Queer *fin de siècle*: Law, Medicine and the Gothic Imaginative Mode' ushers us to the end of the nineteenth century in Queer British Gothic. This time period, and these works specifically, have enjoyed a lot of attention from Queer Gothic theorists; however, Mustafa illuminates new connections and illustrates the myriad ways that juridical and medical language and ideas around criminality, disease and homosexuality play out in Robert Louis Stevenson's *Strange Case of Dr Jekyll and Mr Hyde* (1886), Arthur Machen's *The Great God Pan* (1894) and Bram Stoker's *Dracula* (1897). As Mustafa notes, 'the concept of queerness-as-monstrosity exemplifies how in the *fin de siècle* law, medicine and the Gothic functioned as discursive doppelgängers'. While these texts may represent ultimate examples of fiction in late Victorian Queer Gothic horror, Mustafa also examines Richard von Krafft-Ebing's scientific tome on deviant sexuality, *Psychopathia Sexualis* (1886), as another 'strange case' that, through medical jargon, also makes congenital homosexuality and transsexuality monstrous. The overlap between patients' lived experiences and Krafft-Ebing's reporting of them and the queer fictional characters is profound, and means to ask the reader to consider the ways that laws (which were in part informed by the sexologists) and medical practices not only informed literature, *but the ways that literature informed legal and medical 'truths' and policies.*

Chapter 4 continues to probe Queer Gothic through a sexological lens, but with different results. Dennis Wegner's 'Gothic Cinema and Sexology in the Weimar Republic: Towards a Queer Gothic Aesthetic on Screen' comes to Queer Gothic between 1910 and 1960 via the evolving science of sexology and German cinema produced during the Weimar Republic. Magnus Hirschfeld, who was a student of Krafft-Ebing's, was a gay and Jewish sexologist who headed the Institut für Sexualwissenschaft (Institute for Sexual Studies) in Berlin during the Weimar Republic, prior to the Nazi Party burning the institution down in 1933. Hirschfeld's Institut was one of the reasons that Weimar Berlin has often been seen as one of the most open and queer places to have ever existed. While Wegner analyses German Gothic horror films such as *The Student of Prague* (1913) with its sinister doppelgänger, and the vampiric *Nosferatu: A Symphony of Horror* (1922) for underlying queer readings, he also brings a fresh Gothic perspective to a 1919 queer sex education film featuring Magnus Hirschfeld that was nearly destroyed: *Anders als die Andern (Different from the Others)*.

'Queer Times' concludes with Thomas Brassington's '"Tarting up ideas in costume jewellery": Contemporary Gothic Camp', which explores Gothic camp from 1960 into the twenty-first century. Brassington begins with a look at Sue Zlosnik and Avril Horner's feminist essay about the ways in which older women are often presented as abject in Gothic texts in order to focus on a stock camp figure: the fag hag in Gothic representations. From there, they delve into queer heterosexual family structures via the Addams Family films from the 1990s. Brassington then shifts focus to Black drag queens, who, they argue convincingly, invented camp as they take a look at the campy 1972 *Blacula*, with its blend of vampire and Blaxploitation genres, alongside the twenty-first-century American television show *Pose*, which 'uses Gothic camp to draw attention to systemic injustices and the actions of minoritarian groups'. They conclude the chapter with a look at feminist Gothic camp in *Jennifer's Body* (2009) and the various iterations of *Elvira, Mistress of the Dark*.

The chapters in the second section of this book focus on 'Queer Monsters', beginning with S. Brooke Cameron's 'Queer Vampires: What We Want is in the Shadows'. Cameron's essay begins with Polidori's 1819 *The Vampyre*, in which she considers homoeroticism and friendship within the structure of the vampire tale. From the position of 'friend' and companion, Cameron then traces the trajectory of queer vampire tales through the nineteenth century, where queer vampires of all genders are most often considered fearsome fiends (although there are some excellent questions about the ways in which Le Fanu's Laura might still be pining for Carmilla). As Cameron moves into the twentieth century, she considers two mainstays in creepy depictions of vampiric women: *Dracula's Daughter* (1936) and *Rebecca* (1940), both of which were subject to the Hollywood Hays Code that censored queer themes in American film. From these coded queer films, Cameron moves on to various 1970s international films that include queer women vampires who hearken back to J. S. Le Fanu's *Carmilla*, as some of them also dwell on BDSM imagery: *The Vampire Lovers* (1970), which is a bodice ripper, and *Vampyros Lesbos* (1971), which includes scenes from a queer BDSM club performance. In looking at more contemporary works both from the mainstream (Anne Rice's books) and from an independent queer press focused on pulp fiction (Bold Strokes Books), Cameron traces the ways that the figure of the queer vampire has morphed over time and, in a circular fashion, has gone from friend to fiend and back to friend here in the twenty-first century.

In the second chapter of this section, 'Queer Zombies', Xavier Aldana Reyes utilises 'recent examples of the gay zombie to illustrate the main ways in which this figure has been used to mediate homosexual panic, as is typical of the queer monster, but also anxieties that emerge from within queer communities'. Through the queer theories of Jack Halberstam, José Esteban Muñoz and Lorenzo Bernini, Aldana Reyes contemplates the zombie apocalypse as a 'fictional temporal construct through which it becomes possible to conceive of urgent communitarian forms of queer politics'. Zombie narratives investigated here are the BBC television series *In the Flesh* (2013–14), the Irish film *The Cured* (2017) and the radical queer films of Canadian director Bruce LaBruce, who created *Otto; Or, Up with Dead People* (2008) and *L.A. Zombie* (2010). Aldana Reyes looks specifically to the ways that queer sex needs to be explored outside of the normative parameters that have been choking queer sexuality, and suggests that we need to 'celebrate the transgressive qualities' of queer sex.

Reclaiming queer sex and queer fetishes outside of 'normative' parameters is also the work undertaken by Darren Elliott-Smith in his chapter entitled '"Queer-Wolves and Wolf-Boyz and Were-Bears, Oh My!": Queering the Wolf in New Queer Horror Film and TV'. Elliott-Smith's essay considers four main concerns focused on the queer werewolf: werewolf transformations that represent the ways culture fails in repressing queer desires; 'queerwolves' who are subsumed by hypermasculinity – one could argue toxic masculinity – and who demonstrate 'effeminaphobia'; explorations of the celebration of the hypermasculine 'daddy-wolf' and 'were-bears'; and, finally, trans possibilities for the werewolf. With this essay, Elliott-Smith explores critical issues around stereotypes about queer men, specifically, and the internalised homophobia (and what he refers to as effeminaphobia) that can tend to play out in hypermasculinised situations. His essay's exploration of Bear culture also presents a nuanced queer way of looking at werewolves.

Paulina Palmer's '"Spectrality is, in part, a mode of historicity": Representations of Spectrality in Queer Historiography and Contemporary Fiction' utilises Carla Frecerro's *Queer/Early/Modern* as a theoretical lens through which to inspect queer spectrality in Jeannine Allard's *Légende: The Story of Philippa and Aurelie* (1984), Rebecca S. Buck's *Ghosts of Winter* (2011), Jameson Currier's short story, 'The Country House' (2007) and Rosie Garland's *The Night Brother* (2017). The stories Palmer has chosen all feature contemporary queer characters who are haunted by queer ghosts from the past. This is a theme found in many LGBTQI2+ Gothic literary works post-1969, and exemplifies the notion that history is not linear. Palmer's intertwining the queer spectral with queer historiography opens up new avenues through which to understand queer literature and queer history.

The 'Queer Monsters' section concludes with Silvia Antosa's chapter exploring queer witches: 'Witchcraft, Gender and Queerness in Contemporary British Literature'. Antosa centres her essay on four contemporary British women authors as they 'reinterpret the versatile and iconic figure of the witch through a queer Gothic lens'. The authors and works considered in this chapter are Jeanette Winterson's novel focusing on the Lancashire witches, *The Daylight Gate* (2012); Carol Ann Duffy's poem 'The Lancashire Witches' (2012), which now graces stone pillars along the path the Lancashire witches were said to have trod on their way to execution; Emma Donoghue's 1997 collection of fairy tales, *Kissing the Witch: Old Tales in New Skins*; and Rebecca Tamàs's collection of poems *Witch*, published in 2019 in conjunction with the pagan festival of the Spring Equinox. Through these four diverse and feminist examples of perspectives on queer witches, Antosa explores the obvious queer sexual practices as well as the more covert trans, pansexual and polyamorous possibilities that underly these creative imaginings.

The final section of *Queer Gothic* concentrates on 'Queer Forms', mapping out various Queer Gothic genres or modes of delivery. Clayton Carlyle Tarr's chapter, 'Queer Gothic Poetry', begins this section with his statement, 'the adjectives in this title are tautological because queer poetry is Gothic, and Gothic poetry, queer'. Tarr notes that poetry has often been left aside in studies of Gothic, and his work here is to map out explorations of Queer Gothic poetry that we should consider: 'It is my hope that, rather than limit queer Gothic poetry to a selection of poems from a narrow historical period, these sections instigate a conversation to identify a new genre that is fluid, dynamic, and expansive.' Beginning with Samuel Taylor Coleridge's 'Kubla Kahn' (1797) and tracing through canonical Romantic and Victorian poets, Tarr posits that their forms as well as their content can be read in a queer light. For his second section, Tarr concentrates on the ways that Sapphic desire and Sapphic ballads have come to us through Gothic poetry – most notably Coleridge's haunting *Christabel* (1797) and Christina Rosetti's *Goblin Market* (1862). Finally, in looking at sadomasochism and cannibalism within a Queer Gothic frame, Tarr concludes with Charles Algernon Swinburne's 1866 'Anactoria'.

In the second chapter of this section, Laura Westengard delves into the rich world of Queer Gothic visual art in 'Queer Gothic Visual Art: A Twisted Path from the Eighteenth Century to the Twenty-First'. Westengard begins by analysing Henry Fuseli's 1781 painting *The Nightmare* as a starting point for exploring the emergence of a Queer Gothic aesthetic. In setting up a history of this specific type of aesthetic, Westengard also includes William Blake's 1819–20 *The Ghost of a Flea*. By exploring these late eighteenth- and early nineteenth-century pieces, Westengard also ties visual art to the emergence of Gothic literature by connecting the queer visual aesthetics to the queer aesthetics of the written word in works such as Walpole's *The Castle of Otranto* (1764), Shelley's *Frankenstein; or, The Modern Prometheus* (1818) and Polidori's *The Vampyre* (1819). From this starting point, Westengard's essay moves quickly into twenty-first-century Queer Gothic art, including the work of Jordan Eagles, a white queer artist who utilises blood as his medium and public spaces as his canvas in order to explore continuing blood donation bans against men who have sex with men. Other artists considered are the intersex Black sculptor Vaginal Davis and her *Fountain of Salmacis*, in which she utilises cosmetic products to create grotesque images; Kiyan Williams's installations that use dirt as a medium to interrogate Black trans postcolonial issues; and M. Lamar's queer 'Negrogothic' installations.

Following Queer Gothic visual arts is Gregory Luke Chwala's look at slash fiction in 'Queering Gothic Slash Fandoms: Harry Potter, Ginger Snaps and Worldbuilding'. Chwala begins with a critical look at J. K. Rowling's inflammatory transphobic comments alongside the massive popularity of numerous iterations of the *Harry Potter* tales turned into Queer Gothic slash fiction and visual art (manips and vids). Chwala notes that 'Queer Gothic fiction has always functioned in a truly revolutionary way to question illegitimacy and promote change, but online slash fiction is particularly fertile ground for the visibility and validation of LGBTQIA+ identities because of its capacity for worldbuilding.' The *Harry Potter* slash fiction ranges from works appropriate for teenagers to adult porn sites – but all of the representations embrace queer themes. While the *Harry Potter* series tends to be focused mainly on queer masculine eroticism, the femslash found in *Ginger Snaps* focuses on queer female scenarios and, in popularity, is second only to the *Buffy the Vampire Slayer* femslash. Chwala's main argument is that slash fiction can build inclusive worlds for queer and trans people in order to see themselves in a positive light.

The ability for queer and trans people to see themselves reflected back is equally important in what has been the very cisnormative and heteronormative masculine arena of Gothic video games. Dawn Stobbart's chapter on virtual Queer Gothic, 'Solidarity is More than a Slogan: Queer Representation in the Virtual World', examines current Queer Gothic video games that focus on positive and empowering aspects of the gaming experience. After a brief history of video gaming and gamers (people often also marginalised for preferring virtual worlds), Stobbart goes into depth on games such as *Tell Me Why*, which focuses on a trans protagonist, and *The Last of Us 2*, which offers numerous Queer Gothic possibilities. One of the main points that Stobbart explores throughout is queer solidarity within the constructs of Gothic and the ways that queer aesthetics and Gothic aesthetics come together in the most recent cutting-edge virtual Queer Gothic – and the good news is that this area continues to expand with new games.

Folk horror is another area that has tended to focus on heteronormative situations; however, as Amanda Cruz notes in her chapter entitled '"Y'all ain't from around these parts": Queer Displacement in American Folk Horror', there is a growing body of work that explores queer subjectivity in folk horror narratives. Cruz's focus is on American works, and she begins by reconsidering Thomas Tryon's 1973 classic *Harvest Home* in light of queer possibilities. Cruz's reading of the text looks to the queering of a heteronormative family situation when they relocate from an urban space to a rural town in New England – a town that carries out strange pagan rituals that unbalance the heterosexual and patriarchal family structure. She also considers the closeting of Thomas Tryon himself, who was gay and who died from AIDS-related complications in 1991. From mapping out queer readings in a covertly queer text, Cruz proceeds to look at the ways queer authors have taken folk horror and applied Queer Gothic modes to the genre in Simon Strantzas' 'The King of Stones' and the 2006 young adult book *Dark Harvest*.

Finally, in my own chapter, 'This is What Queer Resistance Looks Like: AIDS Gothic Art', I consider the ways that AIDS has been, from 1981 onwards, read as not only a queer disease, but a Gothic disease. I begin with a look at Jonathan Demme's mainstream Hollywood AIDS film *Philadelphia* (1993), which is not Gothic but utilises Gothic modes to make the protagonist with AIDS a Gothic monstrosity. In the case of this film, I argue, Gothic is weaponised to further a homophobic Hollywood agenda – one that holds (queer) people with AIDS at a distance and considers them to be less than human. From this example, I turn to five artists who resist normative narratives, utilising their queer and sick embodiment to embrace their own perceived queer diseased monstrosity. The artists considered in my chapter are David Wojnarowicz (with Goth music by Diamanda Galás), Ron Athey, Valerie Caris Blitz, Maxime Angel Starling and Luna Luis Ortiz.

It is my hope that the essays in this volume aid the evolution of Queer Gothic theories and that, through the volume as a whole, we are able to visualise the construction of the next iteration of Queer Gothic. Considering José Esteban Muñoz, I would like to think that maybe, like queer, Queer Gothic has not completely arrived yet – it is not something for this present moment. It is my hope that the chapters in this volume will act as those proverbial breadcrumbs that continue to lead us on our way – towards more nuanced forms of Queer Gothic somewhere out there in the future.

Notes

1. Kadji Amin, 'Haunted by the 1990s: Queer Theory's Affective Histories', *Women's Studies Quarterly*, 44.3/4 (2016), pp. 173–89 (p. 175).
2. José Esteban Muñoz, *Cruising Utopia: The Then and There of Queer Futurity* (New York: NYU Press, 2009), p. 1.
3. Amin, 'Haunted by the 1990s', p. 178.
4. LGBTQI2+ denotes the 'alphabet soup' of identities: lesbian, gay, bisexual, transgender, queer, intersex and Two Spirit, which is the term chosen by Indigenous people of the Americas. This is an ever-growing acronym, so the + is there to indicate continuing possibilities.
5. There are numerous sources that discuss the white, cisnormative and homonormative washing of the Stonewall Rebellion. I have covered this topic in chapter 4 of *Introduction to Transgender Studies* (New York: Columbia University Press, 2019), pp. 130–68. See also Jessi Gan, '"Still at the Back of the Bus": Sylvia Rivera's Struggle', in *The Transgender Studies Reader 2*, ed. Susan Stryker and Aren Z. Aizura (New York: Routledge, 2013), pp. 291–301. There are numerous resources online, including videos that also discuss these issues. Most notably, in a 2019 filmed interview about the 50th anniversary of the Stonewall Rebellion, Miss Major Griffin-Gracy, a Black trans woman and one of the few Stonewall veterans still alive, gives a scathing account of the ways that gender diverse people – specifically people of colour – have been left out of the history. See particularly the Trans Oral History Project: https://www.youtube.com/watch?v=O8gKdAOQyyI (accessed 10 April 2022).
6. See Andrea Jenkins and the Trans Oral History Project.
7. Amin, 'Haunted by the 1990s', p. 181.
8. Muñoz, *Cruising Utopia*, p. 1.
9. Map of countries that criminalise LGBT people, https://www.humandignitytrust.org/lgbt-the-law/map-of-criminalisation/ (accessed 6 April 2022).
10. David Punter, 'Introduction', in *The Edinburgh Companion to Gothic and the Arts*, ed. David Punter (Edinburgh: Edinburgh University Press, 2019), pp. 1–11 (p. 1).
11. Ibid., p. 1.
12. William Hughes, *Key Concepts in the Gothic* (Edinburgh: Edinburgh University Press, 2018), p. 3.
13. Ibid., p. 3.
14. Punter, 'Introduction', p. 2.
15. Ardel Haefele-Thomas, *Queer Others in Victorian Gothic: Transgressing Monstrosity* (Cardiff: University of Wales Press, 2012), p. 3.
16. George Haggerty, *Queer Gothic* (Urbana, IL: University of Illinois Press), p. 2.
17. William Hughes and Andrew Smith (eds), *Queering the Gothic* (Manchester: Manchester University Press, 2009), p. 1.
18. Ibid., p. 3.
19. See Jack Halberstam, *In a Queer Time and Place: Transgender Bodies, Subcultural Lives* (New York: NYU Press, 2005).

Part I

Queer Times

Chapter 1

Desiring Deformity in the Romantic Gothic
Jeremy Chow

'And now, friend-reader, you must prepare your heart and your mind for the most impure tale that has ever been told since our world began.'[1] So writes the naughty narrator of Donatien Alphonse François, Marquis de Sade's *The 120 Days of Sodom* (*Les 120 Journées de Sodome*), a text authored during Sade's imprisonment in the Bastille in 1785; unfinished, ensconced in his cell wall and believed destroyed; and then discovered and not fully published until 1904. Despite decades-long censorship, it was declared a *trésor national* by the French government in 2017; indeed Foucault's seminal *The History of Sexuality: Volume 1* opens and closes with nods to Sade.[2]

This erotic masterpiece is not for the faint of heart, squeamish, puritanical or anti-sex crowd. Over four months, four obscenely wealthy libertines enact their most dastardly passions and desires on a coterie of sylphs, ephebes and wives. Nothing is too transgressive for the four, who regularly entertain and engage in sexual violence, incest, pederasty, BDSM, murder, conspiracy, abduction and countless other fetishistic sins. The quartet are accommodated by a group of eight massively endowed 'fuckers' and four unrepentant procuresses, each uglier than the last. The procuresses are introduced by a preface that warns the reader to 'banish all expectation of beauties portrayed [. . .] neither their charms nor their years were the deciding factors, but rather their minds and their experience only be counted, and with what regards the latter [Madame Desgranges], our friends could not possibly have made better choices'.[3] Of the four wizened prostitutes, two bear the marks of pronounced deformity that might characterise such a prefatory warning of ugliness: Madame Martaine and Madame Desgranges. Martaine's life had been devoted 'to sodomitical debauch, and [she] was so well familiarized therewith she tasted absolutely no joy save therefrom. A natural deformity (she had also been blessed with an obstruction) having prevented her from knowing any other, she had given herself over to this kind of pleasure.'[4] Madame Desgranges, on the other hand, possesses an

> ass withered, worn, marked, torn, more resembled marbled paper than human skin, and its hole was so gaping sprung, and rugose that the bulkiest machines could, without her knowing a thing, penetrate it dry. By way of crowning graces, this generous Cytherean athlete, wounded in several combats, was missing one nipple and three fingers. She limped, and was without six teeth and an eye.[5]

Desgranges is 'vice and lust personified'.[6]

This chapter opens with these deliciously crude descriptions to pinpoint how the procuresses' deformed bodies trigger vast opportunities by which to apprehend their erotic preponderance. Deformity, of course, is eighteenth-century parlance for what we now term disability. Helen Deutsch observes that in the eighteenth century,

> Deformity encapsulates the paradox of a visible sign of unintelligibility, a fall from form written by God or nature on the body. It is linked conceptually with 'monstrosity,' which is derived from *monstra*, meaning a warning or a portent of catastrophe to come. 'Deformity,' like 'monstrosity,' is at once sign and story.[7]

The eighteenth-century attention to deformity is meant to be parodic, satirical and downright risible. Simon Dickie, however, cautions us against attempting to conflate all modes of embodied deformity under the contemporary umbrella of disability – there is necessity in specificity. Nonetheless, Dickie acknowledges that 'tormenting the disabled remained ubiquitous and automatic in eighteenth-century culture; printed epigrams and stage routines were profitable parts of its entertainment economy'.[8] Case in point: Sade frames *The 120 Days of Sodom* as a performance – it is a robust entertainment economy that apes all the trappings of the stage and theatre (of which Sade was a regular consumer prior to his incarceration). The narrative introduction of the four libertines, their procuresses and their cast of victims is only in anticipation of the *dramatis personae* that appears immediately before the days commence. In the *dramatis personae*, these elaborate descriptions and reminders of the procuresses' deformities bear repeating. They are replicated almost verbatim. Do not forget, these repetitions seem to reason, these repudiations of able-bodiedness.

This chapter elucidates the literary and material realms by which representations of deformity, womanhood and sexuality cohere in the Romantic Gothic – a genre that I suggest begins with Horace Walpole's

The Castle of Otranto (1764) and bleeds into the early nineteenth century. I am thus interested in frameworks of queer disability studies that have been deftly articulated by Robert McRuer, Alison Kafer, Anna Mollow and Eli Clare.[9] Jason Farr has more recently demonstrated the necessity of this intersectional framework for eighteenth-century studies. In *Novel Bodies*, Farr notes that the recuperative, epithetic use of 'queer' and 'crip' 'undermine the systemic consolidation of heterosexuality and able-bodiedness. Because they are aligned with queerness in this way, crip bodies contest the logic of heteronormativity.'[10] In this mode, and as I have shown elsewhere, specifically with regard to figurations of the eunuch, queer disability intersections enliven opportunities to visualise the deformed eighteenth-century body not as an embodiment predicated on lack or loss but one that is afforded new modes of agency, mobility and autonomy.[11] Extending this work here, I explore how the deformed female body becomes a eroticising lacuna by which to imagine modes of desirability that are predicated on the intersections of disability, age and womanhood. Sade's Madame Desgranges offers a paradigm by which to examine this nexus, though I am not interested in upholding Desgranges or any of the other women discussed here as 'supercrips', a term Clare glosses as a rhetorical exaltation of disabled peoples who 'overcome' their disabilities, thus reinforcing the superiority of the non-disabled body and mind and ultimately 'turn[ing] disabled people, who are simply leading their lives, into [exclusive] symbols of inspiration'.[12] By centring my attention on the erotic lives of the deformed female body, this chapter responds to Tim Dean's criticisms of recent strands of queer theory as unnecessarily sanitised, bereft of the sex that constitutes sexuality and too esoterically abstract. Dean avers, 'There is something about sex – understood not as anatomical difference but as erotic practice – that many scholars in Queer studies find oddly aversive.'[13] By tackling Sade's most provocative work head-on, I seek to reposition sex acts as vital to understanding queer theory and disability studies, especially as they manifest in Gothic narratives that never bat an eye at visions of soft- and hardcore pornography.

But what of the Gothic? While *120 Days of Sodom* is not traditionally positioned within the trajectory of Romantic Gothic, this essay places this banned tome firmly in a Gothic lineage. As Simone de Beauvoir documents in her trenchant foreword 'Must We Burn Sade?', Sade is the forefather of the horror novel, and 'caves, underground passageways, mysterious castles, all the props of the Gothic novel take on a particular meaning in his work'.[14] For Catherine Spooner and Emma McEvoy, the Gothic rejects finite definitional parameters; it is a generic pouch with seams ready to burst. The Gothic is multifacetedly enfolded, they contend, with decay, transgression, aesthetic fear, reality *cum* fantasy and fantasy *cum* reality.[15] Jolene Zigarovich, whose work follows this chapter, has called attention to the Gothic's penchant for 'extreme, perverse, violent, excessive, and masochistic desires' that invariably cohere around formations of gender, sex, and sexuality.[16] And George Haggerty's *Queer Gothic* proffers that queering the Gothic 'disrupts stable notions of *how* to be human' while simultaneously 'challeng[ing] the status quo with the taboo around which the patriarchal system is organized'.[17] Indeed, a common refrain in disability and queer studies is what does it mean to be human and what is at stake in an anthropocentric identification, which invariably upholds Enlightenment-era modalities of (white) colonial embodiment and identity. These concerns are all, without question, painted into the Gothic landscape that Sade authors. By Alyce Mahon's assessment, the Sadean imagination fortifies 'our understanding of humanity [...] through an exploration of humankind's dark, sexually explicit, violent, and cruel nature'.[18] In Sade's queer Gothic, then, we bear witness to new textures of humanity that refuse to uphold normativity in favour of the eroticism of queer, disabled bodies.

While Sade is the centrepiece here, this chapter situates other representations of powerful women who reveal the fecund ways in which queer and crip embodiments flourish in the Gothic. I first look to Hippolita, mother of Conrad and Matilda, and wife to Manfred, the illegitimate ruler in Horace Walpole's *The Castle of Otranto* (1764). While upholding her selfless, uxorial duties, Hippolita is deprecated by Manfred as undesirable and undesirous because of, first, her age, and second, the false accusation that her marriage to Manfred is incestuous. Manfred castigates Hippolita because of 'her own sterility', which positions her outside the heteronormative economy that mandates the reproductive viability and futures of hetero-reproduction.[19] M. G. Lewis's *The Monk* (1796), in turn, recasts these same concerns over sterility and adds to them vaingloriousness, which is disallowed to (aged) women, in Donna Leonella, the ingenue Antonia's ginger aunt. While these two older women are not marked as deformed in the same way that Desgranges may be, I point to these examples to address how the aged female body can be read along the vertices of queer and disability studies – work that Cynthia Port and Jane Gallop have undertaken.[20] I align *The Castle of Otranto* and *The Monk* in order to visualise a Gothic triptych – endowed with misogynistic motifs – in which elderly women are derided and abjured because they seek to remain in or contribute to the heteronormative sexual economy by which they have been refused. By moving from *The Castle of Otranto* to *The Monk* to *120 Days of Sodom*, I offer not a chronology, but rather a mutually informative and accretive modality within which plural representations of misogyny are both extended and remedied in Sade's writing of Desgranges to realise the necessity of the deformed woman to the maintenance and success of a pleasurable economy.

Narrative Sterility

In the first paragraph of Walpole's *The Castle of Otranto*, where we receive a familial introduction, Hippolita is an afterthought. Following descriptions of Manfred, Conrad, Matilda and Isabella, the narrator describes Hippolita thus: 'Hippolita, his wife, an amiable lady, did sometimes venture to represent the danger of marrying their only son so early, considering his great youth, and greater infirmities; but she never received any other answer than reflections on her own sterility, who had given him but one heir.'[21] Manfred's attention to Hippolita then remains enshrouded in his attention to her reproductive shortcomings – she has only borne him one heir and that heir drops dead in the subsequent paragraph.

While Haggerty and Farr have addressed the queer and queer-disability negotiations of Walpole's novel, respectively, they attend only to Conrad, the helmet-decimated heir whose 'great youth' and 'greater infirmities' signal our attention, if only briefly. In Conrad, Haggerty observes, we find that 'the pathetic remains of Walpole's puny weakling can begin to explain something about gothic subjectivity and about queer subjectivity as well'.[22] Farr ups the ante on Haggerty's claim and contends, 'we might also think about the novel as *crip* for the way that it depicts impairment as the critical, resilient center of narrative that haunts healthy, able bodies'.[23] Hippolita, in comparison to her sickly son, may participate in Farr's overview of 'healthy, able bodies', but I would like to push the boundaries of this identification further to pinpoint her sterility as an implicit semaphore of a deformed in/ability to participate in compulsory, reproductive heteronormativity as she had twice previously done – or once, by the standards of Manfred and the laws of primogeniture. Hippolita's recognition as a once-but-no-longer reproductively suitable mate – in other words, her progression into sterility – coincides with Clare's assertion not only that able-bodiedness is a social construction but that disabled-becoming is a temporal inevitability. We will all, Clare implies with the provocative idea of '*temporarily* able-bodied', forfeit our able-bodiedness because of age, trauma, experience, neoliberalism and/or climate change realities.[24] Gallop prefers the term 'late-onset disability', or 'disability beginning in the middle years and beyond'.[25]

Hippolita's characterisation as sterile thus promotes a means by which to understand the inevitable movement of a temporarily reproductively-able body into one that transcends able-bodiedness. Hippolita's sterility exists as an extended conceit – a phantom menace – by which the inhibition of reproduction is both signalled and ironically begat for all other characters. She augurs a narrative sterility that ensures no other reproduction can take place.

What seems to be missing from attention to Hippolita, which has not been missed by feminist critics of eighteenth-century motherhood, is the way Walpole unwittingly rehashes eighteenth-century constructions of congenital deformity for which mothers were purportedly culpable. Marilyn Francus addresses this larger eighteenth-century trope, which the early eighteenth-century satirists Pope and Swift played up with uproarious success. 'Although the progeny in these works [Spenser's *The Faerie Queen* and Pope's *The Dunciad*]', Francus writes, 'do evince an emerging pattern of autonomy, the empowerment of the children primarily provides an extension for maternal authority: the offspring function as agents of the devious maternal self.'[26] Felicity Nussbaum has likewise observed that by mid-century, notions of domestic maternity 'refuse these duties [of procreation and education] and [are] instead capable of heinous acts that threaten lineage and even civilization'.[27] Congenital 'monstrosity', D. Christopher Gabbard and Susannah Mintz reveal in *A Cultural History of Disability in the Long Eighteenth Century*, corroborated a socio-moral conviction that such a 'hideous outcome' had 'impressed itself on the mother's mind during pregnancy'.[28] This was widely accepted until the mid-nineteenth century.

Such cultural contexts inform Walpole's introduction of Hippolita. As Emily Bowles has observed of derogated conceptions of maternity carried over from the late seventeenth century, 'women's bodies were thought capable of deforming or disabling men's bodies through excessive, aggressive, or otherwise non-normative sexuality'.[29] Read this way, Hippolita's sterility serves to threaten the lineage that Manfred and she spawn and that becomes wholly eradicated by the novella's end. To be clear, I do not intend to finger Hippolita as the progenitor through which her son's untimely demise is foretold. Rather, in thinking alongside a Gothic primal scene in which disability and sexuality coalesce, late seventeenth- and eighteenth-century cultural frameworks of motherhood prove useful to address textures of misogynistic deformity that snake their way into the Gothic canon. Put another way, when we take up concerns about ability and sexuality in the novel, we should not forget – to pirate the title of Walpole's play that followed his publication of *Otranto* – the mysterious mother.

Hippolita's reproductive ability and sexuality, though, are determined by their absence: she is sterile. Samuel Johnson records a definition of 'steril' in the 1755 iteration of his *Dictionary*, which stems from the Latin etonym *sterilis* and the French *stérile*, both of which signify barrenness, lack of productivity and infertility, originally in livestock and later in women. Indeed, the Latin root is a cognate for the Sanskrit word *starī*, which refers to a barren cow. To be sterile is to etymologically reckon with modes of belittled womanhood that reek of animal association – an echo of Haggerty's assertion that the Gothic questions and certifies the limits of humanness, in addition to a fluid tie to the calumny that Lewis's Leonella must suffer in possessing a 'leathern paw'. Yet attached to these synonyms for sterility, Johnson posits that the sterile are 'wanting fecundity'.[30] That is, to be sterile is not singularly a cessation of biological reproduction but also a psychological and affective state that longs for hetero-reproduction. Gabbard and Mintz note that a mother's wayward emotional state invariably became incriminated in a child's deformity, which extends classical modes of humoral theory wherein an individual must strive to equipoise the four humours (yellow bile, black bile, blood and phlegm).[31] Despite the fact that Descartes would supplant this theory with mind–body dualism, medical treatises and public frameworks of knowledge remained beholden to humoralism.

Hippolita invariably captures Johnson's definition. Manfred's endeavour to divorce Hippolita and thus instaurate a new bloodline begat by Isabella hinges upon his confession that the two are 'related within the forbidden degrees'.[32] Such an admission hints at Manfred and Hippolita's collective willingness to consummate an incestuous marriage and attends to eighteenth-century juridical contexts in which, as Greta Lafleur reveals, barrenness (in women) and impotence (in men or women) were grounds for the dissolution of marriage and a prohibition of future wedlock.[33] Manfred intends to weaponise the law against his wife. To do so, he flourishes the parameters of the union so as to appeal to Father Jerome, who might consent to, and thus authorise, the divorce:

> It is some time that I have had scruples on the legality of our union: Hippolita is related to me in the fourth degree – It is true, we had a dispensation; but I have been informed that she had also been contracted to another. This it is that sits heavy at my heart: to this state of unlawful wedlock I impute the visitation that has fallen on me in the death of Conrad.[34]

Manfred in these moments (which conjure Henry VIII's supplication to Thomas More) continues to trip over his words as he dives on to the sword of victimhood; his repetition of the passive voice commemorates his passivity, which shifts the brunt of the onus to Hippolita.

Whereas in Hippolita's introduction, her sterility shoulders the fault for the failed lineage, here Manfred points to incestuous consummation as the cause of Conrad's death and the erasure of progeny. These twisted rhetorics are mutually informative: Hippolita's barrenness is the consequence of her submission to incest. Manfred's comeuppance for participating in illicit sex is the death of his son. Despite acknowledging his own complicity in their incestuous marriage, Manfred holds Hippolita singularly responsible. Her determined 'readiness not to oppose the separation' and later acquiescence bespeaks an admission of guilt, which here serves to laminate the accusations wielded by Manfred and simultaneously indemnify him. Put simply, Hippolita's consent to participate in an incestuous marriage and bear the fruit of that marriage leads directly to Conrad's death. By *Otranto*'s weedy logic, incest and sterility join hands to disenfranchise Hippolita. In wanting the fecundity of incestuous relations, Hippolita's body totalises death in its conjunction with deformity: she is rendered barren and both of her children die.

Nicholas Culpeper's *A Directory for Midwives* (1701) further gestures towards larger eighteenth-century cultural constructions of barrenness in women that derived from 'the Womb, and its Infirmities' – what here might be syntactically metaphorised as Hippolita (womb) and Conrad (infirmities).[35] Culpeper's prognostications of barrenness and their antecedents thus anticipate modes of sterility that operate broadly throughout *Otranto*. Culpeper juxtaposes 'natural barrenness' and 'accidental barrenness', so as to separate women's bodies rendered reproductively deformed either by accident or by nature. Whereas the culprit for natural barrenness originates in everything from unhappy marriage to being blood-let before beginning menstruation to too much sex to a poor diet (again humoral theory echoes), accidental barrenness falls squarely on the shoulders of the woman's body. Culpeper adumbrates a series of sources that include too much exercise, obesity, continual sickness, haemorrhoids, ulcers/cancers, hot or cold distemper and 'Care, Fear, Sorrow, and Grief'.[36] As with Johnson's *Dictionary*, Culpeper evidences that barrenness and sterility derive from a plaiting of mental, embodied and affective pangs that better account for how disability is fully embodied rather than resulting from an approportioned body.

So too is this the case for Hippolita. Upon the death of her son, Hippolita bids Isabella – her preordained daughter-in-law – to attend to Manfred who has refused her sight. 'Go, said Hippolita, relieved by a message from her lord: Manfred cannot support the sight of his own family. He thinks you less disordered than we are, and dreads the shock of my grief.'[37] Hippolita's 'disordered' nature proceeds from her outpourings of grief – what Culpeper articulates as an origin point (and undoubtedly an effect) of barrenness. Ironically, it is the care that Hippolita mobilises for both her husband and children that gives rise to sorrow, grief and fear that ultimately defines her by pseudo-medical conceptions of barrenness. *Barrenness is an affective register.* Yet Hippolita's use of 'we' also positions her daughter Matilda within this same disordered and grief-filled framework. During the novella's denouement, Matilda is unintentionally sacrificed, literally on the altar of the church, by her father whose megalomaniacal, psycho-sexual frustrations reach their climax in penetrating his daughter's bosom with a dagger. By Manfred's own admission and later actions, he only penetrates the bodies of those to whom he is connected by forbidden degree. Matilda's premature death prevents her marriage to Theodore and curtails any reproductive value she might possess in furthering an ill-begotten bloodline. The novella seemingly, then, heralds Isabella as the singular, fetishised, reproductively successful woman who serves in direct contrast and competition to Hippolita.

While Isabella might appear as the reproductive surrogate who must be exchanged to counteract Hippolita's incestuous sterility, *Otranto*'s ending reinforces the notion that sterility is narratively contagious. Hippolita's sterility, in this way, sounds a dog whistle by which all reproduction must forcefully stop. My reading of disability and narrative here thus echoes Farr's contention that the eighteenth-century novel engineers both ableist form and rhetoric through sympathetic over-identification with individual characters.[38] I extend this further to suggest that Hippolita's sterility underwrites a crip-narratology wherein all other characters are subject to remain outside of hetero-reproduction. By no means do I suggest that disabled bodies cannot participate in heteronormative reproductive frameworks, but as is clear from my reading of Walpole, the sterile mother begets a narrative in which all others are rendered sterile. Despite Manfred's perverse hope that Isabella might consensually (or not) bear his children and thus endow his illegitimate bloodline with a male heir, we are left not with a birth at the end but rather with a marriage suffused with melancholy. Following Matilda's death and Theodore's ascension as rightful ruler,

> Manfred signed his abdication of the principality, with the approbation of Hippolita, and each took on them the habit of religion in the neighbouring convents. Frederic offered his daughter to the new prince, which Hippolita's tenderness for Isabella concurred to promote: but Theodore's grief was too fresh to admit the thought of another love; and it was not till after frequent discourses with Isabella, of dear Matilda, that he was persuaded he could know no happiness but in the society of one with whom he could forever indulge the melancholy that had taken possession of his soul.[39]

The superimposition of Isabella over Hippolita ultimately fails here along with any lineages that might follow from the bungled and ordained marriages. Hippolita's sterility, articulated by *Otranto*'s first paragraph, invariably reinforces a menacing motif wherein the reproductive female body is altogether forfeited. The ending is not painted with notions of the children that Isabella is threatened to bear. She and Theodore are possessed only by an indulgent melancholy, that by Judith Butler's assessment of melancholia might very well admit auxiliary queer horizons in which Isabella and Matilda are homoerotically enraptured.[40] Hippolita's sterility indexes alternative nodes in which Gothic reproduction becomes an impossibility: Conrad and Matilda, allegedly born of incest, embody the rotten fruit of Hippolita's sterility and wayward womb. If, as Nussbaum has argued, tomb and womb lexically operate as rhyming cultural synonyms in representations of monstrous maternity throughout the eighteenth century, *The Castle of Otranto* continues this legacy.[41] Hippolita's sterility further manifests that lexicon and anticipates a queering of her body and her sexuality that push against what Lee Edelman identifies as 'reproductive futurism' or determinations to reproduce in order to consolidate future heteronormative regimes that replicate ad nauseam and uphold the child as an abstraction of totalising good.[42]

Old Woman, Old Woman, Old Woman, Old Woman

Like Hippolita, Lewis's Leonella exists among similar cultural vectors that would caricature a lustful aged woman for her alleged infringement upon a hetero-reproductive economy from which she has been excluded. Hippolita, Leonella and, as I show later, Madame Desgranges thus typify a chiasmic arrangement of disability and sexuality, which has received its rightful theoretical attention. Jane Gallop's *Sexuality, Disability, and Aging* grounds itself in first-hand situated knowledges of ageing and disability to address how the joining of disability and queer studies at the turn of the new millennium has, only until recently, eclipsed discussions of old age. Gallop's work is then invested in 'later-life sexualities and queer(ness)'.[43] Cynthia Port, in mode, rails against the hetero-futurist narrative Edelman likewise critiques to challenge fetishisations of youth that encode imperial legacies of continuation and expansion.[44] Port's emphasis on the queerness of ageing might realise a queer temporal utopianism proffered by José Esteban Muñoz.[45] And Riva Lehrer poetically homes in on a cultural zeitgeist – one that extends before and beyond the contemporary – that seeks to invisibilise disability, older women and sexual expression. Lehrer writes:

Old women disappear into a slow molasses of obscurity, even when they fight to be seen. I can see the day coming when the shape of my body will be chalked up to age and I will join the ranks of the Invisible Women. Until then, I will be one of the crip girls whose bodies scare the panel of judges. They are afraid that our unbalanced shapes hint of unsanctioned desires.[46]

It is at this nexus that the Gothic novel perches Leonella; her unsanctioned desires justify the derogation she must suffer as an undesirable quinquagenarian.

The first six paragraphs of *The Monk* are punctuated by repeated attention to an 'old woman'.[47] The phrase appears four times and reminds us that Leonella is, well, an old woman who is additionally 'obstinate' and endowed with 'brawny arms' and a persistent 'squint'.[48] In short, the narrative does not ingratiate her to the reader. The opening scene is claustrophobic – everyone in Madrid gathers to witness the splendour of the monk Ambrosio's beauty and oratorical acumen – and the intense heat in addition to the piling up of bodies amplifies the repetition. Leonella's agedness stands in direct contrast to Ambrosio's 'uncommon handsome[ness]' and Antonia's beauty, whose 'dazzling whiteness' (even while veiled) effervesces and 'vied with the Medicean Venus'.[49] The physical, comparative disgust of Leonella's presence is compounded by her over-zealous imagination, which misunderstands Don Christoval's foppishness as a marriage proposal. She coquettishly remarks:

'You may depend upon hearing from me. Farewell, Cavaliers. Segnor Conde, let me entreat you to moderate the excessive ardour of your passion: However, to prove to you that I am not displeased with you, and prevent your abandoning yourself to despair, receive this mark of my affection, and sometimes bestow a thought upon the absent Leonella.'

As She said this, She extended a lean and wrinkled hand; which her supposed Admirer kissed with such sorry grace and constraint so evident, that Lorenzo with difficulty repressed his inclination to laugh.[50]

As with the other old women who people the dark comedy of Lewis's Gothic fiction – Cunegonda, Donna Rodolpha, the Abbess and Dame Jacintha – Leonella exemplifies the butt of the joke (a curious turn of phrase that takes on erotic meaning in the next section).

'Old woman' does not just appear as a pseudonym for Leonella; her 'lean and wrinkled hand' alongside her delusions of grandeur position her as the laughing stock of the young cast who seethe with horny attachments. Don Christoval's response to Leonella's departure is to further malign her:

'What can repay me for having kissed the leathern paw of that confounded old Witch? Diavolo! She has left such a scent upon my lips, that I shall smell of garlick for this month to come! As I pass along the Prado, I shall be taken for a walking Omelet, or some large Onion running to seed!'[51]

If Haggerty offers the queer Gothic as a heuristic by which to test the limits of what and how it means to be human, then here Christoval besmirches Leonella as an animalised sorceress whose touch, smell, taste and appearance become a phenomenological horror. Leonella's supposed vegetal smell conjures up her expiration date: she is embodied detritus that transmogrifies, as witches might, young, eligible bachelors into food. This olfactory expiration additionally signals Leonella's rot from within the hetero-reproductive economy. The fruit that she might bear – but never does – likewise is rotten. The invocation of 'running to seed' seeks to punningly remind us of Christoval's reproductive capabilities, of which Leonella is incapable because of age, appearance and scent. Leonella's agedness, self-confidence and desirousness are the means by which the narrative vilifies her.

These deprecatory resonances become further bandied about when Antonia and Leonella, en route home from the church, are accosted by a gypsy – whose sing-song verses introduce the first ballad interspersed in *The Monk*, one of the novel's very few inclusions that received Samuel Taylor Coleridge's praise in his otherwise lambasting 1797 review. The gypsy's song endeavours to check Leonella's desirousness by repeatedly reminding her of her age.

> Your fortune? You are now so old,
> Good Dame, that 'tis already told:
> Yet for your money, in a trice
> I will repay you in advice.
> Astonished at your childish vanity,
> Your Friends all tax you with insanity,
> And grieve to see you use your art
> To catch some youthful Lover's heart.
> Believe me, Dame, when all is done,
> Your age will still be fifty one;
> And Men will rarely take an hint
> Of love, from two grey eyes that squint.
> Take then my counsels; Lay aside
> Your paint and patches, lust and pride,
> And on the Poor those sums bestow,
> Which now are spent on useless show.
> Think on your Maker, not a Suitor;
> Think on your past faults, not on future;
> And think Time's Scythe will quickly mow
> The few red hairs, which deck your brow.[52]

The gypsy's misogynistic song corroborates the narrative fetishisation of Leonella's age. The juxtaposition of 'vanity' and 'insanity' maligns Leonella's appearance as a mental instability: she is not only vain but her vanity results from a plagued mental health. And in the rhyming of her age – fifty one – with done, the gypsy's words, like Don Christoval's, convey the sense that to be such an age is to knock on death's door. Indeed, time's scythe is invoked at the song's end to metaphorically slash at Leonella while also reminding her that she is to have *no future*. The form of the rhyming couplets, moreover, salt the aural wounds that Leonella must psychically endure; they echo Christoval's ridicule. She is not to partake in coupledom.[53] The rhyming couplet, in other words, goads Leonella's aged singularity. As Howard Anderson notes, the catchiness of this tune extended well beyond the confines of the novel (though unattributed in Lewis), and thus in its attractive aurality we further bear witness to the Gothic's ability to revive criticisms of unmarried, unchilded, older women whose sexual appetites are met with disdain, slapstick humour and ableist-desexualising tendencies.[54] In the depiction of Leonella we find yet another aged woman who must be cast outside the realms of hetero-desirability because of the inflections of disability that are encoded in agedness.

Desiring Deformity

The patterns I have traced thus far in Walpole and Lewis become further complicated, and even inverted, in Sade's depiction of Madame Desgranges. Again, I am not interested in situating identical patterns in which sexuality and disability cohere in the Romantic Gothic; I am instead invested in negotiating their various textures. If Hippolita is rendered a sort of contagious narrative detritus because of her sterility, and Leonella's aged body is undercut and trivialised by lyrical couplets, Madame Desgranges engenders an awe-inspiring representation by which modes of disabled embodiment become welcomed and enfolded into erogenous praxis. Sade, in other words, flips the script.

Desgranges is not the sole disabled character in the cast that populates *The 120 Days of Sodom*; as my introduction noted, her sister procuress, Madame Martaine, maintains her own 'natural deformity'.[55] Two servants, Louison and Thérèse, are additionally described as 'stunted, hunchbacked, blind in one eye, and lame' and possessing 'one twisted arm and limped on one leg', respectively.[56] In this way, the relationship between gender and disability cannot be underestimated and Martaine and Desgranges's roles as harlots who arrange and participate in the titular saturnalias reveal their assistive necessity in bringing forth bodily and sexual effusions (emissions too). The novel's showboating of fetishes aplenty demonstrates that fetishistic play, especially that of deformed bodies, is vital to the success of the 120 days.

Sade paints Desgranges as a spectacle of disorder, deficit and degeneracy. She epitomises Beauvoir's assertion that 'Among the most obvious sexual attractions, Sade includes old age, ugliness, and bad odors. His linking of eroticism with vileness is as original as his linking it with cruelty [. . .] Beauty is too simple.'[57] Desgranges has long ago forfeited 'a beautiful body' to become 'a mere skeleton capable of inspiring nothing but disgust'.[58] Her vagina and anus are excoriated (both literally and figuratively), her emaciated body sports only one nipple, one eye and seven fingers; she is absent six teeth. In correspondence with the narrator's preface to abandon all presumptions of beauty, Desgranges's description bespeaks a commitment to physical and moral ugliness.

> If her body was the picture of ugliness, her soul was the depository of all the most unheard of vices and crimes: an arsonist, a parricide, a sodomite, a tribade, a murderess, a poisoner, guilty of incest, of rape, of theft, of abortions, and of sacrileges, one might truthfully affirm that there is not a single crime in the world this villain had not committed herself.[59]

Desgranges's deformed embodiment comes on the heels of her plural sexual explorations (sodomy, tribadism) and her radical enactment of sins aplenty. If Hippolita's woes lie in her sterility, Desgranges's valour blossoms from her participation in sexual violence and incest as well as the performance of abortion. The ugliness of her soul (precipitated by her actions accounted for here) thus positions her as the ideal candidate to effect the Duc's and his three lecherous companions' lewd intentions. Ugliness is somehow recuperated by the narrative as a physical and moral opportunity that desirably eschews a fascination with and commitment to physical beauty and moral rectitude.

As a result, *120 Days* articulates a passion for ugliness. 'Beauty belongs to the sphere of the simple, the ordinary', the narrator reports, 'whilst ugliness is something extraordinary, and there is no question but that every ardent imagination prefers in lubricity the extraordinary to the commonplace.'[60] Ugliness is not the rejection of beauty; it is a transcendence of beauty to the sphere of the extraordinary. For Sade then, Desgranges's physical and moral ugliness participate in etymological reorderings and simultaneously reify notions of the sublime. Andrew Curran has offered Diderot, Sade's contemporary, as a French Enlightenment figure who taps into accounts of physical monstrosity and deformity, which ultimately births 'sublime disorder'. Curran's titular conception recognises that Diderot's monsters 'are fluctuating figures of uncertainty; their very form is designed to corrupt optimistic philosophy; debunk a static view of nature, and, in certain contexts, question a universal morality based on a normative view of the human body'.[61] Diderot's sublimity moves to 'accept the overwhelming feeling brought on by a cosmos in disarray', all the while exalting its pleasurable and painful interstices.[62] Sade's insistence upon the value of ugliness, especially in its embodied and moral permutations, thus accounts for a similar topos wherein Desgranges's deformities and egregious villainy magnify a sublime corollary that is, yes, fear-inducing, but more importantly, pleasure-inducing.

These collective corollaries embolden Desgranges's participation in the 120 days and she becomes fundamental to bringing sexual congress to fruition. Sade's framing of sexuality, though, is not contingent upon notions of consent, and in fact, most of the sex acts committed by the libertine quartet test the limits of consent – often it is sexual violence that appeals to them. Desgranges assists with this as both procuress and hands-on consigliere. Desgranges's position within modes of sexual contact – both consensual and not – thus pushes against genres of supercrip identity formation that might suggest that her desirable deformity must always be conducted through optimistic, benevolent, rose-coloured (e)utopianism.

In one instance, the Duc commands Sophie, one of the eight in the 'harem of little girls', to be stripped and presented for his algolagnic pleasure. Sophie weeps for the loss of her mother, slain in protecting the girl from abduction, and this lachrymose outpouring fans the ardorous flames of the Duc's priapism.[63] '"Why, fuck my eyes!" the Duc exclaimed, fondling his heaven-threatening prick, "I'd never have believed this scene [Sophie crying over the loss of her mother] could be so voluptuous. Off with her clothes, I tell you to take them off."'[64] When Sophie is unsuccessfully positioned to receive the Duc, Desgranges must accommodate the dandy: 'No one knew what to do, and the more obstacles were encountered, the more the enraged Duc fumed and blasphemed. Desgranges finally came to the rescue; nothing that pertained to libertinage was unknown to that sage old dame.'[65] Desgranges and two servants, in what follows, assist the Duc's rape of Sophie.

Only days later this assistive touch returns when Desgranges has, once again, to prop the Duc and his sexual conquests up to support erotic pleasures.

> The Duc had Duclos [one of the primary raconteurs who 'has the finest ass to be seen'] strip off her clothes, had her bend and lean upon the back of a chair and commanded Desgranges to frig him upon her comrade's buttocks, in such ways that the head of his prick might graze Duclos' asshole with each stroke.[66]

Such an elaborate depiction of sodomy corresponds, Beauvoir contends, with Sade's own predilection: 'he declared aloud in no uncertain terms that the greatest pleasure is derived from a combination of active and passive sodomy'.[67] Though the verb 'to frig' has loosened in contemporary parlance to mean 'to have sex with', the *Oxford English Dictionary* notes that the word's cloudy etymology suggests that it surfaced from onomatopoeic slang that seeks to aurally recreate frike, fridge or fidge, which signify to dance, to rub away or chafe, and to move briskly, respectively. The translation of frig by Wainhouse and Seaver signals manual, masturbatory stimulation. The Duc relies on Desgranges, and her seven fingers, to accommodate the sodomy he perpetrates against Duclos (to which she consents, unlike Sophie), and Desgranges's haptic help allows the Duc 'handsomely served and entirely surrounded, discharged to the tunes of bellowings and shouts which indicated to what a point his mind had been stimulated'.[68] In Desgranges's capable hands, worlds of pleasure discharge.

But Desgranges is not simply a procuring aide to the erogenous praxis homed by the Château de Silling; she is also the recipient of the quartet's taste for polymorphous pleasures. On the fifth day – the one that follows Duclos's sodomising – Duclos narrates another tale that heightens the stakes of disability's eroticism. 'General C***', a brothel client, requires women who

> had to be damaged either by Nature, by libertinage, or by the effects of the law; in a word, he accepted none who were not one-eyed or blind, lame, hunchbacked, legless cripples, or missing an arm or two, or toothless, or mutilated in their limbs, or whipped and branded or clearly marked by some other act of justice, and they always had to be of the ripest old age.[69]

Duclos's description of the anonymised General gives way to the novel's most transparent and evocative statement on the pleasures of disabled bodies. Duclos discloses that the deformed – 'damaged' – body manifests from any number of congenital, social or political causes, thus elucidating a powerful recognition of disability as that which develops alongside bio-sociocultural axes. The General's appetites also amplify the articulations of deformed female embodiment that I have so far traced, in that his desire for, in his words, 'degraded' bodies (to which his list attests) is interwoven with his desire for women 'of the ripest old age'. Perhaps in the General, Leonella would find her just deserts. Duclos's description of the General's predilections is abruptly halted by Curval's announcement, '"behold by the sign of this risen prick, what a flame that passion described ignites in me"'.[70] Durcet, likewise aroused, and Curval thus beckon Desgranges over to reanimate Duclos's retelling of a deformed, aged prostitute embroiled in lustful sex. 'The rest of that worn and wasted body – that ass of parchment or ancient leather, that ample, noxious hole, glistening its center, this mutilated tit, those three vanished fingers, this short leg that causes her limp, that mouth destitute of teeth – everything combines to stimulate our libertine pair.'[71] Durcet and Curval please themselves with Desgranges's body – they simultaneously engage her in cunnilingus and anilingus. The narrator reveals, 'It is with the filthiest and least appetizing object our two rakes, presently beside themselves, are about to taste the most delicious pleasures.'[72]

It would appear that the narration intends to satirically depreciate Desgranges, her appearance and her body, as Leonella must endure in *The Monk*. I want to forestall if not outright reject this reading, because through Sade's authorship we are provided with an opportunity by which to read Desgranges's deformed body as not excluded from the sexual or pleasurable economies that Hippolita and Leonella are. She is instead a central interlocutor through which the Duc, Durcet and Curval – three-quarters of the libertine orchestrators – realise new genres of sexual pleasure that stem from aural, oral and embodied experiences. The degraded laundry list that might characterise Desgranges's deficits instead demarcates vivid descriptions of erogenous anticipation:

> We have two eminent citizens, who, after having given themselves over to the foulest excesses, finally erupt their fuck, and notwithstanding the exhaustion caused by these feats, would very possibly go on to perform other ones of the same crapulous and infamous kind, and perform them without an instant's delay, were it not for the supper bell announcing other pleasure well worth their consideration.[73]

The supper bell signals a respite from the storytelling and concomitant sex acts, and yet the two are not overcome with pangs of regret. Rather, the types of 'crapulous' and 'infamous' eroticisms that the disabled, aged woman's body might provide are those 'well worth their consideration'. In Beauvoir's words, Sade 'made of his sexuality an ethic; he expressed this ethic in works of literature'.[74] In our ugliest passions, Sade proposes, we find a Gothic ethic in which our most lubricious yens are animated.

Queer Crip Gothic Horizons

'Desiring Deformity' is my rallying call for unveiling various modes of embodiment that manifest queer, pleasurable and erotic possibilities in the Gothic. In many ways, the trajectory I have charted here exceeds the loose historical boundaries of the Romantic Gothic, especially for Sade. While written in the eighteenth century, *120 Days of Sodom* was not published until the twentieth – a pattern that likewise pertains to some of William Beckford's most notorious and least studied work. By acknowledging these historical discrepancies, we may further welcome how a queer crip interpretative mode can enliven and update our queer Gothic commitments. While nineteenth-century audiences might have been unfamiliar with Sade's masterpiece (though not his other works or biography), the attention to deformed and disabled bodies – and their erotic connections – is not distinct to any particular historical period. Consider, for example, Byron's *The Deformed Transformed* (1824), Rochester's final disabled form in *Jane Eyre* (1847), countless queer and crip readings of Frankenstein's creature, Laura in Collins's *The Woman in White* (1860), a cohort of characters in Dickens's *Our Mutual Friend* (1865), Hyde's moral and physical ugliness in *Strange Case of Dr Jekyll and Mr Hyde* (1886), and protagonists and supporting characters alike found in Poe, Eliot and du Maurier.

I ask then: how might our attention to the disabled figure vitalise the Gothic syllabus? Much of this enlivening can manifest in the classroom. While many of us who teach the Gothic through a queer studies lens or commitment might regularly approach notions of gender and sexuality, might we be doing our students and ourselves a disservice by not further orienting alternative modalities by which queerness might manifest in the Gothic canon? How might we enfold disability studies and politics into the larger discussion of the Gothic's attendance to sociocultural intersectional identities and queer peculiarities? Queering disability in the Gothic is not the skeleton key to a refurbished syllabus; rather, it is a dedication to further queering our syllabi in hopes of sparking alternative queer crip Gothic horizons.

Notes

1. Marquis de Sade, *The 120 Days of Sodom*, trans. Austryn Wainhouse and Richard Seaver (New York: Grove Press, 1966), p. 253.

2. For Foucault, the expurgation of Sade's work participates in the repressive hypothesis. Additionally, Foucault invokes Sade to plumb how the biopolitics of sexuality emerge literarily and culturally. Michel Foucault, *The History of Sexuality: Volume 1*, trans. Robert Hurley (New York: Vintage, 1978).
3. Sade, *The 120 Days of Sodom*, p. 220.
4. Ibid., p. 221.
5. Ibid., p. 222.
6. Ibid., p. 222.
7. Helen Deutsche, 'Deformity', in *Keywords for Disability Studies*, ed. Rachel Adams, Benjamin Reiss and David Serlin (New York: NYU Press, 2015), pp. 52–4 (p. 52).
8. Simon Dickie, *Cruelty and Laughter: Forgotten Comic Literature and the Unsentimental Eighteenth Century* (Chicago: University of Chicago Press, 2011), p. 45.
9. Robert McRuer, *Crip Theory: Cultural Signs of Queerness and Disability* (New York: NYU Press, 2006); Alison Kafer, *Feminist, Queer, Crip* (Bloomington, IN: Indiana University Press, 2013); Robert McRuer and Anna Mollow, *Sex and Disability* (Durham, NC: Duke University Press, 2012); Eli Clare, *Exile and Pride: Disability, Queerness, and Liberation* (Durham, NC: Duke University Press, 2015).
10. Jason Farr, *Novel Bodies: Disability and Sexuality in Eighteenth-Century British Literature* (Lewisburg, PA: Bucknell University Press, 2019), p. 11.
11. Jeremy Chow, 'Showing the Eunuch: Disability, Sexuality, and Dryden's *All for Love*', in *Castration, Impotence, and Emasculation in the Long Eighteenth Century*, ed. Anne Greenfield (New York: Routledge, 2020), pp. 105–24.
12. Clare, *Exile and Pride*, p. 2.
13. Tim Dean, 'No Sex Please, We're American', *American Literary History*, 27.3 (2015), pp. 614–24 (p . 615).
14. Simone de Beauvoir, 'Must We Burn Sade?', trans. Annette Michelson, in *The 120 Days of Sodom*, trans. Austryn Wainhouse and Richard Seaver (New York: Grove Press, 1966), pp. 3–64 (p. 37).
15. Catherine Spooner and Emma McEvoy (eds), *The Routledge Companion to Gothic* (New York: Routledge, 2007), pp. 1–3.
16. Jolene Zigarovich, 'Introduction: Transing the Gothic', in *TransGothic in Literature and Culture*, ed. Jolene Zigarovich (New York: Routledge, 2018), pp. 1–22 (p. 3).
17. George Haggerty, *Queer Gothic* (Champaign-Urbana, IL: University of Illinois Press, 2006). Italics original, p. 19.
18. Alyce Mahon, *The Marquis de Sade and the Avant-Garde* (Princeton, NJ: Princeton University Press, 2020), p. 1.
19. Horace Walpole, *The Castle of Otranto*, ed. W. S. Lewis (Oxford: Oxford World's Classics, 2008), p. 17.
20. Cynthia Port, 'No Future? Aging, Temporality, History, and Reverse Chronologies', *Occasion*, 4 (2012), pp. 1–19; Jane Gallop, *Sexuality, Disability, and Aging: Queer Temporalities of the Phallus* (Durham, NC: Duke University Press, 2019).
21. Walpole, *The Castle of Otranto*, p. 17.

22. Haggerty, *Queer Gothic*, p. 24.
23. Farr, *Novel Bodies*. Italics original, p. 14.
24. Clare, *Exile and Pride*. Italics original, p. 82.
25. Gallop, *Sexuality, Disability, and Aging*, p. 5.
26. Marilyn Francus, *Monstrous Motherhood: Eighteenth-Century Culture and the Ideology of Domesticity* (Baltimore, MD: Johns Hopkins University Press, 2013), p. 28.
27. Felicity Nussbaum, '"Savage Mothers": Narratives of Maternity in the Mid-Eighteenth Century', *Cultural Critique*, 20 (1991–92), pp. 123–51 (p. 127).
28. D. Christopher Gabbard and Susannah Mintz (eds), *A Cultural History of Disability in the Long Eighteenth Century* (New York: Bloomsbury, 2020), p. 3.
29. Emily Bowles, 'Maternal Culpability in Fetal Defects: Aphra Behn's Satiric Interrogations of Medical Models', in *Recovering Disability in Early Modern England*, ed. Allison Hobgood and David Houston Wood (Columbus, OH: Ohio State University Press, 2013), pp. 43–56 (p. 48).
30. Samuel Johnson, *A Dictionary of the English Language*, https://johnsonsdictionaryonline.com/views/search.php?term=sterile (accessed 14 February 2023).
31. Gabbard and Mintz (eds), *A Cultural History of Disability in the Long Eighteenth Century*.
32. Walpole, *The Castle of Otranto*, p. 69.
33. Greta LaFleur, '"Defective in One of the Principal Parts of Virility": Impotence, Generation, and Defining Disability in Early North America', *Early American Literature*, 52.1 (2017), pp. 79–107 (p. 84).
34. Walpole, *The Castle of Otranto*, p. 51.
35. Nicholas Culpeper, *A Directory for Midwives, or, a guide for women, in their conception, bearing, and suckling their children* (London: Printed for J. and A. Churchill, 1701), p. 63.
36. Ibid., p. 64.
37. Walpole, *The Castle of Otranto*, p. 24.
38. Farr, *Novel Bodies*.
39. Walpole, *The Castle of Otranto*, p. 115.
40. Judith Butler, 'Melancholy Gender – Refused Identification', *Psychoanalytic Dialogues*, 5.2 (1995), pp. 165–80.
41. Felicity Nussbaum, *The Brink of All We Hate: English Satires of Women, 1660–1750* (Lexington, KY: University of Kentucky Press, 1984), pp. 8–42 (p. 29).
42. Lee Edelman, *No Future: Queer Theory and the Death Drive* (Durham, NC: Duke University Press, 2004).
43. Gallop, *Sexuality, Disability, and Aging*, p. 7.
44. Port, 'No Future', pp. 6–7.
45. José Esteban Muñoz, *Cruising Utopia: The Then and There of Queer Futurity* (New York: NYU Press, 2009).
46. Riva Lehrer, 'Golem Girl Gets Lucky', in *Sex and Disability*, ed. Robert McCruer and Anna Mollow (Durham, NC: Duke University Press, 2012), pp. 231–55 (p. 234).

47. Matthew Gregory Lewis, *The Monk*, ed. Howard Anderson (Oxford: Oxford World's Classics, 2006), p. 8.
48. Ibid., p. 8.
49. Ibid., pp. 15, 8–9.
50. Ibid., p. 19.
51. Ibid., p. 19.
52. Ibid., pp. 29–30.
53. Ironically, later in the novel, Leonella is only able to secure a 'young Husband' upon the deaths of her sister and niece. Coupling for Leonella exists only on the backs of her deceased competitors (ibid., pp. 264–5).
54. Ibid., p. 344.
55. Sade, *120 Days of Sodom*, p. 221.
56. Ibid., p. 234.
57. Beauvoir, 'Must We Burn Sade?', p. 26.
58. Sade, *120 Days of Sodom*, p. 222.
59. Ibid., p. 222.
60. Ibid., p. 233.
61. Andrew Curran, *Sublime Disorder: Physical Monstrosity in Diderot's Universe* (Oxford: Voltaire Foundation, 2001), p. 16.
62. Ibid., p. 24.
63. Sade, *120 Days of Sodom*, p. 259.
64. Ibid., p. 294.
65. Ibid., p. 295.
66. Ibid., pp. 257, 320.
67. Beauvoir, 'Must We Burn Sade?', p. 23.
68. Sade, *120 Days of Sodom*, p. 320.
69. Ibid., p. 329.
70. Ibid., p. 329.
71. Ibid., p. 330.
72. Ibid., p. 330.
73. Ibid., p. 330.
74. Beauvoir, 'Must We Burn Sade?', p. 6.

Chapter 2

Queer Gothic: Romantic Origins and Victorian Innovations
Jolene Zigarovich

Queer Romantic Gothic

In Charlotte Dacre's Romantic Gothic novel *Zofloya, or, The Moor* (1806), Victoria di Loredani finds herself punished for her overt sexuality and is imprisoned on her aunt's estate. Concocting a plan of disguise in order to escape, she exchanges clothing with her maid Catau in the walled garden. Dacre's description is intimate and suggestive: Victoria hands Catau her robe and then Catau 'divest[s] herself of her attire' and exchanges with her 'gradually every necessary external part of her dress'.[1] This *deshabillement* is followed by a quasi-lesbian marriage rite: 'The transformation was at length completed; when Victoria, presenting Catau with the promised ring, slightly pressed her hand and said—"My good, my honest Catau . . ."'[2] She then successfully escapes, having 'courted' her aunt's maid to assist her.

I open this chapter with this scene from *Zofloya* in order to underscore the queerness of Dacre's novel. With this female exchange, she rewrites the sexualised unveiling of Rosario–Matilda from Matthew Lewis's *The Monk* (1796). Both novels are rife with homoeroticism, and violently destabilise normative gender roles. With dramatic flourish, they exemplify the origins of queer Gothic. In the late eighteenth century familial and gender relations were being redefined as British culture modernised, the Empire spread, and capitalism emerged. As sexuality and gender were seen in more binary terms, literature often reinforced heteronormativity and cisnormativity. While reinforcing these norms, Gothic literature also dramatised the blatant transgression of desire and challenged social boundaries and regulations. This exploration of tabooed desire was employed by writers in part to reaffirm the power of the normative, but also to carve out spaces for potential non-normative power in eighteenth- and nineteenth-century Gothic. As Ardel Haefele-Thomas puts it, 'Gothic also became a safe location in which authors could investigate ideas about race, interracial desire, cross-class relations, ethnicity, empire, nation and "foreignness" during the nineteenth century.'[3] The aim of this chapter is to highlight the importance of Gothic's queer work, and underscore the complex diversity and social critique embedded in Queer Romantic and Victorian Gothic. Romantic Gothic establishes the queerness of the new genre; its sexual revolutionaries influence later sexual movements and the rise of sexology. Pleasurable and monstrous, violent and homophobic, Romantic Gothic challenges what later would be 'immoral' sexualities. Instituting a 'monstrous sexuality' in the face of a growing sexual binary culture, these texts also provocatively explore queerness before modern moral panics and anxieties were formalised in the Victorian era.

While the Church and state determined the division between licit (legal, marital, reproductive) and illicit (non-reproductive) acts in order to, according to Michel Foucault, 'constitute a sexuality that is economically useful and politically conservative',[4] Gothic literature reinforced heteronormative sexuality and dramatised acts of sexual surveillance. Yet it simultaneously participated in a narrative form of sexology; the Gothic can fruitfully be read as a discursive practice that delineates non-normative sexualities. While legal sanctions multiplied in this era, and psychological taxonomies relegated 'sexual irregularities' to mental illness, heteronormativities were being defined and upheld by numerous discourses (philosophical, legal and literary), including the Gothic. In fact, we might easily align Foucault's list of abnormalities with several well-known Gothic plots. As he writes, 'What came under scrutiny was the sexuality of children' (William Beckford's *Vathek* [1786] and the later *The Episodes of Vathek* [written 1785–86; pub. 1922]), 'mad men and women, and criminals' (Horace Walpole's *The Castle of Otranto* [1764]; Ann Radcliffe's *The Mysteries of Udolpho* [1794]; Matthew Lewis's *The Monk* [1796]); 'the sexuality of those who do not like the opposite sex' (*Vathek, The Episodes*; Radcliffe's *The Romance of the Forest* [1791]); 'reveries, obsessions, petty manias, or great transports of rage' (most Gothic novels, including *Otranto, The Monk, Udolpho*, Thomas De Quincey's *Confessions of an English Opium-Eater* [1821] and James Hogg's *The Private Memoirs and Confessions of a Justified Sinner* [1824]).[5] In order to reinforce norms, these 'peripheral sexualities' were explored (but also condemned) by Gothic authors and deemed 'unnatural'. Later, during the nineteenth century, this would become known as the 'implantation of the perverse', the discursive means through which *scientia sexualis* extended its reach over a range of aberrant pleasures and sexual practices. As George E. Haggerty has aptly put it, 'The connections between the history of sexuality (and the growth of sexology) and the gothic are not necessarily coincidental. They haunt each other with similarities.'[6] Steven Bruhm concurs, maintaining that 'Sexuality, as it comes to us through a history of Freudian, post-Freudian and queer thought, is nothing short of Gothic in its ability to rupture, fragment, and destroy both the coherence of the individual subject and of the culture in which that subject appears.'[7]

The deployment of sexuality thereby produces a continual extension of areas for the maximisation of power and control. 'Unnatural sexuality', from Manfred's near-incestuous desire for his future daughter-in-law Isabella in *The Castle of Otranto* to Victoria's miscegenetic desire for the Moor in *Zofloya*, came to characterise desires and acts that resisted eighteenth-century institutionalised discourses of heterosexual marriage and procreation. Even conservative Gothic, such as Ann Radcliffe's, embeds heavily encoded same-sex desires, though Radcliffe's novels ultimately close with heterosexual marriages and bonds.[8] While novels such as *Vathek*, *The Mysteries of Udolpho*, *The Monk* and *Zofloya* discipline and punish their sexual perpetrators, they concurrently register defiance and resistance to these same institutional norms.

Most critics agree that the Gothic novel powerfully complicates gender divisions, as *The Monk* and *Zofloya* depict, yet as Nowell Marshall, Jeremy Chow and others have argued, these readings are limited because they still work within female and male Gothic parameters.[9] Exploring generic crossings and exposing deviations and transgressions broadens and proliferates these traditional classifications and subgenres. Dacre's *Zofloya* notably straddles, disrupts and reconstructs these binaries; it is one of the first early Gothic novels that we can recognise as trans, as I have argued elsewhere.[10] One of the directions for exploration is revealed in the novel's persistent homoeroticism and violence. In fact, though set in fifteenth-century Italy, *Zofloya*'s contemporary message seems to be that lesbianism and queer sexualities stem from the violent female reaction to the patriarchal constraints of early nineteenth-century culture. Following the death of her ineffective father and her mother's adultery, and before her own 'nymphomania', Victoria di Loredani commences the novel as a stereotypical female heroine: imprisoned and regulated. Keen on escaping through an obscure gate in the garden, she finds comfort with another female. In fact, the novel initially depicts comforting female–female relations in Victoria's interaction with the servant Catau. Though this relationship is hierarchical, and based upon Victoria's own needs, it does allow for physical affection, underscored with Dacre's heavy-handed metaphors, such as this suggestive description of the Edenic garden:

> It so happened that one evening [Victoria and Catau] perambulated to a part of the garden which was yet unknown to Victoria: it was a beautiful close avenue, the sides of the roof of which were interwoven branches of vine and honeysuckle; the entrance was almost concealed by a thick shrubbery, which it required no slight ingenuity to penetrate; and, from the serpentine direction of the path, it appeared wholly impossible to ascertain its extent. Still, having made their way through, they proceeded, Victoria with a vague and indefinable feeling of hope and fear, and Catau merely with that vacant curiosity incident to vulgar minds.[11]

The language of untrimmed vegetation, serpentine paths and hazardous penetration signals Dacre's erotic rhetoric and intention. Calculating and self-interested, through the closeness with Catau, Victoria performs friendship, assumes disguises and shifts class. Disguise is necessary for Victoria's escape, and her preferred means is to exchange clothing with Catau in the garden, as described at the opening of this chapter. Following the exchange of clothing and Victoria's gift of a ring, Victoria bids adieu, which results in Catau's emotional reaction: 'Catau, with a violent burst of tears and sobs, seized the hand of Victoria, and impressed on it a kiss forcible in proportion to the affection it was meant to convey.'[12] Although Dacre never resurrects Catau's character, this interaction demonstrates Victoria's traditionally 'masculine' courtship of a weak and vulnerable female. Dacre underscores Victoria's exploitation of female–female affection and intimacy, an understanding that is finally destroyed by her brutal murder of the innocent Lilla.

Similar to *Zofloya*, Mary Shelley's *Frankenstein* addresses 'the failed leavings of domesticity' which typically propels characters' violent rejection of sexual norms.[13] While *Zofloya* explores a diversity of sexual transgressions and fluid gender representations, and aligns Victoria with female monstrousness (she rejects traditional female roles and commits murder along with numerous other violent and sexual crimes), *Frankenstein* fully develops the conception of the monster as a figure for destabilising gender and sexual norms. Jack Halberstam argues that 'The endeavour of Frankenstein to first create life on his own and then to prevent his monster from mating suggests, if only by default, a homoerotic tension which underlies the incestuous bond.'[14] Halberstam's provocative reading claims that Victor Frankenstein's creation of 'a being like [him]self ... hints at both masturbatory and homosexual desires which the scientist attempts to sanctify with the reproduction of another being. The suggestion that a homosexual bond in fact animates the plot adds an element of sexual perversity to the monster's already hybrid form.'[15] Haggerty agrees, aligning the monster with a common plight of gay men:

> This creature is given life by the mad scientist who then disowns him right after the creature has approached him in his bed: this pattern calls to mind the struggles of a young gay man, monstrous to himself in so many ways and confused about how he has come into being.[16]

Previous to Halberstam's reading of homosexuality and sociopolitical otherness, Anne K. Mellor's discussion of the homoerotic bond between the monster and Victor (which Halberstam charges as having the potential to be discursively homophobic) provides a psychoanalytic interpretation of Victor's rejection of his cousin Elizabeth, which is replaced by a homosexual obsession with his creature.[17] These seminal readings help situate monstrosity as a construction of otherness (along racial, class, sexual and gender lines). And as with eighteenth-century Gothic villains, queer sexuality is aligned with violence, sexual or otherwise. According to Haggerty, 'The creature, like the queer subject, is driven to destroy because he is not allowed the solace of any real companionship.'[18] This anger is critical to understanding the plight of trans and genderqueer experiences.

While Haggerty aligns the creature's experience with that of gay men, Susan Stryker's performance piece and subsequent essay 'My Words to Victor Frankenstein above the Village of Chamounix: Performing Transgender Rage' (1994) profoundly shifted interpretations of *Frankenstein*, and altered the view of the monster's gender malleability in literary criticism. Written in the early 1990s, the essay powerfully expressed Stryker's transsexuality, her physical transition, and her alignment with the Creature: 'Hearken unto me, fellow creatures. I who have dwelt in a form unmatched with my desire, I whose flesh has become an assemblage of incongruous anatomical parts, I who achieve the similitude of a natural body only through an unnatural process ...'[19] This personal, bold exposure of transgender experience paved the way for numerous queer and trans approaches to Gothic literature. And I agree with Stryker and others that monstrous sexualities in modern literature were in response to policed, criminalised and medicalised sexual experiences. As discursive practices delineated traditional gender norms, and Victorian sexologists created sexual taxonomies and outlined deviancies, transgender, gender-fluid and non-binary characters and monsters flourished in literature.

Victorian Sexology and the Incitement to Gothic Discourse

With this eruption of sexual discursive practices and taxonomies (brilliantly and problematically traced by Foucault in Volume 1 of *The*

History of Sexuality) we can locate their inevitable influence on Victorian Gothic. Along with aggressive, monstrous, Sapphic women and ill, nervous, feminised men, Victorian literature houses numerous queer characters who defy sexual and gender categorisation. They help us better understand medical and discursive responses to non-binary and trans individuals, many of the responses attaching biological or psychological explanations. And though the coining of the term 'homosexual' and the wider dissemination of sexologists' work occurred after the publication of mid-century Victorian literature that can be explored through a queer Gothic lens, we can acknowledge that case studies and medical inquiry into sexuality and gender existed from mid-century on, and that Victorian writers consistently depicted numerous gender non-conforming characters.

Austro-German psychiatrist Richard von Krafft-Ebing's conflation of queer sexual orientation and trans gender identity and expression became part of the scientific foundation that informed cisnormative and heteronormative standards not only in medicine and the law, but in the popular imagination. Underlying the landmark taxonomic study *Psychopathia Sexualis with Especial Reference to Contrary Sexual Instinct: A Medico-Legal Study* (1886) is Krafft-Ebing's assumption that 'any departure from procreative heterosexual intercourse represents a form of emotional or physical disease'.[20] Krafft-Ebing regarded homosexuality as a form of gender variance, considering men attracted to men as having female attributes, and women sexually attracted to women as more masculine. Stryker explains in *The Transgender Studies Reader*, 'Krafft-Ebing noted two primary categories of homosexuality – acquired and congenital – and considered each to contain transgender elements to which he applied ornate Victorian labels such as "eviration", "defemi-nination", "viraginity", and "metamorphosis sexualis paranoica".'[21] This latter term refers to the most pathological of disorders, describing individuals who completely identify with the sex they were not assigned at birth and who wish to alter the sex-signifying aspects of their bodies. Stryker continues, 'Krafft-Ebing thought such individuals were profoundly disturbed, and considered their desire for self-affirming transformation to be psychotic.'[22]

Psychopathia Sexualis is one of many taxonomic works from the Victorian era that discursively detail sexual 'abnormalities' and 'deviance' with blatantly subjective narratives. In *Studies in the Psychology of Sex, Volume 2*, Havelock Ellis traces non-normative behaviours of numerous patients, offering a more sympathetic view of sexual and gender variance. Sexologists such as Krafft-Ebing, Ellis and later Sigmund Freud present case studies that are novelistic in their descriptions and explanations, provocatively narrativising sexual anomalies, transvestism, cross-dressing and hermaphroditism (today referred to as intersexed bodies). In their studies, they clearly grapple with and conflate what we would often consider today to be transgender, intersex and homosexual phenomena.[23] Although these theories emerged later in the century, Victorian culture saw an increased visibility of sexual and gender variance, so it is no surprise that reactions and responses to these cultural shifts penetrated the literary landscape, inciting Gothic discourse.

Queering Victorian Femaleness

Having their Gothic origins in Dacre's Victoria, monstrosised female characters include Charlotte Brontë's Bertha in *Jane Eyre* (1847) and the notorious lesbian Miss Wade in Charles Dickens's *Little Dorrit* (1855–57 in serial form). In both novels, these women embody numerous Victorian anxieties and fears: uncontrolled female sexuality, reverse colonisation, miscegenation, mental instability, hysteria and sexually transmitted diseases. While many feminist critics have read Bertha Mason as Jane Eyre's Creole, mad double, it can be productive to read Jane's dehumanised description of Bertha as inflected with the erotic rhetoric of imperial dominance but also queer voyeurism and desire. Prior to the unveiling of Bertha, Jane provides uncomfortably critical descriptions of her rival Blanche Ingram's appearance and behaviour and later spends numerous paragraphs detailing the 'perfect beauty' of her other rival Rosamund Oliver (also tempered with descriptions of her deficient intelligence). Yet it is her problematic description of Bertha's body and behaviour that fully exposes Jane's curiosity and repulsion, as well as Rochester's role in this dynamic. Clearly, Jane's language degrades and dehumanises Bertha ('clothed hyena', 'goblin', 'vampire', 'figure', 'it'), yet it also hypersexualises and obsesses over her physical differences: Bertha's movements are animalistic and erotic ('it grovelled, seemingly, on all fours'), and Jane emphasises this when describing her hair, a Victorian symbol of sexuality ('it was covered with ... a quantity of dark, grizzled hair, wild as a mane, hid its head and face').[24] When Rochester unveils Bertha, who has been imprisoned in the attic at Thornfield, she attacks him. Notably, Jane provides not only vampiric language, but sexually suggestive language: 'the lunatic sprang and grappled his throat viciously, and laid her teeth to his cheek: they struggled'.[25] Reversing traditional gender norms, Bertha is uncontrollable, sexually voracious and violent; her 'attack' and 'virile force' perhaps resembling BDSM practices.

In fact, Jane notes that Rochester engages in submissive tactics and at first refuses to control Bertha's threatening and physical attack: 'He could have settled her with a well-planted blow; but he would not strike.'[26] Having earlier attacked her own brother Richard, biting him 'like a tigress' and 'suck[ing] the blood',[27] Bertha again deploys her teeth, dismantling and appropriating male penetrative power. Once submissive and penetrated, Rochester switches BDSM roles. Jane narrates: 'He mastered her arms ... and he pinioned them behind her: with more rope, which was at hand, he bound her to her chair. The operation was performed amidst the fiercest yells and the most convulsive plunges.'[28] With 'cord' and 'rope' at hand, it seems as if Bertha's lair is well-prepared for these passive/aggressive exchanges and performances. In fact, once Bertha is tied up and no longer a physical threat, Rochester turns to 'the spectators' with an 'acrid and desolate' smile. Clearly, 'the contest' is painfully pleasurable. He even admits that 'Such is the sole conjugal embrace I am ever to know', invoking the present tense as if these embraces are not just relegated to the long past.[29] It is fascinating that the supposedly inexperienced and sexually meek Jane does not run from the 'monstrous' scene; in fact, she stares, intricately describes and interprets the violent exchange for the reader. Even when Rochester flings Jane behind him to supposedly protect her, she chooses to intently observe his interactions with Bertha; instead of escaping in horror, Jane is a passive participant and voyeur, saving her astonishment and demeaning descriptions for the page.

When Rochester later invites Jane to live with him as his lover (an arrangement not codified but already in place), this 'thruppling' again defies institutionalised heteronormativities. By disavowing the rites of Christian marriage, Rochester continues to imagine a queer intimacy shared with both his wife and mistress: Bertha's blatant, physical sexual appetite paired with Jane's quiet but just as enticing strong-willed and deeply felt love and passion. Bertha has in fact initiated Jane into Rochester's sexual fetishes: he desires the wild, untamed, female penetrator who he must eventually tie up and control, as well as the small, fairy-like female who he can physically dominate (Rochester grabs, bruises and manhandles Jane throughout her stay at Thornfield). Yet after Bertha's existence is revealed, Jane also describes Rochester as bound up and dominated: 'But in his countenance I saw a change: that looked desperate and brooding – that reminded me of some wronged and fettered wild beast or bird, dangerous to approach in his sullen woe.'[30] Through the trauma of Bertha's physical containment, Jane finds a way to align the two, who are both 'dangerous to approach' yet fascinating to observe.

In fact, Rochester's non-normative, dominate–submit attractions surface the moment he meets the shy and diminutive Jane: he accuses her of bewitching his horse, which throws and injures him, and he dehumanises her by calling her 'sprite' and 'elf'. In a way, the sturdy, broad Rochester is disempowered by Jane's presence (she admits, 'I felt no fear of him'), and his rhetoric underscores that she has physically forced him into submission. Earlier, in a notorious cross-dressing scene, Rochester penetrates Jane's emotional state through a type of visual and psychological manipulation as an old gypsy fortune-teller. Roles reversed, now Rochester is described by Jane with elfin terms ('elf-locks'), noting that her 'strange talk, voice, manner, had by this time wrapped me in a kind of dream'; 'I got involved in a web of mystification', signifying that now she will be the one controlled and manipulated.[31] Disabling Jane's confidence and self-protection in an intimate manner, Rochester as female Other exposes Jane's vulnerabilities and desires. Emotionally violated, Jane scolds Rochester when he reveals his disguise, yet the violation (along with the other dangers Bertha has posed) does not result in Jane's fleeing Thornfield. She suffers and endures, intrigued by the eccentric man she is falling in love with. Perhaps this is why Brontë chooses to end the novel with gender role reversals: the now 'weaker' and demasculinised Rochester is in a position of physical submission while Jane's body takes on an added strength (she is Rochester's eyes and physical support). Though Bertha is dead and Thornfield destroyed, Rochester creates a new type of BDSM lair at Ferndean: it is wild and overgrown, he is partially blind, disabled and submissive yet still virile, and Jane takes pleasure in her newfound power and mastery over him.

Jane might seem to accept her normative roles as wife and mother, yet Bertha and the queerness she inspired still haunts her narrative. The physical ruins Bertha left in the wake of her suicide are continual reminders of Rochester's queer desires and punishments and Jane's participation in them. While on the surface Brontë deploys a female 'monster' to reinforce Jane's white, English, Christian sensibilities, we can also shift this lens and understand the productive queerness that Bertha inspires through her destruction and reconstruction of normalised ideas of home, marriage, sexuality and femaleness. As the end of *Jane Eyre* attests to, tightly bound with the heteronormative, the Gothic uses the romance plot to temporarily disrupt and then reinstitute this same heteronormativity. Yet sensation and Gothic fiction also dramatise the residue of queerness which haunts, absorbs and lingers, offering new and provocative strategies and potentials that continue to challenge binaries and norms.

Wilkie Collins's Queerness

A prime example of Gothic's response to Victorian cultural formations such as sexology and the increased policing of sexual variance is Wilkie Collins's sensation novel *The Woman in White* (1859). Pointing to both male homoerotic and lesbian elements in the text, D. A. Miller's queer reading of the mustachioed Marian Halcombe is seminal, and has led to numerous queer interpretations of Marian and the novel's other queer characters.[32] Studies such as Miller's and Haefele-Thomas's have helped to illuminate other genderqueer characters in Collins's oeuvre such as *Armadale*'s Ozias Midwinter and Lydia Gwilt, subversive heroines such as *No Name*'s Magdalen Vanstone, *The Dead Secret*'s homoerotic Mrs Jazeph, and *The Law and the Lady*'s genderqueer and disabled Miserrimus Dexter and Ariel. These interpretations signify how queer desire is, like the supernatural, invisible yet hauntingly evident and familiar.

Writing at mid-century, Wilkie Collins was firmly non-conformist: he never married, visited sex workers, had concurrent female partners and had fathered three illegitimate children by the time of his death. Rejecting Victorian values, he celebrated (and sometimes fetishised) the non-conforming in his fiction. Just as his personal, secretive life was something out of one of the plots of his own sensation novels, his genderqueer characters speak to the transgressive capabilities of Victorian culture. His fictional worlds, which hybridise sensation and Gothic forms and tropes, offer spaces for queer and trans characters, spaces that incorporate, accept or, as expected, violently reject them.

For this discussion, it is necessary to briefly address the predominant character who spawned queer readings of Collins: *The Woman in White*'s Marian Halcombe. Though her physical description as given by Walter Hartright has received frequent critical attention, it is necessary to quote it here so we can be reminded of Collins's specific motive in depicting her in a hermaphroditic, androgynous, 'monstrous' manner. Initially, Walter sees her from behind:

> Struck by the rare beauty of her form ... her waist ... was visibly and delightfully undeformed by stays ... The easy elegance of every movement of her limbs and body as soon as she began to advance from the far end of the room, set me in a flutter of expectation to see her face clearly.[33]

Unconventional (not wearing stays or a corset), elegant, and causing Walter's somatic (orgasmic-like) reaction, Marian's body is beautiful, elegant and arousing. Yet Walter's next description of her when she turns around and faces him causes a different type of somatic and emotional reaction:

> The lady's complexion was almost swarthy and the dark down on her upper lip was almost a moustache. She had a large, firm masculine mouth and jaw; prominent, piercing resolute brown eyes; and thick, coal-black hair, growing unusually low down on her forehead. Her expression – bright, frank, and intelligent – appeared, while she was silent, to be altogether wanting in those feminine attractions of gentleness and pliability, without which the beauty of the handsomest woman alive is beauty incomplete. To see such a face as this set on shoulders that a sculptor would have longed to model – to be charmed by the modest graces of action through which the symmetrical limbs betrayed their beauty when they moved, and then to be almost repelled by the masculine form and the masculine look of the features in which the perfectly shaped figure ended – was to feel a sensation oddly akin to the helpless discomfort familiar to us all in sleep, when we recognise but cannot reconcile the anomalies and contradictions of a dream.[34]

Walter's taxonomy of difference, and suggestion that Marian is some atavistic anomaly (large 'masculine' mouth and jaw, low forehead hair), reminds us of the later Victorian sexologists' taxonomies of sexual and gender anomalies (and even Cesare Lombroso's studies of criminality).[35] In fact, Victorian psychological, sexological and evolutionary discourses often interlink, causing the hermaphrodite to be seen as atavistic and unfinished in their development. (Linking the invert to the degenerate was common for sexologists.) And with her majestic female body and masculine, ugly face, Marian is the embodiment of queer difference, as Miller, Richard Collins and others argue.

Marian can also be more specifically read as transgender.[36] In fact, her appealing (yet repellent) androgynous appearance speaks to the Victorian crisis of gender identity. Miller is the first reader of Marian to fully theorise her queerness; his analysis of Walter's description of her 'masculine form' and 'masculine look' are foundational. With this, Miller claims she embodies a symbolic phallus, is a lesbian, 'mannish', and is 'male-identified'.[37] He remarks that Marian's is the 'conspicuously curious case of a woman's body that gives all the signs of containing a man's soul'.[38] Today we can better recognise Miller's gesturing towards a trans reading, locating Marian's difference with transgender concepts and identifications (even perhaps gender dysphoria). Haefele-Thomas's queer reading of Marian aligns her with the Victorian monster or freak (a throwback to the bearded ladies in travelling shows), but also the spinster and superfluous woman (and we can agree in that Marian gestures towards the odd woman and prefigures the New Woman of the *fin de siècle*). Yet she is also the novel's moral compass, the character who reminds Walter of his duty as a man, and the person who all of the novel's male characters rely on in some fashion. Haefele-Thomas remarks that through Marian, 'Collins subverts heteronormative and gender normative constructions of masculinity, femininity, and the stereotypes about relationships between men and women'.[39] With her 'genderqueer position', homoerotic and bonding love with her half-sister Laura, and role as sister-wife at the end of the novel, Marian queers the Victorian family.[40] I wish to extend this reading and suggest that Marian's position in the novel is one primarily of transness. She not only subverts heteronormative constructs and reinforces female–female bonds, she physically defies a sexual binary and appears to male-identify.

The secretive Italian Count Fosco recognises and praises Marian's masculinity. He asks Laura's scheming husband, Sir Percival Glyde, '"Where are your eyes? Can you look at Miss Halcombe, and not see that she as the foresight and resolution of a man?"'[41] Her relation to gender seems to perpetually shift and cross boundaries as she acknowledges the limits of women in her culture. In a notable scene, she refuses to pin her identity down with a series of binary comparisons to the ultra-feminine Laura as she introduces herself to the still-shocked Walter Hartright:

> 'Except that we are both orphans, we are in every respect as unlike each other as possible. My father was a poor man, and Miss Fairlie's father was a rich man. I have got nothing, and she has a fortune. I am dark and ugly, and she is fair and pretty. Everybody thinks me crabbed and odd (with perfect justice); and everybody thinks her sweet-tempered and charming (with more justice still). In short, she is an angel; and I am – Try some of that marmalade, Mr. Hartright, and finish the sentence, in the name of female propriety, for yourself.'[42]

The dash ('and I am –') marks her identity; the narrative draws a line to underscore the gender binary but also slash it. She refuses to self-identify for Walter's comfort, and the dash signifies her power: whatever term the blank is filled with by Walter has no weight or importance for her. She even pronounces to him, 'Dear me, you look puzzled.'[43] Laurel Erickson recognises that Marian defines herself as a marked woman 'but refuses to name her difference', and goes so far as to identify the dash as syntactic replacement for 'a moustache'.[44] She reads Marian with gender indeterminate terms ('she is both man and woman, yet neither man nor woman') and also animalistic similarities, aligning her with the Pig-Faced Lady, Julia Pastrana and other Victorian freaks (as Haefele-Thomas does).[45] These comparisons would of course be common for the

Victorians (and highly offensive today), but when intersected with sexologist taxonomies, Marian's description aligns more with Ellis's eonist and Krafft-Ebing's pseudohermaphrodite.[46] As we have seen, sexologists (and Victorians at large) struggled to categorise gender non-binary people. Collins seems to empower Marian and her trans possibilities; she is fully aware of her difference and ability to destabilise not only Walter, but Victorian norms and binaries.

I'm not suggesting that Collins was directly aware of his culture's medical and scientific approaches to transgender embodiment, but he was well aware of subverting norms through fluid characters. The sensation genre (like the Gothic) allows for and celebrates these subversions, and as in Marian's case, creates spaces for sympathising with non-normative characters. Whereas Erickson argues that she circulates in a 'narrative space that has not already been defined for her', I argue that in the end the narrative forecloses Marian's trans possibilities.[47] She is forced to accept the maternal, feminine role demanded by the text (though in a non-traditional manner as 'sister-wife' to Walter). Once the monstrous, pseudohermaphroditic Other whose incongruous appearance caused 'helpless discomfort', Marian is 'the good angel of our lives' by the novel's last line. Similar to Ariel and Miserrimus in *The Law and the Lady*, whose co-dependent relationship is based on able and disabled capacities, in the end Marian's strength supports Laura, who has suffered emotional and physical trauma. A common arrangement in Victorian families, as helpmate to both Laura and Walter, and surrogate mother to their child, Marian's presence in the relationship is seemingly balanced and normalised. Yet this triad also suggests that in Collins's fictional world, forms of queer families can exist and prosper.

As with Marian Halcombe, Frederick Fairlie and Ezra Jennings, Collins often simultaneously fetishises and 'monstrosises' his non-binary characters, and *The Law and the Lady*'s disabled Miserrimus Dexter is no different. Like Limmeridge House, 'Prince Dexter's Palace' houses trans figures who must necessarily be given atavistic, monstrous descriptors. Similar to Marian, Miserrimus is endowed with homoerotic and trans possibilities; Valeria describes him as 'a strange and startling creature literally the half of a man' and 'like a woman'.[48] He is monstrous ('terrible', 'the halfman'), and like Marian, hyper-sexualised. Valeria repeatedly states that he is 'an unusually handsome, and an unusually well-made man'.[49] Miserrimus crosses several lines of propriety, devouring Valeria's hands with kisses, placing his hands on Valeria's shoulders and, most shockingly for Victorians, around her waist. Collins even resurrects Walter's taxonomic, binary-filled description of Marian with Valeria's portrait of Miserrimus:

> His long silky hair, of a bright and beautiful chestnut colour, fell over shoulders that were the perfection of strength and grace. His face was bright with vivacity and intelligence. His large clear blue eyes, and his long delicate white hands, were like the eyes and hands of a beautiful woman. He would have looked effeminate, but for the manly proportions of his throat and chest; aided in their effect by his flowing beard and long moustache, of a lighter chestnut shade than the colour of his hair. Never had a magnificent head and body been more hopelessly ill-bestowed than in this instance! Never had Nature committed a more careless or more cruel mistake than in the making of this man![50]

Just as Marian's body marks her gender difference and confusion, moustache and all, Miserrimus's body signifies the same disruption and destabilisation of gendered physicality and embodiment. Both bodies are startling in their combination of female and male incongruity and attractiveness; both shock and arouse; and both are in some way disabled and 'unnatural'. Valeria layers her portrait of Miserrimus with gendered terms: he has 'delicate' hands and an 'effeminate' appearance; 'He spoke in the gentlest of voices – and he sighed hysterically when he had done, like a woman recovering from a burst of tears.'[51] Teresa Mangum notes, 'His unclear sexual status and complex gendering are presented as his greatest deformities, motivating the spectator's guilty gaze.'[52]

In another remarkable description, Valeria details his effeminate ensemble:

> His jacket, on this occasion, was of pink quilted silk. The coverlid which hid his deformity matched the jacket in pale sea-green satin; and, to complete these strange vagaries of costume, his wrists were actually adorned with massive bracelets of gold, formed on the severely-simple models which have descended to us from ancient times![53]

Miserrimus explains that he has received Valeria 'in the prettiest clothes I have', and defends his cross-dressing by pronouncing that 'a hundred years ago, a gentleman in pink silk was a gentleman properly dressed'.[54] He further argues, 'I despise the brutish contempt for beauty and mean dread of expense which degrade a gentleman's costume to black cloth, and limit a gentleman's ornaments to a finger ring, in the age I live in.'[55] Here Miserrimus gestures to the Romantic Age, a period before gender norms were firmly established and regulated. At one moment sewing in a pink silk jacket, the next denouncing women for their inability to concentrate their attention 'on any one occupation', and the next cooking truffles in wine for Valeria, Miserrimus defies gender stereotypes while caustically endorsing others.[56]

As Walter is horrifyingly attracted to the moustached Marian, Valeria describes Miserrimus as 'being an unusually handsome man', and says that his blue eyes are 'large as the eyes of a woman'.[57] And just as Walter both eroticises and monstrosises Marian and gives her primordial attributes, Valeria is intrigued by and potentially attracted to Miserrimus, but must temper these emotions by describing him in atavistic terms:

> For one moment we saw a head and body in the air, absolutely deprived of the lower limbs. The moment after, the terrible creature touched the floor as lightly as a monkey, on his hands. The grotesque horror of the scene culminated in his hopping away, on his hands, at a prodigious speed.[58]

Later seized by madness, furiously racing in his wheelchair, Miserrimus is 'Half man, half chair', 'looking in the distance like a monstrous frog'.[59] Valeria even refers to him as 'Thing', 'Object' and 'It'. Eventually incapacitated by his madness, he is placed in an asylum where he soon dies. Whereas Marian is given the opportunity to conform in the end and partially accept Victorian patriarchal and heteronormative norms, Miserrimus's flagrant and transgressive difference cannot be contained by the narrative. Institutions such as asylums punish transgressors, upholding the broader cultural norms challenged by such characters as Marian Halcombe and Miserrimus Dexter.

Queer Bonds: Dickens's Jenny and Lizzie

Similar to Collins, Charles Dickens persistently explores characters who defy sexual and gender norms. For example, *Great Expectations* (1860–61), one of his most 'Gothic' novels, is centred on intimate male friendships, intimacy and violence: Miss Havisham's queer world defies Victorian ideas of motherhood and the home; Pip, Herbert and Herbert's wife Clara create a close-knit thrupple; and numerous male characters are approached and attacked by other men 'from behind'. Dickens's unfinished and darkest novel, *The Mystery of Edwin Drood* (1870), is centred on the violent, incest-laced obsession that John Jasper has for his nephew Edwin. Yet I would like to illuminate a brief moment of female–female intimacy from *Our Mutual Friend* (1865) that speaks to other forms of queer potentials, those not addressed by Sedgwick's landmark reading of the novel in *Between Men: English Literature and Male Homosocial Desire* (1985). While I opened this chapter with the self-interested Victoria's queer 'performance' from *Zofloya*, I wish to close it with a touching, positive queer scene between women. In Dickens's novel, the dolls' dressmaker, Jenny Wren, suffers from a spinal deformity, but she is also endowed with magnificent, golden hair. Noted by critics to be essentially asexual and childish, 'her rich shower of hair' covers men like Eugene Wrayburn in a protective and healing manner. Yet the Victorian sexual associations with hair charge these scenes with potential eroticism (much like Collins's descriptions of Misserimus's flowing golden locks). Both poor and struggling, Jenny and Lizzie Hexam, the corpse-dredger's daughter, take comfort in each others' company, and at the close of laborious days they help each other literally 'let down their hair', unpinning each other's tresses by the fire. It is Lizzie's regular occupation when they are alone to brush out and smooth Jenny's amazing tresses: Lizzie (reminding us of Rossetti's Lizzie from 'Goblin Market') 'playfully smooth[s] the bright long fair hair which grew very luxuriant and beautiful on the head of the doll's dressmaker'.[60] As Rachel Cote recognises, 'It's a sensuous and romantic ritual – two young women basking in their mutual physical charms, silken streams tumbling across shoulders and bosoms as a fire crackles in the dusk.'[61] When Lizzie lives with Jenny, they revel in this companionship and ritual, determining that any husband would pale in comparison to her friend. 'He couldn't brush my hair like you do', Jenny avows, 'or help me up and down stairs like you do, and he couldn't do anything like you do.'[62] Lizzie is the perfect partner, soothing, gentle, and a helpmate for the diminutive and disabled Jenny. Regardless of Jenny's arguments against the benefits of a husband, in the end she does marry the mentally disabled Sloppy. This female intimacy is thereby temporary – Jenny and Lizzie must ultimately accept their heteronormative marriage plots – yet we are reminded of the shared, intense homosocial bond that the erotic symbol of hair generates.

Conclusion

These erotic, sexually ambivalent literary examples in many ways prophesy the provocative literary depictions of sexuality and gender at the *fin de siècle* (discussed in this collection by Jamil Mustafa). In my view, by troubling and extending queer readings of Victorian Gothic, we can better understand genderqueer and trans characterisations and narratives. And with this, we can better understand the diversity of queer possibilities in the culture. Haefele-Thomas insightfully recognises that 'The terms "genderqueer" and "queer" are undeniably useful when looking at Victorian Gothic because they connote a sense of flexibility; they hold the multiple gender identities and sexual behaviours of a Victorian culture that was beginning to rigidly define the connection between identity and behaviour.'[63] Yet figures such as Oscar Wilde who embodied this sexual flexibility and complexity were persecuted by this very same culture, largely in response to the fact that the Victorian era was populated by all manner of non-binary and gender-expansive slippages. Non-conforming figures such as Vernon Lee, Ernest 'Stella' Boulton and Frederick 'Fanny' Park, Michael Field, 'Manchester's female husband' Harry Stokes, and Dr James Barry attest to this fact. The publication of numerous scientific treatises about sexual variants reflects the growing visibility of and cultural interest in sexual and gender fluidity, which resulted in scientific limitations as well as forms of social policing and regulation. Thus Victorian Gothic literature, which consistently depicts and dramatises non-normative sexualities, acts and characters (producing pathology and perversion in Foucauldian terms), ultimately condemns and punishes these potentials and possibilities, often monstrosising gender-fluid characters. While heterosexuality is reinforced in late eighteenth- and nineteenth-century Gothic literature, within its pages we must also illuminate violent, unstable, voyeuristic, celebratory queerness.

Notes

1. Charlotte Dacre, *Zofloya, or The Moor* (Oxford: Oxford University Press, 1997), p. 60 (later Victoria will also demand Lilla's *deshabillement*). For a helpful discussion of Dacre's queer novel, and how to approach it in the classroom, see Ranita Chatterjee, 'Charlotte Dacre's Nymphomaniacs and Demon-Lovers: Teaching Female Masculinities', in *Masculinities in Text and Teaching*, ed. Ben Knights (New York: Palgrave Macmillan, 2008), pp. 75–89.
2. Dacre, *Zofloya*, p. 60.
3. Ardel Haefele-Thomas, *Queer Others in Victorian Gothic: Transgressing Monstrosity* (Cardiff: University of Wales Press, 2012), p. 142. See also William Hughes and Andrew Smith's edited collection *Queering the Gothic* (Manchester: Manchester University Press, 2009). Previous to this, George E. Haggerty, Eve Kosofsky Sedgwick, Ellis Hanson, D. A. Miller and others have suggested that a wide range of late eighteenth- and nineteenth-century writers used 'Gothic' to evoke a 'queer' world that attempts to transgress the binaries of sexual decorum. See more recent book-length studies such as Max Fincher's *Queering Gothic in the Romantic Age: The Penetrating Eye* (Basingstoke: Palgrave Macmillan, 2007) and Paulina Palmer's *The Queer Uncanny: New Perspectives on the Gothic* (Cardiff: University of Wales Press, 2012).
4. Michel Foucault, *The History of Sexuality: An Introduction* (New York: Vintage, 1990), p. 37.
5. Ibid., pp. 38–9. For fuller discussions of Foucault and the Gothic, see Dale Townshend, *The Orders of Gothic: Foucault, Lacan, and the Subject of*

Gothic Writing 1764–1820 (New York: AMS Press, 2007), and Jolene Zigarovich, 'Gothic and the History of Sexuality', in *The Cambridge History of the Gothic, Vol. I: Gothic in the Long Eighteenth Century*, ed. Dale Townshend, Angela Wright and Catherine Spooner (Cambridge: Cambridge University Press, 2020), pp. 382–405.
6. George E. Haggerty, *Queer Gothic* (Champaign, IL: University of Illinois Press, 2006), p. 51.
7. Steven Bruhm, 'Gothic Sexualities' in *Teaching the Gothic*, ed. Anna Powell and Andrew Smith (Basingstoke: Palgrave Macmillan, 2006), pp. 93–106 (p. 93). Portions of this section stem from my previous work 'Gothic and the History of Sexuality'.
8. For further discussion of Radcliffe's queerness, see Jeremy Chow's provocative essay 'Mellifluent Sexuality: Female Intimacy in Radcliffe's *The Romance of the Forest*', *Eighteenth-Century Fiction*, 30.2 (2017/18), pp. 195–221.
9. See Nowell Marshall, 'Beyond Queer Gothic: Charting the Gothic History of the Trans Subject in Beckford, Lewis, Byron', in *TransGothic in Literature and Culture*, ed. Jolene Zigarovich (New York: Routledge, 2018), pp. 25–52. In the same volume, see also Jeremy Chow, 'Go to Hell: William Beckford's Skewed Heaven and Hell', pp. 53–76.
10. See Jolene Zigarovich, 'Transgothic Desire in Charlotte Dacre's *Zofloya*', in *TransGothic in Literature and Culture*, ed. Jolene Zigarovich (New York: Routledge, 2018), pp. 77–96.
11. Dacre, *Zofloya*, p. 53.
12. Ibid., p. 60.
13. George Haggerty, 'Gothic Fiction and Queer Theory', in *Gothic and Theory: An Edinburgh Companion*, ed. Jerrold E. Hogle and Robert Miles (Edinburgh: Edinburgh University Press, 2019), pp. 147–64 (p. 158).
14. Jack Halberstam, *Skin Shows: Gothic Horror and the Technology of Monsters* (Durham, NC: Duke University Press, 1995), p. 42.
15. Ibid., p. 42.
16. Haggerty, 'Gothic Fiction and Queer Theory', p. 159.
17. See Anne K. Mellor, *Romanticism and Gender* (New York: Routledge, 1993), and Anne K. Mellor, *Mary Shelley: Her Life, Her Fiction, Her Monsters* (New York: Methuen, 1988).
18. George Haggerty, 'What is Queer about *Frankenstein*?', in *The Cambridge Companion to Frankenstein*, ed. Andrew Smith (Cambridge: Cambridge University Press), pp. 116–27 (p. 126).
19. Susan Stryker, 'My Words to Victor Frankenstein above the Village of Chamounix: Performing Transgender Rage', in *The Transgender Studies Reader*, vol. II, ed. Susan Stryker and Stephan Whittle (New York: Routledge, 2006), pp. 244–56 (p. 247). Note that I am referring to Stryker's own use of 'transsexual' from the 1990s. Today she refers to herself using *trans* or *transgender*.
20. Susan Stryker, '(De)Subjugated Knowledges: An Introduction to Transgender Studies', in *The Transgender Studies Reader*, vol. 1, ed. Susan Stryker and Stephan Whittle (New York: Routledge, 2006), pp. 1–18 (p. 21).
21. Ibid., p. 21.
22. Ibid., p. 21.

23. Jolene Zigarovich, 'Transing Wilkie Collins', *The Wilkie Collins Journal*, 15 (2018), special issue, 'Heart and Science in Wilkie Collins', ed. Jo Parsons, https://wilkiecollinssociety.org/journal/volume-15/ (accessed 14 February 2023). Note that when referring to historical documents I am following Erickson, Stryker and others by using the terms 'hermaphrodite' and 'hermaphroditic'. Today intersex is a positive and more widely accepted term to describe those with atypical sex attributes.
24. Charlotte Brontë, *Jane Eyre* (New York: W.W. Norton, 2001), p. 250.
25. Ibid., p. 250.
26. Ibid., p. 250.
27. Ibid., p. 181.
28. Ibid., p. 250.
29. Ibid., p. 251.
30. Ibid., p. 367.
31. Ibid., p. 170.
32. See D. A. Miller, *The Novel and the Police* (Berkeley, CA: University of California Press, 1988); Ardel Haefele-Thomas, *Queer Others in Victorian Gothic: Transgressing Monstrosity* (Cardiff: University of Wales Press, 2009); Richard Nemesvari, 'The Mark of the Brotherhood: Homosexual Panic and the Foreign Other in Wilkie Collins's *The Woman in White*', in *Straight Writ Queer: Non-Normative Expression of Heterosexuality in Literature*, ed. Richard Fantina and Calvin Thomas (Jefferson, NC: McFarland, 2006), pp. 95–108; Lauren N. Hoffer and Sarah E. Kersh, 'The Victorian Family in Queer Time: Secrets, Sisters and Lovers in *The Woman the White* and *Fingersmith*', in *Queer Victorian Families: Curious Relations in Literature*, ed. Duc Dau and Shale Preston (Abingdon: Routledge, 2015), pp. 195–210; Martha Stoddard Holmes, 'Queering the Marriage Plot: Wilkie Collins's *The Law and the Lady*', in *Victorian Freaks: The Social Context of Freakery in Britain*, ed. Marlene Tromp (Columbus, OH: Ohio State University Press, 2008), pp. 237–58. For helpful introductions, see Emily Allen, 'Gender and Sensation', in *The Companion to Sensation Fiction*, ed. Pamela K. Gilbert (Hoboken, NJ: John Wiley & Sons, 2011), as well as Ross G. Forman's, 'Queer Sensation' in the same volume.
33. Wilkie Collins, *The Woman in White* (Oxford: Oxford University Press, 1973), p. 25. All subsequent quotes from the novel cite this edition. Portions of this discussion of Collins's queer fiction emanate from my 'Transing Wilkie Collins', and '"A Strange and Startling Creature": Transgender Possibilities in Wilkie Collins's *The Law and the Lady*', *Victorian Review: An Interdisciplinary Journal of Victorian Studies*, 44.1 (2019), pp. 95–108.
34. Collins, *The Woman in White*, p. 25.
35. An Italian physician and criminologist, Lombroso posited a theory of criminal atavism that suggested that criminals embodied physical anomalies and a reversion to a primitive state of subhumanity. Combining phrenology with other pseudosciences, his eugenic, hereditary defect theories were used as frameworks by sexologists such as Krafft-Ebing to 'scientifically' explain human sexual behaviour and abnormalities. For a brilliant discussion of nineteenth-century theories of race, criminality and deviant sexual behaviours, see Kelly Hurley, *The Gothic Body: Sexuality, Materialism,*

and Degeneration at the 'Fin de Siècle' (Cambridge: Cambridge University Press, 1996).
36. While some of the textual evidence may point to trans identification, I wish to clarify that I am not pronouncing this identification for Collins's characters (instead I wish to highlight the possibilities and questions the texts raise).
37. Miller, *The Novel and the Police*, p. 176.
38. Ibid., p. 176.
39. Haefele-Thomas, *Queer Others in Victorian Gothic*, p. 20.
40. Ibid., p. 29.
41. Collins, *The Woman in White*, p. 296.
42. Ibid., p. 27.
43. Ibid., p. 60.
44. Laurel Erickson, '"In Short, She is an Angel, and I am—": Odd Women and Same-Sex Desire in Wilkie Collins's *Woman in White*', in *The Foreign Woman in British Literature: Exotics, Aliens, and Outsiders* (Westport, CT: Greenwood, 1999), pp. 95–116 (p. 100).
45. Ibid., p. 100.
46. Another subversive character, *The Moonstone*'s Ezra Jennings, exhibits transgender possibilities and homoerotic tendencies. Jewish and, like Marian, dark-skinned, Ezra would be seen by his Victorian audience as monstrous 'Other'. See Haefele-Thomas's *Queer Others* for an insightful discussion of Jennings and the Indian *hijra* (a third gender figure that dates back over 4,000 years).
47. Erickson, '"In Short"', p. 100.
48. Wilkie Collins, *The Law and the Lady* (London: Penguin, 1998), pp. 163, 281.
49. Ibid., p. 163.
50. Ibid., p. 163.
51. Ibid., p. 195.
52. Teresa Mangum, 'Wilkie Collins, Detection, and Deformity', *Dickens Studies Annual*, 26 (1998), pp. 285–310 (p. 296).
53. Collins, *The Law and the Lady*, pp. 215–16.
54. Ibid., p. 216.
55. Ibid., p. 216.
56. Ibid., p. 229.
57. Ibid., p. 200.
58. Ibid., p. 194.
59. Ibid., p. 244.
60. Charles Dickens, *Our Mutual Friend* (London: Penguin, 1971), p. 283.
61. Rachel Vorona Cote, *Too Much: How Victorian Constraints Still Bind Women Today* (New York: Grand Central Publishing, 2020), p. 98.
62. Dickens, *Our Mutual Friend*, p. 284.
63. See Haefele-Thomas's chapter 'Queer Victorian Gothic', in *Victorian Gothic: An Edinburgh Companion*, ed. Andrew Smith (Edinburgh: Edinburgh University Press, 2012), pp. 142–55 (p. 151).

Chapter 3

Strange Cases of the Queer *fin de siècle*: Law, Medicine and the Gothic Imaginative Mode
Jamil Mustafa

Opening the Cases

In 1886 legal and medical approaches to queerness developed in parallel yet conflicting ways that helped construct what in the 1890s became homosexuality. In January the Labouchère Amendment went into effect across the United Kingdom, stipulating that any man, 'in public or private', involved in committing, procuring or attempting to procure 'any act of gross indecency' with another man 'shall be guilty of a misdemeanour' punishable by imprisonment 'for any term not exceeding two years'.[1] This statute 'contributed to the social formation of homosexuality by shifting emphasis from sexual acts between men [. . .] to sexual sentiment or thought'.[2] As the law changed focus from acts to feelings, so too did the emerging field of sexology. In *Psychopathia Sexualis* (1886), Richard von Krafft-Ebing stresses that one must 'differentiate between disease (*perversion*) and vice (*perversity*)'.[3] This distinction corresponds to that between '*acquired*' and '*congenital*' homosexuality: those struggling with the former deviate from the sexual norm but may return to it, while those suffering from the latter are so fundamentally '*tainted*' that they cannot be held accountable for their sex crimes.[4] They 'must be removed from society for life, but not as a punishment', though 'Law is, in this, opposed to Medicine, and is constantly in danger of passing judgment on individuals who, in the light of science, are not responsible for their acts'.[5] While compassionate from a late Victorian legal standpoint and progressive from a medical one, Krafft-Ebing's understanding of congenital homosexuality as 'abnormality' rather than 'immorality'[6] promoted the idea that queer men – and, in sexology though not in British law, queer women[7] – were diseased degenerates. Indeed, by construing congenital homosexuals not only as those who commit deviant acts but also as those alienated from normative human nature, as 'step-children of Nature',[8] *Psychopathia Sexualis* helped shape the contemporary perception of homosexuals as monsters.

The concept of queerness-as-monstrosity exemplifies how in the *fin de siècle*, law, medicine and the Gothic functioned as discursive doppelgängers. Andrew Smith explains that 'theories of degeneration which rely on images of perversion, atavism and forms of monstrosity suggest an already Gothicised presence', and he discerns in sexology 'an image of the unstable, divided self which is echoed in the Gothic'.[9] Tabitha Sparks contends that 'by the 1880s and 1890s, a public disenchantment with science' was written into Gothic literature, which 'personifies the suspect power of the scientist or surgeon in figures like Dr. Jekyll and Dr. Moreau'.[10] Law and Gothic fiction were similarly imbricated. As Bridget M. Marshall observes, 'not only do Gothic novels portray courts of law, but seminal legal texts also invoke the Gothic'.[11] Going further, Leslie J. Moran claims that the '[association] between law and the Gothic imagination' not only 'draws attention to their close relationship but also suggests that the Gothic should not be considered solely as a literary genre', and he argues for the Gothic as an 'imaginative mode'.[12] A Gothic imaginative mode that involves law, medicine and fiction provides a potent means of elucidating the construction of homosexuality in the Labouchère Amendment, *Psychopathia Sexualis* and Gothic works by Robert Louis Stevenson, Arthur Machen and Bram Stoker. The case, essential in both law and medicine, is also crucial to how these *fin-de-siècle* Gothic fictions at once align with and diverge from medico-legal representations of queer identity.

Queer Gothic and *Strange Case of Dr Jekyll and Mr Hyde*

In Robert Louis Stevenson's *Strange Case of Dr Jekyll and Mr Hyde* (1886), Henry Jekyll, a distinguished scientist leading a double life, develops a chemical mixture that enables him to transform into the depraved Edward Hyde. Jekyll's friend and lawyer, Gabriel John Utterson, fears that Jekyll is being blackmailed by Hyde, whom Jekyll has made his sole beneficiary. After Hyde murders Sir Danvers Carew, a Member of Parliament and another of Utterson's clients, the lawyer assists the police in their search for the criminal, who disappears. When Jekyll first changes into Hyde without taking his potion, he asks for help from Dr Hastie Lanyon, a colleague from whom he has become estranged due to the unorthodox nature of his research. Having witnessed Jekyll transform into Hyde, Lanyon dies of shock. Before dying, he gives Utterson a letter detailing his encounter with Jekyll/Hyde, to be opened after Jekyll's own death or disappearance. Vainly attempting to create a new batch of the potion and thus maintain his original identity, Jekyll secludes himself for weeks. Poole, Jekyll's butler, comes to suspect that Hyde has murdered his master. He and Utterson break into Jekyll's laboratory, where they discover Hyde, dead from suicide. They also find a letter to Utterson in which Jekyll describes the causes and consequences of his fatal experiment. Through these letters, readers at last realise that Jekyll and Hyde are two aspects of the same man.

Published in the year that the Labouchère Amendment was first enforced and that *Psychopathia Sexualis* appeared in German,[13] Stevenson's *Strange Case of Dr Jekyll and Mr Hyde* best exemplifies connections between the queer Gothic and the case.[14] The novella's title indicates its focus on a single case, though, like so much in the text, this case is doubled: it is at once a medical and a legal case. This medico-legal doubling is redoubled as one of Jekyll's two close friends, Lanyon the doctor, is duplicated by another, Utterson the lawyer. Conversely, the medical and legal professions are conjoined in 'Henry Jekyll, M.D., D.C.L., L.L.D., F.R.S., etc.',[15] who is not only a Doctor of Medicine and a Fellow of the Royal Society, but also a Doctor of Civil Laws and a Doctor of Laws. Jekyll's legal degrees establish his expertise in both civil and canon law; thus, he is at least as credentialed in law as in medicine. This medical and legal expert is involved in a medico-legal case notable for being *strange* – that is, linked with homosexuality. According to the *Oxford English Dictionary*, in 1886 *strange* denoted not only the 'unknown' and 'unfamiliar' but also the 'abnormal' and 'queer' – which latter term had, by 1900, come to mean homosexual.[16] As Elaine Showalter has established, this strange case 'can most persuasively be read as a fable of fin-de-siècle homosexual panic, the discovery and resistance of the homosexual self'.[17] That this study in strangeness is a *case* indicates how the novella functions as a literary double for both the cases of queer men adjudicated after the enactment of the Labouchère Amendment, and the cases of congenital homosexuals in *Psychopathia Sexualis*.

Viewed from a legal perspective, the order of the names in the novella's eponymous title suggests the case of *Jekyll* v. *Hyde*. Jekyll, the plaintiff, is represented by Utterson and testifies against Hyde, the defendant, in 'Henry Jekyll's Full Statement of the Case'.[18] Utterson's theory of the case is that Hyde is blackmailing Jekyll for a 'concealed disgrace'.[19] His crime would be facilitated by the Labouchère Amendment, whose repercussions led to its being popularly known as the Blackmailer's Charter. Enfield also testifies against Hyde, sharing with Utterson an eyewitness account of Hyde's trampling a child, using a key to enter the street door to Jekyll's laboratory, and emerging from 'Black Mail House' with hush money provided by the illustrious doctor.[20] Enfield's 'odd story' focuses on the illicit relationship between Jekyll and Hyde, which is 'connected in [his] mind' with Jekyll's 'door'.[21] This connection is elucidated by the Labouchère Amendment, under whose invasive provisions 'no longer would a locked door sufficiently demarcate the private sphere from the public; no longer would private, consensual acts of a homoerotic [...] nature be "winked at" by the police, the populace, the landlord, or the neighbour'.[22] Exemplifying Stephen Heath's observation that 'the organising image for this narrative is the breaking down of doors, learning the secret behind them',[23] Utterson, representing the force of the law, ultimately breaks down the door to Jekyll's cabinet in order to discover what he and Hyde have been doing behind it, and to punish the latter. He also surveils the street door to Jekyll's laboratory in his 'Search for Mr Hyde',[24] thereby illustrating how the Labouchère Amendment 'aimed at a pre-emptive approach to "gross indecency" [by] expecting non-participants to serve as unofficial police inspectors, since it was possible to be held criminally liable for failing to report acts or anticipated acts'.[25] Yet Utterson, whose involvement in the strange case of Jekyll and Hyde is motivated as much by curiosity and jealousy as by professional obligation, not only embodies but also subverts the Labouchère Amendment.

Utterson reveals unlawful queer desire by doubling both Jekyll and Hyde in ways linked with (metaphorical) doors and keys. 'Jekyll's house, with its two entrances', epitomises how the novella depicts the 'male homosexual body' in 'images suggestive of anality and anal intercourse'.[26] That Hyde enters Jekyll's back door using the key Jekyll has given him fixates Enfield and Utterson. The former is struck by how Hyde '[whips] out a key' to this door; the latter asks, 'You are sure he used a key?' When this question surprises Enfield, Utterson says, 'I know it must seem strange.'[27] While *it* and *strange* refer to Utterson's question, they also imply the strangeness of Hyde's being allowed to insert his key into Jekyll's door. This phallic key not only signifies Hyde's empowerment and penetration of Jekyll's body, but also explains the enigmatic relationship between the two men. Aware of both the sexual and the epistemological implications of Jekyll/Hyde's key, Utterson covets it and the men who possess it. Soon he comes to share Jekyll's 'strange preference or bondage' for Hyde.[28] Utterson '[tosses] to and fro' in bed in his 'curtained room', envisioning Jekyll in his own bedroom, asleep until 'the door of that room [is] opened, the curtains of the bed [are] plucked apart' and 'he must rise and do [Hyde's] bidding'.[29] In what might well be a masturbatory fantasy, Utterson imagines himself as a voyeur watching Hyde violate Jekyll, whose rising suggests his own sexual arousal. Utterson also projects himself into Jekyll's situation, thereby indicating his longing for Hyde. Both men lie in bed, vulnerable behind doors and curtains that can be opened; both are kept awake or awakened by Hyde; both are aroused.

Utterson's erotic identification with Jekyll soon shifts to Hyde. In an uncanny reversal, the lawyer who has been 'haunted' by Hyde himself begins to 'haunt the door in the by-street of shops' where Hyde enters Jekyll's laboratory.[30] By loitering there in the hope of encountering and accosting a strange man, Utterson doubles not only Hyde but also the queer men who cruised late Victorian London's shop-lined streets, looking for sex partners.[31] Like all doppelgängers, these two are at once opposed and complementary. 'If he be Mr Hyde', Utterson thinks, 'I shall be Mr Seek.'[32] Utterson seeks his alter ego out of both curiosity and jealousy, the latter stemming from the fact that their access to Jekyll's front and back doors is inversely proportional. Hyde's increases as Utterson's decreases, until Jekyll's 'door is often shut' to him.[33] When Utterson does finally manage to pass through 'Dr Jekyll's door' and is 'carried down' before being 'at last received into the doctor's cabinet',[34] he takes a figurative trip from mouth to rectum. En route, he '[crosses] the [surgical] theatre'.[35] This is the first time he has entered a theatre of any sort in decades, for 'though he [enjoys] the theatre, [he] [has] not crossed the doors of one for twenty years'.[36] This phrasing emphasises how, until Hyde catalyses his queer desire, Utterson abstains from crossing interrelated physical, cultural and psychosexual boundaries. Repressing his enjoyment of the theatre helps him to repress his own queerness, for in his day the 'theatre had long-standing associations with homosexuality'.[37] Entering Jekyll's theatre, Utterson experiences a 'sense of strangeness' not only because 'that part of his friend's quarters' is unfamiliar, but also because this 'anatomical theatre'[38] uncannily stages Jekyll/Hyde's queer body. The theatre is notable for its anality: it is 'dingy' and cluttered, 'the tables laden with chemical apparatus, the floor strewn with crates and littered with packing straw'.[39] At the end of the theatre is a sphincter-like 'door covered with red baize; and through this, Mr Utterson [is] at last received into the doctor's cabinet'.[40] This elegant door doubles the shabby street door through which Hyde enters and exits Jekyll's laboratory/body. When the door to Jekyll's inner sanctum is later closed to Utterson, he breaks it down, thereby figuratively raping Jekyll. 'I must and shall see you', he cries, 'if not of your consent, then by brute force!'[41] Agreeing with Poole that Jekyll's 'murderer [...] is still lurking in his victim's room', though Poole admits that his suspicions are 'feelings' rather than 'evidence',[42]

Utterson justifies his forceful intrusion by claiming to have heard Hyde's voice behind the door. Thus, while ostensibly acting as an agent of the law, he satisfies both his curiosity and his queer desire by penetrating Jekyll's secrets and body alike.

The door to Jekyll's cabinet is opened more carefully by Dr Lanyon, who shares Utterson's curiosity about their mutual friend's strange case and helps elucidate its medical features. These are first signalled by the contrast between *Dr* and *Mr* in the novella's title, which identifies Jekyll as the kind of 'medical expert' Krafft-Ebing believes should be called upon in 'all cases of sexual crimes' to 'make a psychiatric examination'[43] of the perpetrator. The opposition between examiner and examined is complicated by the fact that this is the case of Dr Jekyll *and* Mr Hyde. A case involving both doctor and patient is strange indeed. This one is made stranger yet when Lanyon, succumbing to curiosity, facilitates and watches Hyde become Jekyll. This transformation elides the distinction between doctor and patient, with disastrous results. After reading Jekyll's letter and experimental notes, Lanyon concludes that '[his] colleague [is] insane', diagnoses a 'case of cerebral disease',[44] and starts to view the doctor as a patient. Similarly, Lanyon observes that Hyde, whom he also treats as 'a patient', is 'wrestling against the approaches of the hysteria'.[45] He fails to note, however, that Hyde speaks to him as if they were colleagues. 'Lanyon', Hyde warns just before taking his potion, 'you remember your vows: what follows is under the seal of *our* profession.'[46] When Lanyon's two patients reveal themselves to be one, and that one a doctor and colleague, the revelation shatters both Lanyon's scepticism of Jekyll's transcendental medicine and his health, soon killing him.

After witnessing Jekyll/Hyde's transformation in the conventional sense, Lanyon does so in the legal one by writing and arranging for Utterson to receive 'Dr Lanyon's Narrative',[47] which is at once the doctor's contribution to a medical case diagnosing Hyde and his testimony in a legal case indicting him. In helping to make both cases, Lanyon employs Gothic terminology shared by Krafft-Ebing. Lanyon first diagnoses Jekyll and Hyde, then avers that Carew has been murdered by the latter '*creature*'.[48] The sexologist would concur with Lanyon's characterisation of Hyde as 'abnormal and misbegotten',[49] since he describes patients ranging from fetishists to sex criminals as 'monster[s]', and frequently calls their acts 'monstrous'.[50] From his perspective, however, the monstrosity of the sexually aberrant is precisely what places them beyond legal jurisdiction. Thus, for Krafft-Ebing the medical case of Jekyll and Hyde would profoundly alter the legal one, since a diseased criminal should not be held responsible for a 'lust-murder'[51] attributable to his innate degeneracy. Jekyll holds a position similar to Krafft-Ebing's, noting that while Hyde's acts are 'monstrous', the 'situation [is] apart from ordinary laws'.[52] Moreover, psychosexual monstrosity may be decoupled from crime, for not all monsters are criminals.

The Strange Case of *Psychopathia Sexualis*

Such is the case in a real-world double for 'Henry Jekyll's Full Statement of the Case', wherein a queer physician/patient vividly describes his transformation into a monster. Though this man has committed no crime, to his 'horror' he has come to feel 'bodily like a woman'.[53] As he writes in a letter to Krafft-Ebing, 'I lost all control, and thought of myself only as a monster before which I myself shuddered.'[54] This doctor's full statement of his own case illustrates how congenital homosexuality can result in a striking 'physical and mental transformation'.[55] According to Krafft-Ebing, in male homosexuals 'neurasthenia induced by masturbation, abstinence, or otherwise' initiates a 'metamorphosis [that] presents [four] different stages' of 'psycho-sexual degeneration' ranging from 'the milder cases', in which the patient presents '[t]races of hetero-sexual, with predominating homo-sexual, instinct', to 'the complete cases', in which the patient experiences 'the delusion of a transformation of sex'.[56]

Both Case 129 of *Psychopathia Sexualis* and 'Henry Jekyll's Full Statement of the Case' are complete cases of congenital homosexuality and transsexuality. As Stevenson suggests in sections of his novella that he later revised, Jekyll has indulged in masturbation.[57] Thus begins a decline that ends in his changing from 'a large, well-made [...] man' into 'a person of small stature' who '[weeps] like a woman'.[58] Similarly, when in youth Krafft-Ebing's doctor practises 'onanism' he '[seems] to [himself] like a double man' whose feeling is 'masculine, but mixed with feminine elements'.[59] Like Jekyll, he '[experiments] with many drugs and methods of cure, always on [himself]',[60] some of which result in a psychosomatic sex change. After bathing to treat his gout, he 'suddenly [changes], and [seems] to be near death' before coming to '[feel] exactly like a woman'.[61] Likewise, Jekyll '[risks] death'[62] when he first transforms into Hyde. In another experiment, the subject of Case 129 takes 'three or four times the usual dose of [hashish], and almost [dies]'[63] before changing, just as Jekyll is forced to 'double, and once, with infinite risk of death, to treble the amount' of his own transformational drug.[64] When the doctor of *Psychopathia Sexualis* transforms, he experiences 'a feeling of unheard of strength and swiftness' and 'unspeakable delight'.[65] When Jekyll changes, he feels 'younger, lighter, happier in body' and 'delighted'.⁶⁶ In both cases, the transformations soon occur on their own, without drugs or treatments. 'I awoke and found myself feeling as if completely changed into a woman', Krafft-Ebing's patient recalls.⁶⁷ Likewise, Jekyll writes, 'I had gone to bed Henry Jekyll, I had awakened Edward Hyde.'⁶⁸ Krafft-Ebing, whose work conflates gender expression, gender identity and sexual orientation, would view these cases as examples of congenital homosexuality that have progressed into irreversible transsexuality. That the masculine Jekyll ultimately finds himself trapped in the body and psyche of the feminine Hyde, and that the subject of Case 129 will think, feel and act as a woman for the rest of his life, align with the sexologist's characterisation of 'eviration', the process by which a queer man becomes, in effect, a woman. 'If, in cases of antipathic sexual instinct thus developed, no restoration occurs, then deep and lasting transformations of the *psychical* personality may occur', Krafft-Ebing writes. 'The patient undergoes a deep change of character, particularly in his feelings and inclinations, which become those of a female [. . .] The possibility of a restoration of the previous mental and sexual personality seems, in such a case, precluded.'⁶⁹

Because neither doctor/patient can reverse his queer transformation, both face uncertain futures. The subject of Case 129 asks himself, 'When a respectable man who enjoys an unusual degree of public confidence [. . .] must go about with his [imaginary] vulva [. . .] what must all this be?'⁷⁰ Moments before being 'finally severed' from his 'own face and nature' and thus his professional and social status, Jekyll wonders, 'Will Hyde die upon the scaffold? or will he find courage to release himself at the last moment?'⁷¹ Jekyll then hurries his case to its conclusion before changing permanently into Hyde, hoping to spare it from his double's 'spite', which Hyde has already expressed by 'scrawling [. . .] blasphemies on the pages of [Jekyll's] books'.⁷² Although Jekyll construes Hyde's writing as a malicious defacement of his own, the Jekyll–Hyde palimpsest might instead be read as the queer alter ego's attempt to overwrite the heteronormative ego in a narrative return of the repressed. The two men share the *Strange Case of Dr Jekyll and Mr Hyde*, and both speak in Utterson's and Lanyon's sections of the case, but 'Henry Jekyll's Full Statement of the Case' silences Hyde.

In so doing, the doctor's testimony repeats with a difference the discursive strategy and structure of Case 129. Whereas Jekyll prevents Hyde from speaking on his own behalf, Krafft-Ebing permits the subject of Case 129 to tell the queer story of his life, and even to argue for its moral and professional significance, before framing his patient's compelling autobiography in a fashion designed to reinscribe its author's abnormality. Offering his own strange case as an object lesson to his colleagues in medicine, beginning with Krafft-Ebing himself, the trans doctor ends it with an appeal to their compassion and sense of justice. 'I hope that [. . .] I may still count myself among human beings who do not deserve merely to be despised', he writes.[73] He also hopes 'to show that one thinking and feeling like a woman can still be a physician', and declares, 'If I could have my way, I should have every physician live the life of a woman for three months [. . .] then he would learn to value the greatness of women, and appreciate the difficulty of their lot.'[74] This extraordinary statement, which evokes Jekyll's initial, short-lived recognition that Hyde is 'natural and human',[75] recognises humanity irrespective of sex, within and beyond queerness and monstrosity. Immediately following and wholly disregarding such a *cri de coeur*, Krafft-Ebing's 'Remarks' are jarringly clinical and intolerant. 'The badly-tainted patient was originally psycho-sexually abnormal', the sexologist observes coldly, and '[t]he abnormal feeling [. . .] received overmastering support in imperative bodily sensations of a sexual change, which now dominate consciousness'.[76] The patient's case is 'remarkable' because 'his ego is able to control these abnormal psycho-physical manifestations', Krafft-Ebing concludes.[77] In other words, Case 129 is strange not only because it involves an imagined change of sex, but also because it illustrates how even a seriously corrupted ego can regulate a still more aberrant alter ego. Krafft-Ebing tacitly approves of his patient's having reached an uneasy truce in his psychomachia, a 'war among [his] members'[78] that Jekyll himself ultimately loses, though, like Krafft-Ebing, he has the last word, '[laying] down the pen and [proceeding] to seal up [his] confession' before Hyde can write upon or destroy it.[79] Both Krafft-Ebing and Jekyll seek to circumscribe or to suppress the queer Other's claim to humanity and expression, the latter going so far as to deny Hyde his status as a speaking subject, and to objectify him as 'the slime of the pit' that only '[seems] to utter cries and voices'.[80] In their attempts to reinforce heteronormativity, both scientists deploy a quintessentially Gothic narrative technique, constructing seemingly rational, objective frames for strange, subjective tales of monstrous transformation and double identity, seeking first to express and then to repress strangeness.

The Strange Cases of Helen in *The Great God Pan*

Gothic discursive complexity likewise characterises Arthur Machen's *The Great God Pan* (1894), which is organised as a series of interlocking narratives told from various perspectives. It begins as a man named Clarke witnesses brain surgery performed by his friend, Dr Raymond, on young Mary, whose mind he hopes to open to the spiritual world, enabling her to experience what the ancients called 'seeing the god Pan'.[81] His experiment succeeds, but Mary is driven mad by her encounter with Pan. Years later, Clarke includes in his collection of real-world mysteries, 'Memoirs to prove the Existence of the Devil', stories about Helen Vaughan, a beautiful but unusual girl.[82] After first seeing her playing in the woods with a strange naked man and then encountering the bust of a satyr, a boy loses his mind. Likewise, after spending time in the woods with Helen, a girl named Rachel returns there and disappears. Years more pass, and in London a man named Villiers encounters his old friend Herbert, who has been psychologically and financially ruined by his wife. Villiers, Clarke and another character, Austin, discover that Herbert was married to Helen, and that a man died from fright after seeing something awful in their home. Herbert is found dead and Helen disappears. After she returns as Mrs Beaumont, she is linked with a number of suicides among seemingly happy, successful men. Villiers and Clarke confront her and demand that she hang herself or risk public exposure. In her death throes, she descends and ascends the evolutionary ladder, wavers from sex to sex, and divides and reunites before finally dissolving into a gelatinous substance and dying. The novella concludes with a letter from Raymond to Clarke, which explains that Helen's mother was Mary and implies that her father was Pan.

Like *Strange Case of Dr Jekyll and Mr Hyde*, *The Great God Pan* is a strange case whose medical and legal aspects are bound up with its complex narrative structure. As Villiers realises while pondering his erstwhile friend Herbert's story, 'A case like this is like a nest of Chinese boxes [. . .] Most likely poor Herbert is merely one of the outside boxes; there are stranger ones to follow.'[83] Though hers is the innermost of these metaphorical boxes, Helen Vaughan, like Edward Hyde, is not permitted to tell her own 'strange story'.[84] Instead, it is presented by a series of presumably heterosexual men beginning with Dr Raymond, whose experiment on Helen's mother Mary opens the novella and whose letter to his friend Clarke closes it. Raymond's comments on Mary's case, like Krafft-Ebing's on Case 129, are clinical, heteronormative, dispassionate and authoritative. Raymond views Mary as an experimental subject to 'use as [he] [sees] fit', and even when the consequences of his brain surgery leave her 'a hopeless idiot', he remains 'quite cool'.[85] The doctor's sex and status allow him to dominate Mary, and his extraordinary medical acumen gives him access to the spirit world. Not surprisingly, the learned Dr Raymond gets the last word, as Drs Krafft-Ebing and Jekyll do. He closes the story by smugly writing to Clarke, 'I was interested in your account, but a good deal, nay all, of what you told me I knew already.'[86] Yet even Raymond is not all-knowing; and, as he admits in the end, he has 'played with energies which [he] did not understand'.[87] The inadequacy of Raymond's knowledge and authority is expressed formally in his framing narrative, which encloses Helen's transgressive tale without containing it. He concludes, 'And now Helen is with her companions . . .',[88] his ellipsis suggesting that her story is not over. She has been killed but not destroyed, and the disruptive forces she represents endure. That she has at least been removed from the material world, and can no longer threaten heterosexuality, aristocracy and patriarchy, is due to the efforts of a small group of well-heeled men who combine to solve her medico-legal mystery.

Helen's medical case involves lesbianism, nymphomania and intersexuality. Her strangeness, like Hyde's, originates in a classically Gothic genealogical puzzle updated to reflect late Victorian anxiety about hereditary degeneration. Helen's mother Mary, who came 'from the gutter',[89] may well have been tainted; her father Pan certainly is. Their degenerate daughter, born from miscegenation and an experiment gone awry, emulates both her biological and scientific fathers by seducing and experimenting upon others. Her second victim is Rachel, who returns home 'half undressed' and tells her mother a 'wild story' that Clarke cannot bear to reveal to the reader because it is 'too monstrous'.[90] His reticence about her nightmarish 'case', echoed in the story's oblique references to 'forces [that] cannot be named', 'nameless infamies' and 'that for which we have no name',[91] bespeaks the love that dare not speak its name and indicates a case of lesbianism involving Rachel and Helen, whose congenital homosexuality aligns with her nymphomania and intersexuality. As Krafft-Ebing explains, among the causes of lesbianism is '[c]onstitutional hypersexuality',[92] and Helen appears to have had sexual encounters with the many men she drives to suicide. Helen's 'Chronic Nymphomania'[93] is more than a diagnosis, given her parentage: her father is a satyr; thus her mother is, in effect, a nymph.

It would make sense to Krafft-Ebing that Helen, a lesbian and a nymphomaniac, would exhibit 'Psychical Hermaphroditism' or 'pseudo-hermaphroditism'.[94] Such '[h]ermaphroditism represents the extreme grade of degenerative homosexuality', at which point the lesbian's 'thought, sentiment, action, even external appearance are those of the man',[95] though her anatomy remains that of a woman. Citing Wilhelm Bernhardi's work on homosexuality, Krafft-Ebing stigmatises '[t]hose practicing active viraginity and hermaphroditism' as '"monsters of masculine gender"'[96] whose monstrosity arises from sexual inversion rather than anatomical anomaly. Yet among these monstrous 'men-women'[97] is Case 160, a lesbian who problematises Krafft-Ebing's distinction between psychical and physical hermaphroditism. Her phallicised 'clitoris [is] rather large', and her 'robust skeleton, powerful muscles and absence of adipose layers [bear] the stamp of the masculine character'.[98] Whereas Case 160 blurs the sexologist's line between the mental and the material, Helen erases it. If Krafft-Ebing were to consider Helen's strange case, he would not be surprised by how, in a sex-role reversal, she emasculates her husband Herbert by taking his patrimony and place. He would, however, be astonished by how Helen's intersexuality is manifest physiologically in her death throes, during which her 'form [wavers] from sex to sex' and 'from woman to man'.[99] As Ann Heilmann and Mark Llewellyn point out, 'The Victorian era was the age of categorization', and this 'category drive' motivated 'sexology, the study of different types of desire, fetish, and "deviations" from the heterosexual norm'.[100] The intersex Helen is monstrous and threatening in large part because she exists outside a biological sex binary and therefore resists sexological categorisation.

Although Helen's medical case is grounded in her monstrous transformation, the legal case against her appears baseless. She is part of 'the Paul Street case',[101] at the centre of her own husband's 'queer case',[102] and implicated in several suicides. Yet, despite her involvement in these strange cases, Helen is guilty of no crimes except those she commits against nature. Unlike Hyde, she has not murdered anyone. Like her queer predecessor, however, she is blackmailed and finally driven to suicide to escape infamy. Her judges and executioners are Villiers, an 'amateur in mysteries',[103] and Clarke, whose transcribed interviews in 'Memoirs to prove the Existence of the Devil' serve as a metonym for the novella: when these testimonies are rendered into a coherent case, they solve Helen's diabolical enigma. As Austin astutely observes, '*She is the mystery.*'[104] Her mysteriousness is a function of her legal invisibility as a lesbian. Krafft-Ebing explains that '[t]he chief reason why inverted sexuality in woman is still covered with the veil of mystery is that the homosexual act so far as woman is concerned, does not fall under the law'. This veil is lifted when Helen's 'human flesh', which 'may become the veil of a horror one dare not express',[105] melts away and reveals her monstrosity. Just as her husband's 'story [needs] no confirmation' because 'he himself [is] the embodied proof of it',[106] so too her own protean body evidences her perversities and indicts her. Poetic justice and heteronormative hegemony alike are served by Helen's condign punishment of suicide. As a queer woman, however, she is past the reach of the Labouchère Amendment. In much the same fashion as Helen's intersexuality positions her outside sexology, her lesbianism situates her beyond the law, rendering her (cases) even stranger.

The Queer Vampires of *Dracula*

In Bram Stoker's *Dracula* (1897), the solicitor Jonathan Harker describes in his journal his visit to a castle in the Carpathian mountains to help Count Dracula buy Carfax, a medieval abbey near London. Harker, who soon realises that his host is a vampire and he himself a prisoner, is menaced by three vampire women. After Dracula leaves his castle for England, Harker escapes from it to Budapest. Meanwhile, letters between Lucy Westenra and her best friend, Harker's fiancée Mina Murray, describe proposals of marriage to Lucy from Dr John Seward, who manages a lunatic asylum; Quincey Morris, an adventurous Texan; and Arthur Holmwood, who becomes Lord Godalming upon the death of his father. Lucy accepts her third suitor and joins Mina in Whitby, where the ship that Dracula has taken from Transylvania runs aground after a storm. Dracula begins vampirising Lucy, who sickens as Mina marries Harker in Budapest. Although Seward's mentor, Prof Abraham Van Helsing, treats Lucy, she dies and becomes a vampire who stalks young children. Van Helsing, Seward, Morris and Godalming confront her, and her fiancé kills her. Harker and Mina return and join the others in Seward's asylum to plan their battle against Dracula, who gains access to the asylum through Renfield, a patient, and vampirises Mina. The men hunt Dracula in London and force him to return to Transylvania, where the group follows him. Van Helsing and Mina go to Castle Dracula, and he kills the vampire women. The men attack Dracula, who is destroyed by Harker and Morris. A note written seven years later by Harker closes the novel by mentioning that he and Mina have a son named Quincey.

Recognising the astuteness of Machen's insight that deviance 'cannot be imagined except under a veil and a symbol',[107] Stoker figures queerness as vampirism. In a scene featuring sadomasochism and androgyny that might have been a case in *Psychopathia Sexualis*, after Harker decides to sleep 'where, of old, ladies had sat and sung and lived sweet lives', he is approached by a vampire who '[arches] her neck' while her 'red tongue' laps 'sharp teeth' and she prepares to 'fasten on [his] throat' while he '[lies] quiet'.[108] This masculine woman's phallic neck, tongue and teeth contrast with Harker's limp, feminised body, which she is about to penetrate. Her active sadism is complemented by his passive masochism, for he awaits her 'in an agony of delightful anticipation'.[109] Harker, who '[seems] somehow to know her face', represses the vampire's uncanny similarity to his fiancée, claiming, 'Faugh! Mina is a woman, and there is nought in common.'[110] In fact, he is drawn to dominant, gender-bending women like Mina, with her 'man's brain' and 'woman's heart'.[111] Dracula also appreciates Mina's androgyny and recognises her corresponding vampiric potential. Like Lucy the nymphomaniac, Mina the androgyne resembles the queer vampire women in Dracula's castle long before she actually drinks blood. In another sadomasochistic scene, Dracula begins – or completes – Mina's transformation into a vampire when he '[opens] a vein in his breast' before '[pressing] [her] mouth to the wound'.[112] Their encounter evokes Case 48 of *Psychopathia Sexualis*, concerning a wife who 'would suck [a] wound' her husband made in his arm and thus 'become violently excited sexually'.[113] Indeed, the sadistic, androgynous female vampires of Stoker's novel align closely with those in Krafft-Ebing's treatise. The sexologist notes that sadism in women is a 'monstrous impulse' and 'a pathological intensification of the masculine sexual character', and speculates that 'the widespread legend of the vampires' may be 'referred to such sadistic facts' as those he relates in Case 48.[114]

Both Mina's erotic experience with Dracula and Harker's with the vampire women are witnessed and disrupted: hers by Van Helsing, his by Dracula himself. That these private sexual acts are made public draws attention to how the Labouchère Amendment invaded privacy, and how sexology revealed what Krafft-Ebing calls 'secrets of married life'.[115] Though both law and medicine intruded into the private sphere, the punitive and diagnostic objectives of their respective incursions were at odds. In *Sexual Inversion* (1897), Havelock Ellis declares that however reprehensible 'it may be for two adult persons of the same sex, men or women, to [. . .] perform an act of sexual intimacy in private, there is no sound or adequate ground for constituting such act a penal offense'.[116] The sexologist's distinction between aberrant sexual acts committed in public and private illuminates how the queer tableaux of *Dracula* engage contemporary medico-legal sexual surveillance. Representing the forces of medicine and law alike, Van Helsing and his fellow vampire hunters follow Utterson's example in the *Strange Case of Dr Jekyll and Mr Hyde* by breaking down the door to the Harkers' bedroom in order to end an illicit sexual encounter and eject a trespasser. 'If the door be locked, I shall break it in', Van Helsing announces, justifying this extraordinary violation of privacy by citing his own medical authority and declaring that '[a]ll chambers are alike to the doctor'.[117] His double entendre prefigures the polymorphously perverse spectacle behind the door. Once Van Helsing and his fellow vampire hunters '[throw] [themselves] against it' and 'with a crash it [bursts] open', they witness a shocking threesome. Harker lies '[o]n the bed beside the window [. . .] his face flushed and breathing heavily', while Mina is '[k]neeling on the near edge of the bed facing outwards' and beside her stands Dracula, 'forcing her face down on his bosom'.[118] This illicit activity is ended immediately by Van Helsing and his colleagues, who – like Utterson, Villiers and Clarke – work to maintain the (hetero)sexual status quo. In contrast, when Dracula bursts in upon Harker and the vampire women, he redirects rather than stops the erotic trajectory of their private moment. 'This man belongs to me!' he declares, and the sexual implications of his assertion become clear when, 'after looking at [Harker's] face attentively', he whispers, '"Yes, I too can love [. . .] I promise you that when I am done with him you shall kiss him at your will."'[119] The circumspection of *Dracula* is exemplified by the fact that the eponymous vampire never penetrates Harker. Likewise, he drinks men's transfused blood through the conduit of a woman's body, and uses Lucy and Mina to triangulate his homoerotic desire.[120] 'Your girls that you all love are mine already', he tells the male vampire hunters, 'and through them you and others shall yet be mine.'[121] Dracula's sadistic desire to possess and dominate is advanced via another sort of triangulation, by which he gains access to Mina through Renfield.

Renfield's relationship with Dracula elucidates both the medical and the legal aspects of the vampire's strange case. 'The case of Renfield' doubles that of Dracula, for both have 'certain qualities very largely developed: selfishness, secrecy, and purpose', and both are classified as 'zoophagous (life-eating)' creatures.[122] Moreover, the two are involved in a case of sadomasochism wherein Renfield vows to Dracula, 'I am here to do Your bidding, Master. I am Your slave.'[123] His language is similar to that of Krafft-Ebing's Case 50, whose subject admits, 'The thought of slavery had something exciting in it for me.'[124] A crucial distinction between Renfield's and Dracula's cases is that the latter is criminal as well as psychiatric. A medico-legal case against the vampire takes shape when Van Helsing explains that '[t]he Count is a criminal and of criminal type', and '*quâ* criminal he is of imperfectly formed mind'.[125] Van Helsing's diagnosis and indictment notwithstanding, Dracula commits no crimes in England. Although the vampire might appear to trespass, he is invited into both Lucy's bedroom and Seward's asylum. Even Dracula's struggle with Renfield is a matter of self-defence. In fact, the vampire hunters and not their quarry are the ones who break the law: evading the police, they 'pick the lock' of Dracula's Piccadilly house, in a criminal act that Van Helsing compares with burglary.[126]

Closing the Cases

As the strange medico-legal cases against Hyde, Helen and Dracula appear to close, these queer creatures are judged both pathological and culpable. The testimonies of their adversaries weigh heavily against them, without counterweight, for they are barred from testifying on their own behalf. Similarly, unlike those who are allowed to speak for themselves in the case studies of *Psychopathia Sexualis* before their accounts are incorporated within Krafft-Ebing's diagnostic frames, these characters are never given the chance to tell their own stories. The fictions of Stevenson, Machen and Stoker are therefore reactionary, insofar as they deploy contemporary discursive practices in law and medicine to render queerness at once unusual and understandable by turning it into a series of strange cases. Their strategy is not entirely successful, however. The multipartite narrative structure of these cases aligns uneasily not only with Jekyll and Hyde's splitting, but also with Helen's and Dracula's ability to change shape and transcend categorisation, thereby suggesting the polymorphous perversity of queerness. Moreover, even as these cases draw together eyewitness and expert testimonies like nets in which to capture queer quarry, interstices remain by which those sentenced to death for their crimes against nature escape into afterlives. The case against Hyde concludes not with Utterson's description of his corpse, but with Jekyll's statement ending his own existence and speculating as to that of his alter ego. Failing to bring his case study of Helen to a complete close, Dr Raymond admits that she continues to exist in spirit. Harker ends his tale by noting that Mina believes their son Quincey to possess some of his namesake's spirit, without mentioning that Dracula's blood flows in the boy's veins. Thus, the strange cases of the queer *fin de siècle* are never fully closed.

Notes

1. F. B. Smith, 'Labouchere's Amendment to the Criminal Law Amendment Bill', *Historical Studies*, 17.67 (1976), pp. 165–75.
2. Richard Dellamora, *Masculine Desire: The Sexual Politics of Victorian Aestheticism* (Chapel Hill, NC: University of North Carolina Press, 1990), p. 200.
3. Richard von Krafft-Ebing, *Psychopathia Sexualis: The Classic Study of Deviant Sex*, trans. Franklin S. Klaf (New York: Arcade Publishing, 1965), p. 53.
4. Ibid., pp. 188, 190, 382.

5. Ibid., pp. 335, 334.
6. Ibid., p. 335.
7. While Krafft-Ebing recognised and discussed female homosexuality, the Labouchère Amendment ignored it. An attempt in 1921 to update the law and include women failed, partly 'on the grounds that publicity would only serve to make more women aware of homosexuality'. See Jeffrey Weeks, *Against Nature: Essays on History, Sexuality, and Identity* (London: Rivers Oram Press, 1991), p. 19.
8. Krafft-Ebing, *Psychopathia Sexualis*, p. 383.
9. Andrew Smith, *Victorian Demons: Medicine, Masculinity and the Gothic at the Fin-de-Siècle* (Manchester: Manchester University Press, 2004), p. 6.
10. Tabitha Sparks, *The Doctor in the Victorian Novel: Family Practices* (Abingdon: Routledge, 2009), p. 112.
11. Bridget M. Marshall, *The Transatlantic Gothic Novel and the Law, 1790–1860* (Farnham: Ashgate, 2011; repr. Abingdon: Routledge, 2016), p. 3.
12. Leslie J. Moran, 'Law and the Gothic Imagination', in *The Gothic*, ed. Fred Botting (Woodbridge: D. S. Brewer, 2001), p. 90.
13. *Psychopathia Sexualis* first appeared in English in 1892, published by F. A. Davis. Since, as Heike Bauer notes, 'sexologists often read each others' works in the original [language]', the 1886 German edition would have been of interest to British physicians. It could also have been read by educated non-professionals. According to Anthony McCobb, 'German books formed the staple reading-diet of the average Victorian intellectual'. See Heike Bauer, *English Literary Sexology: Translations of Inversion, 1860–1930* (Basingstoke: Palgrave Macmillan, 2009), p. 16. See also Anthony McCobb, *George Eliot's Knowledge of German Life and Letters* (Salzburg: Institut für Anglistik und Amerikanistik, Universität Salzburg, 1982), p. 4.
14. I develop and redirect Robert Mighall's insight that Stevenson's novella 'is presented as a "case" in the legal sense, but it is also partly a fictional case-study' (p. 206). See Robert Mighall, 'Diagnosing Jekyll: The Scientific Context to Dr Jekyll's Experiment and Mr Hyde's Embodiment', in Robert Louis Stevenson, *Strange Case of Dr Jekyll and Mr Hyde and Other Tales of Terror* (London: Penguin, 2002), pp. 206–26. Mighall notes parallels between *Jekyll and Hyde* and *Psychopathia Sexualis* first identified by Stephen Heath in 'Psychopathia Sexualis: Stevenson's Strange Case', *Critical Quarterly*, 28.1 (1986), pp. 93–108. While both Heath and Mighall link Hyde's criminal pathology to Krafft-Ebing's concept of lust-murder, neither connects Jekyll/Hyde's transformation to the sexologist's Case 129, with which it is closely aligned. Elaine Showalter does consider *Jekyll and Hyde* together with the case of 'Louis V.', whose personality transformation and hysteria were correlated with queerness. See Elaine Showalter, *Sexual Anarchy: Gender and Culture at the Fin de Siècle* (New York: Viking, 1990), pp. 105–6.
15. Robert Louis Stevenson, *Strange Case of Dr Jekyll and Mr Hyde*, ed. Martin A. Danahay, 3rd edn (Peterborough, Ont.: Broadview, 2015), pp. 38–9.

16. William Veeder, 'Children of the Night: Stevenson and Patriarchy', in *Dr Jekyll and Mr Hyde after One Hundred Years*, ed. William Veeder and Gordon Hirsch (Chicago: University of Chicago Press, 1988), p. 159.
17. Showalter, *Sexual Anarchy*, p. 107.
18. Stevenson, *Dr Jekyll and Mr Hyde*, p. 75.
19. Ibid., p. 44.
20. Ibid., p. 36.
21. Ibid., p. 34.
22. Michael M. Kaylor, *Secreted Desires: The Major Uranians: Hopkins, Pater and Wilde* (Brno, CZ: Masaryk University Press, 2006), p. 55.
23. Heath 'Psychopathia Sexualis', p. 95.
24. Stevenson, *Dr Jekyll and Mr Hyde*, p. 38.
25. Kaylor, *Secreted Desires*, p. 55.
26. Showalter, *Sexual Anarchy*, p. 113.
27. Stevenson, *Dr Jekyll and Mr Hyde*, p. 38.
28. Ibid., p. 41.
29. Ibid., pp. 40–1.
30. Ibid., p. 41.
31. See Matt Cook, *London and the Culture of Homosexuality, 1885–1914* (Cambridge: Cambridge University Press, 2003), pp. 13–15. See also Jack Saul, *The Sins of the Cities of the Plain*, ed. Wolfram Setz (Richmond, VA: Valancourt, 2012), pp. 1–4.
32. Stevenson, *Dr Jekyll and Mr Hyde*, p. 41.
33. Ibid., p. 56.
34. Ibid., p. 51.
35. Ibid.
36. Ibid., p. 33.
37. Cook, *London and the Culture of Homosexuality*, p. 28.
38. Stevenson, *Dr Jekyll and Mr Hyde*, p. 51.
39. Ibid.
40. Ibid.
41. Ibid., p. 66.
42. Ibid., pp. 64–5.
43. Krafft-Ebing, *Psychopathia Sexualis*, p. 336.
44. Stevenson, *Dr Jekyll and Mr Hyde*, pp. 71, 72.
45. Ibid., p. 73.
46. Ibid., p. 74.
47. Ibid., p. 69.
48. Ibid., p. 75.
49. Ibid., p. 73.
50. Krafft-Ebing, *Psychopathia Sexualis*, pp. 55, 69, 144, 377, 4, 35, 53, 56, 85, 88, 130, 292, 334, 335, 374, 375, 403, 408, 418 n. 25.
51. Ibid., p. 351.
52. Stevenson, *Dr Jekyll and Mr Hyde*, pp. 80, 81.
53. Krafft-Ebing, *Psychopathia Sexualis*, p. 213.
54. Ibid., pp. 212–13.
55. Ibid., p. 190.
56. Ibid., p. 188.
57. See Mighall, 'Diagnosing Jekyll', p. 155.

58. Stevenson, *Dr Jekyll and Mr Hyde*, pp. 45, 65.
59. Krafft-Ebing, *Psychopathia Sexualis*, p. 203.
60. Ibid., p. 205.
61. Ibid.
62. Stevenson, *Dr Jekyll and Mr Hyde*, p. 77.
63. Krafft-Ebing, *Psychopathia Sexualis*, p. 205.
64. Stevenson, *Dr Jekyll and Mr Hyde*, p. 83.
65. Krafft-Ebing, *Psychopathia Sexualis*, p. 205.
66. Ibid., p. 78.
67. Ibid., p. 205.
68. Stevenson, *Dr Jekyll and Mr Hyde*, p. 82.
69. Krafft-Ebing, *Psychopathia Sexualis*, pp. 195–6.
70. Ibid., p. 210.
71. Stevenson, *Dr Jekyll and Mr Hyde*, p. 90.
72. Ibid., p. 89.
73. Krafft-Ebing, *Psychopathia Sexualis*, p. 213.
74. Ibid., p. 213.
75. Stevenson, *Dr Jekyll and Mr Hyde*, p. 79.
76. Krafft-Ebing, *Psychopathia Sexualis*, p. 213.
77. Ibid.
78. Stevenson, *Dr Jekyll and Mr Hyde*, p. 76.
79. Ibid., p. 90.
80. Ibid., p. 89.
81. Arthur Machen, *The Great God Pan and Other Horror Stories*, ed. Aaron Worth (Oxford: Oxford University Press, 2018), p. 10.
82. Ibid., p. 16.
83. Ibid., p. 24.
84. Ibid., p. 54.
85. Ibid., pp. 12, 15.
86. Ibid., p. 53.
87. Ibid.
88. Ibid., p. 54.
89. Ibid., p. 12.
90. Ibid., p. 20.
91. Ibid., pp. 20, 47, 45, 53.
92. Krafft-Ebing, *Psychopathia Sexualis*, p. 263.
93. Ibid., p. 323.
94. Ibid., pp. 231, 229.
95. Ibid., p. 264.
96. Ibid., p. 226. See Wilhelm Bernhardi, *Der Uranismus: Lösung eines mehrtausendjährigen Räthsels* (Berlin: Verlag der Volksbuchhandlung, 1882), p. 28.
97. Krafft-Ebing, *Psychopathia Sexualis*, p. 264.
98. Ibid., p. 278.
99. Machen, *Great God Pan*, pp. 50, 54.
100. Ann Heilmann and Mark Llewellyn, 'The Victorians, Sex, and Gender', in *The Oxford Handbook of Victorian Literary Culture*, ed. Juliet John (Oxford: Oxford University Press, 2016), p. 176.
101. Machen, *Great God Pan*, p. 45.

102. Ibid., p. 28.
103. Ibid. p. 22.
104. Ibid., p. 30.
105. Ibid., p. 53.
106. Ibid., p. 24.
107. Ibid., p. 47.
108. Bram Stoker, *Dracula*, ed. Glennis Byron (Peterborough, Ont.: Broadview, 1998), pp. 68–70.
109. Ibid., p. 69.
110. Ibid., pp. 69, 85.
111. Ibid., p. 274.
112. Ibid., p. 328.
113. Krafft-Ebing, *Psychopathia Sexualis*, p. 85.
114. Ibid., p. 87.
115. Ibid., p. 231.
116. Havelock Ellis, *Sexual Inversion* (Honolulu, HI: University Press of the Pacific, 2001), p. 210.
117. Stoker, *Dracula*, p. 321.
118. Ibid., p. 322.
119. Ibid., p. 71.
120. As Christopher Craft observes, 'Dracula's desire to fuse with a male' finds only 'evasive fulfillment in an important series of heterosexual displacements'. See Christopher Craft, '"Kiss Me with Those Red Lips": Gender and Inversion in Bram Stoker's *Dracula*', *Representations*, 8 (1984), p. 110.
121. Stoker, *Dracula*, p. 347.
122. Ibid., p. 103.
123. Ibid., p. 137.
124. Krafft-Ebing, *Psychopathia Sexualis*, p. 105.
125. Stoker, *Dracula*, p. 383.
126. Ibid., p. 333.

Chapter 4

Gothic Cinema and Sexology in the Weimar Republic: Towards a Queer Gothic Aesthetic on Screen
Dennis Wegner

Early Sexology and Queer Culture

The late nineteenth and the early twentieth centuries saw two cultural innovations which, in combination, helped create (or greatly influenced) queer Gothic modes at this time. These were the invention of film and the emergence of sexuality research and queer rights activism. The earliest queer rights efforts fighting against legal discrimination started in late eighteenth-century Germany and culminated in organised and institutionalised activism in the years before the rise of National Socialism in the 1930s. Concurrently, film was invented in the late 1880s and soon evolved into an entirely new way of showing and telling stories. By the 1920s national cinemas had emerged all over the world, among them the cinema of the Weimar Republic, the German state from 1918 to 1933. Weimar cinema not only brought forward filmic innovations that informed Gothic films for many decades to come, but also produced pioneering contributions to queer film history. This chapter will trace the relationship between early Gothic film and societal changes with regard to sexuality and queerness. I will also examine the cultural developments that set the course for the relative productivity of queer depictions and representations in Weimar cinema before examining how and where the Gothic is queered in early twentieth-century film.

Historians of sexuality note the relative visibility of queerness during the Weimar Republic.[1] 1920s Berlin has been painted as an early haven for non-normative expressions of gender and sexuality, an image propagated in popular media such as the 1966 musical *Cabaret* and its 1972 film adaptation, or the more recent neo-noir TV series *Babylon Berlin* (2017–). Both the musical and the TV series, set in Berlin towards the end of the Weimar Republic, depict, among other things, Berlin's cabaret culture and nightlife with its variety of cross-dressing entertainers and queer patrons threatened by the rise of fascism. The famous gay writer Christopher Isherwood, whose 1939 novel *Goodbye to Berlin* would later become the source material for *Cabaret*, fully came to terms with his homosexuality after he moved to Berlin in the 1920s, as he documents in his 1976 memoir *Christopher and His Kind*.[2] Some scholars, such as historian Robert Beachy, whose 2015 book *Gay Berlin* has already become a queer history classic, suggest that homosexuality as an identity fully emerged for the first time in the German capital. What made Berlin so LGBT-'friendly' as to enable such a development?

The precursors of the first gay rights movement in Germany had already emerged well before the Weimar Republic came into being, when Karl Heinrich Ulrichs, possibly the first openly gay man in Germany, wrote a series of twelve pamphlets titled *Studies on the Riddle of Male–Male Love*, published between 1869 and 1880. In these revolutionary pamphlets, Ulrichs theorised his same-sex attraction and invented some of the first terminology for describing queer identities.[3] He did so in response to Paragraph 175 of the German penal code, which criminalised sex between men. One of Ulrichs' interlocutors, Karl-Maria Kertbeny, is credited with first having used the term 'homosexual'. Like Ulrichs, Kertbeny's goal was to replace pejorative terms such as sodomite or pederast with more scientific and neutral vocabulary.[4] Kertbeny's term was popularised by psychiatrist Richard von Krafft-Ebing who drew from Ulrichs' theories and became a pioneer in research on sexuality. Ulrichs ultimately was not successful in overturning Paragraph 175 – in fact, the legal code survived almost into the twenty-first century and was only abolished in its entirety in 1994. However, he did manage to inspire other gay rights activists and researchers of gender and sexuality long before Stonewall.[5]

Although Paragraph 175 remained active, Beachy suggests that the way the anti-sodomy statute was enforced in Berlin at the turn of the century had a major impact on the development of queer culture in the German capital. He writes that police commissioner Leopold von Meerscheidt-Hüllessem, responsible for policing homosexuality at the time, was aware of the recent medical and psychiatric contributions regarding homosexuality. Hüllessem mostly abstained from raiding queer locales, as queer sociability was not prohibited by the anti-sodomy statute, but rather focused on policing male prostitution and the blackmail of homosexuals – thus while the legal code negatively impacted the lives of queer people, arrests for Paragraph 175 violations remained significantly low.[6] Hüllessem even fostered the study of queer nightlife in his policing strategy: 'He literally gave tours of the city's homosexual nightspots and escorted visitors to same-sex costume balls. Berlin came to serve as a kind of laboratory of sexuality, made available for investigation to a range of psychiatrists, sexologists, journalists, and popular writers.'[7] Hüllessem's strategy, intended to improve the surveillance of homosexuality, simultaneously boosted the reputation of Berlin's queer culture. By the early 1900s a few dozen establishments catered to a queer clientele in the capital, ranging from bars and taverns to cafés and venues hosting drag costume balls.[8]

The critical exchange between researchers, activists and public officials is well documented. Sexual researchers such as Richard von Krafft-Ebing and Magnus Hirschfeld, the famous gay, Jewish and polyamorous sexologist and early queer rights advocate, acknowledged Hüllessem in some of their studies. In his monumental 1914 study *Die Homosexualität des Mannes und Weibes* (*Homosexuality of Men and Women*), Hirschfeld thanks Hüllessem and his successor as the director of the Department of Homosexuality and Blackmail, Hans von Tresckow, for always showing their 'friendliest interest'[9] in his work and efforts. It was Hirschfeld who founded the world's first gay rights organisation, the Scientific-Humanitarian Committee (SHC), in 1898.[10] One of the SHC's main objectives was to advocate against legal discrimination against homosexuals via popular education – an approach that would later inform other homophile movements.[11] At the turn of the century, the organisation distributed pamphlets on homosexuality, sponsored public lectures by sexologists, and launched petitions to overturn Paragraph 175 that garnered many signatures but, like Ulrichs' attempt, remained unsuccessful.[12]

By the time Hirschfeld published *Homosexuality of Men and Women*, a colossal 1,000-page work describing research on homosexuality both on the level of the individual and the larger society, research on sexuality had already been productive, albeit not established as a discipline in the academy. Hirschfeld notes in the introduction of *Homosexuality of Men and Women* that in the ten years since the founding of the SHC more than 1,000 original articles, brochures and monographs had been published in Germany and Austria alone.[13] Hirschfeld himself had contributed a large proportion of works to that number, both as an author and as an editor; among them three monographs which laid the groundwork for his major theories, including his view that sexual orientation was biological and not, as many other researchers argued, cultural (i.e. caused by bad parenting or trauma).[14] He also edited the annual periodical *Jahrbuch für sexuelle Zwischenstufen* (*Yearbook for Sexual Intermediates*), which was published from 1899 until 1923 when hyperinflation made printing costs unfeasible. The first of its kind, the *Yearbook* published articles related to solely queer topics ranging from biology and medicine to history and politics, to religion, literature and visual arts. The fourth annual issue includes a collection of intersex studies, source analyses seeking to identify famous historical men who might have been homosexuals, an essay written by an anonymous Catholic clergyman that argues that the Bible opposes legal and social discrimination against homosexuality, and an obituary for Hüllessem, who had died in 1900.[15] Some of these contributions show how the very contemporary queer desires to reinscribe oneself into history or to reconcile queerness and faith have been at the core of queer theorising since the very beginning.

The yearbook's name, moreover, refers to Hirschfeld's major theory, that of sexual intermediates, which he proposed in his 1910 study *Transvestites*, one of the earliest scholarly attempts to distinguish sexuality and gender expression.[16] He employs sexual intermediates as a means to classify sexual alterities on a scale between the two categories of what he calls 'absolute man and woman' using four criteria: 1) sex organs, 2) other physical attributes, 3) sex drive and 4) other psychological attributes.[17] Hirschfeld suggests that the absolute man and woman, that is, individuals who fully embody all of the four criteria to one extreme or the other, are constructs that have yet to be observed in reality, as every single human being contains both masculine and feminine traits to some extent. Hirschfeld, albeit grounded in biological determinism, refutes the existence of essential sex and gender binaries – on the contrary, by multiplying all possible criteria with different variations of these criteria, Hirschfeld estimates the theoretical existence of more than *43 million* sexual and gender identities![18] This number, he writes, might even be too small. Indeed, the number of sexual varieties might even be infinite, as every single individual appears as something special in their combination of physical and mental sexual features.[19]

The examples listed here already exemplify the productivity of writing on queer topics in imperial Germany – the country 'arguably had produced more titles on sexual minorities – scientific, literary, and popular – than the rest of the world combined'.[20] However, the founding of the Weimar Republic in the wake of the First World War and the German revolution in 1918 made possible a series of further advances in terms of sex research and gay rights activism, as the proclamation of the first German democracy under a leftist government entailed the promise of freedom of speech and no censorship. As a result, Hirschfeld opened the Institut für Sexualwissenschaft (Institute for Sexology) in May 1919. Yet another first, the institute was designed to become both a place for medical practice as well as for research in different disciplines related to sexuality – thus to institutionalise sexology. However, because of

German hyperinflation the institute was no longer able to fund research after 1923 and focused only on medical practice and public education.[21] The medical and psychological counselling provided by the institute was not limited to queer issues, but also included counselling for married couples and advice about STIs and reproductive healthcare. The institute also worked on early treatments for what is now described as gender dysphoria and offered the first sex reassignment surgeries.[22] Lili Elbe for example, one of the most famous trans women to undergo early sex reassignment surgery and whose life was portrayed in the 2015 biopic *The Danish Girl*, sought initial counselling at the Institute for Sexology in 1930.[23] Beachy describes the institute as 'one of the singular institutions that helped to define Weimar Berlin'.[24]

The founding years of the Weimar Republic not only helped to further the study of sexuality, but also the cultural representation of queerness. The world's first gay magazine to be sold on newsstands, *Die Freundschaft (Friendship)*, was first published in August 1919 and initiated a substantial queer print culture in Berlin that yielded more than twenty titles between 1918 and 1933.[25] The relative accessibility of queer reading material 'played a key role in the formation of a queer subjectivity and the organization of queer life'.[26]

Cross-Dressers and Vampires: A First Look at Queer Weimar Cinema

This sociocultural development also informed the young medium of film. Clear filmic representations of queerness in the early twentieth century were scarce, but a disproportionally large amount of overall substantially queer depictions in this period were produced in Weimar Republic Germany.[27] Film historians have long established a link between the innovations brought forward by scholarly attention to sexual minorities and the first depictions of queerness in Weimar German cinema.[28] Indeed, the oldest known film to overtly address homosexuality, *Anders als die Andern (Different from the Others)*, released in 1919, was written by Magnus Hirschfeld. Richard Dyer considers *Anders* as well as the 1931 drama *Mädchen in Uniform (Girls in Uniform)* to be the most assertive and positive queer films of the Weimar period. He argues that both films showcase concurrent definitions of homosexuality that see it either as third sex or as a blend of masculinity and femininity, thus corresponding with sexological theories established by Hirschfeld and others.[29]

Scholarship on Weimar German cinema has presented different arguments as to why the German national cinema yielded significantly more films with queer and trans themes than all other national cinemas in the early twentieth century. Pioneering gay rights activism and scholarship enabled by the chaotic legal state of the Weimar Republic certainly figured into the equation. Alice Kuzniar examines a variety of crossdresser comedies made between 1918 and 1933 and argues that these narratives, which she describes as homoerotic fantasies with heterosexual outcomes, were made accessible to mainstream viewers by depicting homosexuality as non-threatening.[30] Take, for example, the 1918 film *Ich möchte kein Mann sein* (*I Don't Want to Be a Man*), whose young female protagonist, Ossi, does not like to behave like a young woman but prefers 'male' pastimes and behaves rather boyishly. Ossi, growing frustrated with the treatment she receives as a woman, decides to dress up as a man, but soon learns that being a man comes with its own set of unpleasant encounters: in the tram, she is scolded for not offering her seat to a woman and when she whines about other men stepping on her feet in the crowded streetcar, the fellow men scold her once again for her 'unmasculine' behaviour. She attends a ball dressed in her tuxedo, where she quickly starts drinking, flirting and eventually making out with another man. Eventually Ossi sheds her costume, enabling a happy heterosexual ending for the pair. This outcome, however, does not take away from the fact that, until the big reveal, Ossi's counterpart believed he was intimate with another man. Indeed, the only ones aware of Ossi's 'true' gender are the audience, as nobody but the camera seems to catch Ossi's womanhood under her disguise.[31] The queer act is made possible for a mainstream audience by hiding it in a heteronormative Trojan horse.

Janet Bergstrom, moreover, believes that German audiences were more accepting of unconventional film than the audiences of other national cinemas. She investigates the role that cinematic conventions relating to sexuality, the spectator and modes of abstraction played in F. W. Murnau's transition from Weimar to Hollywood. Murnau, believed by many scholars to have himself been gay, was one of the most celebrated film directors of Weimar German cinema but failed to achieve similar success in Hollywood. Bergstrom argues that Murnau's treatment of these cinematic conventions led to his success in Germany and his lack thereof in America. A key difference between the two national cinemas during the 1920s was Weimar German cinema's greater tendency towards abstraction, which not only allowed for experimentation but also a spectatorship more willing to positively receive these experiments. Weimar cinema conventionalised ambiguities in editing, camera style and lighting which often correlate with instabilities in class and sexuality.[32]

Murnau's influential horror movie *Nosferatu: A Symphony of Horror* (1922) exemplifies these findings. Indeed, *Nosferatu* has been a popular object of inquiry for queer film scholars. An early unauthorised filmic adaptation of Bram Stoker's *Dracula*, Murnau's film features three central characters, the married couple Thomas and Ellen (Jonathan and Mina Harker), and the vampire Count Orlok (Dracula).[33] Following Eve Kosofsky Sedgwick, the protagonist/antagonist pairing of Thomas and Orlok can be described as a homosocial bond, enabled in a system of triangulation through the female figure Ellen. The vampire lusts after Ellen (and her blood), but early in the film he craves Thomas and manages to bite his neck, forcing himself upon Thomas while his victim is asleep. Queer analyses of *Nosferatu* have not only foregrounded readings of the vampire as metaphor, but also the dichotomies between Count Orlok and Thomas. For instance, film historian Robin Wood advanced a reading of Orlok and Thomas as two embodiments of the same character, in which the vampire figure symbolises repressed sexuality.[34]

A quintessential trope of Gothic fiction, doubles can be found throughout literary history. The trope features significantly in German literature of the Romantic period, which originated the term doppelgänger 'as a means of both representing and critically describing literary and non-literary manifestations of the double'.[35] The doppelgänger, as Andrew Webber suggests, symbolises the Romantic rejection of Enlightenment ideals. It reveals 'what is conventionally discounted or repressed in the cultural heritage of the Enlightenment: the destructive potential of desire, the prevalence of the unknowable, and the corruptible condition of subjective identity'.[36] While the trope is predominantly examined in psychoanalytic readings such as that of Robin Wood's, Richard Dyer suggests that the doubled characters in *Nosferatu* represent two of the most prominent gay archetypes of early twentieth-century gay subculture, the *Tante* (auntie) and the *Bube/Bursche* (boy/lad). As these names suggest, *Tante* was used to label more effeminate gay men while the term *Bube* denoted a more butch and masculine type. In Dyer's reading, Orlok, with his hunched posture, powdered face and mincing steps, is 'a grotesque exaggeration of the effeminized male look'.[37] However, it is the broad-shouldered, butch Thomas who is the passive, sexual object in *Nosferatu*, while the effeminate vampire takes on the active role of the sexual predator. The protagonist thus 'represents the passive, impotent male so common in the Weimar cinema, as Kracauer has observed'.[38] Yet this model of masculinity is presented as more desirable than its effeminate counterpart, coded as monstrous and threatening. I will pick up this binary of contrasting queer identities later in my analysis.

Early Cinema and the Gothic: From Méliès to Caligari

Before returning to Weimar cinema, it is instructive to explore the origins of Gothic film. Film scholar Tom Gunning coined the term 'Cinema of Attraction' to describe the predominant conception in early film (particularly until around 1907 when filmmakers turned to more narrative editing) that harnessed the illusory power of the medium rather than storytelling to attract spectatorship.[39] Many film pioneers exhausted the possibilities of early filmmaking to perform magic tricks and special effects on screen, resulting in often inherently Gothic moments. The infamous myth of the first screening of Auguste and Louis Lumière's documentary film *Arrival of a Train at La Ciotat* (1895) has gained notoriety because of a Gothic effect: It is said that the audience left their seats and ran away in terror when they saw the train getting bigger and bigger while approaching them. Although the story is most likely a legend, one could make a case for viewing the illusion of a train coming directly at the spectators as a precursor of the jump-scare technique popular in more recent horror films.

Arguably the most famous film pioneer of that period, whose filmic illusions went back as far as 1896, was the French filmmaker George Méliès. Film historian James L. Neibaur notes that even his earliest works present Gothic imageries: giant insects, moving objects, the transformation of human bodies. In 1899 he made what Neibaur believes to be the earliest horror movie, *Cleopatra*, in which a man performs necromancy on Cleopatra's mummified corpse to bring her back to life. Film historian Roy Kinnard goes even further by defining 12 additional films directed by Méliès between 1896 and 1899 as the earliest horror films. Kinnard begins his filmography with the two-minute film *Escamotage d'une dame chez Robert-Houdin* (*Conjuring a Lady at Robert Houdin's*), featuring a jump-cut that is used to enact a woman's transformation into a skeleton.[40] Méliès, Neibaur posits, 'comprehended how using darkness to frame carefully lit images could convey an idea, an attitude that was unsettling and scary'.[41] I would like to suggest that Méliès also used Gothic illusions for comedic effects, as in his 1898 film *Un homme de têtes* (*The Four Troublesome Heads*). Méliès created the illusion of a magician severing his head from his shoulders by using stop motion, multiple exposure and blacking out the original head on the magician's shoulders.

The stop-motion technique advanced by Méliès has often been used to enable supernatural depictions of inanimate objects moving by themselves. Bringing the technique to the extreme, French filmmaker Émile

Cohl created films that almost entirely consisted of stop motion. For instance, he uses the technique in his 1910 film *Le Mobilier fidèle* (*The Automatic Moving Company*) to make furniture move around by itself. Made during the narrativisation period of cinema,[42] Cohl's four-minute-long movie tells a clear story, but the spectacle of moving objects constitutes the main attraction of the film. In the first 35 seconds, we see a letter floating across the office of the automatic moving company and landing on a desk, a paper knife cutting open the envelope, the letter with a request for the moving company unfolding, pages of a notebook turning and a pencil writing. The rest of the film shows a driverless trailer arriving at the address; furniture and moving boxes leave the trailer, walk up the stairs and furnish the empty apartment, as if possessed by ghosts. The examples presented here show that Gothic cinema is as old as cinema itself and that the Gothic in film is not limited to the horror genre but could better be described as an aesthetic mode that defies genre.

With the advent of narrative cinema in the 1910s and 1920s, Gothic visuals were further advanced by German filmmakers just before and during the Weimar years.[43] Literary scholar Dietrich Scheunemann documented the revival of the Gothic motif of the doppelgänger in early cinema: 'The *Doppelgänger* did not appear in the tales of the Romantics without the optical instruments required for the projection, reflection and distortion of images.'[44] The technical innovations of cinema, he posits, made possible the production and reproduction of double visions. Film pioneer Paul Wegener discussed this possibility in a 1916 essay: 'and I said to myself that this must also be possible in film and here it would provide the possibility to show E.T.A. Hoffmann's fantasies of the *Doppelgänger* or the mirror image in reality and thus to achieve effects which were not attainable in any other art'.[45] Indeed, the effect was put on screen in Wegener's film acting debut *Der Student von Prag* (*The Student of Prague*). One of the earliest art films, *The Student of Prague* managed to double Wegener on screen, producing a sinister doppelgänger of the film's protagonist. From *The Student of Prague* (1913) to *Nosferatu* (1922), to the *Maschinenmensch* in *Metropolis* (1927), doubles rule supreme in early German cinema.

Early film scholarship has theorised why German film experimented with the visual sphere like no other national cinema. In particular, two influential monographs by Lotte Eisner and Siegfried Kracauer have generated an analogy between German film culture and political history, rendering Weimar cinema haunted by the past and, for Kracauer, the fascist future alike.[46] According to Eisner, poverty, insecurity and the consequences of defeat in the First World War predisposed German artists to 'the apocalyptic doctrine of Expressionism'.⁴⁷ A reaction against both Impressionism and Naturalism, Expressionist artists rejected representations of nature as the point of departure in favour of individualist abstraction. Abstraction, art historian Wilhelm Worringer postulated in his work on Gothic art, 'stems from the great anxiety which man experiences when terrorized by the phenomena he perceives around him, the relationships and mysterious polarities of which he is unable to decipher',⁴⁸ resulting in the desire to separate objects from their natural environments – a practice, Eisner argues, that was predominant in German film in the 1920s.⁴⁹

However, it is important to note that German Expressionism is often conflated with Weimar German cinema in general, when in fact only a portion of all the films produced during that period show clear Expressionist aesthetics. Kristin Thompson and David Bordwell confine the Expressionist movement to a period from 1920, with the release of *Das Cabinet des Dr. Caligari* (*The Cabinet of Dr. Caligari*), to 1927, by which time the Expressionist trend had faded out. Depending on how narrowly one defines formal traits of Expressionism, film historians count merely half a dozen to two dozen films released in that period.⁵⁰ While Expressionist film had a lasting impact on Hollywood's Golden Age, especially on film noir of the 1940s and 1950s, it would be false to limit the cinematic innovations brought forward during the Weimar period to the Expressionist movement alone.

Thompson and Bordwell named Robert Wiene's *Caligari* as the starting point of the Expressionist movement for a good reason. No other film embodies the tenets of Expressionism better than Wiene's horror film, and with its innovative experiments in light, camera and set design, *Caligari* is now considered one of the most influential achievements in cinematic history. The film's *mise en scène* is heavily stylised: 'distorted perspectives, eerie lights and shadows, an angular world of fears and apprehension'.⁵¹ A contemporary film critic for the *New York Times* noted in his review that 'everything is unreal in *The Cabinet of Dr. Caligari*. There is nothing of normalcy about it.'⁵² Disturbances of normalcy, of course, are ripe for queer interpretations. Indeed, the characters navigate a world in which no window is shaped rectangularly, no wall stands upright, no street leads from one place to another in direct lines; in short, straightness doesn't exist on the visual level. Can the same be said about the narrative? In *Flaming Classics*, his ambitious enterprise to queer the film canon, Alexander Doty starts with a queer reading of *Caligari*'s frame narrative, which he describes as 'an older man–younger man cruising scenario'.⁵³ In this opening scene, two men sit on a park bench. The older man begins to tell the younger one, the protagonist Francis, a story: 'There are spirits. They are all around us. They have driven me from hearth and home, from wife and child ...' Who or what are these haunting apparitions that have disrupted the man's 'cozy normative heterosexual life'?[54] This question remains unanswered because Francis interrupts the older man's narration to tell his and his fiancée Jane's story, triggered by her entering the scene: 'What she and I have lived through is stranger still than what you have lived through ...' Doty suggests that Francis attempts to undermine the older man's narrative to assert his own heterosexual narrative. Yet doesn't Francis appear driven from hearth and home himself? After all, while his fiancée Jane may have appeared on screen while he is telling his story, she seems apathetic and lifeless, walking past Francis and the other man like a detached ghost. The opening frame narrative, in any case, establishes what Doty calls 'a disturbed and disturbing queerness'.[55]

This initial situation serves as the point of departure for Francis's story, the main premise of the film. In a long flashback, Francis tells of his encounter with Dr Caligari and the somnambulist Cesare at a fair in the town of Holstenwall. Caligari, who is able to control the sleepwalking Cesare, uses the somnambulist to commit murders around the town, including the killing of Francis's friend Alan. Francis begins to investigate the mysterious scientist, but it is revealed in a twist ending that the entire story has been a figment of Francis's imagination: he, the old man from the frame narrative, his 'fiancée' Jane and Cesare are all patients in a psychiatric hospital – and Caligari is the asylum director. The diegesis of *Caligari*, the twist ending suggests, is far removed from realistic representations of the material world because it depicts Francis's troubled mental state. If we understand the world Francis is navigating as a space void of straightness, as I have suggested above, how can we interpret his return to 'reality' in the frame narrative? In the final scene of the film, Francis is put in a straitjacket – a straightjacket – and brought to a cell, where the director examines him. The doctor concludes: 'At last I understand his delusion. He thinks I am that mystic Caligari! Now I know exactly how to cure him ...' Forcing Francis quite literally into straightness, the film pathologises queerness as a condition that needs to be cured.

But what makes queerness so anxiety-inducing in the film that it needs to be straightened out? We may find the answer in the figure of the somnambulist Cesare, who signifies the queer threat to society woven into the film's fabric. It is Cesare, controlled by Caligari, who strikes fear and terror into the people of Holstenwall. He murders Francis's best friend and threatens to kill his heterosexual love interest in the embedded narrative. Many film scholars have described Cesare, played by

Conrad Veidt, as the easiest point of entry for queer interpretations of the film. Indeed, not long before the release of *Caligari*, Veidt starred as Paul Körner in *Anders als die Andern* and 'became a hero of Weimar's burgeoning gay culture'.[56] But Veidt was popular with heterosexual audiences as well. Playing roles characterised by various degrees of masculinity, he embodied a new type of man, which rendered him desirable for heterosexual women while at the same time making him a role model for heterosexual men.[57] In *Caligari*, Veidt plays an effeminate Cesare who some scholars link to Hirschfeld's notions of the 'sexual intermediate' or, like *Nosferatu*'s monster figure, to the 1920s gay archetype of the *Tante*, similarly reconfigured here 'into the threatening, yet fascinating, androgyne'.[58] Also corresponding to Queer Gothic interpretations of *Nosferatu*, *Caligari*'s queerness can be located in the film's use of the doppelgänger trope. Indeed, doubles are everywhere in the film: there are two versions of the same characters in the frame narrative and the embedded narrative, two incarnations of Caligari, two men fighting for Jane's affection, among many other instances. The central doublings, however, are situated in constellations consisting of Dr Caligari, Cesare and Francis. As Theodore Price argues: 'Caligari and Cesare are *homosexual* Doubles, with Caligari the Active Double, Cesare the Passive, doing whatever Caligari tells him to do.'[59] Alexander Doty adds that both of these figures double Francis, as they stem from his imagination, rendering Francis implicated in both positions. Doty concludes: 'So while the framing story and the fantasy find Francis attempting to assert a heterosexual masculinity, it is consistently troubled by his Doppelgänger connections to Caligari and Cesare, who become expressive of his homosexual fears and repressed desires.'[60] By repressing his own queerness, then, Francis escapes into a fantasy world that configures queerness as murderous and visually haunting.

Reading *Anders als die Andern* as Queer Gothic

Queer analysis shows that the Gothic doppelgänger trope in *Nosferatu* and *Caligari* is employed in similar ways: to establish dichotomies between what is deemed good (heterosexuality) and what is deemed bad (homosexuality). The following concluding look at *Anders als die Andern* will show that this interpretation is not universally applicable to all instances of the doppelgänger trope in Weimar cinema. It is time to return to Magnus Hirschfeld, as he was deeply involved in the production of *Anders*. It might be obvious to locate the impact of advances in sexuality studies and gay rights activism in this film.

However, it is important to discuss the cultural significance of the new medium and its particular conventions in representations of queerness. Hirschfeld himself had noted the importance of film in the fight for social progress and popular education.[61]

Directed by Richard Oswald and co-written by Oswald and Magnus Hirschfeld, *Anders* depicts the tragic life of violinist Paul Körner, who develops a loving relationship with the young man Kurt, but whose bliss is disturbed by an acquaintance from Paul's past. The extortionist Franz, who has blackmailed Paul over his homosexuality in the past, once again demands money from Paul after he recognises his former victim on a happy walk through the park with Kurt. Paul initially meets the blackmailer's demands, but he ultimately reports Franz to the police; Franz in return discloses Paul's violation of Paragraph 175, and both men are arrested and sentenced to prison. While Paul receives the mildest possible sentence of one week in prison, his punishment turns out to be much more grave: his forced outing costs him his career, social standing and the support of friends and family. Paul commits suicide. His devastated boyfriend Kurt would have followed Paul, but his death is prevented by an unnamed sexologist, played by Hirschfeld himself, who urges Kurt to stay alive and fight for justice. Hirschfeld's character appears throughout the film as a voice of reason whose lectures on sexual minorities are attended by the film's protagonists. His lectures serve not only to enlighten the other characters in the film, but also (and primarily) the spectator.

Oswald and Hirschfeld collaborated on a variety of films with this purpose, known as *Aufklärungsfilme*, translated as enlightenment films or social hygiene films. This film genre touched upon taboos and legal problems around topics such as abortion, venereal disease, prostitution or – in the case of *Anders* – homosexuality. Scholarly attention has been paid to the film's (and the genre's) role in social change and political action. Kracauer, for instance, has been entirely dismissive of the genre not only in its artistic but also its moral and political value. He describes the abolition of censorship after the revolution not so much as a catalyst for the transformation of film into a political platform, but rather as making way for a cesspool of filmic depictions of sexual debauchery.[62] More recent scholarship has contested Kracauer and argued that Oswald's social hygiene films played an important role in early twentieth-century political activism, as sex and sexuality were in fact very much politicised during the Weimar Republic years.[63] Germanist Ervin Malakaj, moreover, has described the melodramatic nature of the plot as quintessential to achieving the film's social justice goals, as the 'impossible situation' at the core of the melodrama triggers the spectator's yearning for a better world in which a happy ending is possible.[64] And while the plot of the film is not inherently Gothic in nature, I would like to suggest that the dark story of blackmail, haunting memories and suicide presents Gothic potential worth tapping into. What insights do we gain when we watch *Anders als die Andern* not only as a social hygiene film and a melodrama, but also as a Gothic film, and thus as a pioneering work of Queer Gothic cinema?

The Gothic properties of the film primarily lie in the relationship of its protagonist/antagonist pairing, Paul and Franz, played by Conradt Veidt and Reinhold Schünzel. Paul is introduced as a celebrated violinist who reads about the suicides of various men, including a respectable government official, a factory owner and a bright student, in the morning papers. While no reasons are given for any of the suicides, Paul understands that they all must be the result of legal discrimination against homosexual men. The spectre of discrimination appears to haunt Paul from the very beginning of the film. He goes on to think about other homosexual men in world history, including famous artists and statesmen such as Leonardo da Vinci, Pyotr Tchaikovsky and Frederick the Great, who are described in the intertitles as luminaries. These dead historical figures not only appear at the beginning of the film, but reappear like ghosts in the film's final scenes after Paul commits suicide, haunting and framing the narrative.

This very first scene of the film serves to convey three things: first, to lament the devastating loss to society from the persistent persecution of respectable homosexuals; second, to go back in history in order to establish homosexuality as something as old as humankind itself and thus to reaffirm its normalcy; and third, to place Paul in this list of positively described men. Franz, on the contrary, does not belong on this list. On his first appearance in the film, Franz runs into Paul and Kurt in the park and follows them closely like a dark shadow. Once again, the spectre of discrimination appears to haunt Paul. Franz returns a few scenes later in Paul's quarters. A close-up on Franz reveals unnaturally dark, sunken eyes and a sinister grin – a ghoulish face already suggesting the doom to follow. Franz's unexpected appearance visibly stirs Paul: he moves to the background of the frame while Franz intrudes into Paul's space by lying down on his chaise longue and grabbing his personal belongings. We later learn that this isn't the first encounter of the two: in the past, they met at a queer costume ball and went back to Paul's home together, where Franz revealed himself to be an extortionist demanding money to keep quiet about Paul's homosexuality. In the following sequence, we learn more about Paul's adolescence and young adulthood, characterised by homophobic encounters. Franz's uncanny return to this very home triggers Paul to relive haunting memories of the homophobia he has experienced throughout his life – memories that he had suppressed up until this point. Unlike the protagonist in *Dr. Caligari*, however, Paul does not lose himself in a nightmarish fantasy of internalised homophobia, because he meets the unnamed doctor played by Hirschfeld, who tells him about the normalcy of homosexuality. Unlike the monstrous figure of Franz, Paul is configured as a representative of enlightened thought.

A subsequent scene underlines the stark contrast between Franz and other homosexual men such as Paul. We see Franz sitting at a table in a gay nightclub with same-sex couples dancing in the background. All the patrons of the nightclub seem happy and bright – except for Franz and another sinister-looking man who is approaching his table. The two men begin a conversation about Franz's next plan to extort money from Paul. The *mise en scène* establishes a stark visual contrast between the two ill-boding men in the centre of the shot and the cheerful scene of queer sociability surrounding them. In this gay nightclub, a venue designed to be a queer safe space, the two men forge plans to hurt homosexual men. When Paul ultimately refuses to continue the payments to the blackmailer and both of them are put in the dock in one of the last scenes of the film, the contrast between Paul and Franz is brought to the extreme. Not only does Franz show no remorse for his crimes, but he also seems unfazed by his sentencing to three years in prison for his repeated offences. Paul, on the other hand, follows the proceedings conscientiously, albeit visibly worn out by the affair. The court itself seems to sympathise with him, as the verdict on the intertitle reads: 'A judge can only carry out the law. As long as Paragraph 175 exists, we are not entitled to grant acquittal. The court therefore declares a sentence of one week in prison.' This week of prison is enough to ensure Paul's social death, as he loses his employment, reputation and the support of his family and friends, ultimately driving him to suicide to join the ranks of the dead historical figures from the first scene. The spectre of suicide that loomed over the film from the very first scene returns.

The message is quite clear: even the most minor law and the mildest punishment against same-sex practices will further the severe social repudiation of homosexuality and encourage other crimes such as extortion and blackmail. In its rendition of the Gothic doppelgänger motif, the film presents two very different formations of gay identity generated by and in such an environment: first, the respectable albeit repressed homosexual who cannot survive in a world of social and legal discrimination against homosexuality; second, the sexually unrestricted, but sketchy and shadowy homosexual who takes advantage of the situation to exploit other homosexuals. Viewing *Anders* as a film with a Queer Gothic aesthetic, I understand Franz not only as a double of Paul, but as a double of queer Weimar Berlin itself. But unlike *Nosferatu* or *Dr. Caligari*, the trope's focus shifts from a binary that posits queerness as a monstrous threat to heterosexuality to one in which queerness itself is threatened. In this constellation, the monster is the homophobic blackmailer. The Gothic presence of the latter not only haunts the former, it also helps create a stark binary with formations of queerness worthy of respect and empathy. The contrast between the two undergirds the role of 'normalcy' in this very first gay rights movement. *Anders als die Andern*, a film primarily regarded as a social hygiene film and melodrama as well as a pioneering contribution to queer cinema, is rife with Gothic imagery that, like its didactic and melodramatic components, serves to boost its call for social change and legal reform; but it also reveals that this progress must happen at the expense of non-normative queerness. The attempt seems to have been in vain: *Anders* was banned from public screenings a year after its initial release. The film received an enormous backlash on its premiere and some reviewers even linked the portrayal of homosexuality to Jewishness, demonstrating the proximity of homophobia and antisemitism in Weimar Germany.[65] Thus, it would be false to romanticise Weimar Germany as a place of unequivocal queer acceptance in mainstream society and media.

Hirschfeld's Institute for Sexology and most of its groundbreaking work were destroyed a few months after the Nazi Party took control in Germany in 1933, and Hirschfeld died two years later in exile. Berlin's thriving queer nightlife and publishing industry ceased to exist. Most prints of *Anders* were destroyed and only a 50-minute fragment of the film survives, literally spliced together from different pieces like Dr Frankenstein's monster. Germany's anti-queer laws, which Hirschfeld and so many queer scholars and activists before him sought to overturn, were strengthened under Nazi rule, culminating in a 'hunt against homosexuals'[66] that incarcerated thousands between 1933 and 1945. From the first screening of *Anders*, it took another seventy-five years, and the passing of the Weimar Republic, the Third Reich and the years of two divided German states, until Paragraph 175 was abolished and stopped haunting queer people for good.

Notes

1. See, for example, Robert Beachy, *Gay Berlin: Birthplace of a Modern Identity* (New York: Vintage Books, 2014); Katie Sutton, *Sex Between*

Body and Mind: Psychoanalysis and Sexology in the German-Speaking World, 1890s–1930s (Ann Arbor, MI: University of Michigan Press, 2019); Clayton J. Whisnant, *Queer Identities and Politics in Germany: A History 1880–1945* (New York: Harrington Park Press, 2016).
2. Christopher Isherwood, *Christopher and His Kind, 1929–1939* (New York: Avon Books, 1977).
3. Beachy, *Gay Berlin*, p. 12.
4. Ralph Matthew Leck, *Vita Sexualis: Karl Ulrichs and the Origins of Sexual Science* (Urbana, IL: University of Illinois Press, 2016), p. xii.
5. Beachy, *Gay Berlin*, pp. 12–42.
6. Ibid., p. 72.
7. Ibid., p. 53.
8. Ibid., pp. 56–9.
9. Magnus Hirschfeld, *Die Homosexualität des Mannes und des Weibes* (Berlin: Louis Marcus, 1914), p. xii.
10. Beachy, *Gay Berlin*, p. 74.
11. For an introductory account of the history of the homophile movement, see Annamarie Jagose, *Queer Theory: An Introduction* (New York: NYU Press), pp. 22–9.
12. Beachy, *Gay Berlin*, p. 80.
13. Hirschfeld, *Die Homosexualität*, p. i.
14. For an expansive bibliography of Hirschfeld's works, see James D. Steakley, *The Writings of Dr. Magnus Hirschfeld: A Bibliography* (Toronto: Canadian Gay Archives, 1985).
15. Magnus Hirschfeld (ed.), *Jahrbuch für sexuelle Zwischenstufen unter besonderer Berücksichtigung der Homosexualität* (Leipzig: Max Spohr, 1902).
16. Katie Sutton, '"We Too Deserve a Place in the Sun": The Politics of Transvestite Identity in Weimar Germany', *German Studies Review*, 35.2 (2012), pp. 335–54 (p. 336).
17. Magnus Hirschfeld, *Die Transvestiten: eine Untersuchung über den erotischen Verkleidungstrieb* (Berlin: Pulvermacher, 1910), p. 281.
18. Hirschfeld, *Die Transvestiten*, p. 290.
19. Hirschfeld, *Die Transvestiten*, p. 292.
20. Beachy, *Gay Berlin*, p. 133.
21. Ibid., p. 131.
22. Ibid., p. 132.
23. 'Lili Elbe Digital Archive' http://lilielbe.org/narrative/publicationHistory.html (accessed 7 July 2021).
24. Beachy, *Gay Berlin*, p. 132.
25. Ibid., p. 133.
26. Laurie Marhoefer, '"The Book Was a Revelation, I Recognized Myself in It": Lesbian Sexuality, Censorship, and the Queer Press in Weimar-Era Germany', *Journal of Women's History*, 27.2 (2015), pp. 62–86 (p. 76).
27. Richard Dyer, 'Less and More than Women and Men: Lesbian and Gay Cinema in Weimar Germany', *New German Critique*, 51 (1990), pp. 5–60 (p. 5).
28. See, for example, Dyer, 'Less and More', pp. 5–60; and Alice A. Kuzniar, *The Queer German Cinema* (Stanford, CA: Stanford University Press, 2000). pp. 23–7.

29. Dyer, 'Less and More', p. 12.
30. See Kuzniar's chapter on queer Weimar cinema in *The Queer German Cinema*, pp. 21–56.
31. Ibid., p. 34.
32. Janet Bergstrom, 'Sexuality at a Loss: The Films of F.W. Murnau', *Poetics Today*, 6.1/2 (1985), pp. 185–203 (p. 191), https://doi.org/10.2307/1772129.
33. Character names were most likely changed to avoid copyright infringement issues.
34. Robin Wood, 'Murnau', *Film Comment*, 12.3 (1976), pp. 4–19 (p. 8).
35. Dale Townshend, 'Doubles', in *The Encyclopedia of the Gothic* (John Wiley & Sons, 2012), p. 2, https://doi.org/10.1002/9781118398500.wbeotgd007.
36. Andrew Webber, *The Doppelgänger: Double Visions in German Literature* (Oxford: Clarendon Press, 1996), p. 148.
37. Dyer, 'Less and More', p. 37.
38. Bergstrom, 'Sexuality at a Loss', p. 197.
39. Tom Gunning, 'The Cinema of Attraction[s]: Early Film, Its Spectator and the Avant-Garde', in *The Cinema of Attractions Reloaded*, ed. Wanda Strauven (Amsterdam: Amsterdam University Press, 2006), pp. 381–8, https://doi.org/10.5040/9781838710170.
40. Roy Kinnard, *Horror in Silent Films: A Filmography, 1896–1929* (Jefferson, NC: McFarland, 1995), p. 8.
41. James L Neibaur, 'Gothic Cinema during the Silent Era', in *Gothic Film: An Edinburgh Companion*, ed. Richard J. Hand and McRoy Jay (Edinburgh: Edinburgh University Press, 2020), pp. 11–20 (p. 12).
42. Tom Gunning describes the time between 1907 and 1913 as the narrativisation of cinema, resulting in the emergence of feature films as a primary mode of filmmaking.
43. For a detailed historical overview, see Stephen Brockmann, *A Critical History of German Film* (Melton: Boydell & Brewer, 2020), pp. 43–60.
44. Dietrich Scheunemann, 'The Double, the Décor, and the Framing Device: Once More on Robert Wiene's *The Cabinet of Dr. Caligari*', in *Expressionist Film – New Perspectives*, ed. Dietrich Scheunemann (Rochester, NY: Camden House, 2003), pp. 125–56 (p. 132).
45. Ibid., p. 133.
46. See Lotte H. Eisner, *The Haunted Screen: Expressionism in the German Cinema and the Influence of Max Reinhardt* (Berkeley, CA: University of California Press, 1969); and Siegfried Kracauer, *From Caligari to Hitler: A Psychological History of the German Film* (Princeton, NJ: Princeton University Press, 1947). However, more recent scholarship has somewhat pushed against the interlocking of film culture and political history. In his book *Weimar Cinema and After: Germany's Historical Imaginary* (London: Routledge, 2000), Thomas Elsaesser called this notion a Möbius strip, a self-fulfilling prophecy that has neither beginning nor end.
47. Eisner, *The Haunted Screen*, p. 9.
48. Ibid., p. 13.
49. Ibid., p. 17.
50. Kristin Thompson and David Bordwell, *Film History: An Introduction*, 3rd edn (New York: McGraw-Hill Higher Education, 2010), p. 92.

51. John White, 'Das Kabinett des Dr. Caligari / The Cabinet of Dr. Caligari (1919)', in *The Routledge Encyclopedia of Films*, ed. John White, Sarah Barrow and Sabine Haenni (Abingdon: Routledge, 2015), pp. 287–89 (p. 287).
52. 'The Screen', *New York Times*, 4 April 1921, section Archives, https://www.nytimes.com/1921/04/04/archives/the-screen.html (accessed 12 February 2022).
53. Alexander Doty, *Flaming Classics: Queering the Film Canon* (New York: Routledge, 2000), p. 23.
54. Ibid., p. 23.
55. Ibid., p. 24.
56. Elizabeth Otto, 'Schaulust: Sexuality and Trauma in Conrad Veidt's Masculine Masquerades', in *The Many Faces of Weimar Cinema. Rediscovering Germany's Filmic Legacy*, ed. Christian Rogowski (New York: Camden House, 2010), pp. 134–52 (p. 136).
57. Ibid., 138.
58. Doty, *Flaming Classics*, p. 27.
59. Theodore Price, *Hitchcock and Homosexuality: His 50-Year Obsession with Jack the Ripper and the Superbitch Prostitute: A Psychoanalytic View* (Metuchen, NJ: Scarecrow Press, 1992), p. 318.
60. Doty, *Flaming Classics*, p. 30.
61. Ina Linge, 'Sexology, Popular Science and Queer History in *Anders als die Andern (Different from the Others)*', *Gender & History*, 30.3 (2018), pp. 595–610 (p. 595), https://doi.org/10.1111/1468-0424.12381.
62. Kracauer, *From Caligari to Hitler*, p. 44.
63. Jill Suzanne Smith, 'Richard Oswald and the Social Hygiene Film: Promoting Public Health or Promiscuity?', in *The Many Faces of Weimar Cinema. Rediscovering Germany's Filmic Legacy*, ed. Christian Rogowski (New York: Camden House, 2010), pp. 13–30.
64. Ervin Malakaj, 'Richard Oswald, Magnus Hirschfeld, and the Possible Impossibility of Hygienic Melodrama', *Studies in European Cinema*, 14.3 (2017), pp. 216–30, https://doi.org/10.1080/17411548.2017.1376857.
65. See, for example, Walther Friedmann, 'Homosexuality and Jewishness: The Latest Method of Agitation against "Aufklärungsfilme"', in *The Promise of Cinema: German Film Theory, 1907–1933*, ed. Anton Kaes, Nicholas Baer and Michael J. Cowan (Oakland, CA: University of California Press, 2016), pp. 240–2. In this essay from July 1919, Friedmann condemns the antisemitism implied by the reception of *Anders als die Andern*. However, he joins in on the homophobia by referring to homosexuality as 'certainly an extremely regrettable and, for people with normal sensitivities, a repulsive degeneration of the sex drive, which unfortunately occurs in all social classes, independent of nation, race, and denomination' (p. 241).
66. Whisnant, *Queer Identities*, p. 217.

Chapter 5

'Tarting up ideas in costume jewellery': Contemporary Gothic Camp

Thomas Brassington

'That theatrical way which is, I believe, natural to some people': Introducing Gothic Camp[1]

Gothic has always been campy. Its penchant for melodrama, affinity with superficial expressions of extreme emotion, and preferred locales, set dressings and costumes all collude to craft a camp way of imagining the world. Susan Sontag argued this in 1964, noting that 'the origins of Camp taste are to be found' in eighteenth-century artefacts, with 'Gothic novels' being one of Sontag's many examples.[2] Subsequent criticism further indicates the tremendous tendency of Gothic and horror to be campy. For example, Jack Babuscio argues that horror cinema's camp qualities emerge from the genre's tendency to 'make the most of stylish conventions for expressing instant feeling, thrills, sharply defined personality, outrageous and "unacceptable" sentiments, and so on'.[3] Likewise, Gothic scholars obliquely suggest a contact point between Gothic and camp.[4] Despite this, critical work on Gothic camp is scant.[5] This critical lacuna is even more noticeable within Queer Gothic studies. Considering that the predominant approach that queer Gothicists take when analysing the mode involves a fixation on forms of queer representation and expressions of queer politics interpretable within Gothic work, this gap is arguably understandable – camp is often perceived as light and frothy, and hence at odds with 'serious' creative political endeavours. That said, camp criticism has staged numerous interventions that demonstrate its capacity as a tool for historical, cultural and political critique. For example, Fabio Cleto's fantastic reader *Camp: Queer Aesthetics and the Performing Subject* (1999) and Moe Meyer's edited collection *The Politics and Poetics of Camp* (1994) both expertly outline camp's queer politics.

This chapter explicitly explores the possibilities of camp's queer politics in contemporary Gothic works. Through a range of texts spanning the latter half of the twentieth century to the present day, I shall explore the notion, simply put by Megen de Bruin-Molé in *Gothic Remixed* (2020), that 'camp rehabilitates'.[6] Camp's rehabilitative qualities transform the Gothic into a continually productive site for the expression and creation of different subjecthoods. To begin outlining Gothic camp's range, I present four subsections: the first two find camp among unexpected subjects such as older women and heterosexuals, using *Whatever Happened to Baby Jane?* (1962) and the Addams family, particularly as they are represented in *The Addams Family Values* (1993), as case studies. Following this are two subsections that consider Gothic camp intersectionally by drawing attention to the significance of Blackness and femininities to camp, respectively using *Blacula* (1972) and the episode 'Butterfly/Cocoon' from the television show *Pose* (2019), and *Elvira, Mistress of the Dark* (1988) and *Jennifer's Body* (2009). The period from the 1960s to the close of the 2010s suggests a particularly incisive moment for exploring Gothic camp. The substantial momentum gained by civil rights movements from the 1960s onwards had the concomitant effect of overtly politicising and outwardly expressing minority identities. For example, the 1969 Stonewall Riots function as a historical linchpin on which gender and sexual minority political movements turn. Camp, arguably, transforms at this moment from an open-secret-style practice of queer communication and intra-community identification into a queer practice for publicly expressing queer identities. Therefore, contemporary Gothic camp serves as the most overtly politicised imagining of Gothic camp, and so presents a traceable launching point for exploring the dynamism of Gothic's camp tendencies.

Finding Camp 1: Fag Hags

In 'No Country for Old Women: Gender, Age and the Gothic', Avril Horner and Sue Zlosnik argue that 'Gothic texts often bring to the surface the cultural rejection and abjection of the older woman endemic to the Western world.'[7] Often, older women in Gothic fiction are highly disposable, since they are seen 'as irrelevant and an (increasingly heavy) economic burden'.[8] Older women are not useful to a late capitalist, patriarchal culture because they cannot work or reproduce. Instead, in Gothic fiction, they form part of the supporting cast and window dressing – they are not as 'associated with avenging fire' as younger heroines, implicitly because they are no longer part of the capitalist reproductive economy.[9]

With this in mind, older women arguably share common ground with queer subjects, due to their mutual exclusion from reproductive economies. Such commonality creates a site for camaraderie and the exchange of political strategies such as camp. Here, at this intersection, works such as *Baby Jane* are regarded as camp classics, despite its cast of ostensibly heterosexual women and the rather loathsome queerly coded character Edwin Flagg (Victor Buono).[10] However, it is not Edwin's queer presence, but Jane's (Bette Davis) and Blanche's (Joan Crawford) age that facilitates *Baby Jane*'s campness. Of course, there is something to say about the actresses' respective star quality and their gay iconicity, but I shall not be following this camp thread here. Instead, I wish to consider how the menopausal age of Jane and Blanche transforms them into camp artefacts. In 'The Deaths of Camp' Caryl Flinn argues that a shared quality of camp artefacts is their age: 'the artifact [. . .] cannot be *too* old, for then it might qualify as an object of "proper" anthropological and historical inquiry'.[11] There is a certain period of time in an artefact's life or history when it is particularly capable of camp interpretation, and Jane and Blanche fall within this zone. Both characters are stars in the twilight of their respective careers and both are experiencing or anticipating menopause, if we use Davis's and Crawford's ages at the time of filming to estimate Jane's and Blanche's age (50–54, as Crawford's birthdate is unknown). In other words, Jane and Blanche are at least on the verge of exiting the aforementioned cisheterosexual reproductive economies because their careers and their fertilities are ending. They are too young to be credible artefacts and too old to be (re)productive. Although this suggests a cruel element to Gothic camp, where *Baby Jane*'s campness emerges from a position where old women are laughed at for their cloying attempts to retain relevance, it is worth noting here that such a discussion would not be possible in the first place without a Gothic camp adoration of exactly these kinds of women. Indeed, that queer adoration of women on the cusp of exiting their careers and reproductive lives is exactly what offers such women a moment for career revitalisation. The laughter is not directed at the women, but alongside them at systems that crudely determine relevance centred on signifiers of youth. As Flinn states, 'camp has the power to force attention onto bodies in a culture that seems increasingly interested in burying, suppressing, or transcending them'.[12] Through camp, these films permit a form of comic criticism.

As a camp classic, *Baby Jane* demonstrates that camp's rehabilitative qualities can, in fact, provide a country for old women within the Gothic. Indeed, as Harriet Fletcher argues, 'the Gothic's unsettling nature and celebration of monstrous outsiders plays a crucial role in enabling the ageing actress to break such boundaries'.[13] Hagsploitation as a genre inaugurated this image of older women on screen as monstrous, and necessarily complex. Jane and Blanche's relationship is one of fraught tension, revelling in their respective successes and declines on stage and screen. A camp view of *Baby Jane* draws attention to their mutual exploitation by men, and the systemic injustices that consider women over 40 as, at best, 'gorgons or dragons', to quote Meryl Streep.[14] In the same motion that these injustices are camply made apparent, a sparkling adoration for the star herself manifests. These older women are presented as survivors of a monstrous machine who proceed to thrive (*Baby Jane* partially reignited Davis's and Crawford's careers). Thus, camp Gothic depictions of older women become aligned with a queer politics of survival and persistence. The laughter of camp rehabilitates the Gothic hag into an icon for queer persistence.

Finding Camp 2: Not Straight, just Heterosexual

Camp is a remarkably flexible tool for queer critique that can even infiltrate and affect images of cisheterosexuality. Since Gothic, as George Haggerty argues in *Queer Gothic* (2006), 'def[ies] limits and preconceptions of behavior and offer[s] a usefully uncategorized range of personal, sexual, and emotional behaviors and attitudes', it becomes arguable that Gothic can imagine cisheterosexuality in equally defiant fashion.[15] Naturally, queer studies of Gothic prioritise how the mode imagines queerness. That said, Haggerty's assertion also intimates that Gothic is particularly well suited to imagining alternative figurations of cisheterosexuality. One such figuration is comically suggested by drag queen Trixie Mattel in an episode of her web series 'UNHhhh' when she states, 'you're not straight, you're just heterosexual'.[16] Though originally part of an attempt not to alienate heterosexual viewers, this distinction indirectly suggests that such viewers are not full participants in an oppressive and tasteless straight culture. Those who are already fans of drag and 'UNHhhh' are merely heterosexual. This distinction usefully suggests that camp is not producible or interpretable only by queer subjects, enabling broader horizons for queering. Trixie effectively suggests that straights too can be queered, becoming 'just heterosexual' in the process.

The Addams family present a Gothic image more invested in cisheterosexuality than my other examples. Gomez and Morticia are often cited as an ideal couple, especially in their portrayal in the 1991 and 1993 film adaptations.[17] Their barely contained desire and deep adoration for each other, as well as their affection for their family, evoke an ideal image of a nuclear family, albeit with numerous Gothic touches. In *Gothic Kinship* (2013), Agnes Andeweg and Sue Zlosnik note that 'in Gothic fiction, the family is not the safe refuge of the ideological construct of the private sphere but the site of threat, particularly, as many critics have noted, for its female members'.[18] However, the threat that the Addamses pose is not to the individuals who comprise the family unit, but to the systems that determine such units' behaviour. Indeed, Andeweg and Zlosnik suggest that by 'both contesting and reinforcing notions of the nuclear family, Gothic fiction may offer figurations of alternative kinship ties'.[19] Such alternative figurations are often recognisably queer, but there is also room here to suppose an alternative figuration that is nevertheless recognisably heterosexual. Camp, in the Addams's case, is an important factor for alternative figurations.

Both films are deployments of older images. Initially drawn by cartoonist Charles Addams from 1938, *The Addams Family* aired on ABC from 1964 to 1966, during a period of rapid social development in America centred around a turn to suburban living and the baby boom. This development shifted images of familial domesticity, embodied in the new domestic television sitcom format, which Laura Morowitz argues imagines the American family as 'nostalgic, idyllic, conflict-free and homogenised'.[20] For Morowitz, *The Addams Family* television show presents a highly ambivalent vision of American suburban domesticity, at once mocking the family for their non-conformity, while simultaneously 'expand[ing] the borders of what comprised an acceptable American family unit'.[21] Importantly, the Addams' ambivalent domestic image is composed of historical detritus; *The Addams Family* and rival show *The Munsters* (1964–66) 'are embedded in the old world. This is true of the characters' references (to 1930s movie monsters), to their clothing and accoutrements (Victorian Gothic) and perhaps most pointedly to the fact that they are actually born in earlier centuries.'[22] The Addamses are an image of mid-twentieth-century domesticity interpolated with nineteenth- and early twentieth-century images, reframed yet again in the 1990s. Through this continued recycling, the Addamses resemble an anti-chrononormative vision of the American nuclear family, thus queering that image. Elizabeth Freeman defines chrononormativity as 'a technique by which institutional forces come to seem like somatic facts'.[23] For Freeman, chrornormativity acts through 'manipulations of time [that] convert historically specific regimes of asymmetrical power into seemingly ordinary bodily tempos and routines, which in turn organize the value and meaning of time'.[24] This manifests in forms such as the 9-to-5 workday, which as an institution bifurcates our conception of time as either productive ('working' time) or not, placing importance on the former. Likewise, a chrononormative lifetime revolves around moments in a person's history that are regarded as significant: births, weddings, pregnancies, deaths, sweet-16s, graduations and so on. These milestones privilege specific modes of being, most obviously heterosexual, monogamous and middle class. The Addamses are anti-chrononormative for their continual recycling of historical detritus (itself a Gothic temporal act), which further aligns them with queer senses of time – Freeman describes a 'stubborn lingering of pastness' as 'a hallmark of queer affect', so to continually plumb the images of the past in this camp way renders the Addamses temporally queer.[25]

One of camp's most effective critical tools is its fascination with ephemera that are past their expiration date. Andrew Ross argues that 'camp is a rediscovery of history's waste' that covets 'products [. . .] of a much earlier mode of production, which has lost its power to produce and dominate cultural meanings, becomes available, in the present, for redefinition according to contemporary codes of taste'.[26] Camp's affinity for dated artefacts taps into the resonances of power they once had, redirecting them to new ends. For Ross, this functions as part of a queer strategy for accruing the form of soft power to which queer subjects are often limited.[27] Yet this predilection for the resonances of power signified by certain objects remarkably resembles Gothic's own temporal sites. As Robert Miles argues, Gothic's preferred temporality is a 'period of sensed overlap, where the medieval wanes, and the modern begins', which he refers to as 'the "Gothic cusp"'.[28] On the Gothic cusp, where past meets present, lie piles of historical waste, refracted through contemporary tastes by audiences and/or producers of Gothic work, provoking a camp vision of the Gothic. The Addamses embody this purveying of historical detritus and become detritus through which a late twentieth-century audience/producer then picks, continually mobilising the Gothic cusp through camp actions. In this palimpsestic piling on of different pieces of waste some residue remains, but its presentation is transformed.

The Addamses are a nuclear family in an extremely strict sense. They are Anglo, suburban, wealthy and able bodied. Yet, at the same time, they have become somewhat divorced from the systemic power that is exploited by such units to oppress others. In becoming a camp object, the Addamses shift from a suburban straight family to a suburban heterosexual family, and this transition enables them to partake in types of pleasure and enjoyment not reliant on the oppression and exploitation of others. This is perhaps best exemplified in *The Addams Family Values* (1993), where seemingly any possibly straight American cultural iconography is warped.[29] In the opening sequence, where Morticia (Anjelica Huston) goes into labour, viewers are presented with a classic birthing montage: Morticia announces that she has gone into labour and is swiftly taken to hospital, where doctors tell her to 'push', forceps are called for to assist the birth, and the sequence ends with Gomez (Raúl Juliá) coming into the waiting room, where the rest of the family ask about the newborn's sex. There are numerous alterations to this conventional scene, however. First, Morticia appears to be in barely any pain, or perhaps enjoying the pain associated with labour – when she is asked to 'push', she responds by fluttering her eyes and making a delicate grunting noise. Camp allows Morticia to potentially enjoy her labour, at the same time disallowing audiences the spectacle of the agonies of childbirth that we are used to viewing in such sequences. She makes fun of audience expectations of seeing bodies in pain. At the end of the sequence, in response to the sex question, Gomez gleefully announces that 'It's an Addams', again entertaining the insignificance of assigned sex at birth by comically emphasising the significance of familial identity. In camply evading the question of the baby's sex in this way, Gomez invites a queer moment in which the sex of 'Pubert' is indeterminate, unimportant and no cause for celebration. What is significant and celebrated is a successful birth without casualties, and the expansion of the Addams family.

Black Drag Queens Invented Camp

On the 2019 Met Gala's pink carpet, 'Camp: Notes on Fashion', Lena Waithe wore a custom suit with 'Black drag queens invented camp' embroidered on the back, buttons embossed with the faces of iconic Black music artists, and pinstripes comprised of track titles by those artists.[30] In all, Waithe's sartorial statement highlights the significance of Blackness to contemporary camp. The statement acts as a reminder that contemporary camp, at least in the anglophone Western world, is heavily influenced by intersectional queer Black (sub)cultures. Camp's affinities with Blackness therefore present a rehabilitative method for a Black-centred approach to Gothic.

The case studies in this section, *Blacula* and *Pose*, present two very different orientations of Gothic camp. *Blacula* is a horror film in which camp affects its Black politics, whereas *Pose* sees an eruption of Gothic into an otherwise campy show, enabling a different take on the horrifying decisions facing Black trans women.[31] In *Blacula*, African prince Mamuwalde (William Marshall) requests help in ending the slave trade from Count Dracula (Charles Macaulay), only to be turned into a vampire, renamed Blacula and sealed in a coffin by the Count. In the 1970s two gay antique dealers buy Dracula's estate, Mamuwalde included, to sell the contents in America. They are elated by this relation to the Dracula mythology, since 'the legend of Dracula, that's the absolute crème de la crème of camp' which will increase these antiques' value. In *Blacula*, camp functions to frame how the film engages with and manipulates racist images and their systems of power. It is not lost on the viewer here that Mamuwalde has been purchased, albeit unknowingly, evoking the transatlantic slave trade. These parallels are, of course highly problematic, since Mamuwalde is still turned into a saleable object, but the camp frame here attempts to comically draw attention to this point, rather than simply laugh at these parallels. This comic framing caused by camp rather engages with the politics at hand in Blaxploitation films.

'Blaxploitation', Robin R. Means Coleman writes, 'described an era of Black film offerings which often drew their inspiration from Black Power ideologies', noting that 'in "Black horror" specifically, mainstream or White monsters [...] were purposefully transformed into "agents of Black power"'. Such films 'also often had an anti-establishment message, challenging "the Man's" or "Whitey's" exploitation of Black communities'. Blaxploitation horror films therefore produce a politically inflected Gothic that draws attention to the systemic injustices done to Black people, though such films can fall short when they indict 'a few wicked individuals' rather than the systems that produce such individuals.[32] *Blacula*, then, at once courts mid-twentieth-century African-American political ideologies and camp through the gay antique dealers' excitement at the vampiric mythos, creating a politically inflected Black Gothic camp. Black camp renders Mamuwalde's animalistic body (when hungry he is noticeably hairier and more beastly in manner) a knowing caricature of historically racist representations of Black people. Indeed, such knowing caricaturing of racialised stereotypes is one of the principal bases of Black forms of camp. Sequoia Barnes, in her exploration of Patrick Kelly's Black camp, identifies a strategy whereby his Black queerness is expressed through 'camping the image of the golliwog using fashion as his medium'.[33] Kelly's use of camp plays with and reclaims these racialised stereotypes as a form of comic empowerment. Black subjects use camp as part of a strategy that disempowers discriminatory images and stereotypes. In *Blacula*, this takes the form of a 'rather self-conscious [use of] hateful rhetoric to expose its diminishing effects and to actively rebuke such offenses', in Coleman's words.[34] *Blacula*'s camp functions as a frame which comically disempowers racist stereotypes (Blacula only becomes beastly once a White man curses him with vampirism).

Conversely, camp is a central component of *Pose* – a drama that follows the lives of queer people of colour (predominantly trans women) in the New York City ballroom scene of the 1980s and 1990s. Gothic erupts into this campy drama in the episode 'Butterfly/Cocoon'.[35] This episode's central plot concerns a white-collar client of part-time Dominatrix Elektra Xtravaganza's (Dominique Jackson) dying from an overdose, and the subsequent actions she takes with her found family. First, her daughter Blanca (MJ Rodriguez) advises her to call the police, at which Elektra scoffs. Her other daughter, Candy (Angelica Ross), asks Elektra, 'He white?' Elektra nods, and Candy responds, 'Oh bitch, you fucked.' These simple exchanges make clear to the viewer the prejudices and injustices at play should Elektra take legal action. As a Black trans woman employed at a seedy club, she would be immediately detained and arrested (at best). Instead, Elektra's found family take her to a back-alley doctor (Ms Orlando/Cecilia Gentili), who helps her hide the body. With the support of her community, Elektra mummifies the body in a 'beautiful little cocoon' made of pleather. Camp, here, draws attention to the solidarity between oppressed and disenfranchised groups.

The cocooning process is comically tinted: Ms Orlando demands that the corpse be curled up 'like a baby', the three women clearly struggle and are disgusted by their actions, and Evelyn 'Champagne' King's disco track 'Shame' plays throughout. When they stitch the pleather together, Ms Orlando says there need to be 'no holes, no seams, because when the body starts decomposing, it's gonna spill out all over your heels'. Later in the episode, Elektra confesses to Blanca that she has been having nightmares, and that 'he [the corpse] will be with me for the rest of my life'. Elektra is keenly aware of how this incident has become a literal skeleton in her closet, but is reminded that other options are unavailable for women like her. The monster in the closet, in this instance of Gothic in an otherwise campy dramatic show, is that of the systemic injustices that cause the extreme lengths marginalised groups go to so that they are not victimised by those injustices. Likewise, Elektra's remorse and feelings of guilt about these actions demonstrate a grace that the police would not afford her had she used appropriate legal channels.[36]

Blacula and *Pose* present Gothic camp in two very different capacities. For *Blacula*, camp is a perfunctory note that enhances the film's Black politics, which are displayed through horror tropes. Likewise, *Pose* uses Gothic camp to draw attention to systemic injustices and the actions marginalised groups are consequently forced to undertake. As a camp show that dabbles in Gothic images and moods, *Pose* sits opposite to *Blacula*, and yet their camp politics are similar. They are both concerned with community solidarity, gesture towards systemic injustices done to these communities, and comically disempower images that are emergent from those injustices.

'Excuse me while I indulge myself in a little song and dance'

A thread established throughout these texts is the significance of women to camp. Where Sontag 'has been thus charged by gay critics for turning a basically homosexual mode of self-performance into a degayfied taste', subsequent camp criticism downplays the significance of womanhood and femininities to camp.[37] For Gothic camp, it is especially important to elaborate on women's relationship to it, since the Gothic mode is foundationally indebted to women. To ignore femininities, then, doubly ignores the significance of women to Gothic camp.

In *Guilty Pleasures* (1996), Pamela Robertson stages a feminist intervention on camp, arguing that 'camp has an affinity with feminist discussions of gender construction, performance, and enactment; we can thereby examine forms of camp as feminist practice'.[38] These affinities are located in camp's own affinity with the mutability of (corporeal) surfaces, and tendency towards rendering playful the materials that forcibly inscribe restrictive gendering practises. Through her explorations of Mae West, Ginger Rogers, Joan Crawford and Madonna, Robertson traces how these stars and their female audiences camp up femininity to elicit a form of pleasure that resists a patriarchal curtailing of femininities. Camp rehabilitates images of femininity made repugnant, allowing feminine subjects an opportunity and medium for engaging in a politics of resistance that celebrates femininities. For Robertson, feminist camp often works with imagery pertaining to sex work, arguing that 'the figure of the gold digger is central to camp [and] prostitution is the hidden threat behind feminist camp'.[39] More broadly, a feminine sexuality that is usable as a tool for some level of female emancipation is a staple of feminist camp politics. Like Ross, Robertson also regards feminist camp as a practice of using historical waste.[40] Therefore, a Gothic feminist camp recycles Gothic images of female sexuality and also Gothicises recycled images of female sexuality – Gothic and camp are relational, and their interactions have multidirectional effects.

Elvira, Mistress of the Dark routinely plays with female sexuality and sex work through its eponymous character. Labelled 'a slimy, slithering succubus! A concubine, a streetwalker, a tramp, a slut, a cheap whore!' by the film's secondary antagonist Chastity Pariah (Edie McClurg), Elvira (Cassandra Peterson) is an iconic, and Gothic, embodiment of female sexuality and sex work.[41] Indeed, all an audience might be able to say in her defence is that Elvira is not *not* a sex worker. A joke in the film relies on Elvira misinterpreting the advances of a male character as being for sex work: he drives up alongside her, asking if she would 'care for a ride', to which Elvira responds, 'Buzz off creep, I'm not in the mood.' It turns out that it is her uncle who drove up alongside her. While the exchange is comic for its misunderstanding, Elvira's outburst also indicates that she has a modicum of power as a sex worker, in that she can reject men's approaches and refuse her services. Elvira similarly uses her sexuality to get the neighbourhood children (both masculine- and feminine-presenting) to help repaint her newly acquired dilapidated Gothic manor. She does this by being fun and flirty, by shaking her rear while asking local boys to 'grab a tool and start banging', and by generally providing a frothy atmosphere to the otherwise drab town. To reflect this, the house is repainted in 'fabulous' neon colours – a camp sore thumb amid the surrounding suburban conservatism. In all, Elvira's feminist camp leads men and women to want (to be) her, while also providing Elvira with an agency rooted in a pleasurable and powerful relationship with her feminine sexuality.

As images of female sex work are the principal material that feminist camp recycles, it stands to reason that feminist camp is an embodied practice. Sex work, after all, requires bodies. Obviously, Elvira displays her body throughout the film – her signature costume's plunging neckline and high leg slit ensure this. Likewise, her costuming, hair and make-up all clash with the film's wholesome suburban setting, so that Elvira always stands out. She knows this, saying that 'my appearance is kind of a shock to everybody'. Elvira is looked at, and is aware of this, lining her up with Sontag's notion that 'to perceive Camp in objects and persons is to understand Being-as-Playing-a-Role'.[42] Camp is self-conscious performativity, always in on its own joke, which is where power emerges. Having a palpable sense of self-performance enables the subject to make a mockery of systems of oppression through camp inflection. Elvira knows she is looked at, plays the role of object, thereby negotiating with practices of objectification, since she retains some agency where objectifying practices would efface this.

Feminist camp draws attention to the 'awarishness' [sic] of camp, where 'sexuality is taken at once as a pose or joke and as a real source of power'.[43] The power of posing sexuality is that it alters the composition of objectifying practices, which rely on a unidirectional exertion of power from one actant on to another. In a camp gesture of self-fashioned objectification, power becomes multidirectional. This is most apparent in *Elvira, Mistress of the Dark* through how Elvira's most powerful objects are her breasts and heels. Towards the end of the film, when Elvira is attempting to evade and defeat the film's primary antagonist (Vincent Talbot/William Morgan Sheppard), it is not a rocket launcher that harms the demonic warlock, but Elvira's high heels. The war weapon does nothing, nor does Elvira's *Rambo*-inspired costume at this point enhance her actions or power – masculine power simply will not harm this creature. Yet shortly after this, Elvira trips and then throws one of her high heels at Talbot. The heel pierces his flesh, becoming lodged in his head, giving Elvira vital time to escape. Despite heels' legibility as a phallic object, the fact that more overtly masculine objects such as the wartime images mentioned have no effect on Talbot suggests that it is not the masculinity or phallicisation of the heel that is powerful here. Rather, we ought to consider how heels 'have a masculine lineage, latent in their use by emancipated women eager to rise to men's level', as Camille Paglia writes, and how that power has drifted and become more symbolic of feminine power.[44] High heels, Summer Brennan argues, 'ma[k]e me feel powerful in a womanly way [...] It's a shoe for when we're *on*.'[45] Heels, for Brennan, are a shoe intimately tied to feminine power. Although this power is highly ambivalent, since high heels impact movement and can engage in a politics of disenfranchisement, camp tips the scales towards these empowering affects. For Elvira, in this moment, the shoe's spike heel functions as a weapon that buys her vital time: femininity, and the ephemera of female objectification, are camply tilted towards the empowering end.[46]

Much like her shoes, Elvira's breasts are literally powerful. In the same sequence where her shoe pierces Talbot, Elvira encounters a locked gate. She cannot squeeze through the gap because her breasts are too large. Instead, Elvira expands her chest, causing the lock to break and the gates to open. Gothic heroines famously have a fraught relationship with their clothes, particularly the garments covering their breasts, as Catherine Spooner argues in *Fashioning Gothic Bodies* (2004). In eighteenth-century Gothic works, Spooner identifies decolletage as a site where 'modesty [...] is not only interpretable as sexual invitation but is presented as alarmingly coextensive with sexual invitation'.[47] The revealing of the decolletage functions as an ambivalent symbol of innocence and seduction in older Gothic fiction, an ambivalence that Elvira recycles in her own costume. In recycling this image, Elvira's feminist camp 'still carries traces of the original but is reconfigured, remade for a new purpose'.[48] Titillation and ambivalent sexual politics are retained, though shifted with the historical moment. What is transformed and reconfigured is a greater sense of agency and a focus on the emancipation and freeing up of femininity and female sexuality. Elvira's breasts camply engage with feminist politics by literally breaking the shackles that might allow a man to capture her.

While Robertson's formulation of feminist camp is rooted in how images of female sex work are deployed by camp women, we can easily widen this notion to other aspects of female sexuality. Robertson even acknowledges that the feminist work camp does is firmly located in cultural recycling, arguing that it can 'be utilized in the present to alter the way we perceive sex and gender stereotypes in the future'.[49] Gothic often explores the threat of female sexuality – visible in texts from Matthew Gregory Lewis's *The Monk* (1796), through to the myriad *femmes fatales* of the nineteenth-century *fin de siècle*, and into the present day – though the specific threat is historically contingent. For example, *fin-de-siècle femmes fatales* were intimately linked to the emergence of the New Woman.

Jennifer's Body engages in such a Gothic camp recycling of the threatening nature of feminine sexuality.[50] In this film, the titular Jennifer (Megan Fox) is ritually sacrificed to Satan by an indie band (Low Shoulder) seeking fame. The film riffs on notions of virgin sacrifice, with Satan requiring a virgin as payment in this ritual. The ritual is a success, in that Low Shoulder do become famous, but Jennifer was 'not even a backdoor virgin' when she was sacrificed, and she transforms into a succubus. Jennifer must kill and devour people regularly to sustain herself, and once she has fed she becomes invulnerable and more beautiful. Despite her monstrousness, Jennifer's villainy is presented ambiguously. It must be remembered that these actions are consequences of Low Shoulder's own actions. Indeed, the film parallels Jennifer's capture with sexual assault, and Low Shoulder's fame is built on exploiting the devastation that occurs in Devil's Kettle, the town in which the film is set. Jennifer is at once a victim and a monster, whereas Low Shoulder are exclusively diabolical. Feminist camp here suggests a polyvalent approach to personhood, where a subject such as Jennifer can at once embody apparent opposites, rather than solely present a sexual threat.

Another way in which *Jennifer's Body* engages in feminist camp is in its portrayal of feminine sexual pleasure. As mentioned regarding *Elvira, Mistress of the Dark*, feminist camp is an especially embodied form of camp. Where Elvira deploys a Gothic camp version of sex work to access the embodied nature of feminist camp, *Jennifer's Body* plays on feminine sexual pleasure among horny teens. Undeniably, *Jennifer's Body* is a horny film. Its teenage characters are interested in sex, have sex, can be, and are, tempted by the mere suggestion of sex with Jennifer. This is without mentioning the film's candid portrayal of same-sex eroticism, and Jennifer's campy 'I go both ways' line when she attempts to feed on protagonist Anita ('Needy'/Amanda Seyfried). There is a moment in the film when Needy and her boyfriend are about to have sex. He gets a condom, and she sees that it is ribbed, to which he responds that 'It's supposed to make it feel good for the girl.' This short line explicitly draws attention to how *Jennifer's Body* is often concerned with depicting female sexual pleasure in a fashion uncoupled from a male gaze that pervades Gothic and cinematic displays of female eroticism. It is important here to note that Jennifer and Needy are seemingly psychically linked in the film, with Needy having visions of Jennifer's actions. What this means is that their respective displays of sexual pleasure are linked.

Arguably, Jennifer's feeding on men is monstrous because it is an act of consumption where pleasure is firmly and exclusively for Jennifer. Succubi, according to Mary Ayers, 'drain the life-force from weak-willed men', acting as 'the epitome of depraved sexuality'.[51] Life-draining occurs at the moment of penetration, crafting an image of simultaneous terror and eroticism. The succubus feeding by way of vaginal penetration, while terrifying, is still an erotic image where feminine sexual hunger can only be satisfied by a masculine sexual partner. *Jennifer's Body* recycles and transforms these popular, folk and psychoanalytic images of the succubus, since Jennifer's consumption happens before any moment of penetration. Jennifer is already devouring her partner before penetration can even begin, meaning that her pleasure in feeding loses the titillating component for a cisheterosexual masculine gaze that other succubi have. This feminist camp recycling of the sexuality of *femmes fatales* maintains the eroticism of the woman, while removing misogynistic titillation at witnessing such a display. Jennifer's consumption is monstrous not solely for its grotesquery, but because pleasure is solely hers. She is the threat of female sexual pleasure as envisioned by an insecure patriarchy, and her psychic connection to Needy contrasts this with a mundane and tender exchange between a horny teen couple who are working to create a mutually pleasurable sexual experience. In casting a feminist camp eye on the *femme fatale* like this, *Jennifer's Body* lays bare the misogyny of these viewing practices. Simultaneously, the possibility for feminine eroticism and pleasure on its own terms opens up.

Conclusion

If 'camp rehabilitates', as Bruin-Molé argues, then Gothic as an originator of camp has always been a rehabilitative mode, and, as the contemporary Gothic texts sampled throughout this chapter demonstrate, that rehabilitation is highly dynamic. Contemporary Gothic camp is able to provide complexity and adoration for older women characters, and acts as part of a toolkit for Black, feminist and trans politics. It can even stage interventions into images of heterosexuality. Such a perspective may provide a necessary tonic to current Queer Gothic thinking, which prioritises studying the Gothic's capacity for exploring and resisting queer oppression. For example, Laura Westengard's *Gothic Queer Culture* (2019) argues that 'gothic queer culture resists liberal narratives of wholeness and progress, envisions ways of being that push against assimilationism and limiting conceptual binaries, and gives voice to innumerable experiences of queer insidious trauma'.[52] While such work can illuminate how queer experience can be imagined in contemporary Gothic, it inevitably suggests that queer Gothic imaginations are always already trauma-bound, leaving no capacity for a hopeful or celebratory queer politics, despite such celebrations being a queer political bedrock. Indeed, when the camp aspects of contemporary Gothic are examined, what emerges is a similar political concern with systemic injustice from a more hopeful perspective. In drawing attention to the campy elements of some contemporary Gothic works, a thread of celebratory subversive politics becomes apparent.

Notes

1. J. Sheridan LeFanu, 'Carmilla', in *In a Glass Darkly* [1872] (Bath: Cedric Chivers, 1971), p. 231. The title of this chapter quotes Alan Brien, cited in Andrew Bolton, Karen van Godtsenhoven and Amanda Garfinkel, *Camp: Notes on Fashion*, vol. II (New Haven, CT: Yale University Press, 2019), p. 11.
2. Susan Sontag, 'Notes on "Camp"', in *Camp: Queer Aesthetics and the Performing Subject: A Reader*, ed. Fabio Cleto (Edinburgh: Edinburgh University Press, 1999), pp. 56–7.
3. Jack Babuscio, 'The Cinema of Camp (aka Camp and the Gay Sensibility)', in *Camp: Queer Aesthetics and the Performing Subject: A Reader*, ed. Fabio Cleto (Edinburgh: Edinburgh University Press, 1999), p. 121.
4. See Avril Horner and Sue Zlosnik, *Gothic and the Comic Turn* (Basingstoke: Palgrave Macmillan, 2005); David Punter, *The Literature of Terror: A History of Gothic Fiction from 1765 to the Present Day, Vol. 1: The Gothic Tradition*, 2nd edn. (London: Longman, 1996); *Queering the Gothic*, ed. William Hughes and Andrew Smith (Manchester: Manchester University Press, 2009).
5. See Harry M. Benshoff, *Monsters in the Closet: Homosexuality and the Horror Film* (Manchester: Manchester University Press, 1997), pp. 187–217; Catherine Spooner, *Fashioning Gothic Bodies* (Manchester: Manchester University Press, 2004), pp. 8–9; Catherine Spooner, *Post-Millennial Gothic: Comedy, Romance and the Rise of Happy Gothic* (London: Bloomsbury, 2017), pp. 108–12, 132–8.

6. Megen de Bruin-Molé, *Gothic Remixed: Monster Mashups and Frankenfictions in 21st-Century Culture* (London: Bloomsbury, 2020), p. 99.
7. Avril Horner and Sue Zlosnik, 'No Country for Old Women: Gender, Age and the Gothic', in *Women and the Gothic: An Edinburgh Companion*, ed. Avril Horner and Sue Zlosnik (Edinburgh: Edinburgh University Press, 2016), p. 190.
8. Ibid., p. 185.
9. Ibid., p. 192. The Gothic has a strong thread of fabulous older women whose characterisations betray queer affinities beyond the time period this chapter focuses on. Elizabeth Gaskell's 'The Grey Woman' (1861) relies heavily on cross-dressing, for example. Likewise, LeFanu's 'Carmilla' (1872) describes Carmilla's mother's actions as camp. See Elizabeth Gaskell, 'The Grey Woman' [1861], *Project Gutenberg*, 29 April 2007, https://www.gutenberg.org/files/28636/28636-h/28636-h.htm (accessed 26 January 2022).
10. *Whatever Happened to Baby Jane?*, dir. Robert Aldrich (Warner Bros., 1962).
11. Caryl Flinn, 'The Deaths of Camp', in *Camp: Queer Aesthetics and the Performing Subject: A Reader*, ed. Fabio Cleto (Edinburgh: Edinburgh University Press, 1999), p. 436.
12. Ibid., p. 453.
13. Harriet Fletcher, '"Gothic" TV: High-quality Modern Horror Series Providing Powerful Roles for Hollywood's Older Women', *The Conversation*, 27 October 2020, https://theconversation.com/gothic-tv-high-quality-modern-horror-series-providing-powerful-roles-for-hollywoods-older-women-148870 (accessed 10 February 2021).
14. Jeff Guo, 'Why the Age of 40 is so Important in Hollywood', *Washington Post*, 19 September 2016, https://www.washingtonpost.com/news/wonk/wp/2016/09/19/these-charts-reveal-how-bad-the-film-industrys-sexism-is/ (accessed 10 February 2021).
15. George Haggerty, *Queer Gothic* (Urbana, IL: University of Illinois Press, 2006), p. 202.
16. WOWPresents, 'UNHhhh Ep. 131: Straight People', YouTube, 14 October 2020, 1:56–1:58, https://youtu.be/rXSKCE4-BEI?list=PLhgFEi9aNUb2BNrIEecCGXApgeX7Yjwz8 (accessed 15 February 2021).
17. See Jamie Jones, 'PSA: Morticia and Gomez Addams are Literally the Perfect Couple', *Buzzfeed*, 27 April 2018, https://www.buzzfeed.com/jamiejones/morticia-and-gomez-addams-are-the-perfect-couple (accessed 4 March 2021); Afiya Augustine, 'Five Reasons Gomez and Morticia Addams are Relationship Goals', *Syfy Wire*, 11 November 2020, https://www.syfy.com/syfywire/five-reasons-gomez-and-morticia-addams-are-relationship-goals (accessed 4 March 2021).
18. Agnes Andeweg and Sue Zlosnik, 'Introduction', in *Gothic Kinship* (Manchester: Manchester University Press, 2013), p. 1.
19. Ibid., p. 2.
20. Laura Morowitz, 'The Monster Within: *The Munsters*, *The Addams Family* and the American Family in the 1960s', *Critical Studies in Television: The International Journal of Television Studies*, 3.1 (2007), pp. 35–56 (p. 36).
21. Ibid., p. 36.
22. Ibid., p. 38.

23. Elizabeth Freeman, *Time Binds: Queer Temporalities, Queer Histories* (Durham, NC: Duke University Press, 2010), p. 3.
24. Ibid., p. 3.
25. Ibid., p. 8.
26. Andrew Ross, 'Uses of Camp', in *Camp: Queer Aesthetics and the Performing Subject: A Reader*, ed. Fabio Cleto (Edinburgh: Edinburgh University Press, 1999), pp. 320, 312.
27. Ibid., p. 316.
28. Robert Miles, *Gothic Writing, 1750–1820*, 2nd edn. (Manchester: Manchester University Press, 2007), p. 29.
29. *The Addams Family Values*, dir. Barry Sonnenfeld (Paramount, 1993). It is worth noting here that 'family values' is a common conservative dog whistle used to stir up anti-LGBT+ sentiment. At the time of *The Addams Family Values*' release, the 1992 American Republican presidential campaign was using 'family values' as a central rhetorical theme. 'Family values' rhetoric guided much anti-LGBT+ legislation at this point in America; for example, proposition 9 in Oregon (1992) and amendment 2 in Colorado (1992). See Dana L. Cloud, 'The Rhetoric of "Family Values": Scapegoating, Utopia, and the Privatization of Social Responsibility', *Western Journal of Communication*, 62.4 (1998), pp. 387–419, https://doi.org/10.1080/10570319809374617; Timothy Egan, 'Oregon Measure Asks State to Repress Homosexuality', *New York Times*, 16 August 1992, https://www.nytimes.com/1992/08/16/us/oregon-measure-asks-state-to-repress-homosexuality.html (accessed 26 January 2022); 'Amendment 2', *Colorado Springs Pioneer Museum*, https://www.cspm.org/cos-150-story/amendment-2/ (accessed 26 January 2022).
30. Erica Gonzales, 'Lena Waithe's Met Gala Suit Says "Black Drag Queens Invented Camp"', *Harper's Bazaar*, 7 May 2019, https://www.harpersbazaar.com/celebrity/red-carpet-dresses/a27382445/lena-waithe-met-gala-2019/ (accessed 10 February 2021).
31. *Blacula*, dir. William Crain (American International Pictures, 1972).
32. Robin R. Means Coleman, *Horror Noire: Blacks in American Horror Films from the 1890s to Present* (Abingdon: Routledge, 2011), p. 120.
33. Sequoia Barnes, '"If You Don't Bring No Grits, Don't Come": Critiquing a Critique of Patrick Kelly, Golliwogs, and Camp as a Technique of Black Queer Expression', *Open Cultural Studies*, 1 (2017), pp. 678–89 (p. 685), https://doi.org/10.1515/culture-2017-0062.
34. Coleman, *Horror Noire*, pp. 120–1.
35. 'Butterfly/Cocoon', *Pose*, FX, 25 June 2019.
36. It is also worth noting that the plot of 'Butterfly/Cocoon' is based on the discovery of a mummified corpse in the closet of New York City ballroom legend Dorian Corey. See Edward Conlin, 'The Drag Queen and the Mummy', *Transition*, 65 (1995), pp. 4–24, https:///www.jstor.org/stable/2935316 (accessed 11 February 2021).
37. Fabio Cleto, 'Introduction: Queering the Camp', in *Camp: Queer Aesthetics and the Performing Subject: A Reader*, ed. Fabio Cleto (Edinburgh: Edinburgh University Press, 1999), p. 10.
38. Pamela Robertson, *Guilty Pleasures: Feminist Camp from Mae West to Madonna* (London: I.B. Tauris, 1996) p. 6.

39. Ibid., p. 84.
40. Ibid., p. 142.
41. *Elvira, Mistress of the Dark*, dir. James Signorelli (New World Pictures, 1988).
42. Sontag, 'Notes on Camp', p. 56.
43. Robertson, *Guilty Pleasures*, p. 48.
44. Camille Paglia, 'The Stiletto Heel', *Design and Violence*, 25 October 2019, https://www.moma.org/interactives/exhibitions/2013/designandviolence/the-stiletto-heel/ (accessed 23 March 2021).
45. Summer Brennan, *High Heel* (London: Bloomsbury, 2019), pp. 14–16.
46. Women's apparel is likewise commonly present at sites of queer resistance, to the point that high heels become somewhat mythical weapons thrown at police and anti-LGBT+ oppressors. See Makhesha Hogg, 'Stonewall: 50 Years of Throwing Shoes!', *The Gayly*, 25 June 2019, https://www.gayly.com/stonewall-50-years-throwing-shoes (accessed 29 July 2021); *Screaming Queens: The Riot at Compton's Cafeteria*, dir. Susan Stryker and Victor Silverman (Frameline, 2005).
47. Spooner, *Fashioning Gothic Bodies*, p. 31.
48. Robertson, *Guilty Pleasures*, p. 142.
49. Ibid., p. 143.
50. *Jennifer's Body*, dir. Karyn Kusama (20th Century–Fox, 2009).
51. Mary A. Ayers, *Masculine Shame: From Succubus to the Eternal Feminine* (Abingdon: Routledge, 2011), p. 4.
52. Laura Westengard, *Gothic Queer Culture: Marginalized Communities and the Ghosts of Insidious Trauma* (Lincoln, NE: University of Nebraska Press, 2019), p. 20.

Part II

Queer Monsters

Chapter 6

Queer Vampires: What We Want is in the Shadows
S. Brooke Cameron

From its first appearance in Romantic-era Gothic fiction, the modern vampire has been inextricably tied to queer sexualities. The catalyst for this tradition, John William Polidori's *The Vampyre* (1819), gave us Lord Ruthven (later Lord Strongmore), a human-like vampire whose charm seduced men and women alike. Readers ever since have been fascinated, and the queer vampire thus became a staple of Gothic horror. In its approximation of the living, this modern vampire typically serves as a shadow or mirror reflection of our deepest desires, as well as our fears. 'We look into the mirror it provides and we see a version of ourselves', writes Veronica Hollinger. 'Or, more accurately, keeping in mind the orthodoxy that vampires cast no mirror reflections, we look into the mirror and see nothing *but* ourselves.'[1]

Queer sexuality is at the very heart of those desires reflected back to us through the vampire – and in this regard, I use the term queer to refer to everything from gay and lesbian, as well as bisexual and transgender (LGBTQ+). Indeed, the vampire functions in much the same way as does the concept of queer itself in heteronormative culture: as Judith Butler explains in *Bodies that Matter*, 'much of the straight world has always needed the queers it has sought to repudiate through the performative force of the term'.[2] Queer thus connotes 'Other-ness', or an identity category against which heterosexuality must define itself by naming what it is not or what is tabooed. Just as queer serves as the Other against which straight sexuality is defined (often forcefully, per the often derogatory use of the former term), so too is the vampire a kind of shadow figure for tabooed desires. But it has not always been this way for the queer vampire – it was not always the repudiated Other. Polidori's creature entered the world as a shadow figure, a complement and even companion. It was only after the legal definition of homosexuality as criminal that the vampire was transformed into a figure of queer monstrosity. Certainly, there was throughout the nineteenth century increasing worry over the degree to which the law should prosecute homosexuality, which was illegal in Britain in one way or another from 1533 onwards. However, as scholars such as H. G. Cocks and Angus McLaren note,[3] the rise of sexual blackmail and, in particular, anxieties around cross-class homosexuality in Victorian Britain, led to the 1885 Labouchère Amendment and a subsequent series of highly publicised arrests, including that of the legendary aesthete Oscar Wilde in 1895 – such that queer desire became officially, or openly and in public discourse, defined as criminal and thus 'Other'. This chapter will trace the evolution of the modern vampire figure, from its origins as companion in the early nineteenth century, to the demonisation of homosexuality at the *fin de siècle*, and the queer vampire's gradual social acceptance throughout the twentieth and twenty-first centuries.

Part 1: The Queer Vampire in Nineteenth-Century Literature

Most scholars agree that Polidori invented the modern vampire.[4] What few may realise is that *The Vampyre* also gave us a distinctly queer figure defined by an intense devotion to male–male bonds. Vampires of preceding folklore were grotesque, reanimated corpses who fed upon local friends and family. After Polidori, however, the modern vampire is 1) noted for a human-like appearance, though dead; 2) aristocratic or wealthy; 3) a mobile traveller; and 4) compelling, if not seductive.[5] These new characteristics have much to do with the vampire's homosocial origins, specifically Polidori's relationship with Lord Byron. Polidori was Byron's personal physician and attended the poet during his 1816 summer trip to Italy to visit the Shelleys. This was the famous visit when, one stormy night, the poets devised a horror story competition that resulted in the composition of Mary Shelley's famous Gothic tale *Frankenstein*. Byron and Polidori also participated in the contest, each drafting a similar tale of vampires who bind themselves to another male traveller – in fact, Polidori's tale reads very much like the completion of Byron's fragment. Polidori writes his vampire, Lord Ruthven, as a thinly veiled satire of his employer, right down to the man's aristocratic status and licentious behaviour; at the same time, Polidori's fixation on Byron – at a point when the latter was growing weary of, and often ridiculing, the aspiring writer – reminds one of the conflicted bond between Aubrey and Lord Ruthven.

The Vampyre uses this homosocial bond to paint a picture of the undead Other as a friend, not a fiend. The sworn oath shared between male companions is central to both Byron's and Polidori's tales and serves as a powerful symbol of shared male desire. In extending Byron's earlier attempt, Polidori retains this idea of a vampire who travels with a human; during their shared adventure, this vampire then uses the oath of loyalty to bind himself to the human, and even overcome social hierarchies. The same impulse that led Polidori to fixate on his employer and, subsequently, to complete the latter's story thus makes its way into *The Vampyre* by casting the relationship between revenant and companion as one of homosocial loyalty. Intimate and binding, this oath would certainly unnerve those readers anxious about a human's chosen connection with the Other. Or as Nina Auerbach explains, 'The oath is frightening because it involves not raw power, but honour and reciprocity [. . .] the oath signifies instead a bond between companions that is shared and chosen, one far from the Dracula-like mesmeric coercion we associate with vampires today.'[6] Even the seemingly heterosexual turn towards the end of the story, when Lord Ruthven marries Aubrey's sister, is still about male–male bonds, for the marriage is an opportunity for the vampire to remain close to his one-time travelling companion after their return to society. The marriage is, as Auerbach notes, a kind of prescribed homosocial 'conduit' between the vampire and his male human.[7] As Eve Sedgwick's theory of homosocial desire explains, 'in any erotic rivalry, the bond that links the two rivals is as intense and potent as the bond that links either of the rivals to the beloved'.[8] In the case of Ruthven, the underlying supremacy of this male–male bond is laid bare when the vampire murders his bride on their wedding night in order to exact revenge upon Aubrey. Indeed, the wife in this scenario quite literally, through her drained blood, mediates Ruthven's communion with his true love, Aubrey.

The vampire was not limited to same-sex bonds between men in nineteenth-century literature. Sheridan Le Fanu's *Carmilla* (1872) is perhaps the best-known example of female–female vampirism in this period. This stunning novella contains powerful scenes combining the idea of vampiric feeding, or mixing blood, and the physical act of intercourse. The main events of the story recount the increasingly passionate friendship that develops between a young girl named Laura and her mysterious guest, the eponymous Carmilla. Not long into the visit, Laura starts to have strange dreams that – to the reader – signal Carmilla's nightly feedings in highly erotic terms:

> Sometimes there came a sensation as if a hand was drawn softly along my cheek and neck. Sometimes it was as if warm lips kissed me, and longer and longer and more lovingly as they reached my throat, but there the caress fixed itself. My heart beat faster, my breathing rose and fell rapidly and full drawn; a sobbing, that rose into a sense of strangulation, supervened, and turned into a dreadful convulsion, in which my senses left me and I became unconscious.[9]

Laura's 'rapid' breathing conveys a degree of sexual excitement or stimulation, suggesting that these 'kisses' are not altogether unwanted. Indeed, Laura and her friend share many intimate exchanges while conscious, too (by which I mean when Laura is conscious – for as we discover later, Carmilla was real and conscious all along), with the younger struggling to understand such passion within conventional heteronormative constraints (Laura wonders if she is being seduced by a 'boyish lover [. . .] in masquerade').[10] Still, Laura's complaint is not that Carmilla inverts gender roles but that she remains shrouded in mystery, withholding a portion of herself. When pressed about her past, including prior relationships, all that Carmilla will admit to is 'a strange love, that would have taken [her] life', and she then shushes her lover with a 'kind of shy smile that [Laura] could not decipher'.[11]

Carmilla's refusal to give her 'strange' love a name is not an act of homophobic repression, for such censorship would be anachronistic. Female–female bonds were not viewed by Victorians as a rejection of the heterosexual plot; rather, such intimacies between women were widely accepted in a range of forms, from bosom buddies to romantic love.[12] Instead, we must understand Carmilla's withholding as part of the ongoing story of seduction, drawing Laura into the mystery of the vampire and the sexual intimacy promised by their intense sharing of bodies, blood and feeling. This idea of shared life is Carmilla's promise from the outset: 'I live in your warm life', she tells Laura, 'and you shall die – die, sweetly die – into mine.'[13] Whereas the Byronic vampire of Polidori was a travelling companion, Carmilla's vampire is domestic; she lives in the home with Laura and even replaces the young girl's deceased mother as a source of love. This is a female vampire, as Auerbach explains, who has '[woven] herself so tightly into Laura's perception that without a cumbersome parade of male authorities to stop her narrative, her story would never end'.[14] Even after the vampire is gone, tracked and exterminated by the men, Laura cannot help but feel a persistent desire for the lost lover. '[T]o this hour the image of Carmilla returns to memory', writes Laura, adding that 'often from a reverie I have started, fancying I heard the light step of Carmilla at the drawing room door'.[15] This conclusion is powerful, not least because it leaves the door open to so many interpretations – from fear or concern ('starting') at the vampire's return, to a hint of hope or longing ('fancying') for it.

No discussion of nineteenth-century queer vampires would be complete without reference to Bram Stoker's *Dracula* (1897). The coded queer treatment includes the vampire brides' predation on Jonathan Harker. The scene is rife with references to gender inversion, detailing the brides' 'piercing eyes' and 'brilliant white teeth' against 'the ruby of their voluptuous lips'; these women are active seducers, while Jonathan plays the feminine role of passive recipient, full of 'wicked, burning desire' and 'wait[ing] with beating heart' to be taken.[16] Yet it is the Count's interruption that introduces same-sex desire into the narrative. As he brushes away the brides, he angrily proclaims, 'This man belongs to me!'[17] The Count has been feeding upon Jonathan off-page, and this one exclamation is the closest we come to any admission of male-on-male exchange of bodily fluids. Again, as in Polidori's novella, we have a version of the homosocial triangle wherein heteronormative sexual exchange (between Jonathan and the vampire brides) thus safely mediates (literally, through the transmission of blood) those tabooed desires between men.

That Stoker would code his references to queer desire makes sense when we remember the novel's cultural context. Before 1885 only the act of sodomy was deemed illegal. However, with his introduction of Section 11 of the Criminal Law Amendment Act, Liberal MP Henry Labouchère effectively redefined homosexuality from a forbidden act to a criminal identity. The new legislation was deliberately vague in its reference to acts of so-called 'gross indecency':

> Any male person who in public or private commits or is a party to the commission of or procures or attempts to procure the commission by any male person of any act of gross indecency with another male person shall be guilty of a misdemeanour and being convicted thereof shall be liable to be imprisoned for any term not exceeding two years with or without hard labour.[18]

As Richard Dellamora explains, the 1885 Act stoked social fears around, and culminated in the eventual censorship of, male–male desire 'by shifting emphasis from acts between men, especially sodomy, the traditional focus of legislation, to sexual sentiment or thought, and in this way to an abstract entity soon to be referred to as "homosexuality"'.[19] This 1885 Act was invoked in the infamous 1895 trial of Oscar Wilde, who was found guilty and sentenced to two years of hard labour at Reading Goal. Both the 1885 Act and the fate of Wilde thus spawned a new iteration of the queer vampire, one who is cloaked in metaphor and hidden or repressed from the policing eyes of a now explicitly homophobic Victorian culture.

It is important to note that late Victorian attempts to police same-sex desire differed according to gender. Consider the example of the psychic vampire Harriet Brandt in Florence Marryat's *The Blood of the Vampire*, published the same year as *Dracula*. Harriet is a 21-year-old woman from Jamaica; her father, Henry Brandt, was a white plantation owner and Swiss-educated 'scientist' and vivisectionist who was murdered in retaliation for his sadistic experiments on slaves, while Harriet's mother was of multiracial descent and lived in 'concubinage' with Henry, where she delighted 'to watch the dying agonies of the poor creatures her brutal protector slaughtered'.[20] No names are given for Harriet's mother or her enslaved Black grandmother – as if to drive home the point, through erasure, that Harriet is the product of a violent colonialism mapped on to individual bodies and bloodlines. However, as if in an attempt to displace this violence from aggressor to victim, Harriet's Black maternal bloodline is presented as the source of horror in this novel. Readers learn that her enslaved and pregnant grandmother was scared by a vampire bat, and that this moment of animal imprinting likely caused her mother's insatiable 'lust for blood'.[21]

Although Harriet enjoys financial privilege, thanks to her plantation-owning English father, she is nonetheless marked as Other by her African blood. And like her mother, Harriet feeds upon human suffering. Harriet's earliest vampiric attachments are to women. She forms a bond with her travelling companion, Olga Brimonte, who is near death by the time they arrive in Heyst; then, once in the vacation town, Harriet fixates on Englishwoman Margaret Pullen. The latter is aware of the girl's intense interest:

> She [Margaret] was struck by the look with which Harriet Brandt was regarding her – it was so full of yearning affection – almost of longing to approach her nearer, to hear her speak, to touch her hand! She had heard of such cases, in which young unsophisticated girls had taken unaccountable affections for members of their own sex.[22]

That Margaret is a married woman with a six-month-old baby reminds us of how female–female bonds did not threaten Victorian heterosexual plots. After all, the 1885 Labouchère Amendment only names 'male person[s]'.[23] It was not until 1920 that English law even attempted to rectify this omission by adding a new statute, the CLA Bill, that criminalised sexual acts between women and underage girls.[24] Much of the debate surrounding this proposal centred on the worry that to add such a clause would have the adverse effect of planting lesbian thoughts into otherwise innocent minds. The CLA Bill failed, and the old loophole remained.

Marryat could thus experiment with representations of queer intimacies between women, while Stoker had to censor any depictions of same-sex desire between Dracula and Jonathan because of Victorians' particular anxieties towards male homosexuality. In fact, the bigger source of fear in Marryat's novel seems to be not queer vampiric desire but, rather, potential miscegenation. This is not to say that women in this period could easily transcend heterosexual plots. Even Harriet eventually turns her affection to men – first Captain Ralph Pullen and then socialist/novelist Anthony Pennell, sapping their energy and killing the latter. In the end, however, the novel returns to female–female bonds when Harriet, after taking her own life, bequeaths her fortune to Margaret 'in return for the kindness she shewed [sic] to me when I went to Heyst, a stranger'.[25]

Part 2: Queer Female Vampires in Twentieth-Century Film

With the rise of film in the twentieth century, the vampire migrated to and rapidly reproduced itself in multiple, celluloid iterations. As the most iconic vampire, *Dracula* was the obvious choice for directors interested in adapting the revenant to early film – a list that includes F. W. Murnau's *Nosferatu* (1922) and Tod Browning's *Dracula* (1931).[26] Yet it is the latter's sequel, *Dracula's Daughter* (1936), that gives us the best queer interpretation of the famous narrative.[27] The Countess Marya Zaleska is our eponymous heroine and, like her father, a vampire. However, after Dracula's death, the Countess imagines how she might, like many modern women, be freed from men's authority. To do so, she must overcome her 'horrible impulses' to feed upon humans – of both genders. An early encounter with psychiatrist Jeffrey Garth hints at the idea of vampirism as a metaphor for lesbianism. The doctor urges the Countess to face her desires head-on so that she can overcome such temptations – advice that conjures up images of aversion therapy, which was a popular treatment for homosexuality at the time. The Countess decides to test herself by having a beautiful young girl, Lili, brought back to her studio that night. She asks Lili to model for a bust portrait she is painting, thus exposing the would-be model's neck and naked shoulders. The Countess cannot, it turns out, control herself when faced with such an enticing sight:

> **Lili:** Why are you looking at me that way? Will I do?
> **Countess Marya Zaleska:** Yes, you'll do very well indeed. Do you like jewels, Lily? It's very old and very beautiful, I'll show it to you.
> **Lili:** I think I'll pass tonight. I think I'll go if you don't mind . . . Please don't come any closer! [*She screams*]

The undeniable look of desire mixed with malice in the Countess's eyes, combined with the play of light and shadow across the girl's naked body, presents the moment of vampiric predation as a highly sexualised act. The homophobic gaze of the camera thus links female–female desire with the impulse of murderous lust in a way that firmly brands this queer vampire as dangerously Other.

At the time of its release in 1936, *Dracula's Daughter* would have been subject to the new Motion Picture Production Code – the so-called Hays Code – which essentially banned any homosexual content in movies produced by Hollywood studios. Published in 1930 and enacted in 1934, the first general principles of the Code stipulate that 'No picture shall be produced which will lower the moral standards of those who see it. Hence the sympathy of the audience shall never be thrown to the side of crime, wrong-doing, evil or sin.'[28] Under the specific subheading of 'Sex', the Code goes on to state that '*Sex perversion* or any inference to it is forbidden.'[29] The Code, with its outline of moral standards, was used to justify the censorship of any homosexual content in film. Hence, it is astonishing that *Dracula's Daughter*, with its heroine who seduces women to drain them of their blood, was even made in the first place. Even more shocking is the fact that the film invites viewers to sympathise with the vampire who struggles and fails to overcome her 'horrible impulses'. Certainly, the Countess's failed attempt to follow the doctor's repressive recommendations would seem to critique psychologists' typical treatment for homosexuality. In fact, those moments in this film where the vampire presents the biggest threat to power are less those in which she expresses lesbian desire than those in which she attempts to simulate heteronormative plots. Viewers will recall that, during the same aforementioned meeting, the Countess forms an attraction for Dr Garth, and so when her attempts at self-cure fail, the Countess gives into her vampiric impulses and hatches a plan to lure the doctor to her home in Transylvania (by kidnapping their mutual love-interest, Janet Blake), where she will make him her eternal companion. This seemingly heterosexual plot twist is, then, ultimately queer both in its gender-role reversal (with the woman as seducer) and its sexually fluid or polyamorous love triangle. But perhaps the final sequence, in which Dr Garth saves Janet from the Countess, quelled any possible anxieties over this queer vampire. The doctor wins this battle for sexual authority, and the threat of the female vampire who would undermine the heterosexual plot is extinguished with her death. Indeed, Countess Zaleska's fate effectively signals the death of all lesbian vampires in Hollywood films under the Hays Code. Except for Hitchcock's 1940 film *Rebecca*,[30] with its spectre of lesbian vampirism (Mrs Danvers), we do not see another example of queer women vampires again until Tony Scott's 1983 film *The Hunger*.[31] Of course, this later film appeared well after the Hays Code was finally abandoned by Hollywood in 1968 – after the rise of queer rights' movements in the 1960s and 1970s (on the heels of the

Stonewall Riots, 28 June 1969) signalled a shift in American cultural attitudes and a demand for more queer-positive films.

British and European cinema (which was not subject to the American Hays Code) was already, by the mid-twentieth century, hungry for queer content in film. Hence, the lesbian vampire was resurrected in the 1960s and 1970s with an explosion of *Carmilla*-type vampire films. The 1960 French film *Et mourir de Plaisir* (*Blood and Roses*) is perhaps responsible for starting this trend.[32] It stars Annette Vadim as a young and beautiful Carmilla de Karnstien who is transformed into the legendary vampire after the family's ancient tomb is disturbed. Her deadly desire is safely mediated by a heterosexual love triangle; at first glance, she seems to be infatuated with her cousin, Leopoldo, and thus jealous of his fiancée, Georgia. There is a climactic moment in the film when Carmilla confronts her vampiric identity in a mirror, ripping open her top to expose a bloodied breast (foreshadowing her death by staking), but she is interrupted by her cousin and the two wind up in bed. However, Carmilla turns away from his kisses, for as her vampiric appetite grows so does her preference for female lovers. Later scenes show her gazing longingly at Georgia and, even, passionately kissing her (after they are trapped in a greenhouse by a surprise downpour).

A decade later, other international *Carmilla*-inspired films such as *The Vampire Lovers* (1970, British) and *Vampyros Lesbos* (1971, a West Germany–Spain collaboration) are even more sexually explicit in their representations of female–female desire.[33] Both films abound with exposed breasts and heavy petting between women. The fixation on the breast in these films reads like pornographic fantasies written for the pre-Oedipal male gaze.[34] There is the silly scene in *Vampire Lovers* when Carmilla and Emma (the Laura-character) play-fight over dresses and wind up half-naked and kissing on the bed. Throughout the movie, Carmilla's predation is overseen by some mysterious man on horseback who would seem to be the embodiment of the male viewer. And in *Vampyros Lesbos* there are even more examples of the male gaze leering at women's sexualised interactions. The film opens with a performance of lesbian seduction staged by the Countess, Nadine Carody. In the act, the Countess slowly disrobes while simulating sex with a naked, doll-like woman; the doll-woman is shown to be briefly responsive, though the Countess ultimately dominates – forcing the doll-woman to the ground and biting suggestively at her neck. The mix of pornography and violence helped to establish Spanish director Jess Franco as pioneer of the S&M horror genre. Throughout this and later scenes, the camera cuts back to the Countess in various stages of undress, with her red scarf blowing in the foreground of the shot, a symbolic thread which reappears with and connects her victims. The Laura-character, Linda, is enthralled, but her boyfriend Omar is, throughout the film, extremely possessive. Mixing together elements of *Dracula* and *Carmilla*, the film follows the Countess (Dracula's vampire daughter) as she attempts to lure Linda away.[35] Arriving late to the climax, Omar tries to tell Linda that it was all a dream, but she remains unconvinced: 'No. It wasn't a dream [. . .] The pain will fade in time. But the memory will remain. For as long as I live.'[36] There might be a hint of the original *Carmilla* in this idea of the female lover's persistent longing, but the return to the heterosexual male (gaze) deviates significantly from the original vampire's promise of a shared life between women.

Part 3: Queer Vampires in Contemporary Culture

Back in the United States, Anne Rice's *Interview with the Vampire*, both film and novel, finally presented American audiences with the queer vampire's perspective. Published in 1976, Rice's novel came on the heels of growing civil rights and gay rights movements, but predated the conservative cultural climate and HIV/AIDS pandemic of the 1980s–1990s. Hence, the decision to open with a conversation between the vampire, Louis, and the 'boy'-interviewer from the 'bar' would have looked to many readers in the 1970s as a positive – or rather, non-judgmental – reference to queer cruising culture.[37] Better yet, Louis's quick insistence that 'I won't hurt you' and 'I want this opportunity' to tell his story signals a new era in which the vampire plays the protagonist in control of the narrative and explicitly demanding our sympathy.[38] Louis uses the first person (mediated by the interviewer) to recount the male–male exchange of blood (with Lestat) culminating in his vampiric transformation. And later he paints a picture of himself and Lestat as gay dads to their vampire 'daughter', Claudia.[39] Released twenty-six years after the termination of Hollywood's Hays Code, the 1994 film adaption of Rice's novel amplifies these gay plotlines and thus confirms that American audiences were ready to celebrate advances made by queer rights' activists.[40] The scene where Lestat first bites Louis is absolutely orgasmic as the two men fly into the air, for example, while Lestat later admits that Claudia's transformation is an attempt to bind Louis through family: 'You're mine and Louis' daughter now', he tells her. 'You see, Louis was going to leave us, he was going to go away, but now he's not. Now, he's going to stay and make you happy.' The ploy works, Louis stays, and many 1990s viewers got their first example of gay dads parenting a child.

On the one hand, critics such as George E. Haggerty frame this emphasis on family as an example of the 'uneasy relationship' between conservative politics and queer vampires found in many of Rice's novels.[41] Such a reading also anticipates Lee Edelman's *No Future*, on how modern political discourse is often tacitly defined by a common investment in the promise of a meaning-fulfilling future, as embodied by the child: 'That Child remains the perpetual horizon of every acknowledged politics, the fantasmatic beneficiary of every political intervention.'[42] One's participation in this modern political area thus tacitly requires a shared commitment to sexual (re)production and condemnation of non-(re)productive pleasures as selfish or anti-social. In his defiant response to such heteronormative plots, Edelman instead celebrates what he characterises as queer negativity: '*queerness* names the side of those *not* "fighting for the children", the side outside the consensus by which all politics confirms the absolute value of reproductive futurism'.[43] On the other hand, however, the fact that this gay family is so child-oriented might signal the emergence of a new or mainstream form of vampirism, one not tied to queer Otherness. One can imagine the strategy behind such a bid for inclusion, especially after the devastating effects of political exclusion during the HIV/AIDs pandemic.

In fact, the film *Interview with the Vampire* presents viewers with an almost utopian vision of a queer life that can transcend the horrors of the HIV/AIDS pandemic. The homophobic assumption that HIV/AIDS was a gay disease was *the* major factor in the Reagan administration's refusal to declare a public health emergency for several years, despite the alarming rise in cases. It was not until 1985, with a total of 15,527 reported cases and 12,529 deaths, that President Reagan publicly mentioned AIDS for the first time. Of course, Rice could not have anticipated the AIDS crisis when she originally wrote *Interview with the Vampire* in 1976. Still, the novel is interested in the idea of a vampire who is immune to disease, as suggested by its references to a plague that claims the lives of many Louisianans (including Claudia's mother). In the 1994 movie, the vampire's immunity is stated explicitly when the interviewer asks if Louis minds his smoking. 'I wouldn't assume that it would be [bothersome]', the boy adds. 'Its not like you are going to die of cancer or anything, is it?' Subsequent scenes of men exchanging vibrant red blood immediately confirm for audiences that these queer vampires have nothing to fear from their intimate exchange. It would even seem that the film is defiant in its attempt to provide some hope for a queer-positive future – if not an implicit call for a real cure (effective treatment did not come until 1996, when the CDC and FDA released the first trials of anti-retroviral cocktails; we are still without a cure in 2022) – despite the punishing, homophobic cultural climate surrounding the AIDS pandemic.

At the same time as Rice introduced audiences to sympathetic vampires, Gothic literature of the late twentieth century also pushed back against the traditional canon and gave us vampire stories populated with BIPOC (Black, Indigenous and People of Colour) characters. This shift from the privileged white perspective has much to do with the social influence of postcolonial and Critical Race studies, with their call for us to pay attention to the role of race(ism) and the legacy of European colonialism in literature. Influenced by this critical turn, contemporary Gothic literature on queer themes thus pursues what we now call an intersectional approach that combines analysis of race with sexuality. Jewelle Gomez's *The Gilda Stories* (1991) is among the best examples of this new approach to queer vampire literature. Gomez's novel is told from the perspective of a queer Black vampire who recounts her 200-year-plus history – from escaping slavery in southern Louisiana and being taken in by (and given the name of) the vampire Gilda, to finding a community of like-minded queer vampires in nineteenth-century San Francisco, or companionship among Black political artists in late twentieth-century New York. It is important to note that the original Gilda was a white vampire, and the transference of her name to our hero thus invokes both a history of white supremacy in which white plantation owners often imposed their names on to black subjects, as well as the possible departure from this history by the shifting of power – through narrative control – to a Black subject. In a scene that supports the latter interpretation, the novel's protagonist (at this point an unnamed girl) is taught to read and write by the elder vampire's lover, a Lakota woman named Bird.

> Bird taught the Girl first from the Bible and the newspaper. Neither of them could see themselves reflected there. Then she told the Girl stories of her own childhood, using them to teach her to write. She spoke each letter aloud, then the word, her own hand drawing the Girl's across the worn paper. And soon there'd be a sentence and a legend or memory of who she was.[44]

This moment of shared learning stands as a powerful metaphor for BIPOC women inserting their lives into the annals of history, writing themselves into existence and finding community at the same time. Later, Gilda remakes the girl as her vampire inheritor, asking Bird to complete the transformation and effectively become a kind of mother-lover to the young vampire. This is Gilda's intention, for she does not wish to leave her lover alone after her own death. Carmilla's vision of vampire lovers bonded in enduring familial love (not just raunchy sex) thus finds new and diverse life in Gomez's novel.

This representation of an enduring queer love between BIPOC vampires is especially daring given the conservative cultural climate in which Gomez was writing. In her 'Afterword' to the 2016 edition published by City Lights, Alexis Pauline Gumbs wonders, 'What kind of bravery did it take [for Gomez] to write a novel about a black woman vampire in an era when people were making their political careers off of depictions of how black women and their inner city offspring were sucking the lifeblood out of American capitalism?'[45] Published in the aftermath of Reagan's America, Gomez's novel speaks back to such racist narratives, as its intersectional vampire thwarts the heteronormative gaze marginalising queer desire. 'What kind of bravery', Gumbs continues, 'did it take [Gomez] to write a black lesbian vampire novel in a time when the rise of the religious right was impacting publication norms and restrictive public funding by equating lesbian and gay art with pornography?'[46] *The Gilda Stories* leaves readers with a message of the lasting importance of community and a love that binds.

It is important to note, however, that this emphasis on love can, at times, gloss over some of the more painful chapters in queer history. For example, Gilda begins her account in 1850, and then provides vignettes from 1890 (California), 1921 (Missouri), 1955 (Massachusetts) and 1981 (New York), before jumping ahead to 2020 (New Hampshire) and 2050 ('The Land of Enchantment'). This timeline completely omits the 1980s–1990s AIDS pandemic and its devastating impact on queer communities. Of course, this omission could be the result of burnout in the midst of the crisis, or it could be that *The Gilda Stories* (like *Interview with the Vampire*) wanted desperately to foreground some vision of a hopeful future.

After a hundred years apart, Gilda and Bird are reunited and quickly fall into their familiar relationship. Gilda redefines this vampiric desire as a mutual exchange of love (not predation or perversion): 'this was a desire not unlike their need for blood [. . .] It was not unlike lust but less single-minded', and 'She felt the love almost as motherly affection, yet there was more.'[47] The two vampire women come together in a mix of passion and maternal care, giving readers a picture of a queer bond that infuses the sexual with a deep and almost transcendent intimacy. With this affirmation of love between women, the novel signals its participation in a tradition of queer vampire stories stretching back to *Carmilla* in the nineteenth century; however, we must also remember that our protagonist herself is not lesbian but rather bisexual, and in later chapters she even takes on a male lover. By writing the protagonist as bisexual, then, Gomez challenges binaristic thinking within many gay rights' movements, specifically lesbian communities. By the 1980s and

1990s, many such (usually white) lesbian activists expressed intolerance towards sexual fluidity and even blamed bisexual women for bringing HIV/AIDs into their communities.[48] *The Gilda Stories* refuses the kind of heteronomative thinking that reduces sexuality to monolithic and thus exclusionary binaries of straight or queer – and as a result, it pushes us to expand the latter into a fully inclusive or umbrella term.

Ten years after Gomez's pioneering novel, BIPOC queer vampires found a new home in the virtual bookstore, Bold Strokes Books. Founded in 2004, Bold Strokes is clearly influenced by third wave feminism that is attentive to race as well as Queer Theory's pushback against assumptions of binary (male/female or hetero/homosexual) and cisgendered subject positions (female sexed and gendered). The mid-sized American publisher 'offers a diverse collection of Lesbian, Gay, Bisexual, Transgender and Queer general and genre fiction' (LGBTQ+).[49] Bold Strokes also boasts several works by or about BIPOC, and lists as many as thirty-seven titles on queer vampires alone. This chapter will focus on two recent titles: *A Soul to Keep* (2016) by Rebekah Weatherspoon, and *Hunger for You* (2018) by Jenny Frame.

A Soul to Keep is a modern love story between Black French-Canadian and college junior Jill Babineaux, and Japanese vampire Miyoko 'Tokyo' Hayashi. Both attend Maryland University and are members of Alpha Beta Omega, part of a sorority network in which vampires have consensual feeding relationships with their human familiars (the vampires get blood and the humans get multiple sexual orgasms). Although Jill is bonded as feeder to the vampire Ginger, she forms a non-feeding, sexual relationship with Tokyo. This relationship starts out as a kind of 'experiment', but eventually the bond becomes real as both learn to let down their guard. The story's climax sees Tokyo sacrifice her immortal life in order to save Jill from possession by a demon. Devastated, Jill takes a break from school and, at the same time, decides that she 'never want[s] to be bound to [Ginger] again',[50] as if she cannot bear the thought of another intimate relationship with a vampire unless it is Tokyo. To her surprise, this wish is fulfilled when, upon her return to school, Jill is greeted by Tokyo. In a unique twist, the latter is no longer vampire: 'No more fangs. No blood cravings' and 'I can handle the sun just fine.'[51] But Tokyo is still different from her human counterpart: 'The skin on her hand was suddenly covered in bright blue feathers', and then 'she shook her arm, [and] her hand went back to normal'.[52] Tokyo's continued ability to shape-shift would seem to stand in as a reminder of the vampire's role as a queer or uncanny Other. Interestingly, in this novel at least, the vampire's predation upon the human (blood) must be entirely transcended in order for both to enjoy their happy-ever-after romantic ending. And Jill's emphatic, 'I chose you'[53] signals this move to a new kind of consensual bond.

Published two years later, *Hunger for You* is also interested in the idea of healthy queer relationships, updating this theme in keeping with its fourth-wave feminist context. Readers will remember that the #MeToo movement represents a new era in the fight for gender reform, demanding that survivors of sexual assault be heard and that their voices be validated. The viral campaign gained international recognition in 2017, after several high-profile allegations of rape against Hollywood producer Harvey Weinstein (since convicted of his crimes), but can in fact trace its origins back to 2006 and the work of sexual assault survivor and activist Tarana Burke. The hashtag was first used by Burke while working at Just Be Inc. (a non-profit for young women of colour that she founded in 2003) after a young woman privately disclosed her own sexual abuse. In an interview with CNN, Burke recounted how, after struggling to find the right words, she landed on the phrase Me Too as a way to convey support through shared experience while also empowering individual survivors to share their stories: 'On one side, it's a bold declarative statement that "I'm not ashamed" and "I'm not alone"', she explained, and '[o]n the other side, it's a statement from survivor to survivor that says "I see you, I hear you, I understand you and I'm here for you or I get it."'[54]

Hunger for You responds to the cultural context of the #MeToo movement by giving readers LGBTQ+ vampires who live by a 'sacred rule' of 'consen[sual]' relationships with those upon whom they feed.[55] It is also worth noting, per LGBTQ+ characters, that the primary vampire in this novel, Byron Debrek, is gender-fluid, though uses the pronoun 'she'.[56] It is through her interest in custom-designed men's suits that Byron meets Savile Row tailor Amelia Honey. The attraction is immediate, and the subsequent story focuses on their deepening romance, as Byron learns to share her entire vampire self with Amelia. Though she is named after Byron, the original modern vampire (per Polidori), and though she is clearly capable of mesmerising, this queer vampire instead pursues a mutual and committed relationship with Amelia, her 'Principessa'.[57] In accepting this role as queen, Amelia also unwittingly places herself in the middle of an ages-old feud between the Debrek and Dred vampire clans. Byron's cousin Victorija is head of the Dred clan and desperate to discover the Debreks' secret ability to sexually reproduce. Her ruthless pursuit of this information culminates in the murder of their great-great-grandmother, Lucia, after learning that true love is key to making born vampires. After Victorija flees, Byron seeks comfort in Amelia's arms, and it is suggested that the two will fulfill Lucia's prophecy as parents of a new generation of vampires. *Hunger for You*, in the end, thus brings the nosferatu into the twenty-first century wherein love is paramount and underwrites a new mode of vampiric reproduction based on mutual consent, rather than violence or predation. Like *A Soul to Keep*, *Hunger for You* rewrites the vampire as a figure who integrates into human society and, in the last case, even participates in the kind of reproductive futurity that formerly (according to Edelman) precluded queer voices from political discourse. In the hands of queer authors, and published by independent presses for queer and trans readers, these modern stories model a futurity that is queer-inclusive.

Conclusion

This brings us to current representations of the queer vampire. The mockumentary TV series *What We Do in the Shadows* (2019–) confirms that queer vampires can now even make it in mainstream culture.[58] The show features male–male desire in the relationship between the group's oldest vampire, Nandor, and his devoted human familiar, Guillermo de la Cruz (Nador also claims to have had a sexual relationship with George Washington, 'America's first gay president').[59] There are also explicit scenes and stories of queer sex. During an early interview, for example, both Laszlo and Nadja separately confirm wild sexual encounters with Baron Afanas, an ancient vampire from the Old Country. 'A few hundred years ago, we enjoyed a very intense, very long sexual affair', explains Nadja. 'It was very wild, lots of acrobatic stuff.'[60] Seconds later, Laszlo claims virtually the exact same experience with the Baron: 'A while back, the baron and I enjoyed a very intense sex affair. Very animalistic. Acrobatic stuff, you might say.'[61] Laszlo and Nadja are married, but clearly do not place any kind of sexual prohibitions on each other. Rather, the fact that the Baron does not seem to have genitals implies that their affairs fall completely outside any typical, heteronormative model of marriage.

The idea of queer vampires is so woven into the fabric of the series that, when representatives of GLAAD (an organisation monitoring LGBTQ+ positive representations in the media) contacted producers of the FX series to ask how many of the characters were queer, producer Paul Sims quipped, 'All of them. All of our characters are completely pansexual', adding, 'So we get a 100 percent from GLAAD on the survey. Where's our award?'[62] With approval ratings for season one at 97% (Rotten Tomatoes) and season two at 100% (Rotten Tomatoes), it is little surprise that *What We Do in the Shadows* has since been renewed for another, highly anticipated third season. All of this raises the question, what kind of Gothic creature are we now left with in the new millennium? Indeed, the popularity of the series suggests that queer vampires have come a long way from their former status as fiend (in *Dracula*), and might even be making their way back to that original category of 'friend' (in Polidori's *The Vampyre*). No longer marked as Other by virtue of queer desire, the creature's claim to the Gothic instead seems to rest alone on its status as vampire, our 'shadow' self.

Notes

1. Veronica Hollinger, 'Fantasies of Absence: The Postmodern Vampire', in *Blood Red: The Vampire as Metaphor in Contemporary Culture*, ed. Joan Gordon and Veronica Hollinger (Philadelphia, PA: University of Pennsylvania Press, 1997), pp. 199–212 (p. 200).
2. Judith Butler, *Bodies That Matter: On the Discursive Limits of Sex* (New York: Routledge, 1993), p. 223.
3. Angus McLaren, *Sexual Blackmail: A Modern History* (Cambridge, MA: Harvard University Press, 2002), esp. ch. 1, 'Sodomy and the Invention of Blackmail'; and H. G. Cocks, *Nameless Offences: Homosexual Desire in the Nineteenth Century* (London: I.B. Tauris, 2003), esp. ch. 2, 'Policing Sodomy in the Nineteenth-Century City'.
4. See Carol A. Senf, *The Vampire in 19th-Century English Literature* (Madison, WI: University of Wisconsin Press, 1988); and Nina Auerbach, *Our Vampires, Ourselves* (Chicago: University of Chicago Press, 1995).
5. D. L. Macdonald and Kathleen Scherf, 'Introduction', in *The Vampyre and Ernest Brechtold; or, The Modern Oedipus* (Peterborough, Ont.: Broadview, 2008), pp. 9–31.
6. Auerbach, *Our Vampires, Ourselves*, p. 14.
7. Ibid., p. 18. This also reads like a vampire version of Eve Sedgwick's homosocial triangle, as described in *Between Men: English Literature and Male Homosocial Desire* (New York: Columbia University Press, 1992).
8. Ibid., p. 21.
9. Sheridan Le Fanu, *Carmilla* (Cabin John, MD: Wildside Press, 2005), p. 57.
10. Ibid., p. 35.
11. Ibid., p. 50.
12. See Sharon Marcus, *Between Women: Friendship, Desire, and Marriage in Victorian England* (Princeton, NJ: Princeton University Press, 2007), p. 12.
13. Le Fanu, *Carmilla*, p. 33.
14. Auerbach, *Our Vampires, Ourselves*, p. 45.
15. LeFanu, *Carmilla*, pp. 107–8.
16. Bram Stoker, *Dracula*, ed. Glennis Byron (Peterborough, Ont.: Broadview, 1998), pp. 69–70.
17. Ibid., p. 70.

18. Caryn E. Neumann, 'The Labouchère Amendment (1885–1967)', *glbtq* (2004), http://www.glbtqarchive.com/ssh/labouchere_amendment_S.pdf (accessed 6 February 2021).
19. Richard Dellamora, *Masculine Desire: The Sexual Politics of Victorian Aestheticism* (Chapel Hill, NC: University of North Carolina Press, 1990), p. 200.
20. Florence Marryat, *The Blood of the Vampire* (Kansas City, KS: Valencourt Books, 2009), pp. 82, 83.
21. Ibid., p. 83.
22. Ibid., p. 27. See also Ardel Haefele-Thomas, 'Queering the Female Gothic', in *Women and the Gothic: An Edinburgh Companion*, ed. Avril Horner and Sue Zlosnick (Edinburgh: Edinburgh University Press, 2016), pp. 169–83 (p. 180).
23. Neumann, 'The Labouchère Amendment'.
24. See Sheila Jeffreys, '"Henpecking": Women's Campaigns to Gain Legislation against the Sexual Abuse of Girls', in *The Spinster and Her Enemies: Feminism and Sexuality 1880–1930* (London: Pandora, 1985), pp. 72–85.
25. Marryat, *Blood of the Vampire*, p. 226.
26. *Nosferatu*, dir. F. W. Murnau (Prana Film, 1922), and *Dracula*, dir. Tod Browning (Universal Pictures, 1931).
27. *Dracula's Daughter*, dir. Lambert Hiller (Universal Pictures, 1936).
28. 'The Production Code', in *Movies and Mass Culture*, ed. John Belton (New Brunswick, NJ: Rutgers University Press, 1996), pp. 135–49 (p. 138).
29. Ibid., p. 140.
30. *Rebecca*, dir. Alfred Hitchcock (United Artists, 1940). This was Hitchcock's first American film project.
31. *The Hunger*, dir. Tony Scott (MGM/UA Entertainment, 1983).
32. *Blood and Roses*, dir. Roger Vadim (Paramount Pictures, 1960).
33. *The Vampire Lovers*, dir. Roy Ward Baker (Hammer Film Productions, 1970); and *Vampyros Lesbos*, dir. Jesús Francos (Fénix Films, 1971).
34. See Andrea Weiss, *Vampires and Violets: Lesbians in Film* (Harmondsworth: Penguin, 1993), p. 87; and Auerbach, *Our Vampires, Ourselves*, p. 53.
35. Indeed, the fact that this lesbian vampire is a direct descendant of the Victorian vampire also reminds us of the film *Dracula's Daughter* (1936).
36. *Vampyros Lesbos*, dir. Francos.
37. Anne Rice, *Interview with the Vampire* (New York: Ballantyne, 1997), pp. 3–4.
38. Ibid., p. 4.
39. Ibid., p. 88.
40. *Interview with the Vampire*, dir. Neil Jordan (The Geffen Film Company, 1994).
41. Haggerty, *Queer Gothic* (Chicago: University of Chicago Press, 2006), p. 185.
42. Lee Edelman, *No Future: Queer Theory and the Death Drive* (Durham, NC: Duke University Press, 2004), p. 3.
43. Ibid., p. 3.
44. Jewell Gomez, *The Gilda Stories* (San Francisco: City Lights, 2016), p. 21.
45. Alexis Pauline Gumbs, 'Afterword', in *The Gilda Stories* (San Francisco: City Lights, 2016), pp. 253–9 (p. 255).

46. Ibid., p. 255.
47. Gomez, *Gilda Stories*, p. 139.
48. See Robin Anne Reid, 'Lost in Space between "Center" and "Margin"', in *Feminist Nightmares: Women at Odds: Feminism and the Problem of Sisterhood*, ed. Susan Ostrov Weisser and Jennifer Fleischner (New York: NYU Press, 1994), pp. 343–57 (pp. 348–9).
49. https://www.boldstrokesbooks.com/contact-us (accessed 5 February 2021).
50. Rebekah Weatherspoon, *A Soul to Keep* (Valley Falls, NY: Bold Strokes, 2016), p. 224.
51. Ibid., p. 228.
52. Ibid., p. 228.
53. Ibid., p. 229.
54. Meredith Worthen, 'Tarana Burke', The Biography.com, 1 March 2018, https://www.biography.com/activist/tarana-burke (accessed 14 November 2021).
55. Jenny Frame, *Hunger for You* (Valley Falls, NY: Bold Strokes, 2018), p. 168.
56. Ibid., p. 218.
57. Ibid., p. 97.
58. *What We Do in the Shadows*, creator Jermaine Clement (FX, 2019–).
59. *What We Do in the Shadows*, episode 8, dir. Jason Wollener (FX 2019).
60. *What We Do in the Shadows*, episode 1, dir. Taike Waititi (FX 2019).
61. *What We Do in the Shadows*, episode 1.
62. Daniel Reynolds, 'How *What We Do in the Shadows* Became Cable's Queerest Comedy', *The Advocate*, 15 April 2020, https://www.advocate.com/television/2020/4/15/how-what-we-do-shadows-became-cables-queerest-comedy (accessed 5 February 2021).

Chapter 7

Queer Zombies
Xavier Aldana Reyes

One does not need to be sentient to be a queer zombie, but it helps. The typically frightening quality and voraciousness of the post-Romero undead have made them significant figures in the sizeable roster of contemporary horror. Like late twentieth-century theorisations which saw classic monsters and the patterns of exclusion that narratively construct their bodies and actions as stand-ins for homosexuals, queer zombies can be mined for metaphorical meaning, whether they are capable of complex thought processes or not.[1] The trailer for the comedy horror *Creatures from the Pink Lagoon* (2006) contains all the clues: 'They're horrifying! They're hideous! They're hungry! They're ... homosexual?', the voiceover tentatively asks before boldly proclaiming that viewers' 'blood will curdle at the sight of these depraved man-eating, man-loving monsters', their 'stomach[s] ... churn at the insatiable appetites of these campy cannibals'. Homophobic stereotypes of gay men as promiscuous and gay sex as loathsome, corrupting, degenerate and risky are here parodically turned on their heads to satirise heteronormativity. Such knowing depictions of gay men are not reifications of damaging clichés, however, but rather tongue-in-cheek commentaries on the continuing struggles that queer people face in a world that positions them as necessary exceptions and as repositories of sexual and gendered panic.[2] Since contemporary horror still inscribes monstrosity corporeally and visibly, zombies can be read as supernatural doubles, as queer difference incarnate.[3] However, films such as *Creatures from the Pink Lagoon* can only take the metaphor so far because their living dead still operate as harmful brutes whose inner selves and drives remain inaccessible. Lacking clear stories and identities, they are perceived as sources of danger to eliminate, rather than subjectivities to acknowledge. Self-conscious zombies, who are subjected to the same systems of oppression and discrimination yet can express their feelings, have therefore been more forthcoming.

As the ultimate in monstrous abjection, zombies have been deployed to articulate nuanced messages about discrimination, marginalisation and alienation. Sentient zombies are particularly interesting because they can more easily generate empathy and sympathy than their mindless, bestial siblings.[4] Focalising narratives through zombie 'Others', especially through attractive or otherwise less decayed ones, can nurture feelings of compassion in readers and viewers, especially when their predicaments are recognisably those of certain marginalised human groups. In *Breathers: A Zombie's Lament* (2009), by S. G. Browne, zombies become proxies for the socially disenfranchised, who create Undead Anonymous chapters throughout the US to call for acceptance, integration and civil rights. The novel does not allegorise one unique community, but when protagonist Andy Warner hops on to a bus full of humans (the 'breathers' of the title), he 'wonder[s] if Rosa Parks felt this way'.[5] This is one of various echoes of the long legacy of slavery and segregation in the US. Similarly, Darren Shan's 'Zom-B' series (2012–16) pits the moral growth of its 'revitalized' zombie, a teenager named B, against her dad, whose racist and xenophobic beliefs make him 'a bigger monster than any bloody zombie'.[6] In Daniel Waters' *Generation Dead* (2008), a representative of the Hunter Foundation for the Advancement and Understanding of Differently Biotic Persons criticises the term '*living impaired*' to refer to zombies for its pejorative implications, comparing it to '*handicapped*', a word 'widely recognized as being insulting to differently abled persons'.[7] The sympathetic zombies in these texts do not symbolise any given social cluster, but instead experience the structures of inequality and abuse visited upon various minorities. As beacons of alterity, they encapsulate the detrimental effects of homogenising discourses that privilege certain individuals over others on whatever biases: ethnic, religious, class-based, gendered or sexual, among others. In particular, they concentrate on self-acceptance, ostracism and, invariably, revolution, with heroes resisting injustices and fighting back against a draconian status quo presented as unfair.

It is important to realise that sympathetic zombie stories are rarely straightforward horror. These texts rely heavily on elements from romance and comedy, and generally play out as melodramas and even as superhero narratives. In them, the frightful elements associated with the zombie, such as eating brains to keep decomposition and mental decay in check, either turn into one more pesky inconvenience, as happens for school dropout and pill addict Angel in Diana Rowland's 'White Trash Zombie' series (2011–17), or else into a useful tool that offers a renewed purpose in life, as in the case of the zombie pathologist in the CW's *iZombie* (2015–19). For Liv (Rose McIver), eating brains unlocks the ability to see into the memories of the dead, a skill that motivates her into helping Seattle's police with some gruelling cases. The disavowal of the zombie as object of fear and its refashioning into a likeable underdog with a secret to hide is crucial in the creation of alliances between readers/viewers and fictional monsters. The latter are rethought as fantastic, rather than horrific, benevolent and, most importantly, as characters with a personality and maybe even a sense of humour. Much like sympathetic serial killer texts, where allegiance to 'good' murderers is encouraged by pitting their apparently more ethical codes of conduct against the irredeemable ones of their 'bad' doubles, 'good' zombies are complicated individuals prone to moral conundrums.[8] The Syfy series *Z-Nation* (2014–18) and the novel *The Girl with All the Gifts* (2014), by M. R. Carey, externalise this ontological distinction by separating the 'pure' evil, flesh-eating zombie from psychologically evolved hybrids who end up leading packs of survivors due to their enhanced abilities. In the zom-com *Warm Bodies* (2013), and Isaac Marion's original 2010 novel of the same title, the zombie state can even be reversed through human love and understanding. Conversely, the texts' villains, the 'Boneys', have lost their humanity entirely and are therefore beyond help. Morality, as a cognitive faculty, becomes the main trait separating those truly 'dead' to society from those who can be painstakingly rehabilitated.

Given that sympathetic zombies are self-aware and charismatic, it is inevitable that they would be utilised to tell stories about identity crises. And since gender and sexuality are vital to queer identity, it makes sense that some zombie texts mediate community-specific anxieties such as the process of coming out and the acute rejection that sadly still taints – and in some tragic cases even ends – the lives of many. Corey Redekop's *Husk: A Novel* (2012) illustrates some of the ways in which the sympathetic zombie allegorises such travails. Although the novel is more interested in exploring the ramifications of Hollywood stardom for its undead actor, Sheldon Funk, the author's decision to make the protagonist gay necessarily inflects many of the main events. Sheldon finds it hard to come to terms with his sexuality due to the censorious beliefs of his conservative and devout mother, Eileen, and grows up feeling lonely and like a filial disappointment. Once a zombie, the monster's archetypal insatiability and high infectiousness allegorise pernicious and lingering post-AIDS prejudices. In a telling scene, Eileen calls her son a 'fornicator' and 'Death' itself and warns that 'God will surely punish [him] for [his] sinful ways', effectively equating gay sex with excess, mortality and profanity.[9] Being a zombie doubles for Sheldon's feelings of inadequacy, making the process of building deep and trustworthy sentimental relationships even more difficult. As he goes public with his undead state, his fight for civil rights necessarily reflects that of queer people in the US, especially from 1996 to 2020, a period in which state laws gradually put a stop to controversial bans and levelled out some blatant inequalities.[10] Much later in *Husk*, Sheldon is kidnapped by the world's richest man, Lambertus Dixon, who wants to use the zombie's supernatural abilities to achieve immortality. Also a religious zealot, he chastises Sheldon for not embracing his messianic qualities, only to suggest that his being gay would have made a Second Coming unlikely. He explains that the masses

> would have twisted their beliefs to accommodate a Canadian, they would have found a way to justify worshipping an atheist. You could have been a *woman*, and they'd have reread their texts to allow for it. They would have swallowed you whole and asked for gravy. But a queer? A cockgobbler? ... Not one of them could imagine pledging fealty to a son of God who enjoyed getting fisted. Imagine how the next Testament would read.[11]

In this passage, gay men are constructed as the ultimate figuration of social abjection.[12] *Husk* is broken into seven chapters whose titles reference the various stages of grief: shock, denial, bargaining, guilt, anger, depression and acceptance. While these phases relate primarily to Sheldon embracing his new 'unlife', they also capture his journey towards a sexual self-affirmation that culminates in a fulfilling emotional relationship with actor Duane. In Redekop's novel, recognition of one's gayness is akin to trauma, to the loss of a version of oneself that aligns with society's heteronormative expectations. Due to their incotrovertible physical difference, zombies can mediate unfounded biases and bigotry.

Important as the abjection model is for understanding queer zombie narratives, in this chapter I want to shift the attention to pressing concerns that have emerged for queer artists as a result of the relative advances in visibility and freedom of the twenty-first century. Texts such as the BBC series *In the Flesh* (2013–14) and the Irish film *The Cured* (2017) use horror to comment on the biopolitical discourses that normalise and manage 'acceptable' versions of gender and sexuality. In particular, 'passing' for human in these texts acts as a thinly veiled metaphor for the ways in which queers have had to adapt to fit sociopolitical and legal structures that favour monogamy, reproduction and futurity. For their own part, the radical zombie films of Canadian queercore director Bruce LaBruce, *Otto; or, Up with Dead People* (2008) and *L.A. Zombie* (2010), place the emphasis on the need to rehabilitate gay sex and to celebrate its transgressive qualities. These films also seem preoccupied with homonormativity and with the discriminatory processes underpinning some gay subcultures, and even prod the limits between sex and intimacy. Their ambiguous messages balance the liberating qualities of casual encounters with a scepticism rooted in what may be perceived as the increasing depoliticisation and oppositional nature of queerness. With this in mind, and following the work of Jack Halberstam, José Esteban Muñoz and Lorenzo Bernini, I reframe the zombie apocalypse as a fascinating fictional temporal construct through which it becomes possible to conceive of urgent communitarian forms of queer politics.

(Dis)Integration and Pride

Gay sexuality, marred as it still is in the early twenty-first century by connections to death and disease born out of the AIDS crisis, finds a physical and moral counterpart in the zombie, particularly in the interstitial position of the rehabilitated undead. Queer zombies are either medicated into functional states that suppress their instinctive hunger (*In the Flesh*) or else fully cured (*The Cured*). They are nevertheless perceived as a dangerous minority that threatens the integrity, health and purity of the rest of the population. Their behaviours are closely policed and their freedoms and rights curtailed by the military or local guerrilla groups. Zombie texts with queer characters favour stories about the attempted reintegration of zombies (or post-zombies) and the hostility that arises from those who find the 'returned' intimidating. As with sympathetic zombie texts without major queer characters, such as John Ajvide Lindqvist's novel *Hanteringen av odöda* (2005; *Handling the Undead*, 2009) and the French Canal+ series *Les Revenants* (*The Returned*, 2012–15), these texts are also about loss and nostalgia, but they add queerness to the melting pot. While it is tempting to suggest that *In the Flesh* and *The Cured* metaphorise queerness, the predicament of their zombies also reflects types of discrimination and exclusion visited upon other human groups, such as refugees, migrants or disabled people. It is therefore more useful to think about sympathetic zombies, fully cognisant but actively 'othered', as the victims of monitoring processes that contain and defuse difference. This is not to suggest, of course, that texts with queer zombies do not have something specific to say about gay sexuality.

Labels such as 'gay' or 'queer' are never mentioned in *In the Flesh*, but its main character, Kieren Walker (Luke Newberry), develops romantic attachments with two men throughout its two seasons: Rick (David Walmsley), as a human, and Simon (Emmett J. Scanlan), as a zombie.[13]

These relationships are of vital importance because they help characterise Kieren as sensitive, shy and initially cooperative. In the first season, it is revealed that he committed suicide after finding out that Rick died in Afghanistan while fighting in the military. This moment of self-harm is even more symbolic when spatially concretised in the shape of the cave where both boys used to hang out and which bears the inscription 'REN + RICK 4 EVER'. Kieren's dad will not set foot there because it is the traumatic space where he discovered his son's corpse. Yet, since the series builds up to Kieren's confrontation with his family's – and especially his father's – sheepish acquiescence to Roarton's local management of zombies, his reluctance to revisit the place encompasses a possible rejection of his son's same-sex leanings. Kieren is a PDS (Partially Deceased Syndrome) sufferer, the moniker given to zombies (or 'rotters') who are able to keep their 'rabid' state at bay by taking Neurotriptyline, a chemical compound that suppresses 'their need for human brain cells and restore[s] the balance of neurotransmitters'.[14] Their reinsertion into society relies to a certain extent on their capacity to 'pass' for human; to achieve this, all PDS sufferers are decked with special contact lenses that produce the illusion of wholesome eyes and a cover-up mousse to disguise their pale, capillary-scarred skins.

It is hard not to read such an extreme normalising practice, one that homogenises zombies to the point where they shed their uniqueness, as a commentary on the ways in which queerness has been forced to morph into an acceptable heteronormative simulacrum. The simile becomes more powerful when one considers that PDS sufferers are advised to stay indoors and avoid public life, a recommendation that resonates with queer experience in various ways. On the one hand, it represents the 'hidden' quality of gay and trans life, which has historically had to repress or censor itself to prevent social backlash and the physical threat that still discourages many queers from engaging in public displays of affection, as well as to create tolerant spaces where queerness may be displayed and celebrated, such as gay bars or drag shows. On the other, the injunction to go unnoticed speaks to Leo Bersani's warning that 'visibility is a precondition of surveillance, disciplinary intervention, and, at the limit ... cleansing'.[15] Zombies should avoid being spotted not just for the disruption their mere existence causes to 'the way things are', but for their own safety. In *In the Flesh*, the suppression (and, where possible, elimination) of difference is enforced by the members of the Human Volunteer Force (HVF) and, later, Roarton Protection Service, led by violent and disgruntled straight men who would like to see their town zombie-free. Characters such as Gary (Kevin Sutton) tellingly coerce zombies into an active expression of their secret identities, their true selves – '[t]ime to show me who you really are!' (S2 E6) – before condemning them. The other main ideological state apparatus in the series is the Church. Characters such as Vicar Oddie (Kenneth Cranham) and Abigail Lamb (Rita Tushingham), a parishioner, preach against those they see as sinful and as 'giving themselves over to fornication and going after strange flesh' (S2 E4). These charges are reminiscent of those made against gay people by evangelicals and the Religious Right throughout the 1970s and 1980s, groups whose fight to repeal rights shaped political activism.[16] Finally, MP Maxine Martin (Wunmi Mosaku), a supporter of Victus (a Pro-Living party) who forces all PDS sufferers to engage in community service so they can give something back to the 'society they once helped to destroy' (S2 E2), is more than a stand-in for extremist political parties like the National Front. Maxine can also be read as a figurehead for the government and her treatment of PDS sufferers as redolent of the ways in which queers have long been treated as second-class citizens who have had to fight for basic rights such as marriage, adoption, healthcare or access to assisted reproduction technologies. Queer zombie texts take issue with notions of assimilation that concern the compromises made by queers under heteronormative power structures.

Nevertheless, queer zombie texts are more than depressing tales of authoritarian imposition. The discrimination and the subduing of 'othered' communities inevitably lead to social upheaval and uprisings, especially once zombies decide to take matters into their own hands and resist their oppressors. Part of the journey towards group action begins with self-acceptance. Zombies are depicted struggling to come to terms with themselves and with their pasts once the new medication starts rewriting their brains. In *The Cured*, Senan (Sam Keeley) has 'violent impulses' and 'nightmares', ailments that his rehabilitation officer insists on interpreting as 'remind[ers]' of 'what you did, the suffering you caused'. In *In the Flesh*, Kieren experiences involuntary recurrent memories of his untreated state. These take the shape of vivid flashbacks that elicit guilt and shame due to the essentially immoral acts committed during his rabid phase, such as the maiming and killing of other people. Although doctors keep reminding PDS sufferers that they cannot hold themselves accountable for what happened before their treatments began, this does not stop those like Kieren from feeling inadequate and unhappy. Again, it is tempting to probe such scenarios for further meaning. As critics and historians have noted, shame and guilt have long affected queer identity, even, as David M. Halperin proposes, 'queer resistance'.[17] Equally noticeable are self-harm, depression and suicidal behaviour, a result of the ideological, repressive forces that recognise certain lives as inferior, unviable and even 'unlivable', to use Judith

Butler's term.[18] In queer zombie texts, protagonists overcome inertia. In *The Cured*, intimate friend Conor (Tom Vaughan-Lawlor), leads an army of zombies after he refuses to live 'beaten, and bullied and forgotten'. Although Senan opposes him because he does not endorse Conor's confrontational approach, he himself ends up representing hope, as he saves his sister's son from death. For his part, Kieren goes from the life of a recluse to kissing Simon in public and rejecting the social masking of his undead essence. In a pivotal scene, he decides he belongs in Roarton, the place he has long attempted to escape, and thus forsakes self-pity in favour of shameless pride and a desire to protect other PDS sufferers. *In the Flesh* was cancelled, but series two gives enough indication that change can be accomplished through collective effort.

Queer zombie texts are therefore interesting not only for their proposition that becoming reconciled with one's queerness is a positive, even necessary, step in building a caring community. They cast suspicion on the apparently positive representational and legal advances that have enabled social integration, exposing them as undependable and never guaranteed. This is a salient point in *The Cured*, whose rehabilitated zombies are practically returned to a human state in which they no longer crave brains and cannot pass the virus to others. Still, as the film shows, this does not stop the majority of the public from treating them as dangerous and morally reprehensible. Those like Senan, who interiorise the external rhetoric of blame to the point of doubting whether they 'deserve forgiveness' for what they did to others, remain silent, but the Cured Alliance decides to fight back because they suspect that they will never be left alone, that their lives will be governed by precarity. The cured continue to be constructed as social pariahs, as 'sick' even after they have become resistant and non-infectious.[19] Tolerance, it seems, is only skin-deep, and a regression to earlier forms of regulation, even punishment, is a worrying immanent possibility. In *In the Flesh*, the imposition of the PDS Give Back Scheme makes the important point that rights and freedoms that have been only begrudgingly or narrowly conceded are always provisional and reversible, that queer–straight relations are in perpetual tension.

Gay Sex and Intimacy

Queer zombie texts can also critique the privileging of heteronormative issues and ideals within queer communities, situating those values as sometimes antithetical to more radical, and therefore less hetero-sanctionable, expressions of gender and sexual identity. As Darren

Elliott-Smith explains, this shift in artistic concerns is part of a larger turn inwards in new queer horror.[20] Such an introspective look has translated into an interrogation of sanitised and unthreatening expressions of queerness underpinned by commodification. Lisa Duggan, in her pioneering *The Twilight of Equality? Neoliberalism, Cultural Politics, and the Attack on Democracy* (2003), already questioned the neoliberal principles implicit in the privileging of certain articulations of gayness in the public sphere and the corporatisation of gay civil rights groups such as the International Gay Forum. She described their 'sexual politics' as a '*new homonormativity* . . . that does not contest dominant heteronormative assumptions and institutions, but upholds and sustains them', and that 'promis[es] the possibility of a demobilized gay constituency and a privatized, depoliticized gay culture anchored in domesticity and consumption'.[21] In the UK, the organisation of alternative pride protests that call for a return to activism and freedom-fighting evidences the existence of anti-capitalist, revolutionary sentiments among queer groups.[22] Films such as LaBruce's *Otto; or, Up with Dead People* and *L.A. Zombie* demonstrate a move towards a repoliticisation of queerness that celebrates gay sex while paradoxically pointing out its limitations as an apolitical practice.

Otto is an experimental film, a melange of various styles and genres (avant-garde filmmaking, documentary, horror, pornography, romance), that explores themes such as the superficiality of some gay subcultures and digital alienation.[23] Its running time includes footage from two different intradiegetic films made by avant-garde filmmaker Medea Yarn (Katharina Klewinghaus): one, *Up with Dead People*, a 'political porno zombie' flick shot in black and white and involving the rise of an army of gay zombies, and *Otto*, a documentary that follows the adventures of a maladjusted teenage zombie (Jey Crisfar). Otto could be a real member of the reasoning undead ('a zombie with an identity crisis', as he puts it) or simply a delusional individual. Irrespective of his true ontological state, the protagonist acts as a genuine zombie; he is perceived as 'authentic' and 'different' by others and is portrayed eating the raw meat of roadkill and wild living animals.[24] His fuzzy past unravels over a series of flashbacks triggered by certain objects, places and topics of conversation – happy memories where he is having a good time with ex-boyfriend Rudolf (Gio Black Peter) to the sound of upbeat music. *Otto* begins with the eponymous character coming out of the grave and finding his way to Berlin by pursuing the 'smell of human density, the smell of flesh'. During his time in Berlin, Otto is verbally abused and beaten up by youths, sleeps with two men and has a sobering conversation with his ex. Dissatisfied, he eventually leaves in search of others like him. As a cinematic *Bildungsroman*, *Otto* captures gay intimacy and its dis/connection from/with sex through the figure of an outcast monster who does not fit either heterosexual or homosexual moulds.

Whether Otto is indeed a supernatural being or simply believes this to be the case, LaBruce's film separates him from other men who perform the undead. The first of these is a 'scene gay' dressed up for a zombie-themed night who Otto meets outside a club called *Flesh*. The second is Fritz Fritze (Marcel Schlutt), the star of *Up with Dead People*, who is tasked by Medea with offering Otto 'male companionship'. Neither affair brings much comfort or resolution. The former seemingly ends with the evisceration of the young raver; the latter concludes with Fritz waking up to a drawing of a tombstone marked 'Otto R.I.P.', a species of suicide note and obituary.[25] Straight after his second hook-up, Otto sets off again, cutting the same lonely vagabond silhouette he did at the start of the film. Before jumping on a stranger's car, he tells viewers his rationale for heading north: 'Maybe I would find more of my kind up there and learn to enjoy the company. Maybe I would discover a whole new way of death.' This apparently non-committal ending is rather consequential. Both of Otto's sexual partners embody a hypermasculine version of male gayness, one that is rendered desirable but ultimately revealed to be staged and unfulfilling. It is also set in stark opposition to Otto's fey and fragile sensibility. *Otto* thus pits its protagonist against skin-deep manifestations of the incorporated gay male/zombie. In a knowing exercise in metatextuality, given that *Otto* itself includes explicit images and that *Up with Dead People* ends in an 'orgy of the dead', the film ends by questioning the real political potential of gay pornography and, by extension, sexual desire. This challenge is amplified by Otto's last conversation with Rudolf, in which he finds out that he was dumped because the boy could not (or would not) deal with Otto's 'disorders of the soul' (melancholia, schizophrenia and an eating disorder). At a time when gay clubs and online dating have made gay sex more available than ever, LaBruce queries the capacity for physical gratification to bring real intimacy.[26] In other words, sex, if potentially healing, can be neatly separated from sentiment and care.

L.A. Zombie, LaBruce's follow-up, goes even further to position gay sex, its visualisation and disruptive nature within heteronormative society, as the main catalyst and expression of queer's insurgent spirit. In fact, when asked in a 2010 interview, the director compared his work in the film to both the avant-garde, underground cinema of 1960s gay filmmakers such as Kenneth Anger, Andy Warhol, Paul Morrissey, Jack Smith, Curt McDowell, George Kuchar and John Waters, and to the pornography of Peter de Rome, Wakefield Poole, Jack DeVoe and Fred

Alsgaard.[27] Rescuing gay sex from the barren associational straitjacket that has constrained it since the 1980s, LaBruce's tale of a zombie who emerges from the sea to revive the outlaws of Los Angeles one phallic thrust at a time belongs in the realms of militant X-rated fever dreams. Although *L.A. Zombie* exists in a longer hardcore version that includes traditional porn, the main cut includes enough nudity and sex to distinguish it from mainstream horror cinema. At the same time, the film's decidedly experimental tone, even if ostensibly a result of budgetary constraints and its guerrilla shooting style, destabilises traditional cinematic pleasure. This 'gay zombie gore porn movie' eschews the narrative logic of mainstream film, vouching instead for a series of vignettes in which the zombie ejaculates a black liquid substance (a species of blood and semen hybrid) that resuscitates homeless men, criminals and, in the last main sequence, a group of cruising bondage fetishists.[28] As with *Otto*, whether the protagonist, played by French pornographic actor François Sagat, is really an extraterrestrial being is less important than the overall impression that intercourse between men can be restorative.

The rather obvious revision of HIV discourse, the mutation of consensual 'gift-giving' into a literal gift of life, does not preclude an alternative reading of events as a commentary on the communitarian possibilities surfacing from a shameless sense of queerness that celebrates sex at its most obscene, public (many of the scenes take place outdoors) and least socially acceptable, that rethinks the queer as extreme, reformist and unconcerned with its unpalatability to the heterosexual popular imaginary. *L.A. Zombie* could be dismissed as escapist entertainment, as titillating nonsense intended to stimulate sexual excitement. Yet LaBruce's cinema never jettisons its gung-ho anti-capitalist credentials. Apart from editing discontinuities that generate dissonance, changes to the zombie's appearance that remain unaccounted for and a strange teetering between orders of reality generate a hallucinatory eeriness that forces viewers to question the nature and purpose of the film. Indeed, as Darren Elliott-Smith suggests, 'LaBruce's low rent aesthetic renders sex almost mundane, banal, unerotic, and hollow'.[29] The film's anti-consumerist and non-conformist ethos is reinstated at the end, too, when the unnamed zombie buries himself in a grave marked 'LAW'. This moment underscores the central message: much like the socially excremental bodies of the characters the zombie recovers from the most deprived and peripheral corners of the metropolis, queers cannot escape heterosexual power. *L.A. Zombie* is not a story where the zombie liberates himself from the weight of biopolitical control.

LaBruce's queer zombies pose an intriguing challenge to homogeneous models of gayness; they collapse the 'sexual energy and militant style that really gives strength to more revolutionary movements' with pornography, a proxy for frowned-upon 'extreme sexual behaviour and hedonism'.[30] They also gesture to the limitations of individual endurance against the heteronormative establishment. In his treatise on queer failure, Jack Halberstam highlights the importance of accepting negativity and defeat, but cautions against theoretical models that remain apolitical and foster passivity and apathy. Instead, he calls for the importance of marrying queerness with socialism through messages that promote '[w]ork[ing] together, [r]evel[ing] in difference, [f]ight[ing] exploitation, [d]ecod[ing] ideology, [i]nvesting in resistance'.[31] If the queer apocalypse is to lead to anything more than a nihilistic relish in the dismantling of the present, it must also transform into a collective exercise that makes room for activism and even utopian thinking.

Queer Apocalypticism

In their intrinsic difference and refutation of the status quo, queer zombies practically embody the critical essence of queer theories, understood as 'critical political philosophies that deploy the perspective of sexual minorities and denounce as arbitrary, illegal and intolerable the very regime that produces them as minoritarian in the first place'.[32] The patterns of social, economic and political exclusion visited upon queer zombies literalise processes of oppression that might otherwise remain invisible to those outside queer communities. They also represent anxieties regarding the dictum to assimilate in order to gain access to basic rights, as well as the horrors of the potential de-queering of the subjects interpellated by ideologies built on models of futurity and reproduction that continue to exclude, if not literally then figuratively, queer existence, that produce queers as hierarchically inferior. Queer zombies simultaneously express the difficulty of establishing a sense of intimacy in a neoliberal world in which identities have been reduced to consumable lifestyles. In the hyper-accelerated West, having gay sex safely and unashamedly has become easier, but it is still complex to exist outside authoritative versions of homonormativity. At the heart of the texts examined in this chapter lies the irresolvability between seeking equality within larger systems that regulate individual manifestations of queer identity and the will to be ill-fittingly oneself. Above all, they delineate a growing awareness that 'queer' must reconduct individualising identity politics into a collective political identity, even if this means shattering the veneer of reassuring respectability once needed to advance freedoms.

Given the limitations of heteronormative societies, is it really surprising that so many queer texts have been seduced by the apocalypse? This powerful chronotope signifies more than a dead-end state of affairs or a metaphorical stalemate. Zombie apocalypse narratives typically begin with an overwhelming infectious outbreak that brings about the collapse of known civilisation, and they proceed to chronicle efforts to rebuild some form of society. The fact that the vast majority of post-millennial zombie narratives, from critically acclaimed novels such as Max Brooks's *World War Z: An Oral History of the Zombie War* (2007) and Colson Whitehead's *Zone One* (2012) to the popular AMC series *The Walking Dead* (2010–22), fall short of proposing social arrangements where characters have learned much from the errors of the past or avoid replicating political and economic models reliant on tyrannical expressions of power makes it tempting to suggest that post-apocalyptic narratives are static, even reactionary. They enjoy the destruction of the present yet seem unable to dream up anything truly visionary and progressive. As fantasies of upheaval, they show themselves to be ideologically barren, as failures of the political imagination. Can the queer apocalypse, then, be read any differently, as anything other than a confirmation of the timely adage, popularised by Mark Fisher in his *Capitalist Realism* (2009), that it is 'easier to imagine the end of the world than the end of capitalism?'[33] The answer naturally lies in what the world being supplanted stood for, whose interests and benefits it represented and who remained subdued by its orders of truth. In what remains, I want to suggest that queer apocalypticism, in the form of the queer zombie, can be read more radically – not just as a force for the necessary negation of heterosexist patriarchy, but as a reminder of the duty to think up other queer futures.

The apocalypse in zombie texts is not the biblical one, the coming of judgement; it is always a lot less final than its name suggests. It is not the cessation of human life on earth. The zombie cataclysm broadly puts an end to the structures that govern human life and replaces them with survivalism. As in *In the Flesh* and *The Cured*, humans generally protect their loved ones, their traditions, their sense of worth and moral values. These decisions involve the contentious discernment of who deserves the right to live and die, even what constitutes citizenship. They are tales of tribalism, of warfare, of border-drawing, of the preservation of 'common sense' and of reifications of the 'normal'. If, as Jack Halberstam claims, non-queer (or straight) temporality is ruled by reproductive and generational associations that connect 'the family to the historical past of the nation' and 'the family to the future of both familial and national stability notions', one in which any sense of the future is sublated by the notion of 'reproductive futurism' (the belief that human development and action should be guided by the betterment of the world for the sake of our children), a radical queerness uninterested in normalisation would instead salute its end.[34] In other words, queer zombies bring about the end of heterosexist systems whose political ethos positions them as extraordinary. The future belongs to the nuclear family, valued by capitalism for its perpetuation of consumption and scope for exponential growth. The 'no future' signified by the disruptive figure of the zombie aligns with the oppositional stance taken by critics such as Lee Edelman, who have actively called for an expression of queerness that espouses the symbolic negation of the queer within heteronormativity. This type of antisocial theory, an echo of Leo Bersani's own proposition that queerness should embrace a death drive that values sexual perversion and its unproductivity, champions the most confrontational aspects of queerness.[35] At its most practical and least abstract, antisocial queerness seeks to question the benefits of continuing to engage in political life from the fringes. Queer zombies, in this schema, put a spanner in the works of a straight time and place that allows queerness to manifest only residually, as a surplus that must adapt to dominant discourses of futurity. Queer zombies logically devour the brains of the axiomatic temporality of reproductive majoritarian heterosexuality, leaving nothing but its gruesome ruins.

A complementary, equally radical, reading of the queer apocalypse might envisage it as something other than a tool for destruction and rejection of reigning gender and sexual ideologies – as an invitation to think slant, to visualise a more progressive time to come that might exceed the constraints of the political moment. In *Cruising Utopia: The Then and There of Queer Futurity* (2009), José Esteban Muñoz wrote against antisocial theories and proposed instead a model of queerness premised on utopia. Claiming that '[q]ueerness is essentially about the rejection of a here and now and insistence on potentiality for another world', he emphasises the nurturing effects of queer friendship, relationality and, importantly, the creative power of cultural production in helping us imagine not just a different, better future for minoritarian communities, but also what 'queerness can and should mean'.[36] Starting, as Edelman does, with the argument that 'futurity becomes history's dominant principle', *Cruising Utopia* recasts queerness as a 'temporal arrangement in which the past is a field of possibility in which subjects can act in the present in the service of a new futurity'.[37] For example, centring on the revolutionary demands made by a 1971 issue of the gay liberation journal *Gay Flames*, Muñoz argues that it is precisely what contemporary standards would judge as the manifesto's 'impractical or merely utopian' ideals that can help us think beyond the stultifying models of more pragmatic gay rights.[38] For Muñoz, the project of imagining utopia is exigently communitarian and must resist the narrative of a broken-down present that cannot be repaired and which therefore naturally breeds pessimism and indifference.[39] Tapping into 'collective potentiality' is as valuable as embracing the monstrous state to which the queer has been relegated and can allow us to think outside the parameters of neoliberal, consumer-based identity politics.[40] Similarly, for Lorenzo Bernini, whose *Queer Apocalypse: Elements of Antisocial Theory* (2013, trans. 2017) also looks to zombies for inspiration, 'queer apocalypses represent a collapse of times in which the past rises up in the present' to organise itself.[41] According to him,

> the heteronormative symbolic order of Oedipal civilization assigns sexual minorities the role of representing the end of civilization and the breaking of social ties: it is thus their destiny to be orphans of a community. Nevertheless, they can meet with one another up north, or in a Tuscan agrotourism: in the interstices of the political, where it's not just possible to look obliquely at the world, but it is also possible to create another world within the world – sometimes simple gestures like singing beneath the moon are enough.[42]

Defiance is a unifying, imaginative series of joint efforts to break away from present restrictions.

If the queer zombie is to supersede its current role as symptomatic avatar of discrimination and disaffection, of the rage and anger of oppressed minoritarian communities, of its expectation to remain 'the obscene double of the heterosexual, the waste that confirms the normative', if it is to channel something other than the trauma of being queer in a heterosexual world, it has to eventually move past the liminal finality of the apocalypse.[43] Queer zombies need to shake off their dead skin, the carapace of futility and fear they have been dragging since they became sentient and self-conscious. Queer zombies have to populate texts that allow for solace and can conjure up healing and inventive yet-to-bes. Films such as *Otto; or, Up with Dead People* and *L.A. Zombie* are a good start. *Otto* ends with its protagonist longing for the relationality and understanding of real zombies, not their homonormative imitation. And Sagat's zombie inhabits an alternative fantasy of fleshed-out regenerative sex. Future queer zombies need to surpass the language of mourning, self-pity and inevitable disaster.

The queer zombie texts analysed in this chapter demonstrate that there is a point of disconnect, a disjuncture, between the private and social spheres, between a personal experience of queerness and the asphyxiating grasp of biopolitical dictates. More importantly, these texts signal that 'queerness' as a marker of identity gains meaning principally as a category of political resistance. In an age defined by an expansion of the meaning of 'queer' via trans, non-binary and ever more gender-fluid and porous 'unfolding categories of being' that repudiate reducibility and monolithic labels, queerness will continue to make sense only insofar as it comes to represent the struggle with the heteronormative dominant against which all other forms of gender and sexual identity have been defined.[44] Queer zombies thus need to collectivise action and abandon the atomisation of individualism. Post-apocalyptic reconstruction could begin not with the promise of re-humanisation, of a return to normality, but with the resounding thud of queer zombie feet marching towards a joint dream of a fairer, more inclusive and diverse tomorrow.

Notes

1. Harry M. Benshoff, *Monsters in the Closet: Homosexuality and the Horror Film* (Manchester: Manchester University Press, 1997), p. 4.
2. I use the term 'gendered' because these texts are also concerned with campness and effeminacy. Straight-acting and macho performances of masculinity are still privileged because they are less threatening to patriarchal structures.
3. I follow Jack Halberstam in the view that 'the emergence of the monster within Gothic fiction marks a peculiarly modern emphasis upon the horror of particular bodies', among which the queer body is included. See Jack Halberstam, *Skin Shows: Gothic Horror and the Technology of Monsters* (Durham, NC: Duke University Press, 2006 [1995]), p. 3.
4. The 'sympathetic zombie' has developed significantly in the twenty-first century but has a point of origin in Bub (Sherman Howard), the likeable zombie who is capable of carrying out basic cognitive functions and motor tasks in *Day of the Dead* (1985).
5. S. G. Browne, *Breathers: A Zombie's Lament* (London: Pitkus, 2011 [2009]), p. 151.
6. Darren Shan, *Zom-B*, in *The Zom-B Chronicles* (New York: Little, Brown, 2014 [2012]), pp. 1–184 (p. 177).
7. Daniel Waters, *Generation Dead* (London: Simon & Schuster, 2008), p. 102, italics in original.
8. David Schmid, 'The Devil You Know: *Dexter* and the "Goodness" of American Serial Killing', in *Dexter: Investigating Cutting Edge Television*, ed. Douglas Howard (London: I.B. Tauris, 2010), pp. 132–42 (p. 140).
9. Corey Redekop, *Husk: A Novel* (Toronto: ECW Press, 2012), pp. 91, 93, 92, respectively.
10. I am referring specifically to the period that ranges from the *Romer v. Evans* ruling, which invalidated a homophobic state law, to the *Bostock v. Clayton County* one, which prohibited employment discrimination against gay and transgender people.

11. Redekop, *Husk*, p. 225, italics in original.
12. Naturally, the passage's sexual detail also hints at the possibility of internalised homophobia.
13. Even if *In the Flesh* never uses explicit labels, it gestures at gayness. For example, Amy (Emily Bevan) calls Kieren her 'BDFF (best dead friend forever)', an echo of GBF (gay best friend), and declares that she loves him, but '[n]ot like that, because I know you're not like that, but a love that's greater than that!' She is, of course, establishing her feelings of true friendship and distinguishing them from physical attraction and sexual desire.
14. The words are taken from the 'Understanding Partially Deceased Syndrome' leaflet shown on screen in the second episode, though medication there is called 'Glialformapin (known by the brand name Neurolax)'.
15. Leo Bersani, *Homos* (Cambridge, MA: Harvard University Press, 1995), p. 11.
16. Tina Fetner, *How the Religious Right Shaped Lesbian and Gay Activism* (Minneapolis, MN: University of Minnesota Press, 2008), pp. 119–30.
17. David M. Halperin, 'Why Gay Shame Now?', in *Gay Shame*, ed. David M. Halperin and Valerie Traub (Chicago: University of Chicago Press, 2009), pp. 41–6 (p. 42).
18. Judith Butler, *Undoing Gender* (London: Routledge, 2004), p. 2.
19. The film could thus be interpreted as a critique of persistent negative attitudes towards, and even active professional discrimination against, queers who live with HIV, even where virological suppression has made it undetectable.
20. See Darren Elliott-Smith, *Queer Horror Film and Television: Sexuality and Masculinity at the Margins* (London: I.B. Tauris, 2016), pp. 1–3, 21.
21. Lisa Duggan, *The Twilight of Equality? Neoliberalism, Cultural Politics, and the Attack on Democracy* (Boston, MA: Beacon Press, 2003), p. 50, italics in original.
22. See Lily Wakefield, 'Activists Reclaim Pride in Manchester, Hold Protest on Same Day as Official Festival', *Pink News*, 28 August 2021, https://www.pinknews.co.uk/2021/08/28/manchester-pride-protest/ (accessed 15 November 2021).
23. See Darren Elliott-Smith, '"Death is the New Pornography!": Gay Zombies, Homonormativity and Consuming Masculinity in Queer Horror', in *Screening the Undead: Vampires and Zombies in Film and Television*, ed. Leon Hunt, Sharon Lockyer and Milly Williamson (London: I.B. Tauris, 2014), pp. 148–70; Xavier Aldana Reyes, 'Beyond the Metaphor: Gay Zombies and the Challenge to Homonormativity', *Journal for Cultural and Religious Theory*, 13.2 (2014), pp. 1–12.
24. Otto explains that he wants to consume the living, but he resists this, perhaps due to residual veganism.
25. It is difficult to take either moment at face value. After evisceration, the victim exclaims '[t]hat was amazing! Can I see you again sometime?' The second scene is followed by a sequence in which Otto sets himself on fire, but the immolation is immediately shown to be a stunt performed for Medea's film.
26. For Shaka McGlotten, the film is empowering insofar as it shows how to live with loneliness and proposes an embrace of the 'impersonal sociality' it depicts. See Shaka McGlotten, 'Dead and Live Life: Zombies, Queers

and Online Sociality', in *Generation Zombies: Essays on the Living Dead in Modern Culture*, ed. Stephanie Boluk and Wylie Lenz (Jefferson, NC: McFarland, 2011), pp. 182–93 (p. 187).
27. Bruce LaBruce, interviewed in the DVD featurette 'Bruce LaBruce vs. François Sagat: 63º Festival del Film di Locarno', *L.A. Zombie* (Italy: Queer Frame TV, 2010).
28. The definition is the director's own, as provided in the 'Bruce LaBruce vs. François Sagat' featurette.
29. Darren Elliott-Smith, 'Gay Zombies: Consuming Masculinity and Community in Bruce LaBruce's *Otto; or Up with Dead People* and *L.A. Zombie*', in *Zombies and Sexuality: Essays on Desire and the Living Dead*, ed. Shaka McGlotten and Steven Jones (Jefferson, NC: McFarland, 2014), pp. 140–58 (p. 155).
30. Bruce LaBruce, quoted in Lorenzo Bernini, *Queer Apocalypses: Elements of Antisocial Theory*, trans. Julia Heim (Basingstoke: Palgrave Macmillan, 2017 [2013]), p. 109.
31. Jack Halberstam, *The Queer Art of Failure* (Durham, NC: Duke University Press, 2011), p. 21.
32. Lorenzo Bernini, *Queer Theories: An Introduction*, trans. Michela Baldo and Elena Basile (Abingdon: Routledge, 2021 [2017]), p. 48.
33. Mark Fisher, *Capitalist Realism: Is There No Alternative?* (Alresford: Zero Books, 2009), p. 1. The line first appeared in Fredric Jameson, 'Future City', *New Left Review*, 21 (2003), pp. 65–79 (p. 76). It is important to acknowledge that capitalism can be recognised as a positive force too, as a contributor to the emergence of 'gay' and 'lesbian' as markers of subjective identity insofar as it 'has created the material conditions for homosexual desire to express itself as a central component of some individuals' lives'. See John D'Emilio, 'Capitalism and Gay Identity', in *The Lesbian and Gay Studies Reader*, ed. Henry Abelove, Michèle Aina Barale and David M. Halperin (London: Routledge, 1993), pp. 467–76 (p. 474).
34. Jack Halberstam, *In a Queer Time and Place: Transgender Bodies, Subcultural Lives* (New York: NYU Press, 2005), p. 5; Lee Edelman, *No Future: Queer Theory and the Death Drive* (Durham, NC: Duke University Press, 2004), p. 2.
35. Edelman, *No Future*; Leo Bersani, 'Is the Rectum a Grave?', *October*, 43 (1987), pp. 197–222.
36. José Esteban Muñoz, *Cruising Utopia: The Then and There of Queer Futurity* (New York: NYU Press, 2019 [2009]), pp. 1, xix.
37. Muñoz, *Cruising Utopia*, p. 16.
38. Ibid., pp. 20, 21.
39. Ibid., p. 11.
40. Ibid., p. 189.
41. Bernini, *Queer Apocalypses*, p. xviii.
42. Ibid., p. 181.
43. Ibid., p. 77.
44. Jack Halberstam, *Trans*: A Quick and Quirky Account of Gender Variability* (Oakland, CA: University of California Press, 2018), p. 4.

Chapter 8

'Queer-Wolves and Wolf-Boyz and Were-Bears, Oh My!': Queering the Wolf in New Queer Horror Film and TV

Darren Elliott-Smith

> I saw the best minds of my generation destroyed by madness [...] who bit detectives in the neck and shrieked with delight in police cars [...] who howled on their knees in the subway and were dragged off the roof waving genitals and manuscripts, who let themselves be fucked in the ass by saintly motorcyclists, and screamed with joy [...] (Allen Ginsberg, 'Howl')[1]

The werewolf is but one among many monstrous icons in film and television that have been reclaimed by the queer community via countercultural identification. In Harry Benshoff's work in *Monsters in the Closet* (1997) and in my own extensions into the study of Queer Horror, we both argue that identification with the 'Other' provides a source of joyful self-recognition, a 'powerful pleasure and wish fulfilment fantasy for some queer viewers'.[2] But at the same time, this affinity with the monstrous is not always entirely pleasurable and requires a complex negotiation with prideful/shameful elements that the monstrous metaphor is then reappropriated to represent. The figure of the werewolf allows for a queer celebration of the shared Otherness felt by those marginalised because of their sexual orientation or gender via a hirsute empowerment or furry protest, and also provides a negotiation with the shame felt and provoked those very same associations with queer monstrousness.

The queer legacy of the werewolf as metaphor for non-normative sexuality and gender is arguably well outlined in academic and popular cultural sources, from scholars including Chantal Bourgault du Coudray, Phillip Bernhardt-House and Barbara Creed and, more recently, in Craig Ian Mann's *Phases of the Moon: A Cultural History of the Werewolf Film*.[3] Mann defines the werewolf as 'a human being who, either purposely or against their will, transforms into a wolf. Certain accounts depict a partial transformation into a monstrous hybrid of human and lupine features while others depict a complete anatomical transformation from human to wolf.'[4] Mann's rich study counters Anne Billson's suggestion that, of all the monstrous metaphors, werewolves 'seem less versatile in metaphorical terms than vampires and zombies, which these days can symbolise just about anything [. . .] The werewolf, on the other hand, is basically just the beast within.'[5] Mann argues instead that the werewolf can be read as 'a mutating metaphor that can be seen to shift and evolve in tandem with the fears and anxieties particular to its historical moment'.[6] Indeed, the werewolf as queer, or queerwolf, points towards a more complex understanding that propels the figure beyond a mere reduction of its function to a symptom of 'a war between the civil and bestial sides of the human self'.[7] In fiction, folklore and, more recently, in horror film and TV, the werewolf is often presented as a sympathetic Other. Furthermore, it is often utilised as a representative for dealing with the gender-oriented manifestations of adolescence and puberty (including depictions of menstruation and changes to one's hormones and their effect on the body's changing shape, such as one's voice lowering and hair sprouting in places where there was none) and the emerging feeling of sexual desire, whether normative or non-normative. As such, the werewolf's connection to burgeoning awareness of sexual orientation and problematic biological indicators of gendered and sexual difference makes it a particularly powerful subject for sympathetic identification for the queer spectator.

Bernhardt-House points to the werewolf's 'transgression of species' boundaries in a unified figure' as partial explanation for its frequent adoption as a metaphor for queerness, writing that 'Werewolves [. . .] are a much greater threat to any enduring sense of identity, even for those who might be queer-identified; they can be queers even amongst the queers.'[8]

Marisa Mercurio also argues that the werewolf is 'something ineffably queer'.[9] She contends that the creature is neither human nor wolf, and that the term werewolf itself is a 'spliced together taxonomy that transforms into a concept bigger, looser, and more fearsome than its words suggest separately'.[10] As I have outlined in past writings on monstrous queer icons,[11] eluding fixed definitions is indeed something that can be understood to be intrinsically queer. Such hauntological depictions of queer subjectivities reveal them to be simultaneously at odds with the normative and with the queer worlds. Similarly, I want to turn also to the werewolf as a queer monstrous figure that offers a nuanced take on the monstrous metaphor, allowing for both a paradoxical celebration of repressed non-normative sexual desires and an often ludicrous disavowal of problematic gender tropes for the queer spectator.

For Mercurio, 'Werewolves figure as gender and sexual dissidents, particularly as they represent non-binary embodiments and desires. Their transformations demonstrate the malleability of bodies and their meanings.'[12] The queerness of the werewolf body that evades categorisation as human or beast and is liminal in its gendered presence when seen through the lens of queer sexuality offers a transformative and visceral spectacle via the lycanthropic body as both pleasurable and painful. There is also an abject queer assemblage here of the collapsed boundaries between inside/out and masculine/feminine. The werewolf provides insight into the depiction of queer sexual and gender identities, and indeed of transgender bodies.

The psychologisation of the werewolf figure in fictional representation often points towards an embrace of the psychosis of lycanthropy as being bound up with theories of the unconscious mind. Here the victim of werewolfery can be allied with the marginalisation felt by the queer subject, whose 'deviancy' is often paralleled with the pathology of the human subject who does not fit into patriarchal ideals of heteronormativity. Du Coudray's work outlines the history of the werewolf, covering its emergence from European folklore to find itself later bound up not only within the confines of evolutionary science via Darwin, but also in the world of psychiatry and psychoanalysis in the works of Freud. Though Du Coudray's and Creed's works[13] on werewolves both point to the development of the she-wolf in the proliferation of werewolf literature and film, Mann recognises that, more often than not, the figure of the werewolf 'generally articulates a deep-seated fear of the beast within, werewolfism as symptomatic of repressed masculine aggression'.[14] In *Phallic Panic*, Creed links the werewolf to the concept of the primal uncanny, to femininity and to the abject via its propensity for collapsing the natural with the unnatural. The lycanthrope, Creed argues, is 'a creature who literally gives birth to himself: his fur covers the inside of his skin. Thus, like woman, he carries the signs of nature within his body at all times [...] The werewolf is a feminised male monster, a queer creature aligned to the primal uncanny.'[15] More recently then, the *queer* aspects of the werewolf have been considered in academia. Bernhardt-House reads the werewolf as a liminal and potentially queer figure. He points to the parallel between phobic fears around queer sexuality and the use of werewolves in horror fiction, in that queer sexuality is often associated with canine/lupine symbolism, being attributed a 'beastly, unnatural and atavistic [nature]'.[16]

Throughout the cinematic history of the werewolf, there has indeed been an emphasis on cis male, and implied heterosexual, transformations from man to wolf,[17] with the exception of titles such as *She Wolf* of London (1946), *Werewolf Woman* (1976) and Neil Jordan's depiction of she-wolves in his adaptation of Angela Carter's short story *The Company of Wolves* (1984). Many of these films, if anything, make closeted reference to the representation of lycanthropy as a stand-in for queerness. There are plentiful instances of the queer she-wolf in film and TV, including the implied queer incest between sisters Ginger (Katherine Isabelle, who transforms into a hyper-erotic werewolf) and Brigitte (Emily Perkins) in *Ginger Snaps* (2000); the PG-rated animated folk-fantasy *Wolfwalkers* (2020), with its suggested queer adolescent friendship as the central relationship; the Brazilian queer nanny horror/psychodrama *Good Manners* (2017); and the lesbian queerwolf horror-musical *Bloodthirsty* (2021). Such a developing fascination with the queer she-wolf narrative in film points towards fertile future analysis from a queer intersectional perspective. However, given the connections to my previous research and the sheer number of queerwolf male narratives already released, in this chapter I want to focus largely on cis male or male-presenting queerwolves and those narratives that, due to their depiction of fluid gender transformations, have a particular resonance with trans spectators.

By looking at examples from film and television queerwolf representation, this chapter will reveal contemporary critiques *within* queer communities. First, I want to focus on representations of the werewolf transformation that symbolise the failure of culturally repressed queer and non-normative sexual desires that then literally burst out from the body in lupine liberation. Secondly, this chapter will highlight instances where the queerwolf figure is seen to be bound up with traditional notions of (queer) hypermasculinity which operate to avoid shameful associations with the feminine and portray a degree of effeminaphobia. Thirdly, I will focus on examples of the queerwolf that illustrate the erotic and problematic celebration of hypermasculine 'daddy-wolf' figures or 'were-bears'. Such instances offer a satirical subcultural critique of queer communities that works to stigmatise the wolf as the queer among the queer, revealing a hierarchy within queer culture that privileges traditional notions of masculine attractiveness and white middle-class homonormativity. Finally, the chapter will end with a consideration of the inherent trans-ness of werewolf films (in their clear connections to body dysmorphia and transformation as imprisoning/liberating) which can be seen to represent the feeling of being trapped in a prison of flesh that does not reflect how some individuals identify. The werewolf narrative can signify the feeling of losing control of one's bodily autonomy or feeling it change in ways one never wanted it to.

Phase One: Queering the Wolf

Perhaps the first sympathetic queer/werewolf in cinematic history, and an important film in terms of its representation of repressed homosexual desires, is *Werewolf of London* (1934); as du Coudray points out, it is the first film to suggest that the werewolf's bite transfers its curse to its victims. The bite that infects but also offers a means of queer reproduction is something that has clear resonances in Gothic and horror academia. The queerness implied in this 'unnatural reproduction' is symbolised not only as a means of representing sexually transmitted diseases, and a queer historical association with infectiousness via the AIDS epidemic, but also in the sense of a non-normative method of developing queer communities.[18] The infectious and queer communal aspects of the werewolf bite are also recognised by Alison Peirse in her analysis of *Werewolf of London* as an example of the werewolf narrative that lends itself to a presentation of horror and suffering as a masculine, rather than feminine, form. She argues that, in general, werewolf cinema often locates 'fear, trauma and death upon the male body'.[19] The film provides an early example of homoerotic tension in the narrative, which centres on two competing male botanists, Dr Glendon (Henry Hull) and Dr Yogami (Warner Oland), searching for a rare plant, the *mariphasa lupina lumina*. The presentation of 'strange botany' here presents an early link between plant life and werewolfery, as the sap from the plant is rumoured to provide a cure for the affliction. The film opens in Tibet, where Glendon is stalked and later attacked by a shadowy werewolf-like figure, who is later revealed to be Yogami. The attack is swift yet brutal, and is seen by Peirse as an 'animalistic embrace [whose] primitive communion [. . .] conflat[es] the (yet to be revealed) homosexual desires of the two male werewolves with violence'.[20] Peirse remarks on the film's shift away from the typical Gothic homosocial triangle between two men and an implied female love object,[21] and instead sees the film's couples formulating a love *rectangle* between Glendon and Yogami and Glendon's neglected wife Lisa (Valerie Hobson) and Paul (Lester Matthews), Lisa's childhood sweetheart, whose relationship is presented as a 'natural', that is heteronormative, coupling.

The *foreignness* of queer love is further compounded, not only in the film's opening in Tibet, but also by the implied Orientalism of Dr Yogami (often mispronounced in the film as the more Japanese-sounding 'Dr Yokahama'). It is noted by Benshoff that in early Universal horror films, and specifically those with queer subtexts, 'frequently the queer couple is itself an interracial one, a trope that invariably recasts a light/dark racial hierarchy along with a gendered one'.[22] Queerness is further implied in the scenes between Glendon and Yogami via a mirroring of their matching tailored clothing, and their identical symbolic floral buttonholes. There is also a notable physical closeness between the two when conversing and a sense of queer familiarity rings out in the dialogue:

> **Glendon:** Have I met you before sir?
> **Yogami:** Yes, in Tibet, once, but only for a moment in the dark . . .

Later, Yogami is confronted by Glendon as he attempts to steal the flower in the hope that it will have restorative or curative properties to relieve queer-wolfishness. Yogami explains that he yearns to use the flower to 'save two souls tonight' (referring to himself and Glendon). Peirse recognises a further queer echo in the film's dialogue in a none-too-subtle reference to Oscar Wilde's poem 'The Ballad of Reading Gaol' (1898), written after Wilde's imprisonment for gross indecency with another man, and which contains the phrase 'each man kills the thing he loves'.[23] In *Werewolf of London*, the line is further queered by Yogami who exclaims that 'the werewolf instinctively seeks to kill the thing it loves best'.

In the film's denouement, Glendon becomes increasingly desperate to find a cure, given his frequent 'transvection' (as the film puts it) from man to wolf, and the nightly murders that accompany this change. He is led back to his lab and the promise of the flower within. The final erotically charged set piece revolves not around Glendon's supposedly normative desire for Lisa, but instead the entangled desire and homoerotic violence that spills over between him and Yogami. Having transformed into his wolf-man form, Glendon wrestles with Yogami, eventually murdering him, but not before a vicious mauling of his rival's face which reveals that he does indeed kill the thing he loves most.

Phase Two: Outing the Queerwolf

Mark Pirro's *The Curse of the Queerwolf* (1988) is perhaps the first film to make an explicit link between queerness and werewolfery. This arguably homophobic exploitation satire on Universal's *The Wolf Man* features central character Larry Smalbut (Michael Palazzolo), who is bitten on the buttocks during an amorous clinch with a woman. The woman is later revealed to be a cis man cross-dressing and passing as a cis female prostitute; in the film's dated terminology, she is referred to as a 'transvestite'. After suffering recurring nightmares, Larry eventually changes into the queerwolf in a transformation scene that is equal parts offensive and outrageously camp. In a moonlit montage, we see Larry's comically hysterical response to the changes, which include his nails growing longer and becoming magically painted with varnish; typically feminine face make-up (rouge, eye shadow, lipstick) appearing; and his wrists being forced into a supposedly 'limp' position. Topping off the queer satire, a red handkerchief magically emerges from the back pocket of his jeans in a reference to the gay male SM and leather community's 'hanky code' as a means of sexual advertising on the scene. The film pilfers many of the original Universal story tropes but parodies them in a camp riff on queer stereotypes. For example, the Universal film's mythology of werewolf-ism as part of a gypsy curse makes recurring visual references to the sign of the pentagram which appears on the skin of the cursed person. In *Queerwolf* the pentagram is replaced by the 'pansy-gram' described here as a five-pointed flower.

The film is indicative of the many crossover queer comedy horrors that emerged in the late 1980s and 1990s. In such works there is a clear drive to push queer metaphors out of the closet via parodic reference, but as I have written previously,[24] often these remain poorly received exploitation fare (or as I have suggested, *gay*sploitation fare) that can just as easily be seen as queerphobic. This extends to the work of David DeCoteau, a prolific B-movie horror director who began making slasher and creature feature subgenre horror films with the production company Rapid Heart Pictures, which were often marketed as 'horror films for girls'.[25] Only later coming out as a gay man, DeCoteau then retrospectively re-marketed both his back catalogue and his future films for a more explicitly queer audience. His film *The Wolves of Wall Street* (2002) is indicative of his overall style, which often remains suggestively queer, and more homoerotic than outwardly queer. The film sees newbie stockbroker Jeff (William Gregory Lee) getting into his dream job on Wall Street with a trading company called Wolfe Bros, which, unbeknown to him, is a company of werewolves. After plentiful seduction scenes, Jeff is bitten and thus becomes one of a pack of alpha male financial stockbrokers, causing him to disconnect from his heteronormative life of domesticity with his girlfriend; instead, as part of the wolf pack, he indulges in promiscuous nights of debauchery. DeCoteau states of his films that they celebrate the male form and thus extend their appeal both to straight teenage girls and gay/queer men, but in this film the hypermasculine elements of the werewolf figure combine with DeCoteau's disavowal of masculine identities that are non-normative, instead privileging a straight-acting machismo. As such, his films often reveal an effeminaphobia within queer male culture, in their rejection of feminine association or gendered fluidity in favour of a masc.-for-masc. culture.[26]

This presentation of queerness in seemingly 'normative' Gothic film and TV texts leads to instances of queerwolfery that exist on the margins of the narrative.[27] For example, the film *Cursed* (2005), written by the out gay screenwriter Kevin Williamson, features a scene in which the seemingly straight bully Bo (Milo Ventimiglia) outs himself to the film's central character, a nerdy werewolf in disguise named Jimmy (Jesse Eisenberg). In one scene Bo confesses his secret desires for Jimmy, who then empathises with the bully's closeted turmoil and comically draws parallels with werewolfery and queerness often 'feeling like a curse sometimes'. The Gothic serial drama *Penny Dreadful* (Showtime, 2014–16) also features a surprising scene in the episode entitled 'Demimonde' (S1, E4) in which the seemingly straight, but tortured, werewolf figure Ethan (Josh Hartnett) is seduced by Dorian Gray (Reeve Carney). After enjoying an evening of typically masculine pursuits (in a swooning montage set to Wagner's 'Tristan and Isolde: Mild und leise', they are seen drinking, fighting and smoking), the pair proceed to have passionate absinthe-induced sex. Despite Ethan's alpha-male coding throughout the series, it is revealed in a later episode ('Possession', S1, E7) by Ethan's female love interest Vanessa Ives (Eva Green) that Ethan was the submissive partner in his queer encounter with Gray. This revelation perhaps connects to the ongoing concern in queer culture and queer horror of 'top/bottom' power relations, in that exposing Ethan as the 'bottom' in their sexual encounter offers a subversion of his traditional 'Western' dominant/active male persona. The show shies away from explicitly depicting the penetrative sex act and seems to be aware of the stigma for some men in *being* penetrated. As Leo Bersani states in his influential article, 'Is the Rectum a Grave?': 'to be penetrated is to abdicate power',[28] and so the penetrated subject in gay sex is traditionally seen as passive and, therefore, often associated with shameful femininity. The show perhaps echoes this same aversion to displaying anal sex between men in alluding to the act in the dialogue in a later episode. However, Ethan's stereotypical hypermasculine cowboy, borrowed from the Western genre, is undercut by his predilection for engaging in queer sex acts 'doggy style' in a pun on his canine alter ego.

The inclusion of queer characters and queerwolf content has in recent years emerged in the reboot of the 1980s franchise *Teen Wolf* (MTV, 2011–17) and the spin-off series from *The Vampire Diaries* (The CW, 2009–17), *The Originals* (The CW, 2013–17). There is something to be said about the use of queer sympathetic monsters in such mainstream popular Gothic dramas that are largely aimed at teen and young adult audiences. Despite the shows' links to queer screenwriters (they are all connected to Kevin Williamson), there is arguably an element of *queer-baiting* here both in the casting of (often) straight actors in queer roles and in the trajectory of queer romance that is seen to be ill-fated, thus giving rise to the 'bury your gays' cultural phenomenon of recent years.[29]

Phase Three: Who's Who at the Zoo?

In terms of an explicit 'outing' of the queerwolf figure, Will Gould's *The Wolves of Kromer* (1998) is a low-budget and self-aware fairy tale/ Gothic drama adapted from Charles Lambert's theatrical play. The central narrative focuses on a group of itinerant 'wolves' who are marginalised on the outskirts of the middle-class fishing village of Kromer. The presentation of werewolfery is rendered even more ironic in that the film features a remarkably stagey costume for its queerwolves. Here, elaborate fur coats, complete with furry tails, are loosely worn over the queerwolves' bare chests. However, despite its queer focus, the depiction of queerwolves in Gould's film remains somewhat problematic in the central metaphor of gay/queer men as an ostracised and oppressed 'species'. The central narrative revolves around the tormented love affair between neophyte queerwolf Seth (Lee Williams) and the more experienced Gabriel (James Layton). In an early confessional scene, Seth confides in Gabriel about his coming out as werewolf to his parents:

> **Seth:** They'd always suspected. Mum used to tell me to tuck my tail into my shorts, and Dad used to always tell jokes about 'boys like me'. It's like they'd just hoped it would go away . . . It was a full moon. I just couldn't help myself. I'd locked the door, but they burst in and found me in all my glory. Fur, tail, claws – the lot! I was holding a copy of *Wolf Weekly*. Dad laughed. Mum just sat down and cried.

Despite their initial chemistry, they eventually split up when the bisexual Seth has an affair with a girl from the local town. Seth later returns to the queerwolf den, set up as a makeshift home for the pair, to quarrel with Gabriel over his stifling desire for monogamy. Seth confronts his lover with the painful truth: 'Can you smell her on me? Your little Seth's gone out and fucked a girl. Your little Seth's realised what he's been missing . . . This is what being a man's about isn't it?' The film is perhaps one of the first to begin to use the queerwolf figure as a commentary on monogamous versus promiscuous stereotypes within the queer community, positing Seth as a young queerwolf whose desire is to experience both the wolf scene and the human scene in all their pleasures, and not be restricted to homosexual male romance alone. Gould's film and its presentation of problematic queerwolves walks a line between demonstrating the pride/shame in coming out as queerwolf amid pressures in the queer male community to exhibit traditional masculine tropes, and the gay community's denial of bisexuality or pansexuality which here is seen to be duplicitous.

The film paves the way for more recent representations of the queerwolf metaphor to symbolise fractures within the queer community that reject dominant hegemonic representations of queerness that are often associated with unreal ideals of masculinity and normativity. *Der Samurai* (*The Samurai*) (2014) is a fantasy horror film located in a closed-off community in the woods of a rural German suburb that is terrorised by a bloodthirsty wolf. The central protagonist Jakob (Michel Diercks) is a closeted young policeman who attempts to ensnare the animal by luring it into a trap with large chunks of bloody meat hanging from branches in the woods. Jakob is also repeatedly tormented by a local biker gang who taunt him as ineffectual and make homophobic slurs. Here the 'wolf' that Jakob pursues is depicted as a manifestation of his own repressed queer desires and anxieties. Interestingly though, the wolf-figure is visualised as a queer amalgam of a blonde, long-haired, cis-male, dress-wearing and blade-wielding samurai (Pit Bukowski) who *also* transforms into a wild animal. In the film's denouement, it is eventually revealed that the erotic pursuit of the queerwolf is not entirely real, but a projection of the hated part of Jakob's inner desires and queerness as he and the queerwolf are parts of the same person. In a poetic but rather obvious metaphor, the shame Jakob feels leads him to stalk and slice the queerwolf to bits in the woods in an act that can be interpreted either as an attempt to remove the effeminate 'Otherness' he sees inside himself, or as an excising of the shame that such harmful queer depictions represent.

In more hysterically camp fashion, Tim Sullivan's short film *I Was a Teenage Werebear!* (2013) also depicts the emergence of the queerwolf as an acceptance of repressed homosexuality. *Werebear* takes inspiration from the beach blanket/party films of the 1950s, while revisiting the trend for teen/youth problem films of the same era. The more outlandish of these, *I Was a Teenage Werewolf* (1957) and *I Was a Teenage Frankenstein* (1957), merged Universal Pictures' horrors of the 1930s with the teen-problem film. *Werebear!* follows a newly transferred high school student, Ricky (gay porn star Brent Corrigan), as he battles with his repressed homosexual 'urges', torn between fitting into the conformist group (a gang of wrestling jocks) and the alluring and dangerous biker-coded outsiders led by the appropriately monikered Talon (Anton Troy). Ricky is a curious blend of James Dean's Jim Stark from *Rebel Without a Cause* (1955), clad in a red bomber jacket and even borrowing the famed, and now campy, 'You're tearing me apart!' line from Ray's original film, and *High School Musical*'s Troy Bolton (Zac Efron), complete with floppy-fringed brown hair, naïve demeanour and ability to burst into song.

After a car accident with his girlfriend, Ricky is saved by Talon, and the young teen begins to fall in with Talon's group, developing feelings for the blonde-coiffed leader. Ricky is then warned by the school's nurse, a heavy-accented, stereotypical gypsy-type (played by *Insidious*'s Lin Shaye) to 'stay away from those *animules*'. Nurse Palava recounts an old saying: 'Even a boy that thinks he is straight, yet shaves his balls by night, may become a *Vere*-bear when the hormones rage and the latent urge takes flight.' The curse causes those afflicted to transform into hirsute, werewolf-faced leather daddies when aroused. Talon eventually transforms into a werebear and his crew also turn into rotund, beefy werebears wearing leather studded harnesses and black leather caps. Talon later confronts Ricky, encouraging him to come to terms with his own true nature, and asks him whether 'the bite put the beast in you? Or let it out?' Sullivan's film clearly follows the outrageously comic, performative trend of Gaysploitation Horror and does so in order to remark on the, often exclusive, nature of LGBTQ+ subcultures. The film pokes fun at the established and now clichéd leather scene, but also at other emergent subcultures such as 'Bear culture' and the various subdivisions therein.[30]

In terms of its queer erotic lure, there is a long-standing consideration of certain types of masculinity being foregrounded in relation to the werewolf figure. I have written in the past about the celebration of hypermasculinity in the form of gay daddy types in Queer Horror and, unsurprisingly, the representation of queerwolves also celebrates, albeit problematically, the same hypermasculine traits and tropes and hegemonic masculinity. The recent explosion of queer erotic horror fiction, particularly those subgenres involving 'Shifter Romance', 'MMM Erotica' and 'MPREG Romance', clearly points towards a privileging of largely white, athletically muscular, and often hairless male bodies associated with werewolfery.[31] Subgenres also extend to the fetishisation of more mature, somewhat hirsute 'daddy' types in queerwolf fiction and I want now to consider the, often satirical, depictions of such hypermasculine lupine paternal figures in queerwolf horror and horror comedy.

Phase Four: Wolf-Daddies, Alphas and Queer Pack Mentality

> Men are not gentle creatures who want to be loved [...] they are, on the contrary, creatures among whose instinctual endowments is to be reckoned a powerful share of aggressiveness ... *Homo homini lupus*. [Man is a wolf to man.] (Freud, *Civilisation and its Discontents*)[32]

The recurring narrative tropes in male werewolf texts have often been analysed by academics such as Reynold Humphries as 'castration anxiety' allegories,[33] and these are often born out of connections to Freud's extensive work on castration anxiety, which he later developed in relation to the 'Wolf Man' case in *A History of an Infantile Neurosis* (1918). Freud summarises that for his patient Sergei Pankejeff: 'it was his father at whose hands he feared castration'.[34] Freud's case study centres around a dream from his patient's (whom he names the Wolf Man) childhood in which he sees outside his bedroom window a large tree, in the branches of which sit several white wolves. Freud elaborates on this dream as a symbolic reinterpretation of the traumatic primal scene. He posits that the child had previously witnessed his parents having penetrative sex *a tergo* (from behind) and understood the sex act as traumatic. Throughout the case history, Freud outlines the oscillating identification with his patient's love for and fear of the father as both the victim of and later the exacter of symbolic castration. For Freud, the case study provides a clear study of *neurotically conflicted* male homosexuality whereby the subject 'expresses a feminine tenderness, a readiness to renounce manliness if in return one can be loved as a woman'.[35] He continues that 'from the time of the dream onwards he was unconsciously homosexual'.[36]

In the 'Gay Daddy' chapter of *Homos*, Leo Bersani reconfigures Freud's reading. The Wolf Man's repressed sexual desire for his father and its displacement into threats of castration are reconsidered as a 'genealogy of gay love'. Bersani argues that

> The appeal of the muscular, mature male figure – the Gay Daddy – is complexly tied up with both the frisson of masochistic desire for the punishing, castrating male-father-figure and remarkably tender paternal feelings for Freud's dreaded castrating father.[37]

Following Bersani's queer reinterpretation of Freud's admittedly homophobic case study of the Wolf Man, we can see a running theme in male queerwolf narratives that foreground a gay were-daddy or werebear figure, whereby there is a fascination, albeit satirised, with traditional masculinity (that is, hypermasculine, muscular, dominating, paternal and mature). The male queerwolf body is, at times, overly hirsute in both human and wolf-form and, at others, tends towards a brawny (but hairless) physique.

Produced by Here TV, the queer Gothic soap-drama *The Lair* (2007–09) features an example of the gay daddy/younger male dichotomous relationship that is stereotypically depicted in queer male culture, and does so via the queerwolf figure. Set in a remote Pacific coastal town, the plot revolves around an S/M nightclub which is run entirely by queer male vampires. The show's appropriation of Gothic tropes operates as a satire on stereotypical gay male types. There is a multiplicity of Others here: a cabal of vampires, a murdered vengeful spirit, a male gorgon and a young transient gay werewolf. The town's local law enforcer Sheriff Trout (played by the muscular daddy-type gay porn star Colton Ford) falls in love with Ian (Matty Ferraro), a homeless young drifter, failing to see that he is harbouring a young werewolf who is guilty of killing several innocent civilians across town. The casting of Ford as the hirsute alpha daddy-style Sheriff draws on his porn superstar status as one of the industry's most successful 'tops' and, when set alongside Ferraro's stereotypically younger, smoother, twink-like physique, the show offers a comment on the strong lure of the fetishisation of the twink/daddy imagery in queer male culture.

Such a depiction is more comically parodied in the comedy horror *Faux Paws* (Doug Bari, 2013), which centres on queerwolf couple Brian (Brian Wimer) and Doug (Doug Bari). The film offers a more ludicrously excessive example of a queer generation-gap relationship, with Doug clearly the older partner in the pair. However, the romance is less erotically represented in that Doug and Brian are visually lampooned as unkempt, hippy slackers. The couple escape from a borderline imprisoned existence on a lycanthropic 'reservation', to embark on a road trip across the US to find freedom in Maine, the only state with a sanctioned tolerance of werewolves. The film is a micro-budget road trip comedy, which riffs on the queerwolf couple's coming-out to their family during an overnight full-moon stopover, all the while attempting to elude the law and the werewolf bounty hunters on their *tail*.[38]

Two other short films also feature queerwolf narratives that demonstrate a developing satirical take on the queerwolf/human couple, with both offering a comic horror take on the problematic monogamous relationship between two gay men, one of whom is a queerwolf, driven by a promiscuous lupine drive, and the other a human, who is monogamous, homonormative and takes up a caring role. Karina Farek's animated short *Dirty Paws* (2015) features Aldo (Brian Perry) and his werewolf partner Skelly (Tyler Nolan) preparing themselves for the full-moon night ahead. Aldo is shown chaining Skelly to the radiator in their spare room, preventing him from acting on his carnal desires in the hope that he will not harm anyone. However, once transformed into wolf-form, Skelly escapes and is tracked down by his partner after he finds the carcass of a neighbourhood cat. Upon being scolded for his behaviour, Skelly is running for comfort into the arms of his lover when suddenly his paw is brutally caught in a hidden bear trap. The short ends with Aldo wrapping his queerwolf lover's injured paw in bandages, and the pair lie on their bed, spooning together to pass the rest of the night. This sweet finale clearly marks out queer love's shift towards homonormativity, in that there is a mapping of heteronormative standards of marriage, monogamy, property, propriety and capitalism on to the, now assimilated, queer couple.

Mia-Kate Russell's self-proclaimed 'first gay priest werewolf film' *Swallow* (2014) centres on ex-priest Jim (Kevin Dee), who has found love in the 'big city' with his boyfriend, the more urbane Tom (Jay Bowen), who also happens to be a queerwolf. The couple return home for the weekend to the small backwater Australian town, as Tom puts it 'in the middle of bum-poke nowhere', that Jim had left years before. Jim's departure left the devout Christian locals there without a priest or church to depend on, much to their annoyance. Coming to terms with revisiting such an oppressive and homophobic setting, Jim and Tom attempt to befriend their grotesque, bigoted neighbours Patti (Lulu McClatchy) and Macka (Drew Hobbs) in order to assimilate back into the community. It being a full-moon weekend, Jim chains Tom up in the pastor's pergola to prevent him from feeding once he is transformed.

However, once Patti and Macka discover that Jim is gay, they burst in on their queer neighbours, armed with a shotgun and demanding answers. Finding his lover Tom tied up, they assume Jim is also practising queer bondage. The confrontation meets a premature end when Tom transforms into his queerwolf form and kills and feeds on the homophobic couple. The short ends with Jim chastising his beastly partner for the mess the evisceration has made in their home: 'You see, this is why I don't go out in public with you, honestly Tom, look at this place, I've just had it cleaned, look at the state of mom's rug!' Again, the short follows the typical depiction of the queer male couple attempting to assimilate into domesticated, small-town life, which brings discomfort to Tom, who finds the possibility of a normative, monogamous lifestyle stifling. His desire for flesh, and a non-monogamous life, is symbolised satirically in his werewolfery.

Final Phase: Transitioning, Transforming and the Transness of the Werewolf

Finally, I want to offer a consideration of the usefulness of the queerwolf metaphor, particularly the spectacle of transformation, as a strong identification point for transgender spectators. Indeed, this is especially resonant for those trans individuals whose bodies are felt to be outside of their own control, particularly trans men who may still be experiencing monthly menstrual cycles, and those trans individuals whose transitioning can often be painful and disjointed across time. Caitlin B. Giacopasi's work 'The Werewolf Pride Movement: A Step Back from Queer Medieval Tradition' poses an interesting question that clearly relates to the experience of the trans individual. She asks of the werewolf subject:

> When an individual's species is in constant flux, how can its representation of gender and sexuality remain static? [. . .] Beyond the restrictions of humanity, the werewolf could publicly act and desire in ways which the average man could only dream.[39]

In Zigarovich's collection *Transgothic in Literature and Culture,* Ardel Haefele-Thomas's analysis of three nineteenth-century werewolf tales also points towards the queer potential of the werewolf at the intersection of sexuality, bestiality and transanimality. Zigarovich summarises Haefele-Thomas's championing of the werewolf as a trans representation of 'the constant shift – or migrations – of the boundaries between locations, genders, and species'.[40] The werewolf's transformation, though at times predictable, also suggests a continual process of 'becoming' that perhaps finds parallels in the queer subjective experience. Drawn from posthumanist feminist Rosi Braidotti's work, which itself draws on Deleuze and Guattari's *A Thousand Plateaus,* 'becoming' designates a non-static structure, a repeated performance of gender that allows for the expression of an 'authentic' gendered self declared by the subject themselves, rather than from cultural binaries imposed upon them.[41] The concept of 'becoming' here also reveals instances where gender identity may be unclear, fluid, contradictory and, at times, malleable.

In 'Like and Lycanthropy', Tim Stafford discusses the shift in recent representations of the erotic spectacle of male werewolf transformations, setting out a difference between what he calls the 'Old Pack' and the 'New Pack'.[42] For Stafford, 'Old Pack' werewolf transformations are characterised by a raw, painful and clearly masochistic spectacle, and examples here range from the iconic *An American Werewolf in London* (Landis, 1981) to *The Company of Wolves* (Jordan, 1984). The collapsing of pain/pleasure that is visualised in the skin ripping, contorted bodily distortions and bone-cracking bestial deformations is precisely the voyeuristic desire required by the cinematic spectator of the horror film. Here, the body is caught in the throes of ecstatic suffering, of inside turning outside, and clearly resonates with Linda Williams's work on what she calls 'Body Genres', demonstrating the embodiment of both pornographic spectacle and erotic pain/pleasure.[43]

The 'New Pack' wolves are seen by Stafford to be more in control of the time, place and method of their transformations. There is more of an emphasis on a 'wolf-gift' rather than a 'wolf-curse', whereby the New Pack wolves can be seen as extensions of the superhero figure. Stafford comments that the human form of the New Pack can almost always be recognised by their normative, usually white male, traditionally attractive, lean, muscular and hairless bodies. Their shift from human to wolf is often seen as swift and painless, and transformations do not occur unsolicited and can be performed almost on demand. The New Pack wolves often formulate a pack dynamic that is in stark contrast to the lonely, painful isolation represented in the Old Pack.[44]

As such, the New Pack wolves can be seen as a queer metaphor for the relative ease with which one's own queerness can be openly declared within a largely accepting Western culture, in that 'coming out' as queer is not understood to be as marginalising an act as it once was. Moreover, perhaps, the New Pack wolves can be argued to represent the concept of essentialism in that they do not dwell upon the liminal aspects of werewolf transformation in as tortured a way as the Old Pack depictions. The emphasis here is on the whole and coherent bodily visualisation of either/or, human/wolf. One could argue that this visual binary runs the risk of returning to a more essentialist gendered binary that some more liminal, drawn-out and visceral werewolf transformations have the potential to challenge. The New Pack wolves, then, can be seen to offer a more positive depiction of transformation for trans spectators, one that is not bound up with the voyeuristic spectacle of bodily change, pain and suffering. Yet the Old Pack wolves' problematic objectification of the transformation sequence not only illustrates bodily-centred pain but a cultural struggle too, clearly felt by trans people. More often than not, the Old Pack werewolf transformation sequence wrongly fetishises the non-body or interstitial space as Othered and monstrous which, despite the potential for sympathetic identification, might also be another reminder of painful stigmatisation for queer and trans spectators.

In conclusion, I want to return to Mann's comprehensive study of the representation of the werewolf in film and television. He states that the werewolf film must be understood 'not just in terms of the beast within, but also the beast without, that is, a cultural understanding of the lupine creature as a product of its times'.[45] While queerness and monstrosity have long been interwoven, the contemporary embrace of the horror genre by LGBTQ+ producers and spectators alike over the past twenty years has led to multiple queer reinterpretations of the werewolf in films that embrace '[the werewolf's] identity disrupting hybridity, as well as its atavistic, and thus disallowable sexuality'.[46]

Notes

1. Excerpt from Allen Ginsberg's poem 'Howl', in *Howl and Other Poems* (San Francisco: City Lights, 1956).
2. Darren Elliott-Smith, *Queer Horror Film and Television: Sexuality and Masculinity at the Margins* (London: I.B. Tauris, 2016), p. 14.
3. Chantal Bourgault du Coudray, *The Curse of the Werewolf: Fantasy, Horror and the Beast Within* (London: Bloomsbury Academic, 2006); Phillip A. Bernhardt-House, 'The Werewolf as Queer, the Queer as Werewolf, and Queer Werewolves', in *Queering the Non/Human*, ed. Noreen Giffney and Myra J. Hird (Abingdon: Routledge, 2008), pp. 159–84; Barbara Creed, *Phallic Panic: Film, Horror and the Primal Uncanny* (Melbourne: Melbourne University Press, 2005), pp. 96–153; Craig Ian Mann, *Phases of the Moon: A Cultural History of the Werewolf Film* (Edinburgh: Edinburgh University Press, 2020).
4. Mann, *Phases of the Moon*, p. 1.
5. Anne Billson, 'The Werewolf Howls Again', *The Guardian*, 5 February 2020, p. 7.
6. Mann, *Phases of the Moon*, p. 2.
7. Ibid., p. 2.
8. Bernhardt-House, 'The Werewolf as Queer', pp. 159, 165.
9. Marisa Mercurio, 'Queer Moon Rising: Introducing the Werewolf Reread', *Ancillary Review of Books*, https://ancillaryreviewofbooks.org/2020/10/31/queer-moon-rising-introducing-the-werewolf-reread/ (accessed 8 February 2022).
10. Ibid.
11. See, for example, Elliott-Smith, *Queer Horror Film and Television*, and 'Revolting Queers: The Southern Gothic in Queer Horror Film and Television', in *Queering the South on Screen*, ed. Tison Pugh (Athens, GA: University of Georgia Press, 2020), pp. 88–112.
12. Mercurio, 'Queer Moon Rising'.
13. Barbara Creed, 'Ginger Snaps: The Monstrous Feminine as *femme animale*', in *She-Wolf: A Cultural History of Female Werewolves*, ed. Hannah Priest (Manchester: Manchester University Press, 2015), pp. 180–95.
14. Mann, *Phases of the Moon*, p. 2.

15. Creed, *Phallic Panic*, p. 140.
16. Bernhardt-House, 'The Werewolf as Queer', p. 159.
17. See examples ranging from Universal's 'Wolf Man' franchise (1941–2006), Hammer's period-set *The Curse of the Werewolf* (1961), the US cycle of werewolf films in the 1970s including *Werewolf of Washington* (1973), through to the resurgence of popularity in werewolf cinema in the 1980s from John Landis's *An American Werewolf in London* (1981) to Joe Dante's *The Howling* (1981) and the adaptation of Stephen King's *Silver Bullet* (1985).
18. See, for example, Ellis Hanson, 'Undead', in *Inside/Out: Lesbian Theories, Gay Theories*, ed. Diana Fuss (London: Routledge, 1991), pp. 324–40; and Darren Elliott-Smith, '"Death is the New Pornography!": Gay Zombies, Homonormativity and Consuming Masculinity in Queer Horror', in *Screening the Undead: Vampires and Zombies in Film and Television*, ed. Leon Hunt, Sharon Lockyer and Milly Williamson (London: I.B. Tauris, 2014), pp. 148–70. Both argue that the monstrous metaphor of queerness folds in anxieties about the AIDS epidemic and its impact on queer communities.
19. Alison Peirse, *After Dracula: The 1930s Horror Film* (London: I.B. Tauris, 2013), p. 156.
20. Ibid., p. 156.
21. Eve Kosofsky Sedgwick, *Between Men: English Literature and Male Homosocial Desire* (New York: Columbia University Press, 1985).
22. Harry M. Benshoff, *Monsters in the Closet: Homosexuality and the Horror Film* (Manchester: Manchester University Press, 1997), p. 59.
23. Oscar Wilde, *The Ballad of Reading Gaol* (New York: Brentanos, 1906 [1898]), p. 3, cited in Peirse, *After Dracula*, p. 168.
24. Elliott-Smith, *Queer Horror Film and Television*, p. 89.
25. Taken from the Region 1 import DVD jacket for *Voodoo Academy* (2000).
26. In *Queer Horror Film and TV*, pp. 111–35, I discuss the work of Gaysploitation directors at length for the various ways that their representation of gay masculinity often borrows and plays with depictions of 'straight-acting' masculinity as authentically erotic for the queer male viewer.
27. Here I want to define these normative queer wolf films as texts aimed at cis-normative, largely heterosexual mainstream audiences.
28. Leo Bersani, 'Is the Rectum a Grave?', *October*, 43 (1987), p. 212.
29. 'Bury Your Gays' is a concept that has emerged from Gothic/queer literature and contemporary film and television drama. It entered popular culture as a result of the critical and fan-based reaction to the death of a queer character in the TV series *The 100*. The concept refers to the use of a queer relationship in order to hook queer audiences, only to then result in the death of one or more of the same queer characters. See James McConnaughy, 'What Led to Lexa: A Look at the History of Media Burying Its Gays', *The Mary Sue*, 26 March 2016, https://www.themarysue.com/lexa-bury-your-gays/ (accessed 16 May 2017).
30. Arguably, the first use of the term 'Bear culture' was by George Mazzei in his article 'Who's Who at the Zoo?', *The Advocate*, 26 July 1979. Illustrated by long-time *Advocate* illustrator and cartoonist Gerard P. Donelan, the article also categorises other gay men and lesbians as types of animals in

the zoo. Interestingly, 'Wolves' are included in the categorisation of erotic 'types' within masculinist queer culture. 'Bears' tend to be hairy and large; 'Wolves', on the other hand, are usually hairy too, but slimmer and more defined.
31. MMM Erotic is defined as featuring male/male/male group sex, MPREG refers to male pregnancy romantic fiction, and Shifters/Gay Shifters takes in the wider gamut of werewolves, were-panthers, were-bears, were-cats and shape-shifting humans. See, for example, the self-published titles Reese Corgan, *Red Wolves* (2015) and Krishna Brooks, *A Coyote Among Wolves: Shifter Snacks Gay Menage* (2016); the subgenre of Alpha Gay Werewolf and Wolf-Daddy erotica includes Sy Walker's *Daddy Wolf* (2016) and Guzmasboi's *My Werewolf Daddy* (2016).
32. Sigmund Freud, 'Civilisation and its Discontents', in *Penguin Freud Library 12: Civilisation, Society and Religion*, ed. Angela Richards (London: Penguin, 1991 [1930/31]), p. 302.
33. Reynold Humphries, *The American Horror Film: An Introduction* (Edinburgh: Edinburgh University Press, 2002), p. 21.
34. See, for example, Sigmund Freud, 'The History of an Infantile Neurosis', in *The 'Wolfman' and Other Cases* (London: Penguin, 2002 [1918]), p. 284.
35. Ibid., p. 282.
36. Ibid., p. 263.
37. Leo Bersani, *Homos* (Cambridge, MA: Harvard University Press, 1995), p. 111.
38. The film makes a clear reference to the emerging legalisation of same-sex marriage in 2012 across several US states including Maine, Maryland and Washington (this was, of course, before the Supreme Court ruling in 2015 that required all states to honour same-sex marriage). Prior to this, same-sex marriage had been legalised in Massachusetts in 2004, in California in 2008 and in Iowa in 2009.
39. Caitlin B. Giacopasi, 'The Werewolf Pride Movement: A Step Back from Queer Medieval Tradition', *Theses*, paper 4 (2011), http://scholarship.shu.edu/theses/4 (accessed 8 February 2022).
40. Jolene Zigarovich, 'Introduction', in *Transgothic in Literature and Culture*, ed. Jolene Zigarovich (New York: Routledge, 2018), p. 11. Haefele-Thomas's chapter, '"That Dreadful Thing That Looked Like a Beautiful Girl": Trans Anxiety/Trans Possibility in Three Late Victorian Werewolf Tales', pp. 97–116, discusses the impact of colonial masculinity, Christianity and homosociality on the werewolf figure, by focusing on three texts: Rudyard Kipling's 'The Mark of the Beast' (1890), Clemence Housman's 'The Were-Wolf' (1890) and Eric Stenbock's 'The Other Side: A Breton Legend' (1893).
41. Rosi Braidotti, *The Posthuman* (Malden, MA: Polity, 2013); Gilles Deleuze and Félix Guattari, *A Thousand Plateaus: Capitalism and Schizophrenia*, trans. Brian Massumi (London: Bloomsbury, 1980).
42. Tim Stafford, 'Like and Lycanthropy: The New Pack Werewolf According to Tyler, Tyler and Taylor', in *New Queer Horror Film and Television*, ed. Darren Elliott-Smith and John Edgar Browning (Cardiff: University of Wales Press, 2020), pp. 169–88.
43. Linda Williams, 'Film Bodies: Gender, Genre, and Excess', *Film Quarterly*, 44.4 (1991), pp. 2–13.

44. Stafford's examples of New Pack wolves include those featured in MTV's *Teen Wolf* (2011–17), Hugh Jackman's *Van Helsing* (Sommers, 2004), Alcide (Joe Manganiello) from *True Blood* (HBO, 2008–14) and the shape-shifting wolves from the *Twilight Saga* films (2008–12).
45. Mann, *Phases of the Moon*, p. 10.
46. Mercurio, 'Queer Moon Rising'.

Chapter 9

'Spectrality is in part a mode of historicity': Representations of Spectrality in Queer Historiography and Contemporary Fiction

Paulina Palmer

Spectrality, as well as being a key topic in contemporary queer fiction, including texts with a lesbian, male gay and transgender focus, features prominently in queer historiography, as Carla Freccero illustrates in her study *Queer/Early/Modern*. She employs the topic metaphorically in order to explore the episodic appearances of queer sexuality in earlier centuries – what she describes as 'a particular (and partially imagined) traumatic past' creating a '"hauntology", a spectral approach to an ethico-historical situation'.[1] In addition to acknowledging, like Jack Halberstam, the 'demand [for recognition], a demand to which we must somehow respond' that the queer people who lived in earlier historical periods make on us, she recognises, like George Haggerty, the difficulties that researchers can encounter in investigating their lives and circumstances.[2]

In discussing these problems, Freccero refers to some of the contradictions and ambiguities that queer history can sometimes present to researchers. Records of the lives of upper-class individuals who lived relatively recently, such as Oscar Wilde, Radcliffe Hall and Anne Lister, are, of course, available, although the fact that Lister wrote her diary in a complex code indicates her fear of discovery and, before the code was deciphered, posed problems for readers. There is, however, a significant amount of information from the past that remains lost, especially that relevant to women and the working classes, many of whom, as well as frequently seeking to conceal their sexuality, lacked literacy skills. Historians and critics writing in the period of the Gay Liberation Movement that emerged in the 1960s acknowledged, in fact, the sense of loss that the ignorance of queer history can evoke in people living today. Whereas Gabriele Griffin, writing in 1993, lamented 'the sense expressed by many lesbians that they have no sustained history written by themselves' but feel that they are living in a temporal vacuum, Martha

Vicinus observes that 'The most important and controversial questions [relating to queer history] concern the origins of an individual and group identity.'[3] She urges fellow historians and historiographers to focus their energies on trying to answer them.

The demand voiced by Vicinus that we need to prioritise the discussion of queer history has received a positive response. However, although historiography is now recognised as a key branch of queer studies, historiographers continue to encounter problems. These frequently hinge, as Haggerty argues, on the model they choose to employ in their research. Questioning their utilisation of a 'developmental' model that assumes the growth of queer activity and culture as continuing in a relatively unbroken line from one period to the next, he praises instead the 'cycles of salience' model that Valerie Traub and Freccero both employ.[4] Traub's innovative study *The Renaissance of Lesbianism in Early Modern England*, as well as introducing the reader to a number of interesting events and personages from the sixteenth and seventeenth centuries, vividly demonstrates that the history of lesbianism, 'rather than developing in an unbroken line linking the past to the present', as the 'developmental' model of research implies, tends, on the contrary, to appear episodically, 'emerging at certain moments, silently disappearing from view and then re-emerging in another guise ... as social preoccupations come in and out of context'.[5] Freccero too prioritises a cycle of salience model, constructing it, as described above, on the concept of spectrality. The utilisation of spectrality as a metaphor for the queer inhabitants of the past is, she argues, appropriate, since 'ghostliness and homosexuality have a long history of association'.[6] In addition to citing as an example 'the clichéd and homophobic phrase "the spectre of homosexuality"' which implies that 'the spectre is always lurking in an alley or a bush waiting to pounce on some unsuspecting innocents', she refers to the way in which 'Derrida defines the spectre in terms strikingly reminiscent of homosexual panic, the sense of a not-quite-visible contaminating near-presence that is also an anxious often paranoid projection ...'[7] Terry Castle's discussion of the lesbian's 'apparitional' history is, as Freccero observes, also relevant to the discussion of queer historiography.[8] Castle describes how, as a result of heterosexist society's efforts to exorcise the threat of same-sex female desire, the lesbian became reduced in nineteenth-century fiction to a mere immaterial ghost effect. Referring to the lesbian's 'literary history of derealization', she ironically asks, 'What better way to exorcise the threat of lesbianism than by treating it as ghostly?'[9]

Another strategy, besides engaging in historiographical research, that writers frequently employ in order to access and investigate queer history is, of course, writing creative fiction. In taking this route, they frequently utilise, like Freccero, the topic of spectrality as a vehicle to explore and imaginatively reconstruct episodes from the queer past. Freccero's study *Queer/Early/Modern* furnishes an illuminating context for their discussion. Themes to which she refers, including the tendency of queer people living today to feel haunted by earlier generations, the desire they experience to contact them – even if indirectly – and the sense of 'accountability' they feel they owe them, all feature in these texts. Novels and stories treating topics of this kind include Jeannine Allard's *Légende*, Rebecca S. Buck's *Ghosts of Winter*, Jameson Currier's 'The Country House' and Rosie Garland's *The Night Brother*. Ranging in publication date from the early 1980s to the present day, these works differ radically in storyline, location and, of course, reference to spectrality. The writings of Freccero and other historiographers and theorists furnish, as we shall see, a productive context for their analysis.

Queer Historical Fiction: Jeannine Allard, *Légende: The Story of Philippa and Aurélie*

Works of queer historical fiction published in the past fifty years differ significantly in tone and perspective. Although some are positive in emphasis, others tend to be melancholy. The latter exemplify the kind of writing that, as Jack Halberstam describes, instead of celebrating 'the plucky queer as heroic freedom fighter', as suits the concept of 'gay pride', focuses instead 'on embracing the lonely, the defeated and the melancholic formulations of selfhood' by foregrounding themes of 'longing and loss'.[10] He defends these texts, praising them for creating 'a model of queer history that is . . . resigned to contradictory and complicit narratives' and relevant to earlier generations.[11] Freccero also endorses them, arguing that 'The melancholic model is a response to trauma – the trauma of historicity when "those who are buried will return to haunt us"'.[12] Allard's *Légende: The Story of Philippa and Aurélie*, the earliest published of the four fictional texts that I discuss, though referring on occasion to positive events, on the whole exemplifies the melancholy perspective endorsed by Halberstam and Freccero.

Allard published *Légende* in 1984, the period when different forms of genre fiction, including Gothic fantasy, were beginning to influence lesbian and male gay narratives, supplementing the realist-style texts popular in earlier years. Although some critics opposed this development, rejecting genre fiction as meretricious, others, such as Helen Carr, welcomed it, emphasising the scope for invention that experimentation with different literary forms can promote.[13] Allard too takes advantage of it. She utilises the Gothic mode to create a narrative emphasising the sense of isolation that Aurélie and Philippa, the two lesbian lovers living in a nineteenth-century Normandy, whose story she recounts, frequently experience. Her novel recalls in this respect the plea voiced by the historiographer Heather Love that we 'look on the dark side' of queer history and avoid 'describing it in idealising terms'.[14] Love insists that, instead of ignoring the difficulties that queer people living in earlier centuries experienced, we need to acknowledge and investigate them.

Aurélie, the teenage protagonist of Allard's novel, is portrayed as in certain respects an outsider, since, instead of living by the sea where the majority of the villagers dwell, she resides with her mother on the headland above. Her father and brother are both dead, having been drowned in a storm at sea. The villagers, many of whom are Roman Catholic, regard Aurélie's mother nervously, suspecting her of engaging in witchcraft due to the visits that she makes to the menhirs, a group of ancient standing stones originating from a pagan era. Aurélie herself, on visiting them, regards them as resembling 'massive grey giants'.[15] The uncanny interrelation of different periods, ancient and present-day, that the site evokes fascinates her, for, as Ryan Trimm observes, 'The spectral quality of landscape, one bringing the past into the present ... destabilizes time'.[16] Aurélie's awareness of 'the whispers of those who stood watch' and her recognition that 'the whispers were meant for me'[17] recall Freccero's reference to queer spectrality signifying a 'fantastic model of an otherness struggling to emerge within and sometimes against the self'.[18]

When, on returning home, Aurélie mentions her visit to the menhirs, her mother makes no comment. Several weeks later, however, shortly before her death, she reveals to Aurélie the prophecy relating to her future that she received from them: 'You will marry "one from the north, a foreigner".'[19] However, instead of using the masculine form *étranger*, she unexpectedly employs the feminine *étrangère*. Although Aurélie initially regards this as a slip of the tongue, on later forming a relationship with Philippa she recognises its significance.

Philippa's history differs significantly from Aurélie's. Whereas Aurélie resembles her mother in being associated with the countryside, Philippa has connections with the sea. An orphan with a British father, she was raised in a convent in St Malo but, resisting becoming a nun, left on becoming an adult. Recognising the need to earn a living, she dressed in male attire and, renaming herself Philippe, took a job as a deckhand on one of the ships in the port. She enjoys life at sea and, watching the wake of the ship and the gulls wheeling above it, admits that she 'felt at peace'.[20] Some weeks later, however, when a storm unexpectedly erupts, the ship founders and she is washed up on the nearby beach. On discovering her, Aurélie inspects her injuries and, relieved to find that she can walk, helps her struggle back to her house. Here Philippa encounters Mimi, Aurélie's niece, who is then lodging with her.

Aurélie quickly guesses Philippa's secret – that she is not a boy but a girl in disguise. However, employing the male pronoun, as Philippa herself desires, she admits that she finds 'him beautiful ... with eyes that were always laughing'.[21] She neither understands nor cares how Philippa defines her gender, whether she regards herself as male or female, and, unwilling to invade her privacy and subject her to rigid definitions, she resists enquiring. Allard's avoidance of reference to sexual categories creates another link with Freccero's thought. In his emotive references to the American Brandon Teena and his brutal murder, Freccero criticises the attempts made by the lesbian and gay community to define Teena's sexuality, especially the arguments that erupted after his death about whether he should be portrayed as 'lesbian' or 'transsexual'. Condemning them as signifying an oppressive attempt to entomb Teena in 'regulatory regimes of gender ... that cover over the ghostly, mobile subjectivity that continues to insist beyond those categories',[22] she argues that they signify a crass refusal to accept the fact that Teena was, as C. Jacob Hale describes, 'a border-zone dweller' who, though existing 'in a netherworld constituted by the margins of multiple overlapping identity categories', rejected rigid definitions of gender and sexuality.[23]

Aurélie and Philippa, however, though happy in their relationship, nonetheless encounter problems. Especially urgent is the question of whether or not they should reveal their relationship to Aurélie's niece Mimi. Although Mimi is now an adult and no longer lives with them, she frequently visits their home. However, on eventually disclosing their relationship to her, they are astonished to discover that she too has formed a relationship with a woman. As she explains, 'Knowing their love as I did, their support and reassurance for each other', she found it natural that she should do likewise.[24]

Yet another difficulty that Aurélie and Philippa experience is being hounded by the villagers' accusations that they are living in sin. As a result, though initially resisting the idea and aware of the risk of discovery it involves, they decide to marry. The ruse succeeds and the villagers regard them as man and wife. As Castle, commenting humorously on the difficulty that heterosexuals sometimes experience in recognising queer sexuality, writes in *The Apparitional Lesbian*:

> When it comes to lesbians ... many people have trouble seeing what's in front of them. The lesbian remains a kind of 'ghost effect' in the cinema world of modern life: elusive, vaporous, difficult to spot – even when she is there in plain view, mortal and magnificent, at the center of the screen![25]

However, despite Aurélie's and Philippa's initial success in concealing their relationship, their story concludes sadly. Philippa, who has recently joined the local fishing fleet, is drowned when her boat capsizes in a storm, returning her to the element of water from which she initially came. As Aurélie's mother sagely observed, 'The sea gives ... but sometimes she has to take.'[26] Watching the shipwreck from the headland above the beach and feeling unable to live without Philippa, Aurélie throws herself into the ocean. Her niece Mimi, appropriating the narrative, describes how the villagers construct a commemorative monument to the couple on the beach. However, when rumours spread that they were both women, they crowd on to the shore and savagely destroy it. Unable to bear the sight of their savagery, Mimi escapes to the edge of the waves and, having inherited from Aurélie the gift of second sight, communicates with her in spectral terms. As Freccero observes, 'The past is in the present as a form of haunting. This is what doing a queer kind of history means, since it involves an openness to the possibility of being haunted, even inhabited, by ghosts.'[27]

Rebecca S. Buck, *Ghosts of Winter*: A Haunted House and its Spectral Residents

Unlike Allard, who sets *Légende* in the rural terrain of the Normandy coast and opens with reference to the uncanny events emanating from the pagan world, Rebecca S. Buck focuses *Ghosts of Winter* (2011) on an eighteenth-century country house and the ghosts of the queer people who previously inhabited it. In representing them, she creates what the historiographer Carolyn Dinshaw calls 'an imagined community of the marginal', while exploring the sociopolitical taboos and hurdles that prevented them from revealing their sexuality.[28]

Buck opens the novel by describing the present-day narrator Ros Wynne, a retired history teacher who lives in the North of England, receiving an important piece of news. Although thrilled to discover that her aunt, who has recently died, has bequeathed her the Palladian house Winter Manor on condition that she has the property renovated, her pleasure at the inheritance is overshadowed by grief. As well as having recently experienced two bereavements through the deaths of both her aunt and her mother, her female partner has unexpectedly left her. Looking at the Manor with its cracked windowpanes and moss-covered walls through the trees, she pessimistically wonders, 'Could I rebuild my life and an abandoned country house simultaneously?'[29] On approaching closer, she notices the Grecian-style statue of a young woman with an eroded arm positioned on a pedestal by the front door. The pedestal facing it, where Ros assumes that her 'chiselled lover had once stood', is broken and empty.[30] Perceiving the figure's dejected appearance, Ros murmurs sympathetically, 'I know how you feel, love.'[31]

Like Freccero, who refers to 'the persistence of the ghostly demand to be heard and recognised', Buck hints at the way the ghosts of the earlier residents of the Manor respond to Ros's presence.[32] On spending her first night there, she sleeps badly. As well as feeling nervous about meeting Anna, the architect whom her aunt had assigned to oversee the property's renovation, she is conscious of the eerie way the house 'creaked and groaned around me, as though it was adjusting to my presence'.[33] Though claiming that, rationally, she 'didn't believe in haunted houses', on hearing the mysterious sounds she senses that the spectral inhabitants are 'trying to tell me something'.[34] As Freccero writes, 'The return of the object, demanding to be a person of its own, is one way to think about haunting ... when one is willing to be haunted and inhabited by ghosts.'[35]

Buck's representation of the lives of the individuals who inhabited the Manor in earlier centuries tends to be melancholy, recalling Sigmund Freud's reference to 'All the unfulfilled but possible futures to which we cling in phantasy, all the strivings of the ego which adverse circumstances have crushed.'[36] She portrays Ros, though unable to communicate directly with the ghosts frequenting the house, as nonetheless glimpsing traces of them. The rosewood chest engraved with the initials M.G. that she discovers in an upstairs room furnishes a clue to the identity of Maeve Greville, a neighbour who visited the Manor in the nineteenth century and who exemplifies, as Freccero writes, 'One of the ghostly collectivity of known or unknown strangers' who frequented it.[37] Having secretly formed a relationship with the owner's daughter Catherine and hoping to continue it and live with her, Maeve daringly suggests that she marry Catherine's brother Francis, who has indicated that he loves her. When Catherine indignantly rejects this act of deception, Maeve escapes from the house secretly at night, leaving the chest containing her writing materials behind. The architect Anna, assuming it to be valuable, suggests that Ros sell it, but Ros rejects the idea. Sensing the spectral residents of the house watching her, she explains, 'It would feel like I was betraying someone if I sold it.'[38]

In representing 'the imagined community of spectral strangers that come to haunt us',[39] Buck portrays men as generally more successful than women in forming queer attachments on account of their financial independence and greater freedom of movement. Lord William Fitzsimmons Winter, who initially financed the building of the house and, as we discover, placed the Greek-style statues by the front door, as well as being, as he admits, 'compulsively attracted to his own sex', is also very wealthy.[40] Though worried that he will not have the opportunity to form a same-sex relationship on account of having married in order to sire an heir, a chance encounter with an aristocratic guest who recognises his sexual preference gives him the opportunity he desires. He is overjoyed when, after making love and kissing him prior to leaving, the guest romantically promises, 'There will be other times, my love . . .'[41]

Buck depicts the final episode in the history of the queer ghosts of Winter Manor as taking place in 1927, when radical changes have occurred in the ownership of the property. On account of the death of the male owner in the 1914–18 war, it now belongs to a woman – his sister Evadne. On hosting a house-party there, she fills the rooms with her friends from boarding school. While talking with Edith, with whom she has previously had a brief love affair, she reveals the fact that she is pregnant, though she has no intention of marrying the father. Although Edith, who is still in love with Evadne, experiences a short-lived hope that they will be able to renew their relationship and raise the child together, the two women sadly reject the plan. Although same-sex relationships are becoming acceptable in bohemian circles, the idea of two women bringing up a child in a same-sex partnership remains taboo.

Unlike the earlier female residents of Winter Manor whose attempts to form queer relationships generally end in disappointment, the present-day owner Ros meets, to her surprise, with success. While working on renovating the house together, she and the architect Anna become attracted and embark on a relationship. When Ros admits that, in sensing the presence of the ghosts in the house, she feels that she is 'looking after a legacy' from the queer past, Anna promises to use her architectural skills to assist her to maintain it.[42]

Jameson Currier, 'The Country House': The Haunted House and Military Conflict

The story 'The Country House' by the American Jameson Currier, though resembling Buck's *Ghosts of Winter* in focusing on the topic of the haunted house, differs radically from it.[43] As well as associating spectrality with military conflict, in this case the American Civil War, Currier focuses on a character who, unlike Buck's narrator Ros, far from being interested in queer history, initially ridicules it. The narrative, however, as it develops, illustrates Freccero's recognition that the 'past presses upon us with a kind of insistence, a demand to which we must somehow respond'.[44]

Currier opens the story in the present day, with the unnamed narrator driving from Manhattan to spend the weekend with his friend Arnie in the eighteenth-century house that he has recently purchased. The narrator recounts to his partner Scott the tale of the spectral events that allegedly occurred there. The property, as he describes, was initially constructed by Peter Altermas, who fought on the side of the Unionists in the Civil War. Having been captured in the early years of the conflict, he spent the major part of it incarcerated in a Confederate prison camp near Manhattan where he secretly formed a relationship with one of the guards. The two men, after escaping towards the end of the war, trekked across the countryside together to take refuge in Peter's house. Arriving there late at night, they collapsed exhausted on a bed in an upstairs room and fell asleep in each other's arms. Here they were discovered early the following morning by Peter's wife Emma, the only remaining resident. Having glimpsed the two figures entering the house at night, and assuming them to be enemy soldiers, she decided to get rid of them before they could attack her. Failing to recognise her husband on account of his changed appearance, or perhaps shocked by the sight of two men embracing in bed, she raised the gun that she was carrying in self-defence and shot them both. On recognising with horror that she had accidentally killed her husband, and determined to conceal the fact, she managed, despite their weight, to drag the two bodies downstairs and bury them in the barn. She succeeded in keeping the event secret, revealing it only shortly before her death in a letter she addressed to her daughter.

As the narrator tells Scott, the ghosts of Peter and his partner are rumoured to haunt the house. Although neither Arnie nor his partner have seen them, their appearances have been recorded by previous owners, including an artist who referred to them in his drawings. Scott, however, is unimpressed by the story. Unlike the narrator, who works for a gay journal and is interested in queer history, Scott is a businessman by profession. As Currier describes, he tends to regard homosexuality as a modern-day, psychological invention with little connection to the past.[45] Ridiculing the idea of Peter and the prison guard being lovers, he accuses his partner of 'having read too many gay books', adding mockingly, 'Not everyone in the world is gay!'[46]

By the time that the two men arrive at Arnie's house their bickering has shifted to another topic, one that is also controversial. This is Scott's unwillingness to acknowledge his queer sexuality. Unlike his partner who has been 'out' for years, Scott has recognised his attraction to men only recently. His partner, though initially sympathising with his reticence, is now starting to tire of it.

The weekend they spend at Arnie's house predictably goes badly. Scott and his partner have difficulty concealing their mutual irritation and, as a result, are in no mood to socialise with Arnie and the other guests. By the time Sunday arrives, they are, in fact, on the verge of breaking up. When Arnie suggests that the group spend the evening at the local cinema, Scott opts out and stays at home. As well as hoping to avoid further arguments, he wants to spend the time reading the papers for a conference that he is due to attend the following week.

Halberstam argues that, 'If haunting is an articulate discourse and a mode within which the ghost requires something like accountability, then to tell a ghost story means being willing to be haunted'[47] – and his supposition in this instance proves correct. When Arnie and his friends have left for the cinema and Scott is sitting in his bedroom working on his papers, a storm unexpectedly erupts, with streaks of lightning illuminating the sky. The lights in the room go out and, as he waits for them to return, the room assumes a reddish glow. Two male figures in military dress gradually materialise, lying on a blood-streaked bale of straw by the hearth. Both men appear seriously wounded; one, as Scott perceives, has 'his chest blown apart with a bloody hole' while the other reveals 'a blackened wound at his neck where the bullet must have hit'.[48] As the glow gradually fades, he sees the two figures engage in a fumbling embrace 'as if to draw their bodies closer for warmth'.[49] As Freccero describes, 'The spectre begins by coming back, by repeating itself, by recurring in the present.'[50]

When his partner returns from the cinema later that evening, he finds Scott already in bed. Raising his head from the pillow, Scott murmurs drowsily, 'I'll do it slowly ... the kids first ...'[51] His encounter with the two lovers from the Civil War, as well as illustrating that he can no longer dismiss queer history as fake, prompts him to perceive the importance of acknowledging his queer sexuality. As he emotionally tells his astonished partner, 'They were in love. I saw what they felt for each other. It's how I feel about you. They were simply two guys who felt like us ...'[52] Currier's conclusion to the story, in illustrating Freccero's assertion of 'the reciprocity of haunting and being haunted', creates a sense of reconciliation between the two men.[53] As Scott tells his partner, his unexpected encounter with the two ghosts from the

Civil War has the beneficial effect of 'turning around our relationship' and 'creating a solid union between us'.[54]

Rosie Garland, *The Night Brother*

Rosie Garland's *The Night Brother*, with which this chapter concludes, is a work of historical fiction set in Manchester in the 1890s. Interplaying swiftly paced narrative with humour and racy dialogue, it tells the story of the teenage Edie. A key episode in the text portrays her, on unexpectedly encountering an archaeological item with queer sexual connotations in a local museum, responding to it with astonishment since, as she perceives, it reflects her own sexuality. The episode recalls Thomas A. Dowson's discussion of queer archaeology and its recent development. Commenting on the discovery in 1961 of the representation of two men in the affectionate pose of a same-sex couple on a Fifth Dynasty tomb in Lower Egypt, he observes how, although the concept of queer archaeology then met with homophobic ridicule, it is now generally accepted.[55] Edie's encounter with the artefact encourages her, despite familial disapproval, to eventually accept her own queer sexuality and form a relationship with a woman. As Freccero observes, 'The past may not be present but it is in the present, haunting, if only through our uncertain knowledge of it.'[56]

The novel opens with Edie, whose mother runs a pub in the city, discovering to her surprise that she has a brother – the mysterious Gnome. He materialises unexpectedly in her bedroom at night when she is half-asleep, demanding that she get dressed and 'Come out and play'.[57] Introducing the topic of gender ambiguity that plays a key role in the narrative, Edie puts on the cotton trousers that he insists she wear and follows him down the drainpipe into the street. Their adventures culminate in a visit to the firework display at Belle Vue Stadium, with its 'fairyland' lighting.[58] When, safely back in bed and on the verge of sleep, she hears Gnome giggle, she is uncertain which of them emitted the sound. As she drowsily admits, glimpsing the mysterious nature of their relationship, she is 'unsure where he ends and I begin'.[59] The phrase recalls Freccero's reference to the spectre representing 'an otherness struggling to emerge within and sometimes against the self'.[60]

The mystery of Gnome's identity and her relationship with him puzzles Edie. Although her mother initially refuses to reveal its significance, her grandmother, who lodges with them, moved by Edie's expressions of anxiety, eventually does so. She reveals to her the incredible news that she and Gnome are not, in fact, as Edie had assumed, autonomous individuals but two different facets of a single person, each struggling for dominance. Her mother, though furious with her grandmother for revealing the secret, sulkily endorses her account.

Garland's portrayal of Gnome as representing a secret relating to family history has psychoanalytic significance, recalling Nicholas Abraham's concept of 'the phantom'.[61] As Freccero describes, Abraham makes reference to the phantom's emergence to represent the transference of a transgressive secret from one family generation to the next where, as he describes, 'It works like a stranger within the subject's own mental topography.'[62] Edie similarly depicts Gnome in spectral terms, referring to him as 'a wild and ungovernable creature that has haunted me like a ghost' so 'I'm not sure where he ends and I begin'.[63] Her description evokes connotations of transsexuality, recalling the theorist Jay Prosser's use of spectral imagery to describe the 'phantomic' aspect of the body that the transsexual, prior to transitioning, regards as his 'real' embodiment and seeks to 'liberate'.[64]

Gnome's influence on Edie, however, though worrying her, also has positive effects since it encourages her to liberate herself from familial control. Tiring of his interference and the harassment she experiences from the men frequenting the pub, she increasingly escapes from her mother's surveillance. Rejecting the role of housebound femininity, in episodes recalling the adventures of Nan in Sarah Waters' *Tipping the Velvet*, she explores the city streets alone, sometimes dressing as boy.[65] On one occasion, though fearing that her working-class status will debar her from visiting it, she enters the imposing building that houses the public library and, remembering her teacher's comment that 'Knowledge is power', dips into the books.[66] She also visits the city art gallery. Here, having briefly inspected the displays of 'stuffed beasts, butterflies spreading metallic wings and gigantic shells', she enters the classical gallery where an exhibition entitled 'The Nereid Monument, Lycia 390–380 BC' is on show.[67] She pauses, impressed by the skill of 'the artful hand that teased the marble into flesh', at a sculpted model of two male figures.[68] On inspecting them more closely, however, she is astonished to see that one of them, though having male genitals, also has breasts – and she is gazing at 'a man who is also a woman, a woman who is also man'.[69]

Edie's unexpected encounter with a queer figure in the museum and her uncanny feeling that 'He – or she – calls out to me across the millennia' thrills her.[70] It also heralds a positive change in her fortunes. On leaving the gallery, she encounters in the street a stall with a banner inscribed with the slogan 'Votes for Women'. However, instead of seeing the monstrous harridans that her mother frequently 'rails against as the scourge of society on a mission to drag it to its knees', she perceives to her surprise a group of respectable-looking people of both sexes behaving decorously.[71] She is thrilled by the short speech that one of the women gives and the futuristic image she creates of 'a society where women and men stand side by side as comrades'.[72] However, though impressed by the woman's articulacy and passion, Edie has difficulty concentrating on her words as her attention is increasingly distracted by the beauty of her appearance – 'the fine blades of her cheekbones' and 'her mouth that blooms like a rose'.[73] She discovers that the woman's name is Abigail and, though speaking with her only briefly, happens to meet her again on a later occasion Although the mischievous Gnome, jealous of the couple's attachment, tries to intervene in their friendship and cause trouble, Edie succeeds in eluding his interference – and the novel concludes positively with the two women becoming lovers.

Freccero's discussion in her study of 'the possibilities of spectrality for the project of a queer historiography' creates, as illustrated above, an informative context for discussing works of contemporary fiction that focus on exploring and recreating queer history.[74] The protagonist's encounter with the queer past, as represented in the four works discussed above, takes a variety of different forms. It is exemplified in Allard's *Légende*, the earliest of them, by the visit that the protagonist Aurélie and her mother make to the ancient, pre-Christian site of the menhirs and the prophecy the latter receives of the relationship that Aurélie will form with a woman. In Buck's *Ghosts of Winter* and Currier's 'The Country House' it is exemplified, by contrast, by the motif of the haunted house and the representation of the spectral figures that inhabit the property. Garland's *The Night Brother* illustrates yet another version of the topic, the female protagonist's discovery in a museum of an archaeological artefact representing an episode from queer history. These works of fiction illustrate the fascination that the topic holds for writers and the diversity and imaginative vitality of their representations.

Notes

1. Carla Freccero, *Queer/Early/Modern* (Durham, NC: Duke University Press, 2006), p. 86.
2. Ibid., p. 70; Jack Halberstam, 'Telling Tales: Brandon Teena, Billy Tipton, and Transgender Biography', *A/B: Auto/Biography Studies*, 15 (2000), pp. 62–81; George Haggerty, 'The History of Homosexuality Reconsidered', in *Developments in the History of Homosexuality*, ed. George Mounsey (Lewisburg, PA: Bucknell University Press, 2013), pp. 3–7.

3. Gabrielle Griffin, *Heavenly Love? Lesbian Images in Twentieth Century Women's Writing* (Manchester: Manchester University Press, 1993), p. 694; Martha Vicinus, 'They Wonder to Which Sex I Belong: The Historical Roots of the Modern Lesbian Identity', in *Homosexuality, Which Homosexuality?*, ed. Dennis Altman, Carole Vance, Martha Vicinus and Jeffrey Weeks (London: GMP, 1989), p. 172.
4. Haggerty, 'The History of Homosexuality Reconsidered', pp. 3–4.
5. Valerie Traub, *The Renaissance of Lesbianism in Early Modern England* (Cambridge: Cambridge University Press, 2002), p. 359.
6. Freccero, *Queer/Early/Modern*, p. 77.
7. Ibid., p. 77.
8. Ibid., p. 78.
9. Terry Castle, *The Apparitional Lesbian: Female Homosexuality and Modern Culture* (New York: Columbia University Press, 1993), p. 34.
10. Jack Halberstam, *The Queer Art of Failure* (Durham, NC: Duke University Press, 2011), pp. 150, 148.
11. Ibid, p. 148.
12. Freccero, *Queer/Early/Modern*, p. 71.
13. Helen Carr, 'Introduction', in *From My Guy to Sci-Fi: Genre and Women's Writing in the Postmodern World* (London: Pandora, 1989), pp. 5–12.
14. Heather Love, *Feeling Backward: Loss and the Politics of Queer History* (Cambridge, MA: Harvard University Press, 2007), p. 32.
15. Jeannine Allard, *Légende: The Story of Philippa and Aurélie* (Boston, MA: Alyson Publications, 1984), p. 37.
16. Ryan Trimm, 'Witching Welcome', in *Haunted Landscapes*, ed. Ruth Heholt and Niamh Downing (Lanham, MD: Rowman and Littlefield, 2016), p. 60.
17. Allard, *Légende*, p. 38.
18. Freccero, *Queer/Early/Modern*, p. 101.
19. Allard, *Légende*, p. 19.
20. Ibid., p. 45.
21. Ibid., p. 69.
22. Freccero, *Queer/Early/Modern*, p. 73.
23. C. Jacob Hale, 'Consuming the Living, Dismembering the Dead', *GLQ: A Journal of Lesbian and Gay Studies: Transgender*, 4 (1998), p. 318.
24. Allard, *Légende*, p. 91.
25. Castle, *The Apparitional Lesbian*, p. 2.
26. Allard, *Légende*, p. 17.
27. Freccero, *Queer/Early/Modern*, p. 80.
28. Carolyn Dinshaw, *Getting Medieval: Sexualities and Communities, Pre and Postmodern* (Durham, NC: Duke University Press, 1999), p. 14.
29. Rebecca S. Buck, *Ghosts of Winter* (Valley Falls, NY: Bold Strokes, 2011), p. 32.
30. Ibid., p. 19.
31. Ibid., p. 19.
32. Freccero, *Queer/Early/Modern*, p. 103.
33. Buck, *Ghosts of Winter*, p. 22.
34. Ibid., pp. 33, 47.
35. Freccero, *Queer/Early/Modern*, p. 101.

36. Sigmund Freud, 'The Uncanny', in *The Pelican Freud Library*, ed. Angela Richards and James Strachey, vol. 14 (Harmondsworth: Penguin, 1973–86), p. 358.
37. Freccero, *Queer/Early/Modern*, p. 75.
38. Buck, *Ghosts of Winter*, p. 67.
39. Freccero, *Queer/Early/Modern*, p. 87.
40. Buck, *Ghosts of Winter*, p. 166.
41. Ibid., p. 176.
42. Ibid., p. 266.
43. Jameson Currier, 'The Country House', in *The Haunted Heart and Other Tales* (Maple Shade, NJ: Lethe Press, 2009).
44. Freccero, *Queer/Early/Modern*, p. 70.
45. Currier, 'The Country House', p. 49.
46. Ibid., p. 49.
47. Halberstam, quoted in Freccero, *Queer/Early/Modern*, p. 75.
48. Currier, 'The Country House', p. 52.
49. Ibid., p. 52.
50. Freccero, *Queer/Early/Modern*, p. 85.
51. Currier, 'The Country House', p. 53.
52. Ibid., p. 53.
53. Freccero, *Queer/Early/Modern*, p. 75.
54. Currier, 'The Country House', p. 55.
55. Thomas A. Dowson, 'Queer Theory Meets Archaeology' in *The Ashgate Companion to Queer Theory*, ed. Noreen Giffney and Michael O'Rourke (Farnham: Ashgate, 2009), pp. 286–91.
56. Freccero, *Queer/Early/Modern*, p. 78.
57. Rosie Garland, *The Night Brother* (London: Borough Press, 2017), p. 6.
58. Ibid., p. 6.
59. Ibid., p. 16.
60. Freccero, *Queer/Early/Modern*, p. 101.
61. Nicholas Abraham, 'Notes on the Phantom: A Complement to Freud's Metapsychology', *Critical Inquiry*, 13.2 (1987), p. 287.
62. Ibid., p. 290; Freccero, *Queer/Early/Modern*, p. 86.
63. Garland, *The Night Brother*, p. 14.
64. Jay Prosser, *Second Skins: The Body Narratives of Transsexuality* (New York: Columbia University Press, 1998), p. 85.
65. Sarah Waters, *Tipping the Velvet* (London: Virago, 1998).
66. Garland, *The Night Brother*, p. 100.
67. Ibid., p. 149.
68. Ibid., p. 150.
69. Ibid., p. 151.
70. Ibid., p. 151.
71. Ibid., p. 153.
72. Ibid., p. 153.
73. Ibid., p. 154.
74. Freccero, *Queer/Early/Modern*, p. 70.

Chapter 10

Witchcraft, Gender and Queerness in Contemporary British Literature
Silvia Antosa

Queer Gothic Witches

In the European and Northern American cultural traditions, witches have historically inhabited an unspeakable, liminal space which defies dichotomous categories and clear-cut definitions. The meanings of witchcraft have thus been difficult to define, as they are shifting and unstable. In Malcolm Gaskill's words, witches are 'cultural hybrids, blending learned and popular traditions' as well as 'states of being: life/death, temporal/celestial, good/evil, desire/fulfilment'.[1] Witchcraft discourses have articulated the subordination of women and other oppressed social and religious minority groups in European hetero-patriarchal societies. They are thus crucial to understanding the formation and consolidation of gender hierarchies, sexism and heteronormativity in the modern and contemporary world. In so doing, they also represent and symbolise new forms of queer, fluid identities that challenge class, gender and sexual norms, thus resisting univocal definitions.

From the fourteenth and fifteenth centuries, when witch hunts prevailed in Europe, one of the most popular assumptions about witches was that they were mostly female.[2] This view was strongly supported and disseminated by one of the seminal treatises on diabolical witchcraft, *The Malleus Maleficarum* (1486) or *The Witch's Hammer*, authored by Dominican inquisitors Heinrich Kramer and Jacob Sprenger. Kramer and Sprenger insisted on witchcraft being inextricably linked with the female sex. Significantly, the Latin genitive *Maleficarum* can be translated as 'of *female* evildoers'. Thus, the title of their work crucially interweaves evil and female gender identity in a sort of cause–effect relationship, and gestures towards a persecution based on sex.[3] Its arguments bridged the worlds of theology and popular belief and produced a model of witchcraft that was plausible to and supported by both scholars and ordinary people. In other words, it successfully joined the widespread anxieties about human demonic powers found in traditional European peasant communities to a theological background which made it acceptable to the learned clerical elite.[4] The interweaving of elite theology and popular superstition was supported by the legal system, which had a formative role in the systematic persecution of (female) witches.

Thus, witchcraft undoubtedly had what Clive Holmes has defined as a 'misogynous dimension', based on women's perceived 'natural' weakness and vulnerability to the influence of demonic forces.[5] However, as Holmes and Elizabeth Kent have suggested, witches were not always passive victims.[6] Those who were suspected of witchcraft often contributed to the formation of their own reputations, more or less openly, thus exercising a certain influence upon the life of their community. This can be seen in the case of the Lancashire witches, which has been reinterpreted by Jeanette Winterson and Carol Ann Duffy, as I discuss below. On this point, Geoffrey Scarre has argued that the constraints imposed by patriarchal culture meant that women were more likely than men to resort to magic for sociocultural reasons: 'Witchcraft may have held more appeal for women than for men not because, as contemporaries thought, women were more wicked and more easily led than men, but because their social and economic position imposed greater constraints on their possibilities of action.'[7] The halo of witchcraft and demonic possession could confer on women a social position that would otherwise have been impossible to achieve. This view is supported by Diane Purkiss, who has argued that 'the witch is not solely or simply the creation of patriarchy, but [...] women also invested heavily in the figure as a fantasy which allowed them to express and manage otherwise unspeakable fears and desires'.[8]

About a quarter of those executed for witchcraft were men. They were considered a threat to communal norms and social order as they were perceived as unruly and dangerous. In Oldridge's words, 'As such, they represented a disordered version of manhood: they were quintessentially "bad men", just as female witches displayed a perverted and uncontained femininity.'[9] Etymologically, the word 'bad' in 'bad men' comes from the Middle English, which in turn derives from the Old English *baeddel*, meaning hermaphrodite or 'womanish man'.[10] Significantly, the very notion of being 'bad' is connected to hermaphrodites, or intersex identities, which – like trans identities – challenge conceptual categories by subverting the relations among gender, sexuality and the body and positing the existence of a hybrid, intermediate sex living in an in-between queer space of sexual indeterminacy.[11]

In this way, witchcraft reflects a chaotic and unruly subversion of sociocultural and gender hierarchies. As such, it is marked by excess and transgression, and 'gives form to the deepest fears of society'.[12] Witches – men and women alike – were marginalised and persecuted because they ostensibly violated society's norms and were perceived as deviant and threatening for the social order. Similarly, queer subjectivities have historically defied sex and gender categories to open up new, liminal forms of identity that challenge and resist heteronormative, patriarchal power. Like witches, queer people have historically been silenced, ostracised and persecuted.

The figure of the witch, with its unsettling, defying potentiality, is still a powerful source of inspiration for contemporary writers and artists. It has become a striking metaphor in challenging narratives of female and queer claims of reappropriation of spaces of resistance and empowerment. From this viewpoint, the Gothic has often provided a narrative dimension in which uncanny, queer dilemmas and desires have been represented, and marginalised identities have found their own voice. Historically, Gothic fiction has focused on non-normative forms of sexuality traditionally perceived as deviant and taboo. In this way, in the words of Rosemary Jackson, the Gothic 'pushes us [. . .] towards an area of non-signification [. . .] by attempting to articulate the unnameable and to visualise the unseen'.[13] It also opens up a symbolic space of production and representation of subversive sexual meanings that are conventionally repressed.[14] The close connection between Gothic and queer has been emphasised by William Hughes and Andrew Smith as follows: 'Gothic has, in a sense, always been queer [. . .] The genre has characteristically been perceived in criticism as being poised astride the uneasy cultural boundary that separates the acceptable and familiar from the troubling and different.'[15] According to Eve Kosofsky Sedgwick, 'What makes the Gothic queer, in fact, is its investment in the liminal, the in-between, the brink – particularly, although not exclusively, the line between life and death.'[16] Like the queer, the Gothic gives expression to transgressive, sexually charged desires, which are connected to the exercise of or, alternatively, resistance to dominant forms of heteronormative, patriarchal power.[17]

In this chapter, I analyse a selection of fictional and poetic texts published in Britain in recent years which explore and reinterpret the versatile and iconic figure of the witch through a queer Gothic lens. These include Jeanette Winterson's *The Daylight Gate* (2012), Carol Ann Duffy's 'The Lancashire Witches' (2012), Emma Donoghue's *Kissing the Witch: Old Tales in New Skins* (1997) and Rebecca Tamás's *Witch* (2019). I argue that these texts offer a wide range of queer Gothic revisitations of the powerful, evocative figure of the witch across literary genres, ranging from fictional rewritings of historical events to fairy tales and experimental poetry.

As a liminal figure that does not fit existing categories, the witch is also, as Gaskill has pointed out, 'essentially mysterious, occult – a word meaning "hidden"'; in other words, 'Witchcraft hovers, invisible yet powerful and persistent.'[18] Adapting Marina Warner's definition of the supernatural, by its very nature witchcraft 'is difficult terrain; of its very nature, it resists discourse; or, to put it more accurately, it is always in the process of being described, conjured, made, and made up, without ascertainable outside referents'.[19] The texts that I discuss in this chapter demonstrate this ongoing process of describing, conjuring, making and making up witchcraft, as they explore and actualise it as an open signifier that can be reinscribed in order to give shape and voice to multiple issues and concerns. In so doing, they ultimately create a queer feminist genealogy that represents the lives of liminal individuals, whose 'haunting' presences are intensified by intersecting axes of queerness. Moreover, I investigate how these novels and poems share a number of Gothic tropes in order to enhance their subversive qualities, as well as to explore and articulate women's abuse and exploitation, female and queer same-sex relationships and non-hegemonic forms of masculinity. While there is a lot of theoretical and analytical work on witches and feminism, a reflection on queerness and witchcraft with its powerful potential still needs a proper assessment.

The Daylight Gate, or the Witching Hour

The Daylight Gate was published in 2012 to mark the 400th anniversary of the notorious 1612 trial of the Lancashire Witches, also known as the Pendle Witches Trial, after which eight women and two men were hanged in an outbreak of public hysteria over witchcraft in north-west England.[20] The story is set in the early seventeenth century during the reign of James I, whose *Daemonologie* (1597) had paved the way for the practice of witch-hunting and the persecution of all kinds of dissidents in England, including Catholics, witches, wizards and political rebels. Lancashire, in particular, was regarded as a wild and lawless region. In the words of Rachel Hasted, it was an area 'fabled for its theft, violence and sexual laxity, where the church was honoured without much understanding of its doctrines by the common people'.[21] This area was largely populated by Catholics, who were persecuted by Henry VIII during his reign.

The title of the novel refers to the liminal moment of the day when light and darkness melt into each other. In addition, 'the daylight gate' also hints at the 'witching hour', which is conventionally midnight. This reference reinforces the queer temporal and spatial dimension of the story, and readers are asked to suspend disbelief and enter a world where magic and witchcraft are possible.

The Daylight Gate rewrites historical events by assuming a queer perspective which is 'other' to the official textual source. Winterson depicts a world where power is entirely held by men, who exercise their gender and class privileges through physical and mental abuse, sexual violence and religious and political persecution. In this context, queer identities and desires constitute a space of resistance to heteronormative, patriarchal power.

The novel focuses on a series of events that occurred before the August Assizes in 1612, after which ten convicts were hanged for practising witchcraft. The case was based on an accusation by a local pedlar, John Law, who claimed that a young beggar, Alizon Device, cast a spell on him, causing him to become paralysed. Further accusations of witchcraft between two rival families, the Devices and the Chattoxes, followed. Eventually the accused were all imprisoned and held for months in a dungeon in Lancaster Castle in horrific conditions, before being executed. Among those hanged for witchcraft was Alice Nutter, a gentlewoman and landowner. To this day there is a lack of consensus regarding Nutter's role in the case, and her eventual conviction and death.[22] Winterson's novel revisits and reimagines the story from Nutter's point of view.

In Winterson's novel, Alice Nutter is a self-made woman. As a young widow, she becomes a member of John Dee's research group in alchemical studies. After spending a few years in Manchester, the group moves to London, where Alice lives with her lover Elizabeth Southern, who is also a member of the alchemical research group. Alice and Elizabeth's relationship is fated to end, as Elizabeth is drawn to the darker side of her magical explorations. Years later, after she has returned to Lancashire, Alice's wealth, intelligence and independent nature make her an object of suspicion for the local men. Her past connection with John Dee is similarly perceived as dangerous. She embodies female agency and empowerment, thus exceeding her role as a woman in the local male-dominated environment. Her characterisation is marked by transgressive signs of excess, ranging from her upper-class background to her unconventional sexual identity. Alice lives alone and performs activities and sports that usually pertain to the masculine realm, such as riding horses astride. In this way, she inhabits the outside space and moves beyond the suffocating domestic sphere to which patriarchy has relegated women, thus challenging the (re)production of the gender differences on which the social order is founded.

The novel follows Alice's search for Elizabeth. They are two specular figures, each the double of the other: the former is young and wealthy, whereas the latter is old and abject, as she has offered her beauty and youth to the Dark Gentleman in a sort of gendered revisitation of the Faustian motif. The two women embody a split sexual subjectivity,[23] as Alice is an empowering figure while Elizabeth has rejected her sexuality, ending up being the victim of her internalised homophobia. She chooses to be entrapped in a male-dominated world and to turn herself into a highly sexualised object of male desire. In Judith Butler's terms, this dynamic of self-hatred and uncontrollable sexual violence is inherent to psychic structures themselves.[24]

In her search for her double, Elizabeth, Alice is doomed to fail. As Ruth Parkin-Gounelas explains, in Gothic fiction the encounter with one's double as shadow or image frequently acts as a threat and an uncanny prediction of death.[25] Elizabeth has been imprisoned on suspicion of witchcraft, and Alice goes to visit her. After this encounter, Elizabeth dies in prison and Alice is executed for her association with the Lancashire witches. On the face of it, the final meeting between the two doubles reconstitutes the symbolic divided psychic self and seems to lead to the inevitable physical and symbolic 'death of the lesbian'. But there is another character who constitutes the third pole of queer triangulated desire: Christopher Southworth, a Catholic priest and participant in the Gunpowder Plot, who was Alice's lover in the past. He belongs to the same abject space of alterity and sexual otherness inhabited by the two women. He has been persecuted, tortured and castrated by his oppressors. His scarred body represents the stigmatisation of the Catholics, considered by many as unmanly and sexually deviant individuals. As an outcast and an outsider, Christopher stands for a different, queer model of masculinity.

Christopher goes to Lancashire to liberate his sister, who has also been arrested on the grounds of witchcraft. However, his attempt fails and instead he meets Old Demdike, who turns out to be Elizabeth herself. Christopher returns to Alice's London house to escape from his Protestant persecutors, and encounters the spirits of Alice's and Elizabeth's younger selves. He is the only character who can see the two women's happy, if secretive, love affair. The phantasmatic echoes of their earlier joy together evokes another Gothic trope: the ghosting of abject lesbian identities. The figure of the haunting lesbian, or what Terry Castle has famously defined as the ghost of sexual love between women,[26] calls to mind Diana Fuss's interest in 'the figure of the homosexual as spectre and phantasm, as spirit and revenant, as abject and undead'.[27] Same-sex, illicit desire and spectral, liminal figures are thus inextricably associated. Moreover, the trope of the haunting lesbian further relates to the concept of the unspeakable, which in turn recalls the themes of secrecy and silence. We could here apply the three different meanings of the unspeakable in Gothic fiction identified by Paulina Palmer: 'Something can be unspeakable because the individual lacks knowledge of it, because the knowledge is repressed, or because, though having access to it, s/he dare not admit the fact.'[28] As a consequence, lesbian identities can only be represented, or spoken, through their ghostly versions. All these ideas merge in the sociocultural construction of lesbian identities, whose historical marginalisation and silencing has turned them into secret, hidden, phantasmatic figures.[29]

Significantly, Christopher can see what other men cannot see. His queer masculinity as well as his love for Alice allow him to go beyond the rigid strictures of patriarchal hegemonic culture in order to acknowledge the existence of a relationship between two women, even though through a spectral, supernatural imagery. He is quintessentially a 'bad man' because he displays what his contemporaries judge as 'uncontained femininity', which turns him into a 'womanish man'. It is, however, through Gothic appropriation that the secretive relationship between Alice and Elizabeth can find its verbal articulation and visual representation through Christopher's queer lens. In addition, the Gothic haunting images of the two women's younger selves are a reflection of a past that is becoming present again: it is a queer time in which past, present and future 'melt into each other'. Alice and Elizabeth seem to have found the key to the Great Work envisaged by John Dee: it is through their love that they manage to dissolve corporeal, spatial and temporal boundaries to transform 'one self into the other' in a queer atemporal dimension.

The love triangle between Alice, Elizabeth and Christopher both subverts the normative order and is annihilated by it.[30] The three characters die – Elizabeth dies in prison claimed by the Dark Gentleman, Alice dies by public execution and Christopher kills himself after witnessing Alice's death on the gallows. However, readers are led to believe that they continue to live, even if in a phantasmatic form. The presence of the two happily dancing ghosts in the London room might indicate not only that they continue to live 'in a queer time and space'[31] where time zones overlap, but that Christopher too might soon find himself in this alternative space/time. This is what he wishes for as he commits suicide in the final scene of the novel, where he has, significantly, almost turned into a ghost, ready to join the two women in a queer, albeit phantasmatic, afterlife. This ghastly, final image suggests that Christopher has finally become part of this polyamorous love relationship.

The Daylight Gate is a challenging text that resists a univocal interpretation by offering plural readings. On the one hand, it envisages the idea that homoerotic desire leads to abjection and death. On the other, it provides an alternative story in which Alice and Elizabeth – and Christopher – live their love relationship happily in a queer alternative world that is no longer dominated by patriarchal heteronormative rules. In other words, doomed to live as haunting spectres in their normative reality, as queer subjects they can inhabit an alternative, timeless space where differences can coexist. Winterson's queer Gothic rewriting of history interpellates present-day readers, by offering an empowering cultural history in which all subjects might find their own queer time and space, as well as, to put it in Jack Halberstam's words, 'the potential to open up new life narratives and alternative relations to time and space' conceived as alternative to 'the institutions of family, heterosexuality, and reproduction'.[32]

Witches as Archetypes: Carol Ann Duffy's 'The Lancashire Witches'

The daylight gate, with its queer, magical spatial and temporal dimension connecting past and present, light and darkness, silence and voice, visibility and invisibility, abuse and redemption, belief and disbelief, is also evoked in the poem 'The Lancashire Witches', written by Poet Laureate Carol Ann Duffy in 2012. Duffy's poem is made up of ten tercets that are inscribed on ten mileposts along a newly built 51-mile Lancashire Witches Walk leading from Pendle Hill – site of the alleged witchcraft – to Lancaster Castle where the ten accused of witchcraft were condemned and executed. The queer atmosphere of the witching hour hovering in the places where the events occurred is conjured by the poet in the following lines:

> At daylight's gate, the things we fear
> darken and form. That tree, that rock,
> a slattern's shape with the devil's dog.
>
> Something upholds us in its palm –
> landscape, history, place and time –
> and, above, the same old witness moon
>
> below which Demdike, Chattox, shrieked,
> like hags, unloved, an underclass,
> badly fed, unwell. Their eyes were red.[33]

In Duffy's lines, it is at the witching hour that past and present melt into each other to show the ghastly, spectral shapes of the historical figures who were condemned. Their haunting, supernatural presence lingers in the locations where events took place and speaks volumes about discrimination, abuse and gender violence. In a few powerful lines, Duffy vividly actualises the complex process that led to the sociocultural construction of the stereotype of the witch in the decades to come. As Gaskill has explained, 'In most witch-trials [. . .] misfortunes were not randomly blamed on women who looked like witches, but fitted into specific patterns of social relations involving conflict and fear between neighbours. This explains why young as well as old women were accused, not to mention a significant minority of men.'[34] This is exactly what occurred during the Pendle Witch Trials, where the accused people were 'underclass', or, in the words of Linda Hutcheon, 'the ex-centrics, the marginalised, the peripheral figures of [. . .] history'.[35] They are thus queer figures who challenge the sociocultural order in which they live, as they defy gender roles and even the reproductive function traditionally assigned to women: 'Witch: female, cunning, manless, old, / daughter of such, of evil faith; / in the murk of Pendle Hill, a crone.'[36]

In her lines, Duffy also transforms these outcast historical figures into powerful archetypes 'originating in shared cultural sources and activated by similar experiences and emotions'.[37] Moreover, like Winterson, Duffy evokes and transforms historical facts and characters in order to interpellate readers and stimulate their individual emotional response:

> four seasons,
> centuries, turning, in Lancashire,
>
> away from Castle, Jury, Judge,
> huge crowd, rough rope, short drop, no grave;
> only future tourists who might *grieve*. [my emphasis]

These last few lines hint at the conjunction between literal, physical and symbolic, as the 'future tourists' are both readers and walkers of the itinerary that will see them in the places of the events, which also coincide with the locations where the lines of the poem are installed and can be read. This double reference to the future tourists as readers and walkers turns the lines themselves into a sort of symbolic daylight gate through which readers can access the queer, liminal dimension powerfully evoked by the poet. They can also simultaneously explore the challenging effects of occupying an outsider status, unavoidably similar to queer sexual and gender identities, and be part of those queer subcultures that, in Jack Halberstam's words, 'produce alternative temporalities by allowing their participants to believe that their futures can be imagined according to logics that lie outside of those paradigmatic markers of life experience – namely, birth, marriage, reproduction, and death'.[38]

In addition, the poem concludes with a crucial invitation to grieve those lives. As Judith Butler has discussed, the issue of who we are is closely related to those lives that are considered un/valuable and thus un/grievable:

> One way of posing the question of who 'we' are [...] is by asking whose lives are considered valuable, whose lives are mourned, and whose lives are considered ungrievable. We might think of war as dividing populations into those who are grievable and those who are not. An ungrievable life is one that cannot be mourned because it has never lived, that is, it has never counted as a life at all.[39]

Without grievability, then, there is no life nor mourning. In addition, queer and trans lives are not only never counted as lives at all – sometimes not only silenced by omission – but actively persecuted or snuffed out.

In this light, Duffy's reference to 'grieve' in the very final line significantly aims to restore the visibility, the voice and the dignity of those marginal lives that have been erased and wiped out by history, and actively contributes to the ever evolving creation of 'a constructed memorial to the violence directed at queer and transgender lives'.[40]

Reclaiming Voices, Queering Desires

In 1997 Emma Donoghue published a collection of fairy tales entitled *Kissing the Witch: Old Tales in New Skins*. As the title suggests, the volume consists of new versions of classic fairy tales from authors including Charles Perrault, the Brothers Grimm and Hans Christian Andersen. The final story – which gives the collection its title – is original. Each tale focuses on the adventures of an innocent persecuted heroine, based upon well-known characters such as Cinderella, Snow White and the Little Mermaid, and is told in the first person by the homodiegetic narrator, who is an older version of the protagonist herself. Each story is connected to the previous one as well as to the next, thanks to an interlacing structure that joins tales and voices into an open dialogic frame. At the end of each tale, the narrator turns to one of the characters involved in the story and asks her to tell her own story. In this way, readers experience an oral storytelling exchange and are involved in the process of production and understanding of the multiple meanings conveyed, as the multivocal narrative resists closure and fixed interpretations.

The turning point of these rewritings is the heroines' acknowledgement of their own desires, which is accomplished thanks to the help of another female character. The collection thus explores multiple desires, ranging from same-sex to hetero relationships to the search for a family or even a place of one's own, all of which aim to subvert the patriarchal, heteronormative system embedded in the original fairy tales. As Jennifer Orme has emphasised, 'The radical openness and fluidity of the structure and its troubling gaps, especially as highlighted in the final tale, along with the destabilizing narration and the multiple desires articulated in the text by a plurality of voices invite a queer reading.'[41] In addition, the queerness of *Kissing the Witch* emanates from every aspect of the text; it questions and subverts naturalised constructions of gender and sexuality through tales that focus on non-normative subjects and desires that resist heteropatriarchal ideologies. It reclaims the voices of the female protagonists of classic fairy tales, who become powerful figures who decide for themselves. In this way, the narrative twists their stories in unpredictable, multiple directions.

From this perspective, the final, original tale of the collection, 'The Tale of the Kiss', sums up precisely all these layers of queerness in the figure of the female witch and her narrative strategies. This tale is connected to the previous one, 'The Tale of the Voice', where the figure of the witch makes her first appearance and is eventually asked to tell her story: '*Climbing to the witch's cave one day, I called out, / Who were you / before you came to live here? / And she said, Will I tell you my own story? / It is a tale of a kiss.*'[42] The witch starts to tell her story, and says that as a young woman she found out that she was unable to have children. She knew that she was meant to live a solitary life as an outcast in her community. Therefore, after her mother's death, she decided to leave her village, and found a cave where she settled down. She started enjoying the freedom to be on her own. Not long after, however, she learned that the people of a village nearby believed that she was a witch. She realised that she was given power by the community, a power which grew over the course of time. Her acknowledgement transforms her into the figure they want – and need – her to be. She is aware that her power

> came not from my own thin body or my own taut mind, but was invested in me by a village. Power I had to learn how to pick up without getting burnt, how to shape it and conceal it and flaunt it and use it, and when to use it, and when to steal my breath and do nothing at all.[43]

This power invests the protagonist with a deep sense of responsibility, but at the same time deprives her of her own desires. She eventually claims that she feels complete in her own loneliness and seclusion.

Events take a twist when she meets a red-haired young woman. They strike a bargain. The witch requests that the young woman kiss her in exchange for the advice that she gave to the young woman's parents, which granted her freedom from their constrictions. The girl's kiss breaks the witch's sense of completion and shakes her self-knowledge, by leading her to wonder if '[p]erhaps it is the not being kissed that makes [one] a witch; perhaps the source of her power is the breath of loneliness around her. She who takes a kiss can also die of it, can wake into something unimaginable, having turned herself into some new species.'[44] The kiss has a transformative power, which can even turn the solitary outcast witch into a new being.

Significantly, the protagonist of the story subverts several heteronormative and patriarchal paradigms: she is barren, secluded and, ostensibly, she has fallen in love with a much younger girl. She has rediscovered desire and life takes an unexpected turn. The conclusion of the story points to an open ending that does not give any clear answers. Rather, it opens up a number of unresolved tensions and unanswered questions that are left to the reader:

> And what happened next, you ask? Never you mind. There are some tales not for telling, whether because they are too long, too precious, too laughable, two painful, too easy to need telling or too hard to explain [. . .] This is the story you asked for. I leave it in your mouth.[45]

Moreover, in shifting from the past narrative tense to the present, in which she addresses the listener directly, the witch passes on her own story to each of us, in our own present tense, somehow bestowing on to the readers the same power that had been conferred upon her by the villagers near her cave. This narrative shift actively involves the readers by making them part of the queer narrative frame whereby each story is connected to the others in a never-ending chain. In so doing, it also turns the readers into queer witches who, in telling their own stories of failures and successes, ups and downs, loves and losses, might (re)discover the moment in which desire changed their own lives.

Desire and its transformative power are also at the core of Rebecca Tamás's *Witch* (2019), which was released to coincide with the pagan festival of the Spring Equinox. In her collection of poems, Tamás reclaims and reappropriates the figure of the witch as a powerful archetypal signifier by creating a textual, sacred space in which bodies, desires, nature, gender identities and philosophy are blurred into something new.

Historically marginalised as misfits and outcasts, witches are the vessels through which the poet can experiment with the pushing of boundaries in the embodied, material world. Each poem raises questions about the rules of social oppression, and points to a transgression of rules and norms as the only way towards individual independence and self-assertion. The collection is structured on a number of *spells* alternating with sections centred on the figure of the WITCH (as for example WITCH AND THE DEVIL, WITCH AND THE SUFFRAGETTES and so on). It begins and ends with two hexes: /penis hex/ and /cunt hex/, as well as an opening and a closing interrogation.

The poetic world drawn by Tamàs dismantles certainties and assumptions, as demonstrated by the beginning of the first poem, /penis hex/, where readers are introduced into a space where each element evokes its own opposite:

> the hex for a penis isn't really all about
> the penis
> the penis is not an issue all fine doing its own thing
> ink blot semen   sweet white plaster
> pale peach tartlet
> but when it goes you see   you see a lot of things
> to hex a penis off means taking a laugh out for a walk
> long and blue
> cold as Russia
> laughing and laughing your mouth is open
> let your girlfriend see your tongue.[46]

/penis hex/ is about the deconstruction of the heteropatriarchal system of oppression and the possibility of reclaiming meanings, bodies – especially female bodies – and sensual desires, which are constantly evoked in an expressive innuendo of energy. In particular, Tamàs gives voice and agency to her female witches, who claim independence and unity, while grieving and fighting against a cultural tradition that has kept them as silent, fragmented pieces of a whole. They express their anger but also explore and give voice to a wide range of feelings, thus facilitating readers' participation, as they are interpellated and involved in the poetic process of (de)construction of meanings. In the words of the author:

> Poetry allows us to connect with the possibility of freshness and agency, that is still there underneath all the societal capitalist constructs – the constructs of oppression. There is the possibility that we don't have to be defined or controlled – that we can make things new – that we don't have to label ourselves. I think '/penis hex/' is interacting with that – chipping under the surface of gender. It's not even about valorizing the female. It's about

removing the carapace of the gender entirely and getting down into the mulch where new things grow. Poetic language, interacting with imagery, can create a momentary clash and you see the possibility new shapes of being.[47]

Tamàs gestures towards a physical and theoretical space in which gender and embodiment are no longer the defining factors for identities. Rather, through her poetry, she envisages a queer world in which individuals can freely define themselves, by overcoming labels, boundaries and challenging contemporary understandings of the sexed, gendered and racialised body as it interfaces with society, culture and history.

Queer desire is one of the key themes explored in this collection, as bodies and sexualities are redrawn beyond gender binaries. For example, in the following lines, the intercourse between the witch and the devil challenges and redefines assumed perspectives on gender binaries and sexual embodiment:

> when the witch first met the devil the devil was
> a beautiful man and a beautiful woman [. . .]
> the witch kept having sex with the devil and the devil
> had all the sexual organs you could
> want so the witch could have him inside her at the same
> time as putting his breast in her mouth [. . .][48]

The sexual intercourse between the witch and the devil eventually becomes a joyful, Rabelaisian communion with the rest of the human, animal and natural world ('she felt like everyone / everywhere was getting what they wanted').[49] The historically desecrated and fearful coupling between the witch and the devil is here turned into a positive, regenerative and empowering pantheistic union which confers energy on to beings, animals and natural world alike. Queer desire is thus pivotal in the textual process of redefinition and assertion of the witch. Traditionally perceived as a 'wicked woman' uncannily fusing 'masculine' and 'feminine',[50] the witch is here transformed into a figure on to whom all sorts of meanings, identifications, desires and fantasies can be transcribed and modified.

Conclusion

The texts discussed in this chapter show how the figure of the witch is a powerful archetype that continues to stimulate and challenge writers in countless ways. As liminal beings, witches do not fit into existing normative categories and discourses. As a consequence of their mysterious, occult nature, they are open signifiers that allow the production of meanings that work against established, oppressive systems. The four authors here analysed explore and rewrite the iconic figure of the witch by offering a wide range of queer Gothic revisitations ranging across literary genres, from fiction to fairy tales and experimental poetry. All of them adopt and revisit the queer Gothic mode in order to create a discursive space in which new forms of sexed and gendered identities and embodiments can be explored and challenged in order to forge a new vision of the world. Moreover, Winterson, Duffy, Donoghue and Tamàs demonstrate how the Queer Gothic mode remains crucial in evoking, reassessing and actualising the past by giving voice and visibility to those countless silent and hidden queer figures who have challenged the societies in which they lived. These texts share a number of Gothic tropes which enhance their subversive qualities, as well as exploring and articulating women's abuse and exploitation, female same-sex relationships and non-hegemonic forms of masculinity. The Queer Gothic mode is thus crucial in this narrative and cultural process of transformation of outcast historical figures into powerful queer archetypes, who interpellate contemporary readers and elicit a powerful emotional response. In so doing, they create a feminist and queer genealogy that represents the lives of liminal individuals, whose 'haunting' presences are intensified by intersecting axes of queerness.

Notes

1. Malcolm Gaskill, *Witchcraft: A Very Short Introduction* (Abingdon: Routledge, 2010), pp. 27, 112.
2. Robin Briggs has published an important study on the sex distribution of witchcraft suspects across Europe in the early modern period. See *Witches and Neighbours: The Social and Cultural Context of European Witchcraft*, 2nd edn (London: Blackwell, 2002).
3. The debate on the relationship between witch-hunting and gender relations is fraught with different viewpoints and theoretical assumptions. Among the large number of works written on the subject, it is worth mentioning Christina Larner's seminal study, which famously posited that witchcraft was 'sex-related' but not 'sex-specific', as women were not the only persecuted category. For Larner, it is crucial to understand the wider cultural dynamics at stake in order to grasp the reasons why women were more vulnerable to accusations of witchcraft as well as other crimes such as sexual offences and infanticide. See Christina Larner, *Witchcraft and Religion: The Politics of Popular Belief* (London: Blackwell, 1984), pp. 35–67. Different perspectives are embraced, for example, by Elizabeth Reis's study on witchcraft in puritan New England and Sarah Ferber's work on the persecution of female witches in the context of the Catholic Reformation in early modern France. See Elizabeth Reis, *Damned Women: Sinners and Witches*

in Puritan New England (New York: Cornell University Press, 1997), and Sarah Ferber, *Demonic Possession and Exorcism in Early Modern France* (London: Routledge, 2004). These works demonstrate that both Protestants and Catholics embraced a model of femininity that encouraged and supported the identification of witchcraft with women, who were socially figured as vulnerable vessels for demons and spirits due to their passivity.

4. Hans Peter Broedel, *The Malleus Maleficarum and the Construction of Witchcraft: Theology and Popular Belief* (Manchester: Manchester University Press, 2003), p. 44.
5. Clive Holmes, 'Women, Witches and Witnesses', *Past and Present*, 140 (1993), pp. 44–64 (p. 44). Darren Oldridge notes that the preoccupation with female wickedness shown in the *Malleus* is mostly absent from later demonologies, though there was a consensus on the fact that women were weaker and thus more vulnerable to the Devil's temptations. See Darren Oldridge, 'Witchcraft and Gender', in *The Witchcraft Reader. Second Edition*, ed. Darren Oldridge (Abingdon: Routledge, 2008), p. 251.
6. Elizabeth Kent, 'Masculinity and Male Witches in Old and New England', *History Workshop Journal*, 60.1 (2005), pp. 69–92.
7. Geoffrey Scarre, *Witchcraft and Magic in Sixteenth and Seventeenth-Century Europe* (London: Macmillan, 1987), p. 53.
8. Diane Purkiss, *The Witch in History: Early Modern and Twentieth-Century Representations* (London: Routledge 1996), p. 2.
9. Oldridge, 'Witchcraft and Gender', p. 250.
10. I'd like to thank Ardel Thomas for pointing this out.
11. As Alice D. Dreger and April M. Herndon have pointed out, '[h]istorically, the tendency in the West [. . .] has been to try to keep people sorted into clear male and female roles, and people with intersex seem to have generally participated in that binary sorting [. . .] [As a consequence,] hermaphrodites were strictly required to adhere to one gender (male or female) and to partner only with someone of the other gender, to avoid the appearance of homosexual or other "deviant" sexuality.' Alice D. Dreger and April M. Herndon, 'Progress and Politics in the Intersex Rights Movement: Feminist Theory in Action', *A Journal of Lesbian and Gay Studies*, 15.2 (2009), pp. 199–224 (p. 201).
12. Lyndal Roper, *The Witch in the Western Imagination* (Charlottesville: University of Virginia Press, 2012), p. 17.
13. Rosemary Jackson, *Fantasy: The Literature of Subversion* (London: Routledge, 1981), p. 41.
14. See Mair Rigby, 'Uncanny Recognition: Queer Theory's Debt to the Gothic', *Gothic Studies*, 11.1 (2009), pp. 46–57 (p. 51); Paulina Palmer, *The Queer Uncanny: New Perspective on the Gothic* (Cardiff: University of Wales Press, 2012), pp. 1–22; George Haggerty, *Queer Gothic* (Urbana, IL: University of Illinois Press, 2006), p. 2.
15. William Hughes and Andrew Smith, 'Introduction: Queering the Gothic', in *Queering the Gothic*, ed. William Hughes and Andrew Smith (Manchester: Manchester University Press, 2009), p. 1.
16. Eve Kosofsky Sedgwick, *The Coherence of Gothic Conventions* (New York: Methuen, 1986), pp. 128–34.
17. As Haggerty has emphasised, 'Gothic fiction is not about homo- or heterodesire as much as it is about the fact of desire itself' (*Queer Gothic*, p. 2).

18. Gaskill, *Witchcraft*, p. 3. He adds that the '[m]eanings of witchcraft are so varied because the concept is so versatile' (ibid., p. 3).
19. Marina Warner, *Fantastic Metamorphoses, Other Worlds: Ways of Telling the Self* (Oxford: Oxford University Press, 2002), p. 159.
20. The most detailed account of the Pendle Witches Trial is *The Wonderfull Discoverie of Witches in the Countie of Lancaster* by Thomas Potts (1612). The trial has inspired several accounts over the course of time: William Harrison Ainsworth, *The Lancashire Witches* (1849); Robert Neill, *Mist over Pendle* (1951); Blake Morrison, *Pendle Witches* (1996); 'The Lancashire Witches' by Carol Ann Duffy (2012); and a documentary narrated by Simon Armitage, *The Pendle Witch Child*, shown in August 2012 on BBC 4.
21. Rachel A. C. Hasted, *The Pendle Witch Trial 1612* (Lancaster: Lancashire County Books, 1993), p. 3.
22. See Robert Poole, *The Lancashire Witches: Histories and Stories* (Manchester: Manchester University Press, 2002); and John A. Clayton, *The Lancashire Witch Conspiracy*, 2nd edn (Pendle: Barrowford Press, 2007).
23. On this point, Palmer has emphasised that 'These ideas are pertinent to the lesbian who, encouraged by homophobic attitudes to keep her sexual orientation secret and lead a double life, frequently becomes a figure of psychic division.' Paulina Palmer, 'Lesbian Gothic: Genre, Transformation, Transgression', *Gothic Studies*, 6.1 (2004) pp. 118–30 (p. 119).
24. See Judith Butler, *The Psychic Life of Power: Theories in Subjection* (Stanford, CA: Stanford University Press, 1997).
25. Ruth Parkin-Gounelas, *Literature and Psychoanalysis: Intertextual Readings* (Basingstoke: Palgrave, 2001), p. 109.
26. See Terry Castle, *The Apparitional Lesbian: Female Homosexuality and Modern Culture* (New York: Columbia University Press, 1993).
27. Diana Fuss, 'Introduction', in *Inside/Out: Lesbian Theories, Gay Theories*, ed. Diana Fuss (New York: Routledge, 1991), p. 3.
28. Palmer, 'Lesbian Gothic', p. 120.
29. See Fuss, 'Introduction', p. 1 n. 10; Castle, *The Apparitional Lesbian*; Heather Love, *Feeling Backward: Loss and the Politics of Queer History* (Cambridge, MA: Harvard University Press, 2007).
30. Queer love triangles are frequently adopted by Winterson to dismantle hegemonic representational identity models. Love triangles are discussed by Eve Kosofsky Sedgwick in *Between Men: English Literature and Male Homosocial Desire* (New York: Columbia University Press, 1985). In her analysis of several eighteenth- and nineteenth-century English and American novels, Sedgwick argued that social relations were often built around a triangle between two men and a woman. In her opinion, this is a model of homosocial bonding in which male desire overpowers and ultimately displaces the female subject, who is consequently isolated. A variation of this relational archetype was studied by Terry Castle, who developed Sedgwick's reflections on the triangulation of desire in order to theorise the existence of a female counter-triangulation in lesbian novels. According to Castle, female bonding causes a disruptive effect on the male homosocial order and leads to the formation of a new triangle in which the male subject is isolated from the female-dominated relationship (see Castle, *The Apparitional Lesbian*, pp. 72–4). The shift from male homosocial

bonds to dynamic female/lesbian triangulated relationships is at the core of Winterson's novels, in which they also become symbols of creativity and artistic inspiration. See Silvia Antosa, 'In a Queer Gothic Space and Time: Love Triangles in Jeanette Winterson's *The Daylight Gate*', *Altre Modernità/Other Modernities*, 13 (May 2015), pp. 152–67.
31. See Jack Halberstam, *In a Queer Space and Time: Transgender Bodies, Subcultural Lives* (New York: NYU Press, 2005).
32. Ibid., pp. 2, 1.
33. The text of the poem can be found here: https://literarylancasterpoems2.weebly.com/the-lancaster-witches-carol-ann-duffy.html (accessed 25 June 2021).
34. Gaskill, *Witchcraft*, p. 52.
35. Linda Hutcheon, *A Poetics of Postmodernism: History, Theory, Fiction* (London: Routledge, 1988), p. 114.
36. https://literarylancasterpoems2.weebly.com/the-lancaster-witches-carol-ann-duffy.html (accessed 21 September 2021).
37. Gaskill, *Witchcraft*, p. 112.
38. Halberstam, *In a Queer Space*, p. 2.
39. Judith Butler, 'Frames of War: When Is Life Grievable?', https://www.versobooks.com/blogs/2339-judith-butler-precariousness-and-grievability-when-is-life-grievable (accessed 14 July 2021). See also *Precarious Life: The Powers of Mourning and Violence* (London: Verso, 2006).
40. Halberstam, *In a Queer Space*, p. 23.
41. Jennifer Orme, 'Mouth to Mouth: Queer Desires in Emma Donoghue's "Kissing the Witch"', *Marvels & Tales*, 24.1 (2010), special issue, 'The Fairy Tale after Angela Carter', pp. 116–30 (p. 118).
42. Emma Donoghue, *Kissing the Witch: Old Tales in New Skins* (Harmondsworth: Penguin, 1997), p. 191, italics in the text.
43. Ibid., p. 200.
44. Ibid., p. 210. The reference to the girl's red hair with its symbolic connotations of embodied desire and passion, together with the witch's wish to 'give her [her] heart in a bag and let her do with it what she pleases' (p. 210), call to mind the figure of Villanelle in Jeanette Winterson's *Passion* (1997).
45. Donoghue, *Kissing the Witch*, p. 211.
46. Rebecca Tamàs, *Witch* (London: Penned in the Margins, 2019), p. 13.
47. Alice Hiller, '"I wanted to think about the possibility of a revolution based on female principles": Rebecca Tamàs Speaks with Alice Hiller' (2019), https://alicehiller.info/2019/03/26/i-wanted-to-think-about-the-possibility-of-a-revolution-based-on-female-principles-rebecca-tamas-speaks-with-alice-hiller/ (accessed 31 July 2021).
48. Tamàs, *Witch*, p. 24.
49. Ibid., p. 24.
50. Anne Williams, 'Wicked Women', in *Women and the Gothic: An Edinburgh Companion*, ed. Avril Horner and Sue Zlosnik (Edinburgh: Edinburgh University Press), p. 98.

Part III

Queer Forms

Chapter 11

Queer Gothic Poetry
Clayton Carlyle Tarr

The adjectives in this title are tautological: queer poetry is Gothic, and Gothic poetry, queer. Separating these categories, perhaps paradoxically, creates more confusion. What is queer poetry? Is poetry a queer form of prose? And what about free verse? Does denying metre and rhyme mean queering normative form? Could we read Milton's blank-verse rejection of rhyming couplets – 'the invention of a barbarous age' – as unpairing heteronormative iambic pentameter?[1] Gothic poetry presents similar challenges. Must Gothic poems adhere to the ingredients from an anonymous 1797 Gothic 'recipe' that instructed readers to '[m]ix them together, in the form of three volumes'?[2] Do they even follow Eve Kosofsky Sedgwick's 'coherence of Gothic conventions'?[3] The answer, I think, is no. Gothic poetry, perhaps limited by formal constraints, is not limited by thematic ingredients. A Gothic poem does not need an 'old castle', a 'long gallery', 'murdered bodies', 'skeletons', an 'old woman hanging by the neck, with her throat cut' or 'assassins and desperadoes'.[4] Nor does it even necessitate a monstrosity, the cardinal ingredient of the pre-eminent Gothic novels *Frankenstein* (1818, 1831) and *Dracula* (1897). So is Gothic poetry like pornography, in that we know it when we see it? The answer, again, is probably no. In fact, to understand Gothic poetry is to associate it with queer poetry. What makes a poem Gothic is its queerness, its introduction of a host of uncanny elements that release readers from the normative tethers of ideological reality. Wielding this loose, baggy monster of a definition, my focus in this chapter is to generate categories by which queer Gothic poetry might be recognised. At the very least, I hope to show how some familiar poems might be reassessed as both queer *and* Gothic – or, better yet, queer Gothic.

Recent scholarship has forged valuable links between Gothic and queer that are crucial to the study of queer Gothic poetry. George E. Haggerty was among the first to note the confluence of Gothic fiction with the codification of gender and sexuality. Normative sexuality, Haggerty notes, is 'insistently challenged and in some cases significantly undermined' in Gothic fiction.[5] Since Gothic literature, inaugurated by Horace Walpole's *The Castle of Otranto* (1764), developed into a cultural phenomenon at the end of the eighteenth century, it is important to understand proto-queer representations during the Romantic period.[6] Michael O'Rourke and David Collings note that 'Romanticism and queer theory alike favor the indefinite and the boundless'.[7] Such a reading not only queers the sublime, a mainstay of the Gothic, but also constructs the picturesque, its counterpart, as a normalising framework. Catherine Morland's misunderstanding of the picturesque in Jane Austen's *Northanger Abbey* (1817) makes her a queer pioneer. By rejecting aesthetic boundaries, she supports her own anomalous role of not being 'born . . . a heroine'; in more ways than one, Catherine breaks frames.[8] What is more, the dissolution of the self that accompanies the sublime resembles the Gothic's unnerving impact on readers. Ellis Hanson argues that queer theorists can engage the Gothic for 'the creative transfiguration of the self through the readerly pleasures of fear and abjection'.[9] Indeed, the Gothic and its descendants (sensation fiction, detective fiction, science fiction) draw attention to the embodied reader, who experiences physiological reactions that destabilise notions of the normalised self.[10]

The Gothic's foundational interest in breaking boundaries of genre and selfhood queers regimental literary forms and effects. 'Gothic has', William Hughes and Andrew Smith succinctly note, 'always been "queer"'.[11] Several critics have located queer and Gothic at a site of liminality, noting shared flexibility and resistance to rigid definition.[12] Paulina Palmer emphasises queer connections to the Gothic, which is a 'highly mobile and fluid literary form'.[13] And Ardel Haefele-Thomas observes that both queer and Gothic 'interrogate ideas of what is "respectable" and what is "normal"'.[14] Building on scholarship on queer Romanticism, Haefele-Thomas elsewhere notes that '[t]he Victorian era was teeming with queer possibilities', which were often present in the Gothic's 'queer constructions of monstrosity'.[15] Oscar Wilde's Dorian Gray, both sexually fluid and ontologically unstable, exemplifies the Victorian period's construction of queer monstrosities. Studies of queer Gothic have recently shifted focus into the twentieth and twenty-first centuries, noting how queer expressions continue to evoke Gothic forms. Laura Westengard, for example, notes that 'queer culture [. . .] responds to and challenges traumatic marginalization by creating a distinctly Gothic rhetoric and aesthetic'.[16] Unstated in the rich scholarship on queer Gothic, however, is its implicit emphasis on the novel as the wellspring of gothicism. Gothic poetry's representations of and influences on queer expression and experience have not been fully developed in critical circles, which have been overly reliant on the novel's authority in the genre. Poetry might offer a way to queer queer Gothic.

One path to such a reclamation is to explore the intersections of queer and poetic form. In addition to blank or free verse, other types of rhyming (slant, eye, identical, etc.) queer normative form. In 'Because I could not stop for death', for example, Emily Dickinson uses slant, identical and consonance rhyme to queer the ABCB structure she establishes in the first stanza.[17] Doing so further emphasises the queer Gothic content of the poem, which, among other possible readings, likens heteronormative marriage to death. And this is not to mention experiments with metre and rhythm, plays on stresses, line lengths and numbers, punctuation pacing, and the erotics of oral articulation. The 'sprung rhythm' poetry of Gerard Manley Hopkins exemplifies such formal experimentation. Hopkins's accent manipulation and 'dense chain[s] of alliteration and assonance' encourage certain enunciations that stimulate physiological responses from readers.[18] Gothic elements tinge Hopkins's poems, which stage confrontations between religious devotion and existential crises. But these confrontations also create queer effects when combined with the 'sustained sensual rhapsody'of Hopkins's poetic form.[19] The queer iconography of spondaic (/ /) and pyrrhic (u u) feet is manifest, and this is not to mention the polyamorous dactyl (/ u u) and anapaest (u u /). Modifications of line lengths and numbers also create queer forms. When William Butler Yeats divides the eleventh line of 'Leda and the Swan' (1923), he creates a dramatic caesura, bifurcating the line following its third foot. Doing so violates the structure of the Petrarchan sonnet, making the sestet, generally reserved for answering questions that the octave proposed, ask yet another question: 'Did she put on his knowledge with his power / Before the indifferent beak could let her drop?' (lines 14–15).[20] Yeats reflects the Gothic mysticism of the poem's content through the queering of its form, the sonnet structure itself receiving '[a] sudden blow' (line 1), irreparably divided by Yeats's Zeus-like assault.

While not fully pursuing these queer forms, this chapter nonetheless elevates structure and content over context and intention. Queer Gothic elements, I hope to demonstrate, permeate myriad types of poetry, regardless of the historical moment. Yet one caveat is that my selection of poems focuses exclusively on British authors of the long nineteenth century. There are two reasons for this limited perspective: my own scholarship is regrettably narrow, which restricts my knowledge of and comfort with a host of global poets throughout literary history.

My hope is that more capable scholars will fill the considerable gaps this chapter leaves behind. The second reason is more excusable: the nineteenth century witnessed the development of Gothic poetry, no doubt the offspring of the Gothic novel, but also born from the influence of many other sources, including Anglo-Saxon epics, medieval ballads and eighteenth-century graveyard poems. Samuel Taylor Coleridge, for example, may have founded the Gothic poem in England, translating German tragedies, and supplying the 'supernatural' pieces in *Lyrical Ballads* (1798, 1800).[21] And Alfred, Lord Tennyson, Poet Laureate for over four decades, wrote extensively in the Gothic mode. 'The Lady of Shalott' (1832, 1842) arguably fulfils more Gothic 'conventions' than some noteworthy Gothic novels. Robert Browning's 'Porphyria's Lover' (1836, 1842), to mention one final example, quite explicitly illustrates a performance of erotic asphyxiation, made all the more queer because the 'lover' remains ungendered.[22] Perhaps most important, the nineteenth century also witnessed the discursive categorisation of sexuality, a process best elucidated by Michel Foucault, wherein the systematic normalisation of biological functions and sexual preferences entailed the establishment of divergencies labelled physiologically degenerate and cognitively aberrant. By studying non-normative symbols and themes in nineteenth-century poetry, then, we can discover the origins of queer insurgence. It is no coincidence that both Coleridge and Tennyson write with such queer energy, given the dynamics of their early intellectual partnerships with men.[23]

With an eye towards symbols and themes, this chapter divides into two sections that explore queer elements of Gothic poetry. Admittedly, my use of queer is somewhat limited, engaging mostly with its sexual or bodily connotations.[24] That is, the scope of this chapter does not include non- or anti-normative conceptions of race, ethnicity, class or most of the other 'open mesh of possibilities, gaps, overlaps, dissonances and resonances, lapses and excesses of meaning' that constitute queer.[25] This chapter's first section takes inspiration from what Richard Sha has called 'the vagaries of biological sex' and introduces poems that question the authority of heteronormative bodies and sexualities.[26] Poets represent these queer forms primarily through androgynous combinations of natural images – fountains and caves, thorns and hills, mountains and valleys. The second section highlights moments of sapphic desire in Gothic poetry, specifically observing how erotic interactions between women structure plots of fear, redemption and dissolution. It is my hope that, rather than limiting queer Gothic poetry to a selection of poems from a narrow historical period, these sections instigate a conversation to identify a new genre that is fluid, dynamic and expansive.

Androgynous Forms

This section examines queer Gothic poems that feature what I am terming androgynous forms – that is, they introduce settings or characters with dual, and sometimes duelling, images of male and female sexual/reproductive biology. What I hope to show is that these images, coloured with Gothic touches, suggest anxiety about heteronormative and cisnormative bodies, the process of heterosexual intercourse, and the products of reproduction. Coleridge's 'Kubla Khan' is a good place to begin, as it was composed in 1797, when both the Gothic and Romanticism took shape. Anne Mellor has observed that the fragmentary poem introduces an 'image that is simultaneously ejaculative and parturitive'.[27] This reading demonstrates how 'Kubla Khan' embeds male and female reproductivity within an exotic fantasy that doubles as an erotic nightmare. John Spencer Hill has cautioned readers against 'strained and unwarranted speculation' that attempts to psychoanalyse 'the symbolic significance' of Coleridge's images.[28] But the poem's vivid, yet dreamy, imagery has remained difficult to untether from sexual forms and forces. Indeed, Coleridge's recollection of 'taking his pen, ink, and paper' to reproduce 'the scattered lines and images' doubles as a process of insemination, reflecting the poem's representations of intercourse and reproduction.[29] 'Kubla Khan' juxtaposes natural images that symbolise male and female sexual embodiment. The female-oriented 'pleasure dome' (line 2) and 'deep romantic chasm' (line 12) stand beside the male-oriented 'mighty fountain' (line 19) of 'chaffy grain' (line 22). That this strenuous activity sinks into a 'lifeless ocean' (line 28), however, suggests the impotency of the performance, reflecting Coleridge's incapacity (or impotency) to complete the fragment. The contradiction of a 'sunny pleasure-dome with caves of ice!' (line 36) indicates the failure of the heterosexual copulation that produces '[h]uge fragments' (line 21), like the fragmentary poem. In the fourth stanza, Coleridge introduces the 'vision' of an 'Abyssinian maid' (lines 37–8), whose dulcimer song the poet pointedly cannot reproduce. The female singer accomplishes a sort of immaculate conception, an asexual reproduction that Coleridge cannot equal with his aggressive heterosexual performance.

Wordsworth raises similar stakes in 'The Thorn' (1798). Resembling the positioning of Coleridge's sexualised images, Wordsworth juxtaposes the phallic 'old and grey' and 'erect' thorn of 'knotted joints' (lines 4, 6, 8) against the womblike 'beauteous heap, a hill of moss' (line 35).[30] Wordsworth adds another feature to the landscape, 'a little muddy pond / of water never dry' (lines 29–30), meant to be produced and perpetually refilled by Martha Ray, who 'sits, between the heap', the hill, and the pond in a 'scarlet cloak' (lines 60, 63). Martha, over two decades previously, had been engaged to Stephen Hill, who secretly married another woman. The trauma of Stephen's deceit enflames a 'cruel, cruel fire' that 'drie[s]' Martha's 'body like a cinder. / And almost turned her brain to tinder' (lines 129, 131–2). Abandoned, mad and pregnant, Martha's mental anguish manifests in physical trauma, causing either miscarriage or stillbirth. According to Jennifer Buckley, Wordsworth draws on eighteenth-century theories of the 'maternal imagination', wherein 'the pregnant woman will transmit unwanted qualities to the foetus, or even terminate the pregnancy through her violent emotions'.[31] Local gossips speculate about murder, and the speaker maintains Martha's innocence, but all parties agree that '[t]he little babe was buried there, / Beneath that hill of moss so fair' (lines 219–20). Crucially, the androgynous landscape remains active, though in a different respect to Coleridge's scene in 'Kubla Khan'. Moving mosses that grow upward from the hill 'strive / To drag [the thorn] to the ground' (lines 245–6). The doomed heterosexual union between Martha and Stephen ultimately produces only death, as the mosses attempt to reunite womb and phallus in a macabre dalliance.

In 'Mont Blanc' (1816), Percy Bysshe Shelley enlarges the androgynous landscape to sublime proportions, illustrating not just the life-giving process of glacial movement, but also its catastrophic destructiveness. That Shelley engages the mountain and its surrounding terrain as a metaphor for the activity of the poet's mind shows how heteronormative combinations both stimulate the imagination and breed chaos. Part of this chaos is formal: Shelley queers iambic pentameter with unpatterned rhymes that satisfy neither heroic couplets nor blank verse. This formal contradiction speaks to the opposition at the heart of the poem between the mountain's dual role as provider and destroyer. William Keach observes that 'the syntax and versification' of the poem 'make[] us think differently about the straining swell and flow of Shelley's lines'.[32] The first stanza establishes the influence of '[t]he everlasting universe of things' (line 1) on the poetic mind.[33] Like the titular mountain that eventually feeds the Arve, '[t]he source of human thought' begins as a 'feeble brook' and ends as a 'vast river' (lines 5, 7, 10). The second stanza moves to nature, but not yet to Mont Blanc. Instead, Shelley first locates readers in the 'dark, deep Ravine' (line 12) of the Arve, which echoes Coleridge's 'deep romantic chasm' in 'Kubla Khan'. This 'Dizzy Ravine!' (line 34) brings the poet into a 'trance sublime' (line 35), during which the mind 'receives fast influencings' (line 38), catching flashes of 'things that are' (line 46). This symbol for the female body disorients the poet, freeing his mind to gather images of truth. Again, form comes into play, as the third stanza, the centre of five, rises to view Mont Blanc. The positive sublime of the ravine transitions to the negative sublime of the mountain. The male symbol resists signification, displaying its broken signifiers through destruction: 'how hideously / Its shapes are heaped around! rude bare, and high / Ghastly, and scarred, and riven' (lines 69–71). Shelley continues to trace the destruction of the mountain's movement in stanza four, during which 'glaciers creep / Like snakes that watch their prey' (lines 100–1). This 'flood of ruin' (line 107) drives into 'secret chasms in tumult welling' (line 122) and finally flows into the Arve, '[t]he breath and blood of distant lands' (line 124). Stanza five returns to the poetic mind and '[t]he secret strength of things / Which governs thought' (lines 139–40). Shelley sees both productive and destructive power in the heteronormative coupling of the mountain and the ravine. Like this natural power, Shelley's poetry becomes the 'breath and blood of distant lands'. But what about the destruction this sustenance causes at the source? While the poetic imagination feeds distant readers, it wrenches and divides the poet, who sacrifices stable mental ground.

Similar elements appear in many other queer Gothic poems. In John Keats's *Lamia* (1820), for example, Hermes transforms the eponymous snake into a beautiful maiden, in exchange for the revelation of an invisible nymph he is amorously pursuing. Lamia, in her initial serpentine form, is a Gothic monstrosity with distinctly androgynous attributes: 'Her head was serpent, but ah, bitter-sweet! / She had a woman's mouth with all its pearls complete' (lines 1.59–60).[34] While the serpent form suggests the phallus, the open mouth is vaginal (complete with anxiety over dentata). Denise Gigante observes that the mythical lamia's shape-shifting indeterminacy 'provide[s] an inherent critique of life as merely organization' and signals a 'distinctly Romantic, vitalist concept of monstrosity as too much life'.[35] But reading the poem through a queer lens might also suggest Lamia's transformation as sex affirmation. She identifies as a woman, and Hermes constructs her female form through what Garrett Stewart has called a 'brutal transfiguration': 'The colours all inflam'd throughout her train, / She writh'd about, convuls'd with scarlet pain' (lines 1.152–3).[36] But she is ultimately destroyed by the power of Apollonius's piercing, prejudiced gaze: 'the sophist's eyes, / Like a sharp spear, went through her utterly' (lines 1.299–300). Apollonius, the 'patriarchal superego', rejects Lamia's control over her own identity, weaponising his gaze not just to reposition her as other, but to dissolve her subjectivity entirely: 'with a frightful scream she vanished' (line 2.306).[37] Lamia's inherent queerness – expressed psychologically, biologically and ontologically – cannot exist in the heteronormative world guarded by Apollonius's 'overdetermined masculinity'.[38]

A host of other Gothic poems engage queer settings and characterisations. The tower in Tennyson's 'The Lady of Shalott' (1832, 1842), for example, acts as both phallus and womb, until the doomed figure escapes, stillborn, down the birth canal to Camelot. The Lady of Shalott weaves a 'magic web' of 'shadows' at Camelot, reflected in her 'mirror clear' (lines 38, 71, 46), forming a complex metaphor that reconstitutes, if not radically upends, the stories of Plato's cave and the three Fates. Ensconced and enchanted in the tower, she disregards images of a 'curly shepherd lad', a 'long-hair'd page' and the knights who 'come riding two and two' (lines 57, 58, 62). But 'bold' (line 77) Sir Lancelot proves too beguiling. His 'brazen greaves', sparkling shield, 'gemmy bridle', '[t]hick-jewell'd' saddle, and 'coal-black curls' (lines 76, 82, 92, 103) make him something of a queer idol.[39] That he rides 'between the barley-sheaves', which Tennyson earlier describes as 'bearded', suggests that his 'bow shot', or perhaps the 'mighty silver bugle' that hangs from his 'blazon'd baldric' (lines 74, 29, 73, 88, 87), is vaginally directed. Tennyson's wordplay with 'stay' in line 40 ('A curse is on her, if she stay') renders the Lady of Shalott cursed whether she *stops* weaving or *remains* in 'the silent isle' (line 17). But her sexual awakening ('the water-lily bloom' [line 111]), triggered by a call to heteronormativity, comprises the real curse of her existence. Having 'left the web' and 'left the loom', she descends to a boat 'Beneath a willow' (lines 109, 124), connecting her to Ophelia, similarly doomed by love for a shallow man. Read through the repressive context of female virginity, the 'web' functions as the hymen 'broken utterly' by Lancelot, which causes the Lady of Shalott to waste away: 'her blood was frozen slowly / and her eyes were darken'd wholly' (lines 146–7).[40] Medieval or modern, she is fated either to toil at chaste domesticity or to die for hollow heteronormativity

Robert Browning's poetry might also be read through a queer Gothic lens. In 'My Last Duchess' (1842), the murderous Duke ends his dowry tour by flaunting a statue of Neptune '[t]aming a sea-horse' (line 55).[41] On the one hand, Browning refers to the mythic horses that share the sea-god's domain, the taming of which can be seen in Antoine Coysevox's statue *Neptune* (1705). On the other hand, Browning pits the Roman god against the diminutive fish, illustrating the Duke's perceived dominance. That female seahorses deposit their eggs into males, however, suggests the Duke's misconception about his power, which remains tied to the animated blush of his 'last Duchess painted on the wall, / Looking as if she were alive' (lines 1–2).[42] Browning's 'Childe Roland to the Dark Tower Came' (1855) features similar queer symbols, its landscape unmistakably androgynous. The poem chronicles the titular knight's journey through a psychic hellscape. Isobel Armstrong asserts that '[n]o women enter the poem except through hints of adultery which may as well suggest homosexual relations'.[43] But the phallic tower, the search for which has trapped Roland's fellow knights in ghostly purgatory, is surrounded by female landmarks, including the 'little river' where the knight thinks he hears a 'baby's shriek', the 'two hills' and the 'tall scalped mountain' (lines 109, 126, 176, 178).[44] Roland's suicidal quest is not restricted to the tower's 'phallic power', but also expresses anxieties about the female body, thus questioning heteronormative structures.[45]

Sapphic Forms

This section examines queer Gothic poems that depict forms of sapphic desire. The purpose of representing this desire varies widely, ranging from condemnation to celebration. That these poems, generally speaking, code this desire (through hedging, resistant, anti-normative manoeuvres) marks them as queer rather than homosexual. They share, in other words, an interest in exploring subjectivities that lie beyond heteronormative structures, without necessarily announcing themselves as wholly lesbian. Terming such modes sapphic (after the Ancient Greek poet Sappho) rather than lesbian emphasises the significance of the imagination and potentially frees readers to understand representations of this desire as something closer to Adrienne Rich's 'continuum' than to more rigidly erotic associations.[46] To begin once again with Coleridge further establishes his role as a progenitor of queer forms. That he composed 'Kubla Khan' and *Christabel* in the same year, moreover, marks 1797 as arguably the inaugural year for queer Gothic poetry. Readers have long identified the sapphic storyline in *Christabel*. Terry Castle calls the poem 'one of the strangest sapphic fantasias in all of European literature', which reveals Coleridge's 'lifelong, enigmatic fascination with lesbian sexuality'.[47] Indeed, Andrew Elfenbein has revealed that Coleridge and Wordsworth, while composing *Lyrical Ballads*, shared possession of *The Frisky Songster* (c. 1770), a collection of lecherous verses. Elfenbein observes that the text's 'obscene moments of women exposing themselves to women provide a hitherto unacknowledged background for Christabel's vision of disrobing Geraldine'.[48] The scene to which Elfenbein refers structures the dramatic climax of the poem's first part. Christabel, lovesick and night-time wandering, encounters Geraldine, who claims to have been abducted. The pair sneak into

Christabel's chamber, and Geraldine exposes herself while preparing for bed, thereby placing Christabel under a curse.

Coleridge provides clues to the poem's sapphic themes well before the disrobing scene. Mourning under an oak tree, Christabel hears a 'moan', which Coleridge (or perhaps Christabel herself) attributes initially to 'It' (line 39), as if the utterer has already been othered out of subjectivity.[49] That Geraldine hides behind the 'broad-breasted' (line 42) tree prefigures the significance of breasts in the poem. Christabel also finds Geraldine, '[b]eautiful exceedingly' (line 68), in a state of undress, wearing only a 'silken robe', and revealing her 'stately neck', bare arms and 'blue-veined feet' (lines 59, 62–3). Geraldine narrates her story of abduction at the hands of unidentified, villainous 'warriors' (line 81) and implores Christabel to 'share your couch with me' (line 122). Geraldine thereafter faints at the 'threshold' (line 132), in a scene that critics have read as vampiric, and recovers only after Christabel carries her across. Sneaking past Leoline, her slumbering father, Christabel appears already under Geraldine's thrall, seeing nothing but 'the lady's eye' and 'the boss of the shield of Sir Leoline' (lines 160, 162). The 'boss' here is a convex adornment at the centre of a shield, which might resemble the nipple or areola of a breast.[50] Christabel then trims her lamp, perhaps a symbol for castration, and lies in an inviting pose as Geraldine prepares for bed. Geraldine undoes a clasp and

> Her silken robe, and inner vest,
> Dropt to her feet, and full in view,
> Behold! her bosom and half her side——
> A sight to dream of, not to tell!
> O shield her! shield sweet Christabel! (lines 249–53)

To 'shield' recalls the 'boss' on the shield, but more important is the line Coleridge removed following the long dash: 'Are lean and old and foul of hue'. By excising the description of Christabel's breasts, Coleridge invites readers to speculate on the horror (or perhaps charm) that 'worketh a spell' (line 267) on Christabel. For Elfenbein, this blank 'marks an event so burdened with sublime horror that it cannot even be spoken'.[51] Geraldine refers to the unrepresented affliction as a 'mark of my shame' (line 270), suggesting that some secret sin has physically materialised on her breast. Christabel, having gazed on Geraldine's nude torso, subsequently takes on the burden. 'Sure I have sinned!' (line 381), she wails. In the poem's second part, Coleridge adds serpent imagery to Geraldine's increasingly supernatural appearance, anticipating Keats's *Lamia*. In the end, Christabel manages to resist the curse just long enough to plead with her father to banish Geraldine, a request Leoline rejects as an affront to his honoured guest. Of the many potential readings of the poem, ones that address its homoerotic impulses remain most convincing. Christabel's 'sin' is her desire for Geraldine, her attraction to the naked breast. And Geraldine's original sin, that which led to her possible banishment, is her own sapphic desire, which she fails to suppress in the company of Christabel. Coleridge, in a patriarchal move still familiar today, seeks simultaneously to fetishise and to condemn lesbian desire, which is both arousing and sinful. Although Geraldine's breast goes unrepresented, it is nonetheless the poem's focal image – 'A sight to dream of, not to tell!' (line 252).

Whereas *Christabel*, at best, defines sapphic desire ambiguously, Christina Rossetti's 'Goblin Market' (1862) expresses the essential vitality of sororal devotion. Lizzie saves her sister Laura through corporeal sacrifice, braving violent, rapacious goblin men to ensure the safety and endurance of their maternal society. Yet, as Terry Castle remarks, the children's poem remains 'shockingly homoerotic'.[52] Other critics have questioned such readings. For Jeannette Howard Foster, the poem's 'vivid narrative is too symbolic for precise sexual interpretation'.[53] And Sandra M. Gilbert and Susan Gubar have referred to its 'covertly (if ambiguously) lesbian world'.[54] This ambiguity makes 'Goblin Market' fundamentally queer, more concerned with sisterly devotion than lesbian desire. That is, conspicuously erotic lines, including '[h]ug me, kiss me, suck my juices' (line 468), are less important than the closing lines that depict the coterie of women maintained and propagated by Lizzie's sacrifice.[55] Helena Michie observes that Lizzie, in order 'to reconstruct a shared sororal space', in fact 'fuses with Laura in the act of replacing her'.[56] This fusion might explain how the sisters manage to produce 'children of their own' (line 545), despite the absence of non-goblin men. In Rossetti's female utopia, it seems, women reproduce asexually, able not only to fuse, but also to bud.[57] Thus, we might read Lizzie's heroic encounter as cross-pollination, wherein the goblins figure more like bees, and Laura's subsequent feeding triggers the germination of her own seeds.

The queer Gothicism of 'Goblin Market' also emerges pictorially and formally. Rossetti's brother, Dante Gabriel Rossetti, provided illustrations for the 1862 collection *Goblin Market and Other Poems*. Joseph Bristow has noted that this commission gave Dante Gabriel an 'ideal opportunity to represent the potentially transgressive intimacy embodied in sisterhood', including details not conspicuously present in his sister's poem.[58] And Herbert Tucker has deftly pursued the poem's 'virtual orality', which involves 'adhesive memorability' and the 'seductive merger of gustatory with verbal oralities'.[59] Indeed, the 'iterated jingle / Of sugar-baited words' (lines 233–4) not only makes the goblins poets, but also suggests Rossetti's goblin-ness, as she has similarly lured her readers to purchase her wares and 'to listen and look' (line 328). Thus, we should reconsider the customary move to read Christina Rossetti and her sister Maria as models for Lizzie and Laura (or vice versa). Instead, we might see Christina and Dante Gabriel (if not William Michael Rossetti, who edited Christina's poems in 1904 and added his own sugary recollection that 'she did not mean anything profound by this fairy tale') as goblins, 'cooing all together // With their shrill repeated cry, / "Come buy, come buy"' (lines 78, 89–90).[60]

I would like to conclude with brief words about one more poem, which is perhaps the best representative for queer Gothic poetry. Algernon Charles Swinburne's 'Anactoria' (1866), in many respects a sister poem to 'Goblin Market', dismantles Rossetti's themes of sororal devotion, and reconstructs them as macabre obsession. For Antony Harrison, the poem represents 'one of Swinburne's more obviously carnal lyrics'.[61] Swinburne, who considered Sappho 'the very greatest poet that ever lived', expresses Sappho's desire for Anactoria through sadomasochism and cannibalism.[62] Anactoria's infidelity triggers in Sappho a range of destructive emotions, but the speaker ultimately writes herself out of mourning by realising the immortality of her poetry, which infuses the natural landscape: 'I Sappho shall be one with all these things' (line 276).[63] While Anactoria, who has caused Sappho such misery, will die, Sappho boasts: 'I say I shall not die' (line 290). The unparalleled queer Gothic energy of the poem's content only increases when we consider the dynamics of authorship. According to Yopie Prins, Swinburne's fascination with Sappho was so profound that he became her 'very reincarnation'.[64] In 'Anactoria', Swinburne inhabits Sappho's body and mind, using her as a mouthpiece to challenge Victorian heteronormativity. Thäis Morgan argues that Swinburne 'imagines homosexual practice between men through the analogy of lesbian coupling'.[65] The levels of narrative transmission conflate Ancient Greece with nineteenth-century England, unite Sappho and Swinburne, and bind lesbian and gay. Images of disintegration, consumption and fusion come to be less about Sappho and Anactoria than a queer Gothic dissolution of time, subjectivity and sexuality, rupturing hegemonic categories of normalcy.

Conclusion

I began this chapter by arguing that 'queer' and 'Gothic' are tautological, mutually inclusive models that have proved symbiotic, sympathetic and synergistic. I also suggested that 'poetry' might complete a multimodal triumvirate. If to be a poem is to be queer, and to be queer is to be Gothic, then, by the transitive law, to be a poem is to be Gothic. That the last connection might be a bridge too far demonstrates the significance of 'queer' as the central atom, chemically speaking, of a triatomic molecule. Queer, in other words, must be present to bond Gothic and poetry. Such an imbalanced relationship should prompt critical reconsideration of capitalisation customs. 'The Gothic' acquires precedence that is not afforded to 'realism', 'science fiction', 'the sentimental novel' or 'the sensation novel', to name only a few examples. Thus, 'queer gothic poetry' subtly loosens the subjugative shackles of 'queer Gothic poetry', much as bell hooks, k. d. lang and danah boyd have resisted the patriarchal oppression of capitalisation. Any resistance to the adoption of this proposal reveals the hegemonic erasure of 'the/a queer', as if only heteronormative or homonormative people can be subjects. Perhaps it is best to mimic the title of this chapter, no matter the position of its individual parts: Queer Gothic Poetry.

Notes

1. John Milton, *Paradise Lost*, ed. Gordon Teskey (New York: Norton, 2005), p. 2.
2. 'Terrorist Novel Writing', *Spirit of the Public Journals for 1797*, vol. 1 (London: James Ridgeway, 1802), pp. 227–29 (p. 229).
3. Sedgwick explains: 'You know something about the novel's form: it is likely to be discontinuous and involuted, perhaps incorporating tales within tales, changes of narrators, and such framing devices as found manuscripts or interpolated histories.' Eve Kosofsky Sedgwick, *The Coherence of Gothic Conventions* (New York: Arno, 1980), p. 8.
4. 'Terrorist', p. 229.
5. George E. Haggerty, *Queer Gothic* (Urbana, IL: University of Illinois Press, 2006), p. 3.
6. Richard Sha, working to counter the tendency to erase the Romantic period from the history of sexuality, argues that 'Romanticism was central to [homosexuality's] emergence'. Richard Sha, 'Romanticism and Sexuality – A Special Issue of Romanticism on the Net', *Romanticism on the Net*, 23 (2001), para. 1–12 (para. 7).
7. Michael O'Rourke and David Collings, 'Queer Romanticisms: Past, Present, and Future', *Romanticism on the Net*, 36–37 (2004–05), para. 1–42 (para. 4).
8. Jane Austen, *Northanger Abbey*, ed. Claire Grogan (Peterborough, Ont.: Broadview, 2002), p. 37.
9. Ellis Hanson, 'Queer Gothic', in *The Routledge Companion to Gothic*, ed. Catherine Spooner and Emma McEvoy (Abingdon: Routledge, 2007), pp. 174–82 (p. 175).

10. D. A. Miller notes that the sensation novel 'address[es] itself primarily to the sympathetic nervous system, where it grounds its characteristic adrenaline effects'. D. A. Miller, *The Novel and the Police* (Berkeley, CA: University of California Press, 1988), p. 146.
11. William Hughes and Andrew Smith, *Queering the Gothic* (Manchester: Manchester University Press, 2009), p. 1.
12. E. L. McCallum underscores the queer Gothic's 'investment in the liminal, the in-between, the brink – particularly, although not exclusively, the line between life and death'. E. L. McCallum, 'The "Queer Limits" in the Modern Gothic', in *The Cambridge Companion to the Modern Gothic*, ed. Jerrold E. Hogle (Cambridge: Cambridge University Press, 2014), pp. 71–86 (p. 77).
13. Paulina Palmer, *The Queer Uncanny: New Perspectives on the Gothic* (Cardiff: University of Wales Press, 2012), p. 11.
14. Ardel Haefele-Thomas, *Queer Others in Victorian Gothic: Transgressing Monstrosity* (Cardiff: University of Wales Press, 2012), p. 2.
15. Ardel Haefele-Thomas, 'Queer Victorian Gothic', in *Victorian Gothic: An Edinburgh Companion*, ed. Andrew Smith (Edinburgh: Edinburgh University Press, 2012), pp. 142–55 (pp. 152, 143).
16. Laura Westengard, *Gothic Queer Culture: Marginalized Communities and the Ghosts of Insidious Trauma* (Lincoln, NE: University of Nebraska Press, 2019), p. 3.
17. The first stanza's B rhymes are 'me' and 'Immortality'. But the remainder, if rhymes at all, are irregular: 'away' | 'Civility'; 'Ring' | Sun'; 'Chill' | 'Tulle'; 'Ground' | 'Ground'; 'Day' | 'Eternity'.
18. Martin Dubois, *Gerard Manley Hopkins and the Poetry of Religious Experience* (Cambridge: Cambridge University Press, 2017), p. 104.
19. C. Day Lewis, 'A Hope for Poetry', in *Gerard Manley Hopkins: The Critical Heritage*, ed. Gerald Roberts (London: Routledge, 1934), pp. 276–83 (p. 282).
20. William Butler Yeats, 'Leda and the Swan', in *The Collected Poems of W. B. Yeats*, ed. Richard J. Finneran (New York: Scribner, 1996), pp. 214–15 (p. 215, lines 14–15).
21. In *Biographia Literaria* (1817), Coleridge recalls that his poems were 'directed to persons and characters supernatural, or at least romantic', while Wordsworth would 'give the charm of novelty to things of every day'. Samuel Taylor Coleridge, *The Major Works*, ed. H. J. Jackson (Oxford: Oxford University Press, 2000), pp. 155–482 (p. 314).
22. See Catherine Ross, 'Browning's Porphyria's Lover', *Explicator*, 60.2 (2002), pp. 68–72; and Clayton Carlyle Tarr, 'Pleasurable Suspension: Erotic Asphyxiation in the Nineteenth Century', *Nineteenth-Century Contexts*, 38.1 (2016), pp. 55–68.
23. Wayne Koestenbaum argues that Coleridge's short-lived writing partnership with Wordsworth 'emerged from a moment of unexamined fraternity and heat'. Wayne Koestenbaum, *Double Talk: The Erotics of Male Literary Collaboration* (New York: Routledge, 1990), p. 74. And Tennyson's stimulating, and ultimately devastating, university relationship with Arthur Hallam has been labelled both homosexual and queer.

24. Ardel Haefele-Thomas offers a more useful and expansive definition, writing that queer theory 'supplies room for multiple, potentially polyvalent positions, conveying gender, sexuality, race, class, and familial structures beyond heteronormative (and often bourgeois) social constructs' (*Gothic*, p. 4).
25. Eve Kosofsky Sedgwick, 'Queer and Now', in *Tendencies* (London: Routledge, 1994), pp. 1–20 (p. 8).
26. Sha, 'Romanticism and Sexuality', p. 14.
27. Anne Mellor, *Romanticism and Feminism* (Bloomington, IN: Indiana University Press, 1988), p. 7. Barry Milligan clarifies Mellor's claim, noting that 'Kubla Khan' is 'wildly, even dangerously orgasmic' and that it 'hearken[s] perhaps more readily to seminal emission than to late eighteenth-century understandings of female ejaculation'. Barry Milligan, *Pleasures and Pains: Opium and the Orient in 19th-Century British Culture* (Charlottesville, VA: University of Virginia Press, 1995), p. 37.
28. John Spencer Hill, *A Coleridge Companion: An Introduction to the Major Poems and the* Biographia Literaria (London: Palgrave Macmillan, 1983), p. 100.
29. Coleridge, 'Kubla Khan', in *The Major Works*, ed. Jackson, pp. 102–4 (p. 102).
30. William Wordsworth, 'The Thorn', in *The Major Works*, ed. Stephen Gill (Oxford: Oxford University Press, 2008), pp. 59–66 (p. 59, lines 4, 6, 8).
31. Jenifer Buckley, *Gender, Pregnancy and Power in Eighteenth-Century Literature: The Maternal Imagination* (London: Palgrave Macmillan, 2017), p. 213.
32. William Keach, 'Rhyme and the Arbitrariness of Language', in *English Romantic Poetry*, ed. Harold Bloom (New York: Chelsea House, 2004), pp. 129–48 (p. 141).
33. Percy Bysshe Shelley, 'Mont Blanc', in *Shelley's Poetry and Prose*, ed. Donald H. Reiman and Neil Fraistat (New York: W. W. Norton, 2002), pp. 97–101 (p. 97, line 1).
34. John Keats, *Lamia*, in *Keats's Poetry and Prose*, ed. Jeffrey N. Cox (New York: W. W. Norton, 2009), pp. 413–29 (p. 414, lines 59–60).
35. Denise Gigante, *Life: Organic Form and Romanticism* (New Haven, CT: Yale University Press, 2009), p. 209.
36. Garrett Stewart, '*Lamia* and the Language of Metamorphosis', *Studies in Romanticism*, 15.1 (1976), pp. 3–41 (p. 5).
37. Bruce Clarke, 'Fabulous Monsters of Conscience: Anthropomorphosis in Keats's *Lamia*', *Studies in Romanticism*, 23.4 (1984), pp. 555–79 (p. 573).
38. Paul Endo, 'Seeing Romantically in *Lamia*', *ELH*, 66.1 (1999), pp. 111–29 (p. 117).
39. Alfred, Lord Tennyson, 'The Lady of Shalott', in *Tennyson's Poetry*, ed. Robert W. Hill Jr (New York: W. W. Norton, 1999), pp. 41–5 (pp. 42–3, lines 76, 82, 92, 103).
40. The 'web' being 'broken utterly' appears in the 1832 version of the poem, lines 178–9.
41. Robert Browning, 'My Last Duchess', in *The Penguin Book of Victorian Verse*, ed. Daniel Karlin (London: Penguin, 1998), pp. 207–8 (p. 208, line 55).

42. Browning would have known about this exceptional phenomenon. In the early nineteenth century, Georges Cuvier, famed French naturalist, explained: 'it is to be observed that in all the species [of seahorses] it is the male, and not the female, which has the pouch, and hatches the eggs'. Georges Cuvier, *Cuvier's Animal Kingdom* (London: W. M. S. Orr, 1840), p. 327.
43. Isobel Armstrong, *Victorian Poetry: Poetry, Poetics and Politics* (London: Routledge, 2002), p. 309.
44. Robert Browning, 'Childe Roland to the Dark Tower Came', in *The Penguin Book of Victorian Verse*, ed. Karlin, pp. 234–41 (pp. 238, 240, lines 109, 126, 176, 178).
45. Armstrong, *Victorian Poetry*, p. 209.
46. Rich defines the 'lesbian continuum' as a 'range [...] of woman-identified experience'. Adrienne Rich, 'Compulsory Heterosexuality and Lesbian Existence', *Signs*, 5.4 (1980), pp. 631–60 (p. 648). These experiences do not necessarily mean genital sexual stimulus, but rather encompass a wide variety of circumstances and emotions: 'all women [...] exist on a lesbian continuum [...] whether we identify ourselves as lesbian or not' (pp. 650–1). Ultimately, Rich argues that heterosexuality has been 'both forcibly and subliminally imposed on women' (p. 653), with the result that women live a 'double life', an 'apparent acquiescence to an institution founded on male interest and prerogative' (p. 654).
47. Terry Castle, *The Literature of Lesbianism: A Historical Anthology from Ariosto to Stonewall* (New York: Columbia University Press, 2003), p. 360.
48. Andrew Elfenbein, *Romantic Genius: The Prehistory of a Homosexual Role* (New York: Columbia University Press, 1999), p. 184.
49. Samuel Taylor Coleridge, *Christabel*, in *The Major Works*, ed. Jackson, pp. 69–87 (p. 70, line 39).
50. I am indebted to Nelson Hilton, eminent scholar of William Blake and Romanticism, for this connection.
51. Elfenbein, *Romantic Genius*, p. 177.
52. Castle, *The Literature of Lesbianism*, p. 443.
53. Jeanette Howard Foster, *Sex Variant Women in Literature* (Baltimore, MD: Diana Press, 1975), p. 75.
54. Sandra M. Gilbert and Susan Gubar, *The Madwoman in the Attic: The Woman Writer and the Nineteenth-Century Literary Imagination* (New Haven, CT: Yale University Press, 1979), p. 567.
55. Christina Rossetti, 'Goblin Market', in *The Penguin Book of Victorian Verse*, ed. Karlin, pp. 473–88 (p. 486, line 468).
56. Helena Michie, '"There is no Friend Like a Sister": Sisterhood as Sexual Difference', *ELH*, 56.2 (1989), pp. 410–21 (p. 418).
57. Many fruits reproduce asexually. And coral reproduces through a process known as budding, which was known in Rossetti's time. In 1853 the famed American naturalist James Dwight Dana described the process: 'The bud generally commences as a slight prominence on the side of the parent [...]; enlargement goes on till the young finally equals the parent in size. Thus by budding, a compound group is commenced.' James Dwight Dana, *Coral Reefs and Islands* (New York: G. P. Putnam, 1853), p. 50.

58. Joseph Bristow, '"No Friend Like a Sister"? Christina Rossetti's Female Kin', *Victorian Poetry*, 33.2 (1995), pp. 257–81 (p. 265).
59. Herbert Tucker, 'Rossetti's Goblin Marketing: Sweet to Tongue and Sound to Eye', *Representations*, 82 (2003), pp. 117–33 (pp. 119, 123).
60. William Michael Rossetti, *The Poetical Works of Christina Georgina Rossetti* (London: Macmillan, 1904), p. 459.
61. Antony Harrison, 'Swinburne's Losses: The Poetics of Passion', *ELH*, 49.3 (1982), pp. 689–706 (p. 699).
62. Algernon Charles Swinburne, 'Sappho', *Saturday Review*, 117 (1914), p. 228.
63. Algernon Charles Swinburne, 'Anactoria', in *Poems and Ballads & Atalanta in Calydon*, ed. Kenneth Haynes (London: Penguin, 2000), pp. 47–54 (p. 54, line 276).
64. Yopie Prins, *Victorian Sappho* (Princeton, NJ: Princeton University Press, 1999), p. 112.
65. Thäis Morgan, 'Male Lesbian Bodies: The Construction of Alternative Masculinities in Courbet, Baudelaire, and Swinburne', *Genders*, 15 (1992), pp. 37–57 (p. 49).

Chapter 12

Queer Gothic Visual Art: A Twisted Path from the Eighteenth Century to the Twenty-First

Laura Westengard

The 'Shocking' Emergence of Queer Gothic Aesthetics

Henry Fuseli's monstrous 'bedroom scene' in *The Nightmare* (1781) depicts the body of a woman draped lifelessly on a bed while a demon-like figure crouches on her chest and an ominous horse looks on.[1] The scene is intimate, frightening and erotic. Its atmosphere is dark and gloomy, and the bedroom has become its own uncanny double as the blissfulness of sleep transforms into a paralytic nightmare. Viewers are invited to peek voyeuristically into the intimacy of a young woman's boudoir as she succumbs to the monstrously threatening forces that render her helpless and exposed. The gaze of the demon meets the viewers' eyes directly as if threatening to infiltrate their bedrooms next. It evokes a swirl of sensations akin to the extreme affective experience of the Burkean sublime, causing it to be received as 'shocking', to echo Horace Walpole's terse annotation in his copy of the catalogue for the 1782 show at which it was first shown.[2] Fuseli traversed boundaries of decorum in both his artistic content and his personal life as one dedicated to darkly eroticised paintings as well as orgiastic sexual experimentation.[3]

The feelings of shock and terror that *The Nightmare* produced caused controversy and debate regarding its meaning and artistic value, but its horrifying subject matter was not unheard of in artistic and literary productions at the time. The same Horace Walpole who judged the painting as 'shocking' had written *The Castle of Otranto* in 1764, and with that landmark publication created the Gothic romance, a popular fiction genre that established the characteristics that have come to be recognised as 'Gothic'.[4] Notably, Walpole is known not only as a Gothic literary figure but also for his gender-transgressive 'effeminacy' and queer relationship to sexuality.[5] While gothicism is most commonly

Figure 1 Henry Fuseli, *The Nightmare* (1781). Courtesy of Detroit Institute of Arts

associated with British and US Gothic fiction from the eighteenth and nineteenth centuries, Walpole's novel presented many of the formal and aesthetic attributes that continue to be associated with Gothic creative productions that exceed any bounded literary period, genre, location or historical moment. In other words, the tropes and aesthetics established in eighteenth- and nineteenth-century Gothic fiction continue to appear in the contemporary moment and across a variety of cultural forms, including fiction, poetry, film, television, visual art and beyond. Indeed, the Gothic never stayed contained within generic categories, as is made clear with the decidedly Gothic characteristics of Fuseli's painting.

Scholars of gothicism such as George E. Haggerty and Maggie Kilgour note that the Gothic is an 'affective form' with a primary purpose of 'creat[ing] a feeling or effect in its readers by placing them in a state of thrilling suspense and uncertainty'.[6] Queer studies pioneer Eve Kosofsky Sedgwick spent her early academic career exploring Gothic conventions, describing the Gothic as both 'paranoid' and 'unspeakable', two characteristics that she also associated with queerness, and in *Queer Gothic*, George Haggerty explains that 'transgressive social-sexual relations are the most basic common denominator of gothic writing'.[7] The Gothic preoccupation with affective and formal excess, thrilling risk and uncertainty, paranoia and the unspeakable makes gothicism appealing for those who wish to create, reflect or reframe queer worlds and experiences. Queerness plays a central role in Gothic art and literature, and gothicism is likewise present in contemporary queer visual art, which contains echoes of the aesthetics and tropes established in the eighteenth and nineteenth centuries.

Gothic queerness has traditionally functioned with a dual purpose – transgressive and conservative at once. Initially, the formal excess and monstrous uncertainty of the Gothic was deemed disruptive to eighteenth-century aesthetics and the impressionable minds of readers. However, these concerns made it no less popular. Further, the transgressive elements of Gothic narratives often served as horrifying departures from normative existence, departures that elicited both titillation and judgement. The monstrous Gothic villain represents the social outsider marked by its otherness and 'excess of meaning' and serves as a screen upon which readers can project simultaneous 'fear and desire'.[8] Gothic's conservative mode, however, means that these outsiders are generally destroyed in the end in order to re-establish the status quo and ensure the 'restoration of a norm, which after the experience of terror, now seems immensely desirable'.[9] Regardless of the narrative conservatism of eighteenth- and nineteenth-century Gothic narratives, the 'twisted path that leads to this reestablishment

Figure 2 William Blake, *The Ghost of a Flea* (1819–20). Courtesy of Tate Images

of norms is, nonetheless, queer' since it is the transgressive elements that occupy the majority of the narrative.[10]

William Blake's *The Ghost of a Flea* (1819–20) exhibits a charged, vampiric animalism that, like Fuseli's *The Nightmare*, both excites and threatens the viewer.[11] *The Ghost of a Flea* depicts a sinewy and muscular creature against a dark backdrop of draped curtains and shooting stars in a night sky. The creature gazes into a bowl of blood held in one hand, tongue extended, as if viewers have stumbled upon a scene in which they discover the creature indulging in illicit and perverse desires, giving it a distinctly masturbatory and voyeuristic effect. Blake claimed that he was visited by a vision of this creature who 'told the artist that all fleas were inhabited by the souls of men who were "by nature bloodthirsty to excess"'.[12] At times exhibited as *A Vampire*, the painting evokes a number of Gothic tropes – a monstrous figure endowed with markers of excessive masculinity, a dark, gloomy atmosphere, the spectral nature of Blake's vision, and an allusion to vampirism.[13] Its homoeroticism comes across through these Gothic elements that evoke a mixture of fear and desire as well as an excess of meaning, as the 'amalgamation of man and beast suggests a human character marred by animalistic traits' and ultimately queers the line between human and animal.[14] Unlike Fuseli's known sexual experimentation, Blake's personal sexual proclivities are up for debate. However, the expansive sexual imagination he demonstrates in his work 'encompasses the humanly odd, grotesque and outlandish and it confounds narrow, natural norms through a "wondrous Art" that consciously declares its aim to capture humanity's awesomely diverse erotic and emotional proclivities'.[15] Recent scholarship has explored Blake's queer eroticism and many consider his work to have queer themes and aesthetics.[16] It is notable that the queer aspects of his work also frequently intersect with a distinctly Gothic aesthetic.

The excessive appetite of the flea marks it as a vampire, a Gothic monster that represents foreign, threatening, non-normative sexuality. Decades before Bram Stoker's *Dracula* (1897), John Polidori penned *The Vampyre* (1819) after appropriating a fragmentary story written by Lord Byron as part of the famous ghost story competition between himself, Lord Byron, Mary Shelley and Percy Shelley while visiting Geneva.[17] While Mary Shelley's *Frankenstein; or, The Modern Prometheus* (1818) may be the best-known product of that challenge, Polidori's story had great influence on popular culture after its publication.[18] *The Vampyre* presented the masculine, aristocratic Lord Ruthven as a man with dangerous and excessive appetites who leaves a path of death and destruction in his wake. Along the way, he becomes an object of fascination for the young Aubrey, and together they 'traverse the explosively tense line between compulsory homosocial relations and the culturally prohibited horrors of homoerotic desire'.[19] By depicting a naked, sexualised and hypermasculine creature that tempts viewers' erotic gaze, Blake's painting blasts through the 'tense line' between homosociality and homoeroticism, but walks a distinctly Gothic line in which his vision is simultaneously monstrous in its excessive desires while bulging and pulsing with masculine vivacity. The vampire as a sexualised cautionary figure re-emerges in Stoker's Count Dracula, who threatens to penetrate those around him as well as England itself with his foreign and feudal power. Dracula's legacy continues into the twentieth and twenty-first centuries through the frighteningly erotic figures of fiction, film and television, such as *Daughters of Darkness*, *Interview with the Vampire*, *The Hunger*, *Twilight*, *True Blood* and countless others.

The dual function of gothicism has also persisted into the twenty-first century, as cultural producers continue to use Gothic aesthetics to marginalise difference as well as to reclaim and even celebrate the inherent queerness of Gothic tropes. It is important to note that queer Gothic literature, art and culture may be topically, formally or aesthetically queer, it may be created by queer cultural producers who use gothicism to reflect their queer identity and worldview, or it may be a hybrid of these queer elements. There is no monolithic definition of what makes queer art 'queer', and this chapter will examine a range of queer Gothic visual art that is not limited to the biographically queer but that takes queer as an 'open mesh of possibilities, gaps, overlaps, dissonances and resonances, lapses and excesses of meaning' expressed via Gothic aesthetics and metaphors.[20] This chapter will highlight several Gothic aesthetic through-lines by first locating them in eighteenth- and nineteenth-century Gothic art and literature, and then tracing their reverberations into twenty-first-century queer visual art from the United States. By highlighting the presence of gothicisms such as vampirism, monstrosity, spectres, live burial and sadomasochism, the chapter uncovers how the Gothic in contemporary visual art functions as a strategy for exploring queer genders and sexualities as they intersect with race and trauma, both historical and ongoing.

Queer Gothic Reverberations in Contemporary Visual Art

Jordan Eagles, a New York City-based artist who uses blood and resin to explore the 'aesthetics and ethics of blood as an artistic medium since the late 1990s', plays with the historical association of the Gothic

Figure 3 Jordan Eagles, *Illuminations*, installation view, High Line, New York, NY. Photographer David Meanix (2016). Courtesy of the artist

vampire, blood and queer sexuality. He uses both 'animal blood from slaughterhouses' and 'donated human blood', often to draw attention to discriminatory bans on blood donations from gay and bisexual men.[21] Eagles' *Illuminations* series includes installations in which he lights preserved blood from behind, projecting it on to spaces and people. In 2016 he illuminated the High Line, a public park built on a historical elevated railway line in Manhattan, effectively turning the public space into a sublime bloodbath, both lush and horrifying.[22]

Bloody Nick, a photograph of a man whose torso and head are soaked in projected blood, mirrors Blake's flea in its hues and themes.[23] A dark tongue of blood snakes from his neck to his navel, evoking at once the path of a sensual caress and a chilling gush of pouring blood. While the flea's tongue flicks towards the bowl of blood as viewers observe from a critical distance, *Bloody Nick*'s sensual drip of blood paired with the subject's direct and invitational gaze asks viewers to take on the position of haematic consumer. As the photograph elicits desire, it at the same time evokes fear and even disgust for those who have an aversion to blood or who find themselves eroticising the bloodbath. Further, the dark spots of blood on ivory skin also call to mind Kaposi sarcoma lesions, the gut-wrenching telltale sign of HIV infection that was so much part of queer consciousness in the 1980s and 1990s, made more relevant in light of Eagles' explicit project to use donated LGBTQ+ blood to 'advocate for fair blood donation policies, anti-stigma, and equality' in the ongoing AIDS crisis.[24] The spectre of vampiric appetites

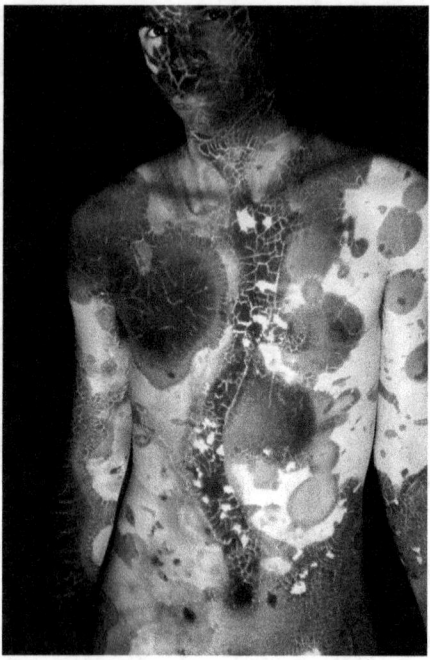

Figure 4 Jordan Eagles, *Bloody Nick* (2009). Courtesy of the artist

and eroticism links Blake's and Eagles' work across centuries, but while Blake's flea condemns to a life of monstrosity the 'souls of men who were "by nature bloodthirsty to excess"', Eagles asks viewers to identify with the bloodthirsty appetite while reminding us of the dangers of blood-related stigma.

In *Illuminations* and *Bloody Nick*, viewers' bodies are bathed in the bloody projections or are invited to engage in the erotic spectatorship of a bloodied body, making both vampiric in the way they collapse the distinction between audience and art. This dynamic of collapse reflects an aspect of Bram Stoker's *Dracula* in which the Count collapses the distinction between his mind and Mina's by both feeding on her blood and forcing her to feed on his, resulting in a muddied distinction across boundaries of gender, ethnicity and humanity. This unholy intimacy queers heteronormative assumptions about the unidirectional power dynamics of penetration, and that is part of its frightening eroticism, making it distinctly Gothic. Though Eagles' projections only visually soak the audience, viewers may feel threatened by the spectre of bloody penetration. The visual sense that one's body is covered in blood paired with the artist's claim that his blood is obtained from those donors who are banned from blood donation due to 'high risk' potentially activates the discomfort of audience members who hold lingering assumptions about the link between queer people and blood made unsafe by HIV infection. As a medium upon which the blood is projected, the audience members' bodies become inescapably bloodied, and no amount of scrubbing will remove the stigmatised image pervading their person. This experience can be potentially traumatising for those who are squeamish around blood as well as those who have developed careful delineations between their own identities and those who have been framed as 'deserving' of infection. The threat of this bloody projection lies in the collapse of presumptive boundaries between art and audience, innocent and perverse. As audiences are encouraged to think about the stigma of LGBTQ+ blood donation, the bloody projections also encourage them to imagine how they might feel about receiving blood donated by stigmatised groups. In this imaginative exchange, the blood becomes threatening to audience comfort and even to their sense of themselves as impenetrable, as it 'penetrates the audience *affectively*, confronting them with the complexities of their own feelings, assumptions, and reactions and drawing attention to the precariousness of identity and interdependence of existence'.[25] Like the interchange between Dracula and Mina, the imagined two-way exchange of blood collapses the separation between bodies and threatens notions of individuality. However, any threat they might perceive from this collapse depends upon a kind of 'penetrative fantasy' in which the audience imagines that they are exposed to the blood.[26] Eagles' bloody art, like the figure of the vampire, breaks open the imaginary boundaries of the human form and collapses distinctions, a dynamic that Carla Freccero describes in the context of historiography as 'penetrative reciprocity', a simultaneously uncomfortable and expansive approach to traumatic histories.[27]

Like Stoker's Count Dracula, the creature from Mary Shelley's *Frankenstein* has appeared in numerous forms in the centuries following the introduction of the monster into the popular consciousness. Monsters queer the very nature of existence and the boundaries of humanity. They are 'disturbing hybrids whose externally incoherent bodies resist attempts to include them in any systematic structuration. And so the monster is dangerous, a form suspended between forms that threatens to smash distinctions.'[28] Because of their incoherence and difference, Gothic monsters have served as metaphors of alterity, representing the figure of the 'other' at a 'certain cultural moment – of a time, a feeling, and a place'.[29] As a culturally contingent figure the monster is a shape-shifter as well, taking the form of the anxieties and desires of the time and place in which it appears. The Frankensteinian monster is the epitome of monstrous multiplicity in that it is literally a hybrid body created by piecing together bits and pieces gathered from the 'living animal' as well as the 'unhallowed damps of the grave'.[30] Contemporary queer artists have turned to the Frankensteinian monster as a reappropriation of difference-as-monstrosity and a response to the violence that such an equivalency enacts. Susan Stryker explains that she, as a 'transsexual woman', has a complex relationship with monstrosity:

> Like the monster, I am too often perceived as less than fully human due to the means of my embodiment; like the monster's as well, my exclusion from human community fuels a deep and abiding rage in me that I, like the monster, direct against the conditions in which I must struggle to exist.[31]

Rage and struggle but also power and beauty circulate in the figure of the queer Gothic monster, and queer visual artists gravitate to this figure partially because of its ambiguousness and complexity.

Vaginal Davis is a black, intersex, genderqueer art-music icon whose disruptive aesthetic was named 'terrorist drag' by theorist José Esteban Muñoz and whose recent work adopts queer Gothic monstrosity.[32] She is a 'performer, painter, curator, composer, writer, cultural antagonist, film scholar, and erotic provocateur' who 'stages a clash of identifications within and against both heterosexual and queer cultures, and Black and Hispanic identities'.[33] Her 2015 New York exhibition, *Come On Daughter Save Me*, features 'sixteen clay-and-nail-polish frieze sculptures' in which faces and other semi-recognisable forms seemingly emerge from the gore of human entrails.[34] The sculptures are composed from the trappings of gendered beauty, forming viscerally grotesque monstrosities out of the items that are marketed as tools for attaining idealised femininity. *Fountain of Salmacis*, for example, is composed of clay, stucco fragments, Wet&Wild Brickhouse nail varnish, Neon nail lacquer, Rival deLoop Nylon nail enamel, hydrogen peroxide, glycerin, witch hazel, Pam, Aquanet Extra Strength hair spray and Jean Naté perfume.[35] Like the pieces of dead flesh that Victor Frankenstein salvaged from the charnel houses, the conglomeration of beauty products creates a series of sculptures that appear as dismembered fragments rather than a coherent whole, creating a paradoxical experience in which the tools of beauty culture come together to create pieces that appear fragmented and grotesque rather than conventionally aesthetically pleasing.

The paradox of beauty is present in Shelley's *Frankenstein* as well. Victor describes his careful selection of flesh pieces as designed to create a beautiful creature, making the living result of his experiment both a hideous surprise as well as an ego-shattering disappointment. In Greek mythology, the fountain of Salmacis was the site at which Hermaphroditus was merged with a beautiful nymph and was said to make men who drank from it effeminate, and with this classical reference, the piece speaks to the impossible push and pull of racialised and gendered expectations for those whose bodies and identities do not fit neatly into binary cisheteropatriarchal white supremacist standards. Davis designs these oozing, gory sculptures to pull together narratives of racial and gender hierarchies, policing and violence with the seemingly innocuous items used to construct femininity today, and asks viewers to think critically about the potential for beauty in bodies commonly deemed unruly and undesirable.

As Kilgour notes, Gothic fiction in its narrative drive towards destruction and deviance is often 'better at dismemberment than re-memberment', and Davis's work uses the Gothic monstrosity of dismemberment to disrupt narratives of natural and constructed beauty, to queer sex and gender, and to destabilise our understanding of conventional binaries.[36] She explains that she embodies the status of outsider herself: 'I don't fit into mainstream society, but I also don't really fit into "alternative culture," either . . . I was always too gay for the punks and too punk for the gays. I am a societal threat.'[37] Muñoz notes that Davis's interstitial status includes a racial dislocation as well, explaining that her 'blackness and queerness render her a freak among freaks. Rather than be alienated by her freakiness, she exploits its energies and its potential to enact cultural critique.'[38] Like her drag performances, Davis's sculptural work employs the Gothic characteristic of simultaneously conflicting emotions – fear and desire, beauty and terror – to create 'an uneasiness in desire, which works to confound and subvert the social fabric'.[39] Indeed, the Gothic monster's incoherence positions it as a 'societal threat', but Davis locates the paradoxical beauty in incoherence and

Figure 5 Vaginal Davis, *Fountain of Salmacis* (2015). Courtesy of INVISIBLE-EXPORTS/New Discretions

refusal by creating dismembered and fragmented sculptures as pieces of a 'sacred mythology for the outsider'.[40]

Contemporary queer Gothic art does not always rest in Gothic dismemberment, however. If Davis's sculptures show us a kind of dismembered monstrosity, artist Kiyan Williams, who 'works fluidly across sculpture, performance, and video', utilises monstrosity in order to re-member subjects that have been objectified and erased by colonial violence.[41] Williams's installation *Dirt Eater* (2019) 'resurfaces the act of geophagy, consuming dirt, practiced among enslaved Africans in the Caribbean and American South'.[42] The installation includes a sculpted figure created out of 'soil, bricks, and debris from the ruins of a plantation in St. Croix' and an accompanying video in which the artist engages in geophagy and wears a torture mask reproduced from nineteenth-century drawings.[43] The *Dirt Eater* sculpture is an armless human form constructed out of soil, with suture lines running through in a lighter coloured material. The figure has a metal collar around the neck, and the lower half bells out in a dress-like shape studded with candles, incense and pieces of torture materials based on those used on enslaved people. The piece not only evokes a figure re-membered from fragments of abandoned, devalued and once-forbidden materials, but the ephemerality of its construction is spectral since the soil feels impermanent and ready to crumble at any moment. Williams creates an ancestral figure, both grounded and ghostly, out of a violently obscured history, pulling the historical past into the present moment.

Williams reflects on the act of digging up dirt for the site-specific piece *Reaching Towards Warmer Suns* (2020), featuring 'a cluster of exaggeratedly long dirt stalks, each culminating in an outstretched dirt hand, that rise like zombie arms from the earth'.[44] Digging is an encounter with the traumatic 'violence inflicted upon African slaves centuries ago and the violence inflicted upon "Black trans people" today in the US, with the implication that the latter should be understood as part of the former's "unwanted inheritance"'.[45] The moulded and sutured, dress-clad, feminine form in *Dirt Eater* rests at this traumatic intersection as well, reinforcing the inextricability of race and gender and pointing towards 'chattel slavery as a constitutive grammar to express sex and gender as effects of racial science'.[46] Williams uses dirt to exhume lost figures buried in history and stands them up to gaze back at viewers, evoking a defiant and empowered version of the living dead. Both enslaved people and postcolonial Black trans people have been viewed as disposable and linked to 'immanent and imminent death'.[47] The resulting 'representations of blackness become the symbol, par excellence, for the less-than-human being condemned to death'.[48] Williams's work

Figure 6 Kiyan Williams, *Dirt Eater* (2019). Courtesy of the artist

makes this relationship visible, and points to the necropolitical status of Black trans-feminine descendants of enslaved people who are subject to '*death-worlds*, new and unique forms of social existence in which vast populations are subjected to conditions of life conferring upon them the status of *living dead*'.[49]

Living death is tied in the Gothic imagination to live burial, and this is but one of the tropes introduced in Matthew Lewis's Gothic tale *The Monk* (1796) that have come to characterise queer Gothic visual art.[50] The novel depicts a corrupt monk, Ambrosio, who indulges in his depraved desires through a relationship with the devil. Along the way, he is seduced by a demon in the form of Matilda, a woman who is passing as a novice monk, but he soon tires of her and sets his sights on innocent Antonia. His drive to possess Antonia culminates in a scene that combines disempowered female vulnerability, rape, live burial in subterranean catacombs, implied necrophilia and incest. Live burial is also introduced in the narrative of Agnes, a nun who becomes pregnant and is buried alive with her infant in a locked catacomb by the powerful and sadistic Prioress. The explicit violence and eroticised power dynamics made this novel both popular and controversial on its publication. It also established a distinctly Gothic sadomasochism in which power flows in incoherent, threatening and erotic ways. In the midst of all of the Gothic tropes circulating in *The Monk*, sadomasochism as an expression of eroticised unequal power is perhaps most central. In Gothic novels, sadomasochistic 'desire is expressed as the exercise of (or resistance to) power. But that power itself is charged with a sexual force – a sexuality – that determines the action and gives it shape.'[51] Sadomasochism can be a kind of queer orientation to sexuality, and contemporary queer artists have certainly gravitated towards Gothic sadomasochism to reflect on the swirl of consensual and non-consensual power-infused experiences that constitutes queer life in homophobic and transphobic cultures.

Both sadomasochistic power dynamics and live burial make an appearance in the explicitly queer Gothic work of artist M. Lamar, a 'composer who works across opera, metal, performance, video, sculpture and installation to craft sprawling narratives of radical becomings'.[52] He describes himself and the aesthetic of his work as 'Negrogothic', as it often employs signifiers of contemporary subcultural gothicism as well as a Gothic romanticism that blends romance and horror in order to address the lived realities of existing as a queer Black man in the United States today. Lamar explains that he has 'always been obsessed with this romance and this horror: I mean, I'm living through it'.[53] As I explore in detail in *Gothic Queer Culture*, Lamar's use of Gothic sadomasochism is at the forefront of his series of photographic stills entitled *Mapplethorpe's Whip* taken from his film *Surveillance Punishment and the Black Psyche*. The images depict Lamar as the 'Overseer' in a hooded black cloak posed among several shirtless white men in a stark landscape that vaguely evokes a cotton plantation. The Overseer holds a large, phallic, black whip in his hand, which is depicted at times emerging from the Overseer's crotch, severed by a guillotine, resting in a basket of cotton, and anally inserted into the kneeling shirtless men.[54] In these images, Lamar 'juxtaposes the Romantic elements of gothicism and sadomasochistic eroticism with the horrors of black history' by showing scenes with 'classic sadomasochistic props and postures – whips, hoods, torture devices, kneeling submission [. . .] paired with a sexualized nostalgia in the scenes of racialized master-slave relations, cotton picking, whips, and anal penetration'.[55] The display of eroticised and racialised power bridges the divide between historical horrors and their present-day effects, and it asks viewers to encounter their assumptions about race, sexuality, white supremacist history, and their own role in contemporary manifestations of these histories.

Figure 7 M. Lamar, *Mapplethorpe's Whip III* (2014). Courtesy of the artist

Lamar also uses the Gothic trope of live burial as an element of horror that represents, at least in part, the stifling weight of historical racism on present-day Black queer men. *Legacies*, a forthcoming film by Lamar, uses many of the Overseer images from *Surveillance Punishment and the Black Psyche*, including the guillotine and whip imagery, but it also incorporates footage of Lamar in a nineteenth-century-style coffin featuring a viewing window through which his living face can be seen.[56] At the end of the film he rises up, in a nod to the nightly undead resurrections of Count Dracula. In *Negro Antichrist*, Lamar sings and plays piano across black and white clips of him wearing black leather collars, cuffs and spikes.[57] The video features recurring images of his body rising stiffly from a freshly dug grave, shedding the black soil from his head and chest, and singing with the grimace of a scream. The inability to breathe when buried alive certainly evokes the language circulating around Black Lives Matter, and Lamar's buried body notably refuses to remain contained. Whether it is through undeath or a resistance to the forces that would see his body disappeared and buried, Lamar's nod to Gothic live burial is both an indulgence in the morbid beauty of gothicism and an active resistance to ongoing forces that threaten the physical existence of those who are intersectionally marginalised as both queer and Black.

A Culture of Incoherence and Destabilisation

Gothic metaphors and aesthetics were traditionally used to identify and ostracise those who occupied the status of 'other', creating a logic by which gothicism itself 'produces the deviant subjectivities opposite

Figure 8 M. Lamar, *Legacies*, video still. Courtesy of the artist

Figure 9 M. Lamar, *Negro Antichrist*, video still. Courtesy of the artist

which the normal, the healthy, and the pure can be known'.[58] Queer Gothic visual art paradoxically uses the metaphors and aesthetics produced by the Gothic to negotiate the challenges, traumas and pleasures of the queer, thereby reappropriating those historically marginalising strategies that condemned the deviant and perverse to a life of monstrosity, entombment and isolation. In this way, queer Gothic visual art may be said to employ a 'freak theory' that 'undermines a logic of norm and deviation in that it produces or confirms the norm by deploying highly unstable narratives about the "other", so that a kind of pleasure arises precisely from the instability of the narrative'.[59] The monstrous incoherence of Gothic narrative is itself an eighteenth-century Gothic convention, and artistic destabilisation uses that very gothicism to challenge and unground the normative and binary worldviews once produced by the Gothic, a move that adds complexity and nuance to Gothic frameworks while both reflecting and creating queer experiences from the eighteenth century to today.

Notes

1. Henry Fuseli, *The Nightmare*, 1781, oil on canvas.
2. Christopher Frayling, 'Fuseli's *The Nightmare*: Somewhere between the Sublime and the Ridiculous', in *Gothic Nightmares: Fuseli, Blake, and the Romantic Imagination*, ed. Martin Myrone (London: Tate Publishing, 2006), pp. 9–20 (p. 10).
3. For more on Fuseli's documented sexual experimentation, see Matthew Craske, *Art in Europe 1700–1830* (Oxford: Oxford University Press, 1997).
4. Horace Walpole, *The Castle of Otranto* (Oxford: Oxford University Press, 1998).
5. Max Fincher, *Queering Gothic in the Romantic Age: The Penetrating Eye* (New York: Palgrave Macmillan, 2007), p. 24.
6. George E. Haggerty, *Gothic Fiction/Gothic Form* (University Park: Pennsylvania State University Press, 1989), pp. 7–8; Maggie Kilgour, *The Rise of the Gothic Novel* (London: Routledge, 1995), p. 6.
7. Eve Kosofsky Sedgwick, *The Coherence of Gothic Conventions* (London: Methuen, 1986) p. 6; Eve Kosofsky Sedgwick, *Between Men: English Literature and Male Homosocial Desire* (New York: Columbia University Press, 1985), p. 92; George E. Haggerty, *Queer Gothic* (Urbana, IL: University of Illinois Press, 2006), p. 2.
8. Jack Halberstam, *Skin Shows: Gothic Horror and the Technology of Monsters* (Durham, NC: Duke University Press, 1995), p. 2.
9. Kilgour, *The Rise of the Gothic Novel*, p. 8.
10. Laura Westengard, *Gothic Queer Culture: Marginalized Communities and the Ghosts of Insidious Trauma* (Lincoln, NE: University of Nebraska Press, 2019), pp. 9–10.
11. William Blake, *The Ghost of a Flea*, 1819–20, tempera and gold on mahogany.
12. *The Ghost of a Flea* gallery label, Tate, updated May 2011, https://www.tate.org.uk/art/artworks/blake-the-ghost-of-a-flea-n05889 (accessed 19 January 2021).
13. Martin Butlin, *William Blake 1757–1827*, Tate Gallery Collections, V (London, 1990); *The Ghost of a Flea*, catalogue entry, Tate, https://www.tate.org.uk/art/artworks/blake-the-ghost-of-a-flea-n05889 (accessed 19 January 2021).
14. *The Ghost of a Flea* gallery label.
15. Helen P. Bruder and Tristanne Connolly, 'Introduction: What is now proved, was once only imagin'd', in *Queer Blake*, ed. Helen P. Bruder and Tristanne Connolly (Basingstoke: Palgrave Macmillan, 2010), pp. 1–20 (p. 4).
16. See Bruder and Connolly (eds), *Queer Blake*; and Christopher Z. Hobson, *Blake and Homosexuality* (Basingstoke: Palgrave Macmillan, 2000).
17. Bram Stoker, *Dracula* (New York: W. W. Norton, 1997); John Polidori, *The Vampyre; A Tale* (Project Gutenberg, 2009, https://www.gutenberg.org/files/6087/6087-h/6087-h.htm).
18. Mary Shelley, *Frankenstein; or, The Modern Prometheus* (London: Penguin, 1992).

19. Mair Rigby, '"Prey to some cureless disquiet": Polidori's Queer Vampyre at the Margins of Romanticism', *Romanticism on the Net*, 36–37 (2004), para. 2, https://www.erudit.org/fr/revues/ron/2004-n36-37-ron947/011135ar/ (accessed 16 February 2021).
20. Eve Kosofsky Sedgwick, *Tendencies* (London: Routledge, 1994), p. 7.
21. Jordan Eagles, 'About', jordaneagles.com, https://jordaneagles.com/about (accessed 21 January 2021).
22. Jordan Eagles, *Illuminations Installation View, High Line, New York, NY*, 2016, photograph by David Meanix.
23. Jordan Eagles, *Bloody Nick*, 2009, digital c-print.
24. Eagles, 'About'.
25. Westengard, *Gothic Queer Culture*, p. 131.
26. Ibid., p. 129.
27. Carla Freccero, *Queer/Early/Modern* (Durham, NC: Duke University Press, 2006), p. 99.
28. Jeffrey Jerome Cohen, 'Monster Culture (Seven Theses)', in *Monster Theory: Reading Culture*, ed. Jeffrey Jerome Cohen (Minneapolis, MN: University of Minnesota Press, 1996), pp. 3–25 (p. 6).
29. Ibid., p. 4.
30. Shelley, *Frankenstein*, p. 53.
31. Susan Stryker, 'My Words to Victor Frankenstein above the Village of Chamounix: Performing Transgender Rage', *GL/Q: A Journal of Lesbian and Gay Studies*, 1 (1994), pp. 237–54 (p. 238).
32. José Esteban Muñoz, '"The White to Be Angry": Vaginal Davis's Terrorist Drag', *Social Text*, 52/53 (1997), pp. 80–103 (p. 80).
33. Press release for Vaginal Davis, *Come On Daughter Save Me* at Invisible-Exports, New York, 20 November–20 December 2015; Dominic Johnson, Vaginal Davis Biography [online], vaginaldavis.com, http://www.vaginaldavis.com/bio.shtml (accessed 28 January 2021).
34. Invisible-Exports, press release, *Come On Daughter Save Me*, 2015.
35. Vaginal Davis, *Fountain of Salmacis*, 2015, mixed media, 6 × 18 × 5 in. (15.2 × 45.7 × 12.7 cm), VD15 7. Collection of Indiana State University.
36. Kilgour, *The Rise of the Gothic Novel*, p. 31.
37. Cyrus Grace Dunham, 'The "Terrorist Drag" of Vaginal Davis', *New Yorker*, 12 December 2015, para. 8, https://www.newyorker.com/culture/culture-desk/terrorist-drag-vaginal-davis (accessed 2 February 2021).
38. Muñoz, '"The White to Be Angry"', p. 96.
39. Ibid., p. 86.
40. Dunham, 'The "Terrorist Drag" of Vaginal Davis', para. 11.
41. Kiyan Williams, 'Bio', kiyanwilliams.com, http://www.kiyanwilliams.com/bio (accessed 2 February 2021).
42. Kiyan Williams, *Dirt Eater*, 2019, sculpture and HD color video with sound; Kiyan Williams, 'Dirt Eater', kiyanwilliams.com, http://www.kiyanwilliams.com/dirt-eater-1 (accessed 2 February 2021).
43. Williams, 'Dirt Eater'.
44. Louis Bury, 'Kiyan Williams Digs Into the Meaning of Soil', *Hyperallergic*, 7 November 2020, para. 2, https://hyperallergic.com/586039/kiyan-williams-digs-into-the-meaning-of-soil/ (accessed 4 February 2021).
45. Ibid., para. 1.

46. C. Riley Snorton, *Black on Both Sides: A Racial History of Trans Identity* (Minneapolis, MN: University of Minnesota Press, 2017), p. 41.
47. Cristina Sharpe, *In the Wake: On Blackness and Being* (Durham, NC: Duke University Press, 2016), p. 13.
48. Ibid., p. 21.
49. Achille Mbembe, 'Necropolitics', *Public Culture* 15 (2003), pp. 11–40 (p. 40).
50. Matthew Lewis, *The Monk: A Romance* (London: Penguin, 1998).
51. Haggerty, *Queer Gothic*, p. 2.
52. M. Lamar, 'Biography', mlamar.com, https://www.mlamar.com/biography/ (accessed 26 January 2021).
53. Emily Nathan, 'Southern Gothic and Goth-Kid Makeup: M. Lamar on Racialized Art and Black Leather', *Observer*, 16 February 2015, para. 8, https://observer.com/2015/02/southern-gothic-and-goth-kid-makeup-m-lamar-on-racialized-art-and-black-leather/ (accessed 25 January 2021).
54. M. Lamar, *Mapplethorpe's Whip III, Surveillance Punishment and the Black Psyche, Part Two, Overseer*, 2014, digital video still.
55. Westengard, *Gothic Queer Culture*, p. 153.
56. *Legacies*, dir. M. Lamar, cinematography Fatos Marishta, M. Lamar and Mivos Quartet, 2017.
57. *Negro Antichrist*, dir. M. Lamar and Taylor Clark, cinematography Annie Malamet, M. Lamar, 2012.
58. Halberstam, *Skin Shows*, p. 2.
59. Renate Lorenz, *Queer Art: A Freak Theory* (New Brunswick, NJ: Transaction Publishers, 2012), p. 162.

Chapter 13

Queering Gothic Slash Fandoms: *Harry Potter, Ginger Snaps* and Worldbuilding
Gregory Luke Chwala

J. K. Rowling, author of the *Harry Potter* books that gave rise to one of the largest franchises of Gothic fantasy ever recorded, caused an uproar on social media in June 2020 when she posted several controversial tweets perceived by many as being directed towards the trans community: 'people who menstruate. I'm sure there used to be a word for those people . . . Wumben? Wimpund? Woomud?'; 'If sex isn't real, there's no same-sex attraction'; 'my life has been shaped by being female. I do not believe it's hateful to say so.'[1] Seemingly missing the argument of decades of queer and trans scholarship distinguishing sex assigned at birth from gender, and disregarding the existence of intersex people, Rowling's refutation of her transphobia relies on the insistence that gender is solely determined by biology. Many LGBTQIA+ fans who came to find solace in her stories were alarmed by this apparent misunderstanding of trans experiences, assumption that all trans people aim to have gender-affirmation procedures, and apparent insistence that trans men are somehow tied to misogyny and patriarchy. They felt that Rowling had insulted them. LGBTQIA+ fans find resonance in Rowling's stories of marginalised characters with secrets and differences which come to be their great strengths in overcoming cruelty and evil. Yet fans grew tired of waiting for LGBTQIA+ representation in the *Harry Potter Wizarding World* franchise, and over time, came to create and consume a *Harry Potter* slash fandom.

Harry Potter slash fiction emerged online shortly after the first film, and today Potter fandoms offer perhaps the most prevalent online Gothic slash content. Slash fiction, a fan fiction that pairs two or more characters of the same gender in a romance or sexual relationship, has for quite some time been a means for fans to live vicariously through their favourite characters as they pursue their erotic and queer unfulfilled desires and fantasies, though its content is not a new phenomenon. Scholars and readers of Gothic fiction have scrutinised texts for queer content for decades, and much scholarship proposes that writers of Gothic fiction even produced homoerotic coding in foundational Gothic texts such as Horace Walpole's *The Castle of Otranto* (1764) and Matthew Lewis's *The Monk* (1796) that inform the earliest vestiges of queer intertextuality found in Gothic fiction because of the perceived sexuality of the authors. Eve Sedgwick and George Haggerty have speculated about the homosexuality of Walpole and Lewis. Haggerty argues that 'the contradictory nature of Otranto reflects a conflict inherent in the emergence of a homosexual identity', and that 'for Lewis sexuality seems so deeply rooted in aberrant desire and guilt-ridden fear that no easy expression of sexual identity is possible'.[2] Although not often literal or even apparent, early Gothic works featured characters who many fans today read as queer. Haggerty speculates upon the homoerotic description of Lucifer and the cross-dressing character Rosario/Matilda in *The Monk* (1796).[3] James McGavran surmises that queer desire is represented in Mary Shelley's *Frankenstein* between Victor and his Creature, as has Talia Schaffer between Harker and Dracula in *Dracula*.[4] Oscar Wilde's *Dorian Gray* contains so much homoerotic coding that it was used in court to convict him of gross indecency.[5]

Whether one agrees or not with the queer readings of these foundational Gothic masterpieces, the desire to see queerness in their characters via their creators is not unlike what creators of online Gothic slash fiction yearn for today. Several Gothic slash pairings have emerged in online fandoms, including Sherlock Holmes and John Watson from *The Adventures of Sherlock Holmes*; Buffy and Willow from *Buffy the Vampire Slayer*; Dean Winchester and Sam Winchester from *Supernatural*; Edward Cullen and Jacob Black from *Twilight*; Brigitte and Ginger Fitzgerald from *Ginger Snaps*; and of course, Harry Potter and Draco Malfoy from *Harry Potter*. Scholars and consumers of Gothic fiction have offered up fan fictions and created slash identifications. Characters, plotlines and tropes of Gothic texts have come together to create queer fandoms that offer a path forward in worldbuilding by which society can progress, heal and remake that which has been censored and oppressed. Similarly, though largely ignored by queer theorists in the past, slash fiction offers a resistance to the expectation of heterosexuality and cisgender relationships, and it destigmatises LGBTQIA+ identities. Online fandoms are often the only spaces where young people can be out and explore their identities with low risk because of the anonymity online platforms offer. The Internet has allowed young people to take adolescent Gothic content wherein the expectation is heterosexuality and recreate their favourite stories and characters to allow them to explore themselves more fully. Additionally, adults who revel in these stories have used online spaces to create erotic/pornographic Gothic slash as a means of challenging heteronormative restrictions. Reading queer desire in characters not necessarily intended to be queer is at the heart of online slash fan fiction, and Gothic fiction offers the perfect context into which reimaginings and wish fulfilments can emerge because it already inherently challenges the status quo and a preoccupation with sexual taboos and anxieties.

This chapter uncovers the crucial ways that online fan fiction of the twenty-first century has reimagined Gothic monsters and figures as queer through romantic and sexual relationships. I posit that online Gothic slash fiction can be therapeutic while at the same time challenging oppressive and discriminatory precedents; queer fandom offers safe spaces where reimagined fictional characters can be used to enrich diversity and build queer communities. After providing a brief background of online Gothic slash fiction in the next section, I examine a few popular *Harry Potter* slash pairings of characters in prose, manips (manipulated photos), slash fan art and vids (video splices/images set to music). I reveal how online Gothic slash fiction has moved from gay to queer as fans in recent years more prominently account for expansive genders, bisexuality, polyamorous sex, and queer family dynamics in *Ginger Snaps* fandoms. Online fandoms, I argue, have created spaces wherein the meaning of queer can evolve and adapt. Queer Gothic fiction has always functioned in a truly revolutionary way to question illegitimacy and promote change, but online slash fiction is particularly fertile ground for the visibility and validation of LGBTQIA+ identities because of its capacity for worldbuilding. Moreover, the places where LGBTQIA+ visibility and validation are needed most fall short of this need almost without exception, notably in the large franchises such as *Harry Potter* and *Ginger Snaps*. Queer fandoms offer a means of rewriting, recasting and recreating Gothic fantasy that is inclusive of LGBTQIA+ representation. The evolution of slash fictions in online spaces illustrates this need for change.

Online Gothic Fandoms Evolve

Slash fandoms have used online social platforms to remake and remould the queer Gothic. Since the publication of works such as Jack Halberstam's *Skin Shows* (1995) and George Haggerty's *Queer Gothic* (2006), which brought to the surface the rich queer contexts and possibilities of Gothic fiction, there has been an increased appetite for imagining and embracing queered monsters, and this is largely because of the Internet. Queer representation has moved from analogy to outright queer relationships, from socially conditioned fears generated by a shared sense of otherness and loss as the foreclosure of homoerotic possibility, to rewritten stories that feature queer relationships between popular heterosexual characters in Gothic fiction. The most popular examples of online Gothic slash include reimaginings of queered relationships involving werewolves in the *Harry Potter* series (2001–11) and the *Ginger Snaps* trilogy (2000–04), the latter producing slash fiction that speculates on an incestuous lesbian relationship between the Fitzgerald werewolf sisters. Fans have interpreted the relationship between Sirius Black and Remus Lupin in and out of werewolf forms in queer ways in the online fan fiction series *Stealing Harry Verse Collection*, in which Sam Starbuck rewrites the storyline to have Remus and Sirius raising Harry Potter as their child, and fans have furthermore reimagined a romantic relationship between Harry Potter and Draco Malfoy (what fans refer to as Drarry). Slash fan fiction has reinvented a need for queer monstrosity and Gothic stories, but this would not have been possible without twenty-first-century technology.

Though fan fiction in general has been around since the early twentieth century, slash fiction is believed to have originated from the speculative fiction franchises of the late twentieth century, notably *Star Trek*.[6] However, as the fandom website *Fanlore* notes, it was the Internet that allowed slash fiction to flourish as it moved from fanzines, fan-edited non-profit print copies sold at fan conventions, to forums, message boards, social media, and eventually to websites that produced fandoms and open-source repositories for creators and creations of fan fiction. Queer storylines, collages, remixes and discussions quickly found a home in the twenty-first century.[7] The Internet offered spaces where queer identities could be readily formed and forged in slash fandoms. Kristina Busse notes that 'The early 2000s were a time among online media fans that saw an increased focus on queer identification, both in terms of fans coming out and discussing their sexualities in online fandoms such as *LiveJournal*, and an increase in meta discussions about queer fans.'[8] As slash fiction evolved online, the second decade of the twenty-first century enabled slash fiction of the first decade to flourish not only because of the proliferation of media-literate users and platforms, but also because of the ease of use of new technologies, the means of publication, and the changing dynamics of the meaning of queer. Fans have created queered content that moves beyond traditional M/M (male/male) slash and femslash, resulting in fan fiction such as genderfuck and intersex fiction, BDSM and kink memes, explicit smut/porn/erotica and other queered configurations. Romano notes the different tags that are used to describe popular tropes, such as genderswap (characters switching binary genders), Mpreg (male pregnancy), incest, OT3 (one true threesome), OT4 (one true foursome), enemyslash, smut (distinctly sexual content), and even cargo (relationships between a person and an inanimate object) and crossover (pairings of characters from different media who have never interacted).[9] Creators of today's online slash fiction can easily contribute in a number of ways.

Open-source repositories such as *Archive of Our Own* (AO3) and social networking services such as *LiveJournal* (LJ) have been providing online slash fiction writers with platforms for over a decade. These platforms enable writers of Gothic slash to explore their creative possibilities, engage with readers in fandoms (subcultures composed of fans with common interests), access feedback that guides their spin-offs, and impact queer communities in ways that mainstream fiction has not. Written predominantly by cisgender heterosexual women and accounting for most of the Gothic slash fiction on the web, online M/M Gothic slash has changed queer representation to offer queer romances and sex between cisgender male characters from heteronormative fictional series such as *Harry Potter* and CW's *Supernatural*, and this in turn has impacted the confidence of queer youth and strengthened both online and offline communities. Femslash has also offered lesbian representation using characters from Gothic stories such as the film trilogy *Ginger Snaps*. The spaces wherein fans read these slash fictions and engage in discussions build fandoms and offer spaces for visibility and community. As Busse argues, 'Fandoms have become safe spaces not just for geeky behavior but also for expressing one's identities and sexualities.'[10] Gothic slash and femslash have thus provided a mode of healing from the trauma many LGBTQIA+ people have experienced from marginalisation and a lack of representation in mainstream Gothic fantasy fictions. In recent years, creators of *Harry Potter* and *Ginger Snaps* online Gothic slash fiction and fandoms have moreover moved beyond a critique of traditional Gothic slash to examine queer family dynamics, bisexual, intersex, Mpreg and polymorphous slash.

Harry Potter Gothic Slash

Harry Potter has one of the largest fanbases on the web, and slash Potter fanfiction is perhaps the most popular, as Tosenberger notes, because 'Potter fandom, due in part to its sheer size, but also to the great diversity of ages and sexual orientations of its members, is ideal ground for exploring many varieties of non-heteronormative discourses in fandom'.[11] Although many consider the novels and film adaptations to be fantasy, *Harry Potter* is rife with Gothic tropes: a medieval castle full of turrets, dungeons and secret passageways; ghosts, monsters, witches, werewolves and demons; death, morbidity, fear, terror and horror; an orphaned protagonist; a past which is haunting the present; and doppelgängers and uncanny things. A quick Google search will reveal massive amounts of Harry Potter slash fiction, including erotica, smut, porn, BDSM, kink memes, manips, slash fan art and vids. Drarry erotica is the most popular *Harry Potter* slash erotica, but it is not the only kind found on Internet fandoms; erotic slash content featuring Severus Snape, Ron Weasley, Sirius Black, Remus Lupin, Lucius Malfoy, Gellert Grindelwald, Albus Dumbledore and even Lord Voldemort can also be found. Most *Harry Potter* slash is M/M, but *Harry Potter* slash erotica also includes OT3, OT4, Mpreg, genderswap and intersex slash erotica. It would likely take years for one to work through all the *Harry Potter* slash prose on the web. I share just a few slash stories below.

Sam Starbuck's (aka copperbadge) slash series, *The Stealing Harry Verse Collection*, is perhaps the most popular M/M Gothic slash on the web and is appropriate for all audiences. His work became so popular that it can now be found as an online eBook compiled and published by Chandri MacLeod via *LiveJournal* for EPUB download and officially bearing Starbuck's name rather than his online pseudonym, copperbadge. This series is 1,185 pages long and includes four parts: 'Stealing Harry', 'Tales from the River House', 'Laocoon's Children' and 'Unfinished Tales and The Rest'.

'Stealing Harry', initially published via AO3 in 2004 and edited in June 2020, imagines a scenario in which Sirius Black never went to the Azkaban prison, and when Sirius realises that Harry is being mistreated in the Dursleys' house, he rescues him to be raised in a household with Remus Lupin (a werewolf) and himself. Thus, this Gothic slash positions the heteronormative household as a danger to a young boy and provides him a safe haven with queer parents; Sirius can be read as bisexual, and Remus is depicted as gay and deeply in love with Sirius. Black runs a bookshop, Sandust Books, which Harry is forbidden to enter, but Harry soon discovers that Mr Mooney, the alias of Remus Lupin, is running the store, and its dog, Padfoot, is actually Sirius in shape-shifted form. Sirius and Remus protect Harry. When Molly Weasley proposes that Sirius marry a woman to provide a proper home for Harry, the idea disturbs Remus because he finds it hard to restrain his love for Sirius, who copperbadge notes is 'not interested in girls so much'.[12] The two men eventually kiss when Sirius seduces Remus; yet Remus refuses to be used for Sirius's exploration of his sexuality, as is evidenced when he says, 'I'm not a toy,

Sirius ... I'm not going to let you fool around with me because I'm in love with you.'[13] Although copperbadge stops short of overt sex scenes in 'Stealing Harry', including only additional attempts by Sirius to seduce Remus in rather erotic scenes, for early online Gothic slash of 2004 the text is remarkable for its depiction of two men raising a child, protecting that child from harm, and dealing with the difficulty of resisting a sexual relationship that is clearly desired by a refashioned heterosexual character from the original *Harry Potter* series. 'Stealing Harry' is a queered romance in a Gothic setting with queer family dynamics.

While 'Stealing Harry' is a Gothic slash fic with queer storylines appropriate for an underage audience, some *Harry Potter* slash is sold as slash erotica that is far more graphic and aimed at an adult audience. On the site *Adult-FanFiction.org*, one will find OT3 stories with graphic sex between Harry, Draco and Severus, such as this story by Ophiuchus Malfoy, a passage of which reads:

> With a cry Draco pulled out several inches and shoved home, beginning a tandem motion thrust and retreat with Severus ... Harry was the first to break. He came hard, screaming in release, balls tightening painfully as they emptied in a rush. His ass clenched in time to his spurts, milking Draco and Severus to an explosive completion of their own.[14]

Malfoy includes a note before the story that reads, 'This story also contains a healthy (more than) amount of smut, including figging [inserting ginger root into the anus], rimming, double penetration, blindfolds, and sex. Lots of sex. Read at your own peril if legal for you to do so.'[15] The Bistander Ben's 'Horny Harry and Life before Hogwarts' showcases James and Lily Potter as intersex characters: James 'one of the uncommon wizards to have a pussy', and Lily 'one of the rare witches to have a cock ... longer and thicker than any man, [that] ... made James wet [and] ... tremble'.[16] James gives birth to an intersex Harry; intersex wizards are 'known to be very strong magically ... as rare as a metamorphmagus [able to change appearance via free will without spells or Polyjuice] and almost as sought after'.[17] They name the baby Harry Lilith Potter. netrixie's story features an Mpreg story in which Draco gets Harry pregnant: 'No, no, no!! I am not pregnant! [Harry says.] Guys can't get pregnant! ... What do you mean wizards can get pregnant?'[18] Prose *Harry Potter* slash erotica such as that found in these three stories has reworked Gothic fantasy as queer fantasy from original content lacking queer visibility.

Harry Potter slash erotica is also offered in the form of manips and vids. It is often hard to distinguish manipulated photos from original images. The most famous Harry/Draco (Drarry) manip is Eneada's image, which can be found widely on the web in online articles, blogs and fandom websites.[19] The website *Fanlore.org* lists this image as a fair use photo and links it to their pages 'Harry/Draco' and 'Harry Potter Art', which provide numerous links to other visual *Harry Potter* slash forms.[20] In Eneada's image, Harry's and Draco's faces look as if they were derived from film images, but the creator has shown their bodies in an erotic, naked embrace, Draco's eyes staring seductively at the viewer, his body language bearing a dominant expression as he locks Harry in his embrace. The black background and unfocused borders of the image draw the reader's attention to the now very famous faces of the actors Daniel Radcliffe (Harry Potter) and Tom Felton (Draco Malfoy). The online persona Lady Saika describes this image on her fandom page *Lady Geek Girl and friends* as 'the most famous manip in H/D fandom'.[21] However, such images do tend to erase bisexuality and reinforce heteronormative (or even homonormative) gender roles; Lady Saika argues that 'using "everyone is gay" to retcon a paring they don't like ... [is] ... sloppy writing as well as bisexual erasure ... [and produces] the problem of gay fetishization'.[22] In other words, though Eneada's Harry/Draco manip helps to establish queer possibility and normalises queerness in mainstream Gothic-themed fantasy, the problem with this image, and with much M/M visual slash, is its tendency to fetishise gay pairings by portraying slash characters in a heteronormative way, often reinforcing gender binaries of masculinity and femininity. Although on the one hand Eneada's Harry/Draco manip reinforces the Gothic tropes of a damsel in distress and knight errant, the image also reclaims this trope as queer, though at the same time it erases bisexuality and normalises cisgender M/M erotica.

While many M/M slash manips do reinforce heteronormative tropes, they also challenge the mainstream media's ownership of romance and sex in speculative fictions. One such way that fans challenge heteronormativity is through fan art. Red Rahl, who has been posting slash fan art for over a decade, has many depictions of M/M slash anime from *Harry Potter* to *Teen Wolf* on his *Tumblr* blog, red_rahl's fanart. One of Red Rahl's Drarry slash anime posted on pklovesdw's blog[23] is set as a Veela mating party and challenges heteronormativity by placing Harry in a sexual situation with a magical creature (Draco as a Veela). According to *Fanlore.org*, Veelafic is a *Harry Potter* slash trope wherein one of the characters is revealed to have Veela powers and ancestry, Veela being magical creatures with enhanced sexual allure.[24] This trope is often used as a plot device to show how Veela mating instincts can lead to a couple having sex. Looking closely at Red Rahl's Drarry manip, one notices that Draco has a tail, perhaps pointy ears and fangs. Two girls and one boy react to stumbling upon Draco (as a Veela) and Harry in the act of intimacy: one character is jealous ('No, Harry's supposed to be mine!'), one has a realisation ('This actually explains a lot . . .'), and the other seemingly finds it amusing as he points and laughs at the couple. Harry humorously tries to cover things up, exclaiming, 'Guys?! It's not—Well it is what you think. Give me a second to calm my ferret down', while Draco grasps Harry in a possessive embrace, exclaiming, 'Grrr!!! MINE!!!'[25] The clothing insinuates that the scene is at Hogwarts since the onlookers are in their school uniforms. Harry appears to be naked and wrapped in a blanket. The Gothic tropes of shape-shifting, supernatural powers and ancestral curses are apparent in the Veela, and its queerness and sexual allure are akin to that of Gothic monsters such as Dracula. The Draco Veela uses his power to seduce and possess Harry.

Fanvids or fan films are yet another means through which *Harry Potter* fans have challenged the ways that the films portray romantic relationships. *Harry Potter* fanvids consist of footage from the *Harry Potter* films and other films or images set to a variety of songs and music. According to *Fanlore*, four popular places to find *Harry Potter* vids are YouTube, *LiveJournal*, fanwork archives such as *ArtisticAlley* and fan sites such as *Veritaserum*. Some vids feature puppets, such as *Potter Puppet Pals*, parody musicals, such as *The Very Potter Musical Series* by StarKid Productions, and filk parody (folk fandom vids) such as *It's Quidditch* and *Friday*.[26] Among the most popular *Harry Potter* slash fanvids are Drarry vids. Some of these vids focus on Harry and Draco's romance, some on sex, and some on a combination of the two. Sapphiamur's 'Suffocating' (2012) is one of the more superior vids with over 361,000 views and 808 comments.[27] Sapphaimur's vid begins with the caption, 'The War is Coming. This could be the last chance to be with someone you love' written over an ocean and land backdrop with a lighthouse, and pensive music, Red's 'Already Over', playing in the background. It then cuts to a scene of Harry's friends who say, 'How does it feel Harry', insinuating that they are asking him about love. There are images of Draco and Harry together throughout the vid, in several of which they are kissing, including a newspaper image with a caption surrounding a heart reading, 'Harry Potter's Secret Heartache', as a disapproving press takes photos of the boys. Captions tell the viewer the month and year as the vid moves through the story of their romance. The story basically follows the plot of the film series but adds the insinuation that Draco and Harry fall in love in their fifth year of knowing one another. At one point, Draco is shown holding Harry's dead body before Harry is brought back to life. At the end of the vid, the caption reads, 'Second Wizarding War 1995–1998: We Were Fighting for Love', and Draco and Harry are shown in an embrace. The vid invests the viewer in imagining possibilities for queer romance.

vochina's 'My Sweet Prince' and SciFiNerd92's 'Choke' are focused on lust and sex. 'My Sweet Prince' (2011) has over 404,000 views and 620 comments.[28] Placebo's song 'My Sweet Prince' plays in the background: 'Never thought you'd make me perspire. / Never thought I'd do you the same. / Never thought I'd fill with desire. / Never thought I'd feel so ashamed.' The vid uses only black and white footage, and it shows clips of Hogwarts juxtaposed with scenes of Harry and Draco having passionate sex accompanied by throbbing background music. White static lines and black screens act as transitions between erotic sex scenes showing bodies entangled, but never showing the faces of the characters. The combination of the dark music, black and white footage, and Gothic imagery of the castle adds to this vid's Gothic tone. 'Choke' (2011) uses the instrumental song of the same name by Hybrid to tell the story of Harry turning into an incubus (a male demon believed to have sex with its victims).[29] The Gothic undertones here are obvious. Harry is evil in this storyline, and he craves Draco after picking up on his scent. Draco likes the attention. The description of the vid reads, 'So they both live and have angsty smexy smex all the live long day.' A Gothic caption at the beginning of the vid reads, 'Medieval legend claims that incubus demons sexually prey on human beings, generally during the night when the victim is sleeping. Religious tradition holds that repeated intercourse with an incubus may result in the deterioration of health, or even death.' This vid is almost pornographic, and the shots of two men having sex can easily be mistaken for Harry (Daniel Radcliffe) and Draco (Tom Felton). SciFiNerd92 has produced other Drarry slash erotica that is even steamier.[30] The worldbuilding offered by such *Harry Potter* fanvids helps to make visible and validate LGBTQIA+ identities in major Gothic fantasy franchises where LGBTQIA+ visibility is most absent.

Ginger Snaps Gothic Femslash

Ginger Snaps slash, much like *Harry Potter* slash, fulfils the same need by addressing a similar void. Though far less well-known than *Harry Potter* online slash fiction, the Canadian film trilogy *Ginger Snaps* (2000–04) has morphed into large online fandoms, perhaps the second largest Gothic femslash next to *Buffy the Vampire Slayer*, and though femslash manips and vids are noticeably harder to find than they are for *Harry Potter* online slash, since M/M slash still dominates Gothic slash fandoms, femslash prose and discussions are not. The story and characters are strongly Gothic. Aside from the plotline revolving around lycanthropy and werewolves, the sisters are preoccupied with death and stage death scenes with one another from the time they are children. The series also adds a Gothic twist in its prequel by setting the stage for a curse from the past being revisited upon the Fitzgerald family.

The trilogy consists of *Ginger Snaps* (2000), its sequel *Ginger Snaps 2: Unleashed* (2004) and *Ginger Snaps Back: The Beginning* (2004),[31] which acts as a prequel to the original film. *Ginger Snaps* is about the Fitzgerald sisters, Ginger and Brigitte, battling lycanthropy in 1999 after Ginger (Katharine Isabelle) is bitten by a werewolf that has been terrorising the town of Bailey Downs in Ontario, Canada. In *Ginger Snaps 2: Unleashed*, Brigitte (Emily Perkins) struggles to save herself from lycanthropy after the death of her sister at the end of the first film. The prequel, *Ginger Snaps Back: The Beginning*, which takes place in 1815 around Fort Bailey and the Canadian wilderness of Northern Ontario, provides an explanation for the origin of the modern werewolf and its curse on the Fitzgerald family by explaining how ancestors of the Fitzgerald sisters (also sisters named Ginger and Brigitte) became infected with lycanthropy after stumbling upon a fort in which several men have been massacred by werewolves. As with the *Harry Potter* books and franchise, none of the characters in the *Ginger Snaps* trilogy are overtly queer; however, scholars have argued for the queerness of the Fitzgerald sisters in part due to their inseparability, and fans have imagined and rewritten the werewolf sisters as more overtly queer and in an incestuous relationship, which is not hard to do considering all the homoerotic Gothic images produced to market the film.[32]

Phillip A. Bernhardt-House argues that the werewolf is a signifier of homoeroticism (as a constructed form of unnatural, bestial homosexuality),[33] and though this argument certainly helps to support a queer Gothic reading of *Ginger Snaps*, the fact that the werewolf has traditionally been a queer masculine metaphor is problematic. Yet, at the same time it is reinvented in its queer female representation in *Ginger Snaps*, as Tanis MacDonald notes:

> The film's exploration of the female werewolf as a sign of lesbian eroticism suggests a convergence of gender, alternative sexuality, and transbiology, a triumvirate of competing taboos that cannot be ignored. *Ginger Snaps* may still be first and foremost a horror story about the transformation of adolescence, but, by offering a resolutely intimate representation of incestuous adolescent same-sex desire that destabilizes horror-film convention, *Ginger Snaps* frames female relationships in all their queer(ed) intensity.[34]

Xavier Mendik further argues that *Ginger Snaps* brings 'lesbian iconography to the werewolf genre', and April Miller suggests that the sisters' 'uncommonly strong bond' is suggestive of the homoerotic.[35] In fact, it is not hard to read the relationship between the Fitzgerald sisters as homoerotic in scenes such as the one in which Brigitte climbs on top of Ginger to pierce her navel as Ginger writhes beneath her; the secret that the girls keep about Ginger's lycanthropy construed as their secret lesbianism; when Ginger crawls on top of Brigitte and whispers in her ear, 'We're almost not related any more';[36] and Ginger's constant reminder that the sisters are bound by a blood pact, 'together forever, united against life as we know it'.[37] The sisters constantly challenge heteronormativity and the stereotype of the feminised teenage girl – until Ginger learns that she can use this image to entrap her victims and eat them. The transformation of Ginger into a werewolf can moreover be read as a trans experience; Ginger begins to grow hair out of wounds; she becomes dominant and develops strength and musculature; and she grows a tail that can be read as a phallic symbol, which she hides by taping it to her leg.[38]

However, this isn't the kind of queerness that *Ginger Snaps* fans and fandoms are interested in reading and creating. *Ginger Snaps* slash fics wish to remix the original story to more appropriately address the assumption that the Fitzgerald sisters are heterosexual, casting aside the moral concern that a slash relationship between them is incestuous. Kaleigh Fleming argues that assuming that the girls are heterosexual just because they show an interest in sex with boys misses the point, because this sex is used to seduce their victims; furthermore, this completely erases bisexuality and privileges heteronormativity:

> Straight people tend to view ambiguously queer folks as straight, hands down, no further questions asked . . . If altering a character's sexual orientation is unsettling, we should ask ourselves why. And why not use these rich, fictitious opportunities to explore, to learn, and to broaden our perspectives of the world? . . . Bisexual identities [furthermore] get erased with overwhelming frequency even within the queer community, and straight people tend to forget that bisexuality exists altogether . . . Bisexuals are [also] still considered invalid . . . or problematic because they are often (incorrectly) thought to exclude trans, nonbinary, intersex, and other gender identities.[39]

As Fleming notes, there are many assumptions and erasures of identity made by *Ginger Snaps* fans who refuse to consider the possibility that the Fitzgerald sisters might be queer, but creators of slash fiction are able to address the real root of the problem – a lack of visibility and imagination. By imagining sex between werewolves and humans, and between females and sisters, fans have remixed storylines to contribute to Gothic slash that queers boundaries, not only by recasting these presumed heterosexual characters as lesbian or bisexual, but also by taking up identities that include polymorphous identity.

Remixes of *Ginger Snaps* are prevalent on the Internet in spaces such as *AO3, Fanfiction.net* and *Adult FanFiction.org*. Much like the M/M slash of *Harry Potter*, *Ginger Snaps* femslash stories that feature the Fitzgerald sisters are intimate and pornographic. Blisterdude's 'Ginger Snaps: The Last Straw' subtly alludes to a growing eroticism between Ginger and Brigitte that never fully comes to fruition:

> Ginger . . . carefully slipped her fingers under the waist of Brigitte's tracksuit bottoms. Hell, they'd spent three years apart. Brigitte thinking she was dead, Ginger realising she couldn't live without her. It had been a little surprising to find Brigitte was thinking about her in a blatantly sexual way, at first, she'd even masturbated thinking about her.[40]

In a much longer novel-length story of 37 chapters entitled '*Ginger Snaps*: The Feral Bond' (2010), madman fred offers smut that is a bit less graphic. Ginger and Brigitte are presented as bisexual and polymorphous in that the characters gain sexual gratification outside of normative sexual behaviours, mostly achieving orgasm via their kills, though as Brigitte turns more towards her lycanthropy, she views the male body with revulsion: 'She tore open his pants and underwear, saw his erect cock, felt her fur all over her body shift. She looked away in disgust. It annoyed her that with her radical transformations, her nausea about penises hadn't changed at all.'[41] Lyssandra_Med's story 'Bonds' begins with BDSM and ends with Gothic eroticism between the Fitzgerald sisters: 'Brigitte dug her tongue inside, nipped with too-sharp teeth. Above her, Ginger moaned and growled, panting harshly when she became too lost for anything else while a howl was ever-present on the tip of her tongue.'[42] As these examples illustrate, the ways in which slash about *Ginger Snaps* is written varies from suggestive to overt.

It is a bit more difficult to find overtly erotic *Ginger Snaps* slash manips and smut vids, which is again likely because M/M erotic slash and smut manips and vids dominate Gothic slash fandoms. Although there are many images of Ginger and Brigitte together on the web, one would expect this since they are sisters and equally protagonists in the films, and one suspects that there is more hesitancy to produce images of two sisters engaged in sex than there is to create *Harry Potter* slash between Draco and Harry. Nonetheless, fans have created fanart images that suggest homoeroticism. Yuri-World-Ruler's 'G and B' shows the Fitzgerald sisters in a very erotic pose.[43] A member of *Deviant Art* since 2011, Yuri-World-Ruler writes that this image has been created using XNALara+Blender. The first comment on the image suggests that the two characters could be mistaken for lesbians, and, in fact, it is not hard to see this. Ginger has her arm around Brigitte and her other hand touches her lower lip. Her eyes stare enthralled at Brigitte, a nail of her werewolf transformation showing as she does so. She is dressed scantily showing her abdomen, and Brigitte stands stoically with legs spread, suggesting a dominant demeanour, the kind she takes up in the sequel to *Ginger Snaps*. Ginger is shown with iconic white highlights in her otherwise red hair from the initiation of her transformation into a werewolf. This image certainly does not seem what one might expect as a portrayal of sisters. Another fanart image by sirhc6997 shows the Fitzgerald sisters in a stained-glass format, standing in front of a full moon, arm in arm, wearing provocative clothing.[44] A meme created by CharityDingle replays the scene where Ginger straddles Brigitte, repeating 'I said I would die for you!'[45] A cartoon by daaku-no-tenashi shows the sisters in prison-like frames with dialogue bubbles reading, 'It's like we're not even related any more' (Ginger) and 'You're fucked' (Brigitte), and the caption below reads their slogan, 'Out by sixteen, or dead in this scene. Together forever.'[46]

There has clearly been some thought put into the perception of Ginger and Brigitte in these examples of queer Gothic slash that take up the Gothic's tendency to queer characters and blur the boundaries of horror and violent sexual acts. The monster is a stand-in for queer transgressions, as it has been since the beginning; however, with online queer Gothic slash fiction, the negative connotations shift. The queer monsters become the heroes of their sagas. They do not meet their ends in death. They create families and forge queer relationships. *Ginger Snaps* is a werewolf trilogy that inspires mostly young fans craving queer representation. Where it has not been found, fans have created queer content themselves, and this worldbuilding has helped to muster confidence and the exploration and development of queer identities in safe spaces of anonymity on the web. Much like *Harry Potter* queer Gothic slash, *Ginger Snaps* fans push boundaries and transgressions to remake Gothic worlds as queer and reinvent meaning from that in which LGBTQIA+ people have not found representation.

Conclusion

Queer fan fiction has produced online spaces wherein Gothic slash can thrive. Mainstream franchises often do not represent queer culture or people, notably in series and franchises largely marketed to an underage audience such as *Harry Potter* and *Ginger Snaps*. Fans have found a way to circumvent this lack of representation, censorship and oppression by worlding and remixing fiction that imagines their favourite characters in queer(ed) relationships. SciFi has had slash fandoms for decades, but now Gothic slash of the twenty-first century is seeing this form of therapeutic creativity, building communities between straight and queer fans in virtual spaces, exploring the meaning of queer, and challenging what monsters and Gothic worlds might do. Fans have imagined Gothic slash that moves beyond M/M and F/F relationships, manipulating gender norms and barriers with Mpreg, intersex, polymorphous and incestuous storylines and tags. Nonetheless, Gothic slash is still dominated by M/M slash, notably in visual representations such as manips and vids, indicating that to move towards a truly diverse queer futurity, more inclusivity and representation is needed across the LGBTQIA+ spectrum. More trans representation is needed, and fans are working hard to remix Gothic stories with trans characters and to create online fandoms that are more trans-inclusive. Trans bodies and queer sexualities, once coded, indirect monstrosities in Gothic fiction, are shifting into the limelight of the twenty-first century as they are taken up by fans, remixed, and used for queer worldbuilding. While blockbuster Gothic film and fiction franchises may continue to subvert, ignore and insult queer identities, LGBTQIA+ fans can remix content, produce crossovers, and speak to neglected markets through online fandoms to reinvent the queer Gothic.

Notes

1. Abby Gardner, 'A Complete Breakdown of the J.K. Rowling Transgender-Comments Controversy', *Glamour*, 20 July 2021, https://www.glamour.com/story/a-complete-breakdown-of-the-jk-rowling-transgender-comments-controversy (accessed 16 December 2021).
2. George E. Haggerty, 'Literature and Homosexuality in the Late Eighteenth Century: Walpole, Beckford, and Lewis', *Studies in the Novel*, 18.4 (1986), pp. 345, 349.
3. George E. Haggerty, *Queer Gothic* (Urbana, IL: University of Illinois Press, 2006), pp. 10–13, 26–30.
4. James Holt McGavran, '"Insurmountable barriers to our union": Homosocial Male Bonding, Homosexual Panic, and Death on Ice in Frankenstein', *European Romantic Review*, 11.1 (2000), pp. 46–67, doi.org/10.1080/10509580008570098; Talia Schaffer, '"A Wilde Desire Took Me": The Homoerotic History of *Dracula*', in Bram Stoker, *Dracula*, ed. Nina Auerbach and David J. Skal (New York: W. W. Norton, 1997), pp. 470–82.
5. Neil McKenna, *The Secret Life of Oscar Wilde* (New York: Basic Books, 2005), p. 362.

6. Fanlore, 'History of Slash Fandom', *Fanlore*, 9 September 2019, https://fanlore.org/wiki/History_of_Slash_Fandom (accessed 26 May 2021).
7. Ibid.
8. Kristina Busse, *Framing Fan Fiction* (Iowa City: University of Iowa Press, 2017), p. 16.
9. Aja Romano, 'Canon, Fanon, Shipping and More: A Glossary of the Tricky Terminology that Makes up Fan Culture', *Vox*, 7 June 2016, https://www.vox.com/2016/6/7/11858680/fandom-glossary-fanfiction-explained (accessed 1 May 2021).
10. Busse, *Framing Fan Fiction*, p. 196.
11. Catherine Tosenberger, 'Homosexuality at the Online Hogwarts: *Harry Potter* Slash Fanfiction', *Children's Literature*, 36.1 (2008), pp. 185–207 (p. 186), doi.org/10.1353/chl.0.0017.
12. copperbadge, 'Stealing Harry', Harry Potter slash fan fiction, *Archive of Our Own*, 1 May 2004, https://archiveofourown.org/works/987408 (accessed 10 May 2021).
13. Ibid, pp. 81–2.
14. Ophiuchus Malfoy, 'Excerpts from On the Plethora of Uses for Zingiber officinale by S. Snape, PM; with notations by D. Malfoy, App', Harry Potter slash fanfiction, *Adult-FanFiction*, n.d., http://hp.adult-fanfiction.org/story.php?no=600007817 (accessed 10 May 2021).
15. Ibid.
16. The_Bistander_Ben, '"Horny Harry and Life before Hogwarts": Part I of the *Harry Potter and a Life of Lust* series', *Harry Potter* slash fan fiction, *Archive of Our Own*, 16 May 2021, https://archiveofourown.org/works/31321055 (accessed 11 May 2021).
17. Ibid.
18. netrixie, 'Come Kid With Me', Harry Potter mpreg slash fiction, *FanFiction*, 25 March 2008, https://www.fanfiction.net/s/4154664/1/Come-Kid-With-Me (accessed 10 May 2021).
19. Eneada, HarryDraco Manip.jpg, Harry/Draco photo manipulation, *Fanlore*, 5 October 2011, https://fanlore.org/wiki/File:HarryDraco_Manip.jpg (accessed 10 May 2021).
20. See Fanlore, 'Harry/Draco', *Fanlore*, 2021, https://fanlore.org/wiki/Harry/Draco (accessed 1 May 2021). See also Fanlore, 'Harry Potter Art', *Fanlore*, 2020, https://fanlore.org/wiki/Harry_Potter_Art (accessed 1 May 2021).
21. Lady Saika, 'Sexualized Saturdays: The Everyone is Gay Trope in Fanfiction', *Lady Geek Girl and friends*, 20 April 2013, https://ladygeekgirl.wordpress.com/2013/04/20/sexualized-saturdays-the-everyone-is-gay-trope-in-fanfiction/ (accessed 1 May 2021).
22. Ibid.
23. pklovesdw, 'Drarry masterlist', fanfic blog featuring Drarry Veela animae fanart and fanfic synopses, *Tumblr*, n.d., https://pklovesdw.tumblr.com/post/36687401572/drarry-masterlist (accessed 27 May 2021).
24. Fanlore, 'Veelafic', *Fanlore*, n.d., https://fanlore.org/wiki/Veelafic (accessed 27 May 2021).
25. Ibid.
26. Fanlore, 'Harry Potter Art', *Fanlore*, 2020, https://fanlore.org/wiki/Harry_Potter_Art (accessed 1 May 2021).

27. Sapphiamur, 'Suffocating', online video recording, YouTube, 10 June 2012, https://www.youtube.com/watch?v=dLR0cWlUyZE (accessed 10 May 2021).
28. volchiha, 'My Sweet Prince', online video recording, YouTube, 17 January 2011, https://www.youtube.com/watch?v=y5eE0SLZBW0 (accessed 10 May 2021).
29. SciFiNerd92, *Choke*, online video recording, YouTube, 19 February 2011, https://www.youtube.com/watch?v=f3p8wO_FIr4 (accessed 10 May 2021).
30. See SciFiNerd92, 'Late At Night', online video recording, YouTube, 11 October 2009, https://youtu.be/Htwc_8njQh0 (accessed 10 May 2021).
31. See *Ginger Snaps*, dir. John Fawcett (20th Century–Fox, 2000). See also *Ginger Snaps Back: The Beginning*, dir. Grant Harvey (Nice Doggle, 2004), and *Ginger Snaps II: Unleashed*, dir. Brent Sullivan (Lion's Gate, 2004).
32. See *Ginger Snaps*, DVD cover, in 'Horror Movie Review: *Ginger Snaps* (2000)', Games, Brrraaains & a Head-Banging Life, 2 July 2019, https://www.gbhbl.com/horror-movie-review-ginger-snaps-2000/ (accessed 26 May 2021).
33. Phillip A. Bernhardt-House, 'The Werewolf as Queer, the Queer as Werewolf, and Queer Werewolves', in *Queering the Non/Human*, ed. Noreen Giffney and Myra J. Hird (Abingdon: Routledge, 2008), pp. 187–212.
34. Tanis MacDonald, '"Out by Sixteen": Queer(ed) Girls in *Ginger Snaps*', *Jeunesse: Young People, Texts, Cultures*, 3.1 (2011), pp. 58–79 (p. 76), doi.org/10.1353/jeu.2011.0001.
35. Xavier Mendik, 'Menstrual Meanings: Brett Sullivan Discusses Werewolves, Hormonal Horror and the Ginger Snaps Audience Research Project', *Film International*, 4.21 (2006), pp. 78–83 (p. 81); April Miller, '"The Hair that Wasn't There Before": Demystifying Monstrosity and Menstruation in *Ginger Snaps* and *Ginger Snaps Unleashed*', *Western Folklore*, 6.3–4 (2005), pp. 281–303 (p. 284), https://www.jstor.org/stable/25474753.
36. *Ginger Snaps*, dir. John Fawcett (20th Century–Fox, 2000).
37. Ibid.
38. See Kate Jackson, 'Ginger Snaps', still of sisters from the film Ginger Snaps, *Wordpress*, 19 November 2014, https://sorryneverheardofit.wordpress.com/2014/11/19/ginger-snaps/ (accessed 26 May 2021).
39. Kaleigh Fleming, 'Queering Brigitte Fitzgerald', *An Injustice: Voices, Values, and Identities*, 17 June 2020, https://aninjusticemag.com/queering-brigitte-fitzgerald-98738f7b6628 (accessed 25 May 2021).
40. Blisterdude, 'Ginger Snaps: The Last Straw', Ginger Snaps slash fan fiction, *Archive of Our Own*, 3 February 2017, https://archiveofourown.org/works/9397847/chapters/21422711 (accessed 26 May 2021).
41. madman fred, 'Ginger Snaps: The Feral Bond', Ginger Snaps femslash fiction, *FanFiction*, 1 February 2010, https://m.fanfiction.net/s/5709622/1 (accessed 26 May 2021).
42. Lyssandra_Med, 'Bonds', Ginger Snaps femslash fiction, *Archive of Our Own*, 17 March 2021, https://archiveofourown.org/works/30107151 (accessed 26 May 2021).
43. Yuri-World-Ruler, 'G and B', Ginger Snaps aanart, *Deviant Art*, 19 July 2015, https://www.deviantart.com/yuri-world-ruler/art/G-and-B-547442564 (accessed 26 May 2021).

44. sirhc6997, 'Ginger Snaps', Fitzgerald sister fanart, *Deviant Art*, 14 September 2007. https://www.deviantart.com/sirhc6997/art/Ginger-Snaps-64917444 (accessed 26 May 2021).
45. CharityDingle, 'I said I would die for you!', digital meme, *Tumblr*, 4 October 2020, https://filmreel.tumblr.com/post/631068395428839424/ginger-snaps-2000-dir-john-fawcett (accessed 26 May 2021).
46. Daaku-no-tenshi, 'Ginger Snaps Poster', Ginger Snaps fanart, *Deviant Art*, 17 September 2003, https://www.deviantart.com/daaku-no-tenshi/art/Ginger-Snaps-Poster-3073559 (accessed 26 May 2021).

Chapter 14

Solidarity is More than a Slogan: Queer Representation in the Virtual World

Dawn Stobbart

In the 2011 novel *Ready Player One*, protagonist Parzival is given a Virtual Reality headset called an ONI. Significantly improving on the VR technology of the near-future setting of the novel, the ONI creates a direct neural link between a human brain, a computer and the Internet, which results in the user being able to taste, touch and feel. This technology also allows the wearer to passively experience the physical feelings and emotional reactions to events that another person records via their ONI. On their first use of the ONI, Parzival discovers that there are several recordings of sexual 'memories' pre-installed on the system. These allow a user to engage with the feelings of several individuals, including those with a different gender, biological or sexual identity. The demonstration includes 'see[ing], hear[ing], feel[ing], and smell[ing] everything – every sensation' that the original contributor had when recording the experience.[1] While a device such as the ONI or the (in)famous Holodeck of the *Star Trek* universe is confined to fiction, the virtual environment that we inhabit is one that can be a haven, an escape and a refuge from everyday life for a diverse range of people – for good or ill. For some queer people, this is the only chance they have to be authentic in a world that can sometimes punish a person for not upholding the social and gendered norms of their lived environment.[2]

It cannot be denied that the perception of the virtual realm has historically been that of a domain inhabited by the cis male, and as such has reflected his gendered and sexual norms. Stories of teenage boys in the family garage, building computers and games to play on them, or playing those games in dark, musty bedrooms, permeated game culture's early days; the heteronormativity engineered into the soul of this medium offers little respite for the rest of us who do not fit into this demographic.[3] 'Sexuality is an integral part of video games', writes Tereza Krobová et al., 'and it is easy to see that heterosexuality is the default setting'.[4] This heteronormative foundation can be seen in every aspect of the virtual world: social media platforms, videogame design and production, and, despite the reality, the perception of a predominantly male user base – although this is slowly beginning to change. However, this view does not reflect the whole picture of the virtual world, where LGBTQIAP+ people have been involved in the medium since it first began. It must be noted though that there still exists content in the virtual realm (as with the physical) that is unkind, homophobic and hateful to people in the LGBTQIAP+ community.

As the lessons of feminism, gay liberation and queer theory were realised in the 1990s, the Gothic became a rich literary source for more explicitly thinking about how sexual differences are inherently relative and unstable. Authors such as Sarah Waters (*Affinity*) and Billy Martin writing as Poppy Z Brite (*Drawing Blood, Lost Souls*) were writing explicitly queer Gothic novels. These novels, and more recently a growing presence online and in videogames, provide an opportunity to challenge the boundaries of conventional fiction, even the genre itself. It allows the representation of different points of view, and to contemporise traditional Gothic tropes through a medium that brings an intimacy to the narrative through direct interaction with the characters and narrative; something the 2020 videogame *Tell Me Why* has attempted with its story of twins Alyson and Tyler, which will be discussed later.[5]

This chapter chooses to predominantly focus on the positive aspects of the queer Gothic virtual world, the ability of the user to engage with aspects of their identity that might be hidden in everyday life, and to explore perceptions of gender and sexual identity – either their own or others to more broadly understand another's position. In some cases, the queer Gothic virtual world enables the player/user to consider abstract concepts concerning gender and sexual identity and expression.

Early LGBTQ Virtual Spaces

In the early (1980s!) days of the online world, before the Internet existed as it does today, virtual spaces for online interaction were predominantly found on a bulletin board system (BBS). These often text-based spaces were frequently run from home. People would connect to each other's computer to play games, post messages and upload or download files. In these early years, a user would access a BBS (often physically through an acoustic coupler) by attaching a computer to a telephone line, which then allowed the user's system to link with another computer that was also attached to the telephone system.[6] More than this though, access to the BBS would allow a user to find information and support for a seemingly endless list of needs, and to engage with like-minded people in private spaces. While not created for the queer community specifically, BBSes were used across the world by people who were oppressed, marginalised, and in places where open communication was hindered or even suppressed. BBSes were often private platforms and not easily accessible to people outside a specific group, and so were vital to communities such as LGBTQIAP+, as a place where someone could explore their identity freely, without fear of being ridiculed, subject to homophobic slurs, or even murdered.

As part of the foundations of the Internet, BBSes cannot be discounted for their importance in creating the virtual world as we know it. A labyrinthine system of connections directing a user to information and social spaces still underpins the Internet. And these spaces (whether BBSes or any of the myriad other platforms that have come and gone) are themselves Gothic, haunted by the ghostly presence of users past; their likes and dislikes, opinions and prejudices remaining long after a real person abandons a platform: an imprint of users long forgotten. Myspace.com, for example, continues to function, despite losing most of its millions of users when Facebook overtook it in 2008,[7] and remains accessible both to the original user and to the intrepid Internet explorer, should they wish to engage with that past.

While traversing the remains of these spaces, the virtual world is not in itself frightening. However, Gothic in the virtual world can and does employ many of the same genre devices as other media to generate the uncanny and unnerving. And, despite their computer-generated nature, these sometimes expansive, immersive environments can produce genuine sensations in a player: delight and enchantment, or anxiety, discomfort and fear – often mirrored in that of the avatar being controlled on the screen.

The control of the player over the avatar is itself a Gothic construct explored by Ewan Kirkland in his current research, which examines the link created between the player and the character on screen. The player and protagonist perform a series of movements seemingly in tandem: pressing buttons on the control pad (or keyboard) results in movements on the screen, with the player possessing and embodying the character through this activity. This embodiment can be seen in Diane Carr's notion that avatars can create 'forms of uncanny resonance', in her comment that 'all players, surely, have found themselves flinching when an avatar bangs its head . . . or recoil when an avatar plunges over a cliff'. She implies a link between the player and the character they are controlling, which players can be keen to engage with.[8] Closely aligned with this stance, and drawing on Myron Krueger, Tom Boellstorff considers that avatars in the virtual world are important to the player as a representation of the self, and users carefully choose attributes ranging from eye colour and shape, through hairstyles, gender, sexuality and even species before play begins, creating a version of oneself to exist in the virtual world.[9]

It can be further reasoned that the link between player and character that Carr notes, alongside Boellstorff's understanding of avatar creation, shows that an individual can and does create a persona more aligned with their imagined self when establishing their online persona, whether that is a subjective self-portrait, or a metaphorical understanding of their persona to represent them online. As Krobová et al. note: 'avatars, in this sense, are the access points for creation of a player identity, gender identity included'.[10] Here, the status of the avatar as a Gothic double, with 'the experience of oneself *as* a foreign body' or 'a sense of ourselves as double, split, at odds with ourselves', is manifest.[11] As Michael Hancock explains, 'we constantly construct virtual doubles of ourselves through which we communicate with other people'.[12] The uncanny, then, is seen in the relationship between an avatar and the controlling human, which is then placed into an environment where 'embodiment ha[s] become central to online selfhood' and 'presence enacts itself as an embodied activity'.[13] These embodied avatars can allow a person to engage with the virtual environment and other users across the world, often anonymously in terms of a 'real' identity – and the possibilities for experimentation are endless, including exploring gender and sexuality.

Before the Internet as we know it in the twenty-first century, and in the absence of being able to access a BBS, the main way that a person could interact with a 'virtual' reality in the 1980s and early 1990s was through playing a videogame. Queer representation was not common in mainstream media, and while there were television programmes and films that explored queer issues, such as the groundbreaking US TV film *That Certain Summer* in 1972, and the UK television broadcaster Channel 4, which 'has allowed for greater gay, lesbian, and bisexual visibility than its terrestrial competitors in both its fictional and documentary output',[14] this openness was not initially reflected in videogames, where heteronormativity meant the representation of a white cis male.[15] Furthermore, historically, narrative embodiment in videogames has involved a series of 'explicitly *male* fantasies ... where the imagined body remains male' (original emphasis), and this has hindered the representation of any other group of people.[16]

The virtual world, whether in videogames or in a social environment such as Twitter or Facebook, is being reshaped by the queer community. Anna Antrophy (aka Auntie Pixelanta), for example, is a trans woman pushing boundaries with her game *Dys4ia*, which allowed her to recount her experiences of gender dysphoria and hormone-replacement therapy.[17] Games such as *Dream Daddy: A Dad Dating Simulator* and *Coming Out on Top* are made by smaller studios, and enable users to explore gay themes, such as coming out and dating as a gay dad.[18] There has been a recent surge in games in the indie market that are centred around queer spaces and people, and these are predominantly positive games, filled with humour, acceptance and support for the rights of all people, rather than the heteronormative image that the virtual world originally portrayed. This change can be seen in things such as the backlash from Twitter users when people such as J. K. Rowling voice their own views publicly, which are then used to attack others, and the platform coming together to voice their feeling that such words are unacceptable. Here, the power of the virtual world is manifest – sharing a game such as *Dys4ia*, which deals with specifically trans content, is empowering, allowing the voices of trans people to be heard, and voices can be raised in support of people when they are discriminated against, harassed or bullied online.

Queer Gothic Gaming

The online world, then, is an emotionally complex environment that the player engages with, which can support or divide people, and each person brings their own opinions and beliefs with them. 'We all', Alayna Cole and Dakota Barker explain, 'have the capacity to feel empathy for the fundamental truths underpinning the lives of others' in our lives, and this can be used to create virtual environments and videogames so that 'the player's actions and interactions are explicitly linked to the messages that a game conveys'.[19] Videogames let players take on the role, and to some extent the identity, of a protagonist, and in doing so they are able to explore events from an unfamiliar (or indeed othered) perspective – such as a different gender, sexuality or even species.[20] Through this interaction, a videogame can highlight an ideological position, or align players with a character to enable an empathetic reaction to events in the game from a particular perspective. Videogames such as these often tell stories that put a specific individual at the heart of the narrative, with the player controlling a PC (playable character) and being asked to play 'as' the character. These characters have set identities that the player cannot alter, with sometimes elaborate backstories and histories that the player interacts with, such as in *The Last of Us* franchise, which contains several queer characters, including the protagonist Ellie, or the 2020 game *Tell Me Why*, the first big-budget videogame to feature a trans protagonist.

There is a distinct difference between an avatar that the user creates in a virtual world such as *Second Life* or an RPG (role-playing game), and the playable characters in games that feature a stronger narrative structure. These playable characters are, in the main, heteronormative in their construction – both narratively and through the rule systems that govern them (although this chapter shows that this is changing). These videogames can present complex attributes in a character, which at first appear to be adhering to a stereotypical role, but are in fact critiquing aspects of society.

The first big-budget videogame to feature a queer woman as protagonist was the post-apocalyptic *The Last of Us 2* (*TLOU2*), a Gothic story of revenge in the zombie apocalypse.[21] The protagonist Ellie and her girlfriend Dina escape the confines of the heteronormative community (signalled by the dominance of heterosexual relationships, and the explicit cat-calling that Ellie receives during cut-scenes because of her sexuality) for the 'freedom' of the post-apocalyptic world. Although at first glance this seems to signal a positive representation of Ellie as a queer character, this is not the case. The narrative structure enables Ellie's revenge on the antagonist Abby after she kills Ellie's father-figure Joel – a typical revenge plot across media and history. Yet at the same time it highlights a typically gendered masculinity, with Ellie in the role of avenger, situating her as masculine-presenting and fulfilling the role of a male character. In videogames, as with a lot of other media, the avenging character is typically male. Even if this is not the case, a male (even where there is a female protagonist) serves as 'protector, guide, or actually performs most of the action while the female serves as sidekick', and while this is actively undercut in this game through both central characters, Ellie and Dina being female, at the same time the creators of the game are adhering to typical heterosexual standards of representation.[22]

According to Cole and Barker, physical representations of a queer character in videogames are often designed to appeal to a heterosexual male audience. In games such as these, the queer female character wears 'practical clothing' and has a 'thin, curvy body ... and soft feminine facial features', an appearance that Ellie conforms to in *TLOU2*.[23] When taken alongside the role Ellie has as revenger, she is male-presenting, providing a typical heterosexual videogame reading of a queer female character: designed to appeal to a heterosexual male player. While this might suggest a superficial and ill-thought-out means of including a queer character in a major videogame, it also allows the person playing to explore gender and sexuality from a queer perspective, asking questions such as whether it matters that Ellie is female, in terms of her actions and reactions, and whether her behaviour is deviant or transgressive, and more widely whether the gender or sexuality of a person is relevant to the outcome of actions that take place, notably revenge and survival in the post-apocalyptic world of *TLOU2*.

A Positive Trans Experience?

Another character that *The Last of Us 2* presents in a masculine light is the antagonist, Abby – although this moniker of antagonist is not as clear-cut as her being the bad guy. She is a strong, muscular and confident character, who functions as a Gothic double for Ellie, thus allowing the player to see the same traits in the two and to question the long-term problems with revenge. Both women want revenge for the death of a father – Ellie's 'father' Joel killed Abby's father to save her at the end of the first game, and Abby kills Joel in revenge early in the second game. As with Ellie, Abby has a companion – although this is a platonic relationship: Lev, a young man from a religious tribe called the Seraphites. Lev was cast out of his tribe when he shaved his head and refuted his gender and birth name, Lily. Within the context of *TLOU2*, head-shaving is something that only the men of the Seraphites are allowed to do, and Lev's mother and the wider clan do not accept this breaking of the rules. Throughout the game, Lev goes through immense personal suffering (as do all the characters): his sister dies, and the game leads him to kill his mother. For Lev, this suffering is augmented by the suffering caused by his complete ostracisation for his 'crime', and constant dead-naming by his former allies when in conflict with them. The game takes pains to portray Lev as a sympathetic character, one whose actions the player can understand as she interacts with him and with the persecution he experiences. He is a deeply religious person; his belief is not shaken even in the face of that religion persecuting him – but this persecution is visible to the player, whom the hatred seems to be aimed at while they are controlling Lev. The player cannot help but be moved by the actions taking place on the screen, and to empathise with his plight as a human being.

In a game with revenge as its primary theme, Lev stands out as one of the only morally positive characters, despite the trauma he endures. Lev's suffering mirrors the experiences of trans people across the world. They too can be ostracised from entire communities; friends, parents and siblings disown them – sometimes telling the trans person that they are dead to them, or simply refusing to acknowledge a new name and gender but punishing them for it nonetheless. The player comes to know Lev's feelings and the torment he suffers for trying to break free of a group that tries to impose a false identity on him and his core beliefs through conversations that take place while performing mundane tasks such as climbing or running. At the end of the game, it is Lev that emerges as the 'winner' – he is not interested in retribution or the violence that comes with it, he just wants to be able to live as himself. In a positive turn on the stereotype that Lev is, the player only ever interacts with Lev's chosen gender – there is no indication (other than the dead name and spoken history) that he is anything other than as presented – but the player comes to understand exactly who he is, physically, mentally and emotionally, and to empathise with his suffering.

Ellie, on the other hand, seemingly ends the game alone, her desire for revenge robbing her of a settled life with Dina. Abby has come to terms with her desire for revenge, but she is still hunting for the Fireflies – an almost mythical militia group founded in the wake of the apocalypse. The comparison is explicit: the character who is given the 'happiest' ending in a post-apocalyptic, violent and dangerous world is the one who is accepting of who they, and others, are.

Of course, Lev's portrayal in this game is indicative of the trauma that cis-written trans experiences are endowed with on a wider scale: a stereotypical rendition of suffering that is bequeathed to trans people, with 'trauma, tragedy, and outright slaughter' being 'staples within trans representation across media'.[24] While the player comes to understand Lev, his history and his beliefs, he is still punished more than any other character – despite being a fairly minor one, something relatively common in Gothic novels, where often 'conventional moralities and identities are proclaimed as triumphant'.[25] Conversely, the 2020 videogame *Tell Me Why* allows the medium to show a positive trans experience, with protagonist Tyler being a trans man – the first time this has happened in a big-budget videogame.[26]

More than a Slogan: Diversity and Recognition in *Tell Me Why*

In *Tell Me Why* there is a clearly proactive approach to trans representation: Tyler, the protagonist and trans character, is voiced by trans man August Black, who contributed to the way the character is portrayed. This included editing the script to be more reflective of a trans person's lived experience. Game studio Dontnod Entertainment also involved GLAAD (Gay and Lesbian Alliance Against Defamation) to ensure that the game would resonate with a wide and diverse audience, including trans people themselves.[27] The game itself is steeped in trauma, as befits a Gothic narrative: the mother (Mary Ann) of Tyler and his twin sister Alyson is killed when the twins are 10 years old, and Tyler is convicted of her murder. This trauma does not result in Tyler being trans, but rather Tyler's trans status, while crucial to the narrative, is not its central theme – which also encompasses trust, poverty, memory, race and mental illness.[28] As the game progresses, the player learns that Tyler was already expressing himself as masculine to his sister, telling her that he felt 'more like a brother' to her than a sister, and asking to be called Ollie, his first chosen name. Interestingly, the game never refers to Tyler by anything other than his chosen names – his birth name stays dead throughout, even in flashbacks and cut-scenes where it might seem 'natural' to use it – in contrast to *The Last of Us 2* in which Lev is dead-named repeatedly.

Tell Me Why relies on the player making choices as part of the play element of the game. These decisions are usually at points where Tyler or Alyson are at an emotional crossroads. While these decisions do not necessarily mean that the narrative itself changes, the choices the player makes on Tyler and Alyson's behalf do affect relationships – both positively and negatively. This becomes clear when considering the relationship Tyler and Alyson have with their mother's best friend, Tessa.

Early in *Tell Me Why*, Tyler and Alyson try to talk to Tessa about their mother. After ludically triggering memories that relate to Tessa (visually showing the player instances of Tessa being kind, caring and even forgiving to the twins and their mother, and balancing this with Tessa and Mary Ann disagreeing), they approach her with their questions. Controlling Tyler's responses, the player asks several questions to which Tessa responds. If the player – and therefore Tyler – acts in a hostile manner, Tessa also becomes hostile, and eventually asks the twins to leave. If instead, the player chooses a different set of dialogue options, then it is possible for Tessa to admit to giving Mary Ann a leaflet promoting conversion camps for Tyler, though she states that she was ignorant about what happened there. Rather than the destructive places they are, Tessa says that she genuinely believed that they were positive and helpful. This then changes the relationship between the two positively, enabling a relationship between Tessa and Tyler later in the game.

At the end of the game, this decision is directly associated with Tyler's relationship with Tessa going forward – and her recognition of his transition. If Tyler has been hostile in the earlier scene, Tessa says that she is not able to accept Tyler as a man. However, if the conversation has been constructive earlier, she indicates a wish to build a relationship with him. This is somewhat awkward: the game is trying to show that Tyler's actions as an adult have repercussions for the relationships he has with those around him, regardless of his trans status. However, to tie that with the acceptance of his trans status is problematic in a game that is trying to portray a positive experience.

Alongside this problematic portrayal, there is an argument to be made that Tyler's story in *Tell Me Why* is one of a privileged transition. Despite being sentenced and incarcerated for the murder of his mother in the US state of Alaska, he undergoes a transition from female to male in the Fireweed Residential Center with no negative impact on his mental health, and when he is released, he continues to live and work there for another three years, with no discrimination for his crime or transition. The people he encounters in the game might not understand why Tyler has transitioned, yet they all appear to treat him with respect (it must be noted, however, that this game has a branching narrative, and so different actions can and do bring about different endings that may not have been found while researching this piece). For example, Tyler is never dead-named, and the only childhood name used for him is Ollie, his first chosen name, or his first-person pronoun, which discards notions of gender. He is also never mis-gendered, even through ignorance. There is also only one episode of explicit transphobia, part of the story arc concerning Tessa, mentioned earlier.[29] Within this idyllic acceptance, even the circumstances of his mother's death are given clarity. Memories are uncovered that enable Tyler and his sister to be freed of her ghost, and along with it the notion that they both had that she was against Tyler's trans status.

While the game is not focused solely on Tyler's gender, it *is* a major theme, and there are several situations in which the player controlling Tyler has to navigate conversations and interactions with people who do not understand how to talk to him or can be hostile. The choice-based structure allows for the dialogue the player chooses to influence future relationships, as shown through Tessa, and so the player has an influence on the emotional outcome of the game, and how the twins' futures will play out.

Polar Gothic

The Gothic condition of *Tell Me Why* is one that is not instantly evident. However, the game is filled with Gothic, which a superficial consideration makes manifest. First, the setting calls to mind Polar Gothic, in which a journey to the Arctic (or Antarctic) pits the protagonist against the landscape, the climate and, of course, their own frailty. This is exemplified in *Frankenstein*, with a framing narrative set in the Arctic, several scenes set in polar-like conditions (for example, the scene on Mont Blanc where the creature and his creator meet) and, of course, the ending, in which Frankenstein chases his creation across the Arctic tundra to his death, his body unable to withstand the harsh elements of the glacial region. Alaska, the setting of *Tell Me Why*, fits directly into this tradition. With an opening that shows the Alaskan landscape, Tyler returns to his hometown on a ferry. This landscape offers Tyler the threat 'of entrapment and persecution' and the town of Delos can be seen as an 'outpost of civilization', offering support for the concept of this game as Polar Gothic.[30] Alongside this, an encounter with an exaggerated reflection of Tyler's repressed 'uncivilized' self encourages this view.[31] On arriving in Delos, Tyler comes face-to-face with the self he could have been when he is greeted by his (formerly) identical twin sister, whom he has not seen for ten years – an uncanny resonance that permeates the whole game, and which is heightened by the player controlling both characters throughout the game.

Tyler's return to Delos, then, is shrouded in Gothic. His return, his reuniting with his twin sister, the uncanniness of being shown how he could have been, and of course the setting highlight a Gothic that permeates the entire game. This return also underscores another common aspect of the Gothic, the preoccupation with the past, especially a past that is shrouded in mystery and that threatens the protagonist's future. Tyler and his sister want to understand their mother and the events leading to her death, and to do so they must uncover these through conversation and their own unreliable memories. This is achieved through having the player 'replay' memories such as those mentioned earlier with regard to Tessa, more traditionally invoking the Gothic with its use of haunting and reliving memory.

Gothic texts are designed, according to Jennifer Andrews, to draw audiences in, to make the reader identify with what he or she reads, and it follows that this will also allow the reader to question their own emotional and moral decisions within the context of a fictional representation.[32] In this game, the player is asked to make such emotional and moral decisions, which are then used to show how they affect those around them. What makes videogames stand out from other fiction is the ability to place the player in a position where they can be shown their own behaviour reflected back at them – just as Andrews considers Gothic fiction does. The decisions the player makes involve several factors that the player must engage with, one of these being to consider how something such as the desire to transition is received – including how people might react. For a trans person who might not have access to resources or a community, this might be their only way of exploring their own identity and feelings, and the reactions they might expect once the process has begun.

Less Story, Bigger Haunting

Ellen Moers considers that one of Gothic fiction's aims is 'to get to the body itself, its glands, muscles, epidermis, and circulatory system, quickly arousing and quickly allaying the physiological reactions to fear'.[33] The Gothic, she tells us, is able to evoke a physical response. This same response reaction can be seen in videogames, a medium that demands bodily activity from its users. It is a medium where players react, often without conscious thought, to sudden changes in circumstances, and a rigorous session of gameplay can often be a physically exhausting ordeal. I argue in *Videogames and Horror* that videogames are able to evoke reactions such as fear through play, sound, setting and the need for the player to physically respond to stimuli, creating a tense atmosphere that the player is engaging with.[34]

Atmospheric tension can be a major storytelling technique in gaming – as can be seen in the 2013 game *Gone Home*.[35] Taking the role of Katie, the player explores the empty family home, and must figure out where everyone has gone. There is a duality in *Gone Home*, as the player quickly realises. The game is founded on the discovery of the whereabouts of the family – Katie's mother, father and sister Sam – when they are inexplicably not there to greet Katie when she returns home for the first time in a year. However, the game is centred on Sam's disappearance and the events leading up to the note she leaves for her sister with the chilling 'don't try to find me' content.

In *Gone Home*, Gothic is evoked through the player's interaction with the empty mansion that figures across Gothic fiction, with its hidden rooms and secrets, using the principles of environmental storytelling pioneered by Henry Jenkins, and expanded on by Stobbart among others, and the atmosphere the game is created with.[36] As the player explores the old mansion known locally as the Psycho House, they are treated to many familiar Gothic tropes: the floors creak, there are odd noises and lights flicker – all of which leads the player to believe *Gone Home* to be a game in the style of *Silent Hill* or *Resident Evil* – a survival horror game in which the player creeps around to avoid being killed. This idiom is used deliberately to heighten the tension that the player feels while exploring – and to suggest the expectation of death that is commonly part of this structure. However, in *Gone Home* this is used instead to explore Sam's recent history, including their coming out and initially feeling that they are rejected by their parents. Being placed in close perspective with Katie, the player experiences the aftermath of these events, and has to piece everything together through clues left around the house. The emotions the player feels when playing a game such as *Amnesia: The Dark Descent* are recalled in the player's subconscious and the reactions are replayed via the story being told on the screen in front of them – they feel the same rising terror in exploring the house with Katie as when controlling the protagonist in *Amnesia*.

While not a game as these are typically reckoned (it has no combat, action, threat or any way to die or otherwise influence the narrative), *Gone Home* instead immerses the player in the environment in order to engage with it. With none of the usual stimuli, the player instead focuses on the house itself and the several stories that exist within. Through interacting with the contents of the house, Katie learns what has been happening to her parents and sister, Sam, while she has been travelling for a year. As Katie searches the house, she finds evidence of her mother's attraction to another man, her father's financial and creative problems, and Sam's struggle with and revelation of their sexuality. All of this is revealed to Katie as the player controls her passage through the family home via a first-person perspective that lessens the narrative distance between the player and Katie, and which situates the player as sympathetic to Sam. Despite this narrative closeness, however, the reactions are all Katie's – the player is as passive as in any other narrative. There is no option to change the outcome of the game, no one wins or loses; instead, the player is exposed to the emotional content of the game at close proximity and is invited to empathise with Sam's coming out through interacting with the environment.

Throughout the game, certain objects can trigger a spoken aspect to the narrative, which forms the basis for the queer elements of *Gone Home*. In these segments Sam relates events that have taken place while Katie has been away, such as the negative reaction to Sam coming out to their parents. With these audio segments coming from the 'I' perspective, this enables the player to empathise with Sam: to share their perspective and to 'walk a mile in their shoes', so to speak. It is Sam that the narrative concentrates on: *Gone Home* tells Sam's story, coloured by the aftermath of a bad coming out, and the player is explicitly intended to empathise with them. Sam's is the voice the player hears talking, as they share the joy of falling in love, and the sadness and anger of a negative coming out.

The atmosphere of *Gone Home* is distinctly Gothic – the house is central to the game, and as with many Gothic narratives, it offers a labyrinthine space, filled with secrets. As with other Gothic media, there is a duality to this familiar setting. For videogame Gothic, this duality contains the ludic element of conquering the space, which means controlling Katie in exploring the old house, making it familiar or *Heimlich*.[37] At the same time this exploration evokes the terror of having to enter the dark corners of the house, where the threat of violence and harm coexist with the urge to conquer the space. Stereotypical tropes such as flickering lights and a storm outside foreground this Gothic atmosphere, acting as a further semiotic marker to the Gothic genre.

The atmosphere of the game, the narrative and the Gothic tropes all lend themselves to a suggestion that there is a death at the heart of the game, and as the player draws closer to discovering Sam's whereabouts, they are directed to the attic – a space that the Gothic has long called home, calling to mind Bertha in *Jane Eyre* and Madeline in *The Fall of the House of Usher*, among many other characters and Gothic texts. However, in the final scenes of the game, we learn that there is no Gothic mystery and that no one has died: Sam and Lonnie have simply left to build a life together.

Gone Home, then, uses the Gothic structure to underpin Katie's discovery of her sister's sexuality and recent history, using the connotations that the player associates with the Gothic to suggest the fate of Sam, and to create sympathy in the player for Sam and the struggles they have faced in coming out. Here, as with *Tell Me Why*, the player is placed in a position that sympathises with the character so as to gain an understanding of the problems that they face.

Conclusion

Queer representation has been a factor in the virtual world since its earliest incarnation. Despite the prevalence of heteronormative content across the virtual world, queer culture has been at the foundation of the Internet. Alongside this, storytelling in videogames allows a player to engage with a narrative premise such as queerness on a level closer than that of most fiction, with the addition of an interactivity not readily achieved in other media. Here, then, the distance between the player and the onscreen avatar or playable character is lessened to give the perception that the two are the same person – an uncanny state where the player 'endows' the character or avatar with thoughts, feelings, desires and even an identity, thus allowing the player to engage with the experiences of another in a closer approximation of living their experiences, like Parzival in *Ready Player One*. Such an approach offers the opportunity for an individual to gain an understanding of another's life: their trauma, persecution and the personal history that has made each character who they are. This can be seen across the videogames examined in this chapter: the persecution Lev is subjected to in *TLOU2*, the past and the different memories that Tyler and his sister share, and, of course, the rejection that Sam feels when they tell their parents of their sexuality. Each of these games offers the player an insight into the mind of the character, and furthermore gives them an understanding of these events *as* that character, rather than watching (or reading) about them in the third person.

In the virtual world, then, there is a level of solidarity with the queer community that has always existed, even if it could not be seen, and when aligned with the Gothic, whose tropes are eminently suitable for interrogating and exploring this solidarity, a unity with the queer community is not only evident, but allows creators to share their own lived experiences and often to find support and positive reinforcement of the self that might be undermined or denied to the queer person in the real world.

Notes

1. Ernest Cline, *Ready Player One* (New York: Crown, 2011), p. ??.
2. Janet Murray, *Hamlet on the Holodeck* (Cambridge, MA: MIT Press, 1997).
3. Janine Fron et al., *The Hegemony of Play*, proceedings of DiGRA Situated Play, https://ict.usc.edu/pubs/The%20Hegemony%20of%20Play.pdf (2007) (accessed 30 March 2021).
4. Tereza Krobová, Ondrej Moravec and Jaroslav Švelch, 'Dressing Commander Shepard in Pink: Queer Playing in a Heteronormative Game Culture', *Cyberpsychology: Journal of Psychosocial Research on Cyberspace*, 9.3 (2015), https://doi.org/10.5817/CP2015-3-3 (accessed 30 March 2021).
5. Dontnod Entertainment, *Tell Me Why* [videogame] (Xbox Game Studio, 2020).
6. This can be seen in the 1983 film *Wargames*, starring Matthew Broderick as a teen hacker.
7. Esteban Ortiz-Ospina, 'The Rise of Social Media' (2019), https://ourworldindata.org/rise-of-social-media (Accessed 30 March 2021).
8. Diane Carr et al., *Computer Games, Text, Narrative, Play* (Malden, MA: Polity, 2006), p. 68.
9. Tom Boellstorff, *Coming of Age in Second Life* (Princeton, NJ: Princeton University Press, 2008), pp.129–130.

10. Krobová, Moravec and Švelch, 'Dressing Commander Shepard in Pink'.
11. Nicholas Royle, *The Uncanny* (Manchester: Manchester University Press, 2003), pp. 2, 6.
12. Michael Hancock, 'Doppelgamers: Video Games and Gothic Choice', in *American Gothic Culture: An Edinburgh Companion*, ed. Joel Faflak and Jason Haslam (Edinburgh: Edinburgh University Press, 2016), pp. 166–85.
13. Boellstorff, *Coming of Age*, pp. 134–5.
14. *That Certain Summer*, dir. Lamont Johnson (Universal Television, 1972); Natalie Edwards, 'From Minority to Mainstream: Channel 4's Queer Television', *e-Media Studies*, 2.1 (2009), https://journals.dartmouth.edu/cgi-bin/WebObjects/Journals.woa/1/xmlpage/4/article/325 (accessed 30 March 2021).
15. Michelle Zorrilla, *Video Games and Gender*, thesis, https://www.academia.edu/5594515/Video_Games_and_Gender_Game_Representation_Gender_Effects_Differences_in_Play_and_Player_Representation (accessed 30 March 2021).
16. Helen Thornham, *Ethnographies of the Videogame* (Farnham: Ashgate, 2011), p. 4.
17. Anna Anthropy, *Dys4ria* [videogame] (Newgrounds, 2012).
18. Game Grumps, *Dream Daddy: A Dad Dating Simulator* [videogame] (Game Grumps, 2017); Obscurasoft, *Coming Out on Top* [videogame] (Obscurasoft, 2014).
19. Alayna Cole and Dakoda Barker, *Games as Texts* (London: CRC Press, 2021), p. 8.
20. Christoph Klimmt, Dorothée Hefner, Peter Vorderer, Christian Roth and Christopher Blake, 'Identification with Video Game Characters as Automatic Shifts of Self-Perceptions', *Media Psychology*, 13.4 (2010), https://www.tandfonline.com/doi/abs/10.1080/15213269.2010.524911 (accessed 30 March 2021).
21. Naughty Dog, *The Last of Us Part II* [videogame] (Sony Interactive Entertainment, 2020).
22. Zorrilla, *Video Games and Gender*.
23. Cole and Barker, *Games as Texts*, p. 56.
24. Sara Elsam, 'Trans Games Professionals Explore *Tell Me Why*'s Landmark Depiction of Trans Identity' (2020), https://www.gamesindustry.biz/articles/2020-09-15-trans-games-professionals-explore-tell-me-whys-landmark-depiction-of-trans-identity (accessed: 30 March 2021).
25. William Hughes and Andrew Smith, 'Introduction: Queering the Gothic', in *Queering the Gothic* (Manchester: Manchester University Press, 2009), p. 1.
26. Cynthia Silva, '"Tell me Why": Video Game Features Transgender Lead Character' (2020), https://www.nbcnews.com/feature/nbc-out/tell-me-why-video-game-features-transgender-lead-character-n1239123 (accessed 30 March 2021); Elsam, 'Trans Games Professionals'.
27. GLAAD, GLAAD, https://www.glaad.org/ (accessed 28 December 2021).
28. James Batchelor, 'Dontnod's *Tell Me Why* Aims for a Transgender Story not "Rooted in Pain or Trauma"' (2020), https://www.gamesindustry.biz/articles/2020-07-24-dontnods-tell-me-why-aims-for-a-transgender-story-not-rooted-in-pain-or-trauma (accessed 30 March 2021).

29. Tellmewhygame.com, FAQ (2020), https://www.tellmewhygame.com/faq/#:~:text=No%2C%20Tyler's%20birth%20name%20does,Alyson's%20nickname%2C%20%E2%80%9CAly.%E2%80%9D&text=No (accessed 30 March 2021).
30. Mariaconcetta Costantini, 'Polar Contagion: Ecogothic Anxiety across Media in the Twenty-First Century', *Lingue e Linguaggi*, 44 (2021), pp. 67–80, http://siba-ese.unisalento.it/index.php/linguelinguaggi/issue/current (accessed 29 December 2021).
31. Katherine Bowers, 'Haunted Ice, Fearful Sounds, and the Arctic Sublime: Exploring Nineteenth Century Polar Gothic Space', *Gothic Studies*, 9.2 (2017), pp. 71–84, https://euppublishing.com/toc/gothic/19/2 (accessed 29 December 2021).
32. Jennifer Andrews, 'Native Canadian Gothic Refigured: Reading Eden Robinson's *Monkey Beach*', *Essays on Canadian Writing*, 73 (2001), pp. 1–24.
33. Ellen Moers, 'Female Gothic: The Monster's Mother', in *Frankenstein*, ed. J. Paul Hunter (New York: W. W. Norton, 1996), p. 90.
34. Dawn Stobbart, *Videogames and Horror: From Amnesia to Zombies, Run!* (Cardiff: University of Wales Press, 2019), p. 28.
35. Fullbright, *Gone Home* [videogame] (Fullbright, 2013).
36. Henry Jenkins, 'Game Design as Narrative Architecture' (2002), http://web.mit.edu/~21fms/People/henry3/games&narrative.html (accessed 30 March 2021); Dawn Stobbart, 'Playing the Future History of Humanity: Situating *Fallout 3* as a Narratological Artefact', in *On the Fringes of Literature and Digital Media*, ed. Irena Kalla et al. (Leiden: Brill, 2018), pp. 123–34.
37. Sigmund Freud, 'The Uncanny' (1919), https://web.mit.edu/allanmc/www/freud1.pdf (accessed 30 March 2021).

Chapter 15

'Y'all ain't from around these parts': Queer Displacement in American Folk Horror
Amanda Cruz

Defining Folk Horror

As a genre, folk horror resists strict categorisation, much like queer identity. By and large, however, the 'folk horror chain' holds true: emphasis on landscape, a skewed belief system and a violent climax all combine to discomfort the audience, prompting them to interrogate their own ideas of 'normal'.[1] This interrogation pushes the boundaries of the allowable, shrinking the distance between self and other. Folk horror as a subgenre of Gothic fiction offers a rich space for further study to advance the understanding of the Queer Gothic.

Folk horror is relatively new as a genre of study, although the term 'folk horror' has been around far longer. Most sources credit a 2003 *Fangoria* interview with Piers Haggard, the director of *The Blood on Satan's Claw*, as the moment the term was coined.[2] Haggard's film is often referred to as a member of the unholy trinity of folk horror cinema: *Witchfinder General* (1968), *The Blood on Satan's Claw* (1971) and *The Wicker Man* (1973).[3] These films are treated as foundational texts for defining the genre in cinema. At their base level, these three unrelated films are connected by their use of rural British settings and themes of pagan worship.

The unholy trinity draws on the literary tradition of British folk horror, but this genre hardly belongs to the British Isles. The legend of *La Llorona* (The Crying Woman) is a Mexican folk tale of a woman who drowns her own children and dies afterwards, cursed to wander near bodies of water, weeping over her loss and drowning any who come close.[4] In South Korea, the 2016 horror film *The Wailing* tells the story of a policeman investigating a series of small-town murders caused by a strange infection, or perhaps a supernatural evil. Folk horror is a vast landscape of stories reflecting a culture's values and fears. For the purposes of this chapter, I will focus primarily on American folk horror and its relationship to queer identity in the United States. American folk horror draws on the transatlantic literary scene, as well as European paganism. British authors of supernatural horror such as Arthur Machen and Algernon Blackwood were noted influences for American authors such as H. P. Lovecraft and Stephen King. American folk horror also reflects the colonial impact of Puritanism and westward expansion in its use of the forest as an evil-laden wilderness beyond civilisation. The harvest is a common theme in American folk horror with its symbolic representation of death and rebirth. The rural setting that is typical of a large portion of folk horror relies alternately on the woods as a symbolic space of transgressive behaviour, and cultivated fields as spaces of civilisation. Both are dangerous, and both represent a threat to the individual in their own contexts.

In 2014 Adam Scovell posited a new way of identifying folk horror in his presentation at the 'Fiend in the Furrows' folk horror conference at Queens University Belfast. Scovell argues for the existence of a folk horror chain, a trio of narrative features that signal a work's belonging in the genre: landscape, a skewed belief system and a happening or summoning.[5] While not exclusive to works of the genre, these three traits are commonly found in some combination in a work of folk horror, producing atmospheric tension and a sense of the surreal and scary. Scovell's chain breaks down into three distinct units. The first connective thread is the use of landscape. Folk horror narratives are frequently set in idyllic-seeming rural spaces, with an emphasis on isolation. This rurality, often used to invoke pastoral calm and simplicity, hides (and enables) the skewed belief systems and morality that govern the population. The wrongness of the belief systems is emphasised by the protagonist's role as intruder or misfit, creating a feeling of dis-ease and growing tension. Finally, there is a happening or a summoning; the tension peaks as there is a violent, often supernatural event. In *The Blood on Satan's Claw*, this is the summoning of the demon. In *The Wicker Man*, it is the ritual sacrifice of the protagonist in a burning, human-shaped structure. In *Witchfinder General*, it is the brutal murder of the witch-hunter as both Sara and Richard lose their sanity after the horrors that the witch-hunter has committed.

Scovell's folk horror chain is particularly useful because of his acknowledgement of its limitations. He writes that to rigidly define the parameters of the genre is 'conceivably impossible' and would limit the scope of interconnected works detrimentally.[6] This allows for works that ostensibly subvert the formula, but still 'feel' as though they belong within the genre. Andy Paciorek argues that the aesthetic and atmosphere, specifically the feeling they create in the audience, are more important to a work's inclusion in the genre than how successfully they can be codified.[7] By thinking of the folk horror genre itself as an offshoot of Gothic fiction, its resistance to categorisation begins to make more sense. As Ardel Haefele-Thomas writes in 'Queering the Female Gothic', 'as a genre, Gothic thrives on complications and constantly throws what we think we know and believe into confusion'.[8] The undermined expectations for genre classifications mirror the eeriness of subverted expectations that the protagonists in folk horror stories experience throughout the narrative. By considering folk horror within the bounds of Gothic literature, Scovell's chain becomes a narrative framework for folk horror to produce the uncanny effects of the Gothic genre. The pastoral landscape initially invokes a sense of simplicity and refuge from the perils of the urban world, but its isolation leaves the protagonists stranded without help in an increasingly hostile, possibly supernatural environment. The traditional values and old-fashioned ways of the community hide sinister secrets, often involving neo-paganistic rituals that unsettle both protagonist and audience. Finally, the happening or summoning reveals the full extent of the horror. This chain is therefore how folk horror achieves the Uncanny, defined by Freud as that which is both familiar and unfamiliar.[9]

George Haggerty's *Queer Gothic* is critical for understanding the deep ties between the Gothic and queer theory. The terror in Gothic fiction 'is almost always sexual terror', with desire 'expressed as the exercise of (or resistance to) power'.[10] Haggerty's use of queer here is less about hetero- or homosexual desire, and more about the ways in which the stories work to destabilise the 'sexual status quo'.[11] As a subsection of the genre, folk horror dramatises the cultural forces that produce 'proper' subjectivities (and sexualities) while disciplining those who refuse to conform. Jacques Derrida posits that beyond the simplistic definition of the monster as something hybrid or chimerical, 'a monster is a species for which we do not yet have a name [. . .] it frightens precisely because no anticipation had prepared one to identify this figure'.[12] The hybridity of monsters rejects comforting binaries and defies understanding because of its abnormality. The rejection of monstrous humanity from within the system is an attempt to reinforce the meaning of the self through dehumanisation and demonisation of the Other.

However, as Derrida argues, monstrosity is unstable, relying on its separation from the normal and its imperceptibility to remain monstrous.[13] Once seen, monstrosity can be compared to the norm, and it begins the 'movement of acculturation, precisely, of domestication, or normalization'.[14] In other words, to know a monster is to remove some of its monstrosity and begin the process of normalising the abnormal.

Things that used to shock and terrify become banal over time with understanding, and reflecting on the things that used to elicit terror helps to understand the way normalcy is constructed and maintained, and how that has changed over time. This chapter will focus on the ways that gender and sexuality are performed in folk horror, exposing the constructed nature of normalcy and challenging the sexual status quo. This chapter will also examine how uncanny monstrosity is used to repel or elicit sympathy from the reader, and why the uncanny monster is sympathetic from a queer perspective.

The Urbanoid versus the Rural Enclave

One way in which folk horror dramatises opposing cultural forces is through the dichotomy of urban and rural settings. With folk horror's reliance on isolation and landscape, it's no wonder that a lot (although crucially, not all) of folk horror takes place in rural settings. The rural backdrop creates a landscape that is alien to most urban audiences. While this alienation is useful for the Gothic sense of dis-ease, it points to an urbanoid perspective. Urbanoia, coined by Carol Clover, describes the recurring theme of stories in which city dwellers venture into the backwoods or similarly rural spaces, only to be attacked and murdered by the locals.[15] Frequently called 'hillbilly horror' or 'hillbilly slashers' in American film, this genre is a permutation on Puritan notions that civilisation exists on the border of a wilderness that is populated by devils and evil spirits. It also reflects the very real trend of queer people flocking to cities to live safely and authentically, away from insular communities that are hostile to 'difference' from the status quo. This divide both reflects and exacerbates the cultural divide and alienation between American urban and rural populations, but to what end? The conception of an Other, something distant and unfamiliar, is the negative image by which the normal is defined. Community is defined as much by what it includes as what it rejects. From the perspective of an urban audience, the 'fantasy of rural separation and remoteness' allows for 'preservation of the arcane and sinister'.[16] The use of antiquated farming equipment emphasises the feeling of being stuck in the past; scythes and pitchforks populate these stories rather than tractors and threshing machines, and they are wielded by the superstitious locals who threaten urban interlopers and keep their own communities compliant with their skewed belief systems. The mythology of the small town is a space where tradition and community, in isolation, can become corrupted into something sinister and violent. This mythology also relies on the assumption of a binary where urbanity is synonymous with modernity, in contrast to outdated rurality.

Thomas Tryon's 1973 novel *Harvest Home* tells the story of Theodore 'Ned' Constantine as he moves his family to a tiny farming town and away from New York City. The town of Cornwall Coombe is welcoming, but Ned discovers sinister paganistic rituals at the heart of their belief system, all occurring under the watchful eye of Widow Fortune, the town matriarch. While his wife and daughter adapt and join the community, Ned resists. His decision to remain an outsider ultimately leads to his mutilation at the hands of the town's women at the peak of their harvest ritual.

The town of Cornwall Coombe is 'nestled among some low hills' and 'its roads seem hardly traveled, but for an occasional truck or farm wagon'.[17] The tiny town seems idyllic in comparison to the narrator's apartment in New York City, which now feels dark, cramped and depressing. Ned calls the villagers of Cornwall Coombe 'a tightly knit, insular group, these corn farmers, apparently determined to cut themselves off from the rest of society in an effort to preserve their own folkways'.[18] Ned's dismissive condescension towards the townspeople gives way to suspicion that their naivety is a cover for something sinister. In addition to isolating Ned from the town, his suspicions and unwillingness to integrate into the community isolate him from his wife and daughter as they begin to adopt the local customs and social practices.

Ned as protagonist is urbane, educated and a successful patriarch of his family. He hopes the rural setting will be a balm from the corruption of the city, but the change in setting only exposes the real problem: Ned himself. In the isolation of the small town, he begins to lose control over the things that defined him in the larger structures of the world. This town is matriarchal and paganistic, and while his wife Beth and daughter Kate adapt and thrive in the community, he grows suspicious. As Ned's rage and suspicion grow, he focuses this on Tamar Penrose, a local woman who Ned derisively considers a 'sex fiend'.[19] Tensions peak when Ned learns that the women of the town are responsible for cutting out the tongue of the local peddler. Tamar confirms Ned's suspicions that she personally saw to the mutilation, and killed another woman during the previous Harvest Home ritual. The woman, Gracie, had been intended as the Corn Maiden, but she was disfigured by an illness before the ceremony. Tamar killed her to keep her ugliness from tainting the harvest. As Tamar confesses all this, she is seducing Ned, provoking both his anger and his lust. In a fit of impotent rage, Ned attempts to murder Tamar by drowning, and then by raping her. He exhausts his rage against her, trying to violate her even as she invites his violence and takes pleasure when he intends to inflict pain. He weeps as he orgasms, finally realising that the power which he has never had to doubt within a patriarchal social framework is absent here, and he has become a 'man, unmanned, defeated by the woman'.[20] He doesn't succeed in violating her, or taking anything from her, because she is a creature of the earth, belonging to the Mother Goddess. Just as the earth cannot be dominated, neither can she. This moment of failing to commit corrective rape is the beginning of Ned's fall.

Ned's last attempt at control occurs on the night of the Harvest Festival; he hides himself in the woods to witness the last secrets of the town, the secret of the Sacred Mother. As Ned watches the women of the town dance and chant in tongues, he is filled with 'hatred for their stupid, primitive beliefs'.[21] He bursts from his hiding place when he realises that his wife is at the centre of the ceremony. The women capture him, and the matriarch forces him to witness that which he came to spy on: the 'making of the corn'.[22] His wife, in the role of Corn Maiden, and his best friend, in the role of Harvest King, perform ritualised sex for the blessing of Mother Earth before the women cut the Harvest King's throat, watering the ground with his blood. The women blind Ned and cut out his tongue in the aftermath as punishment for having witnessed their sacred secret, removing the last of his agency and power. At the end of the novel, Ned is a ghost in his own home. Blind and muted, he is an afterthought for his wife as she and their daughter thrive without him.

The patriarchal and matriarchal systems are both based in gender binaries and inequity that harm those who resist. The horror of a man engaging in this matriarchal system only to be emasculated, with no recourse to his own gendered power, dramatises the naturalised oppressive structures that Ned is familiar with. Here, the relationship between natural/feminine and urban/masculine is underscored with a threat of sexual violence that targets men. The Harvest King is the most quintessentially masculine man in town, and this masculinity is revered at the same time as it is destroyed. Desire and power are in the hands of the women, and any resistance is met with gruesome violence.

Thomas Tryon's own experiences with compulsory heterosexuality may have influenced Ned's tragic fate at the hands of the women of Cornwall Coombe. Tryon was queer and HIV-positive, though not out publicly or to his family during his lifetime. Ned is an embodiment of frustration within the heteropatriarchal roles offered to men and symbolises Tryon's own insecurities as a closeted queer man. Ned's inadequacies in his masculine roles of husband, father and community member parallel Tryon's own failed marriage. By framing the entire story as Ned's internal thoughts, knowing that he will never be able to voice them, Tryon subtly evokes a very queer fear: the fear of erasure from the narrative, of dying unseen and unmentioned, excised by the community at large. The excessive monstrosity of the climax of the novel (Ned's attempted rape of Tamar, the erotic violence of the Harvest Festival and Ned's symbolic castration) render the small town uncanny. It is not a refuge from the violence and danger of the city as Ned had once thought, just a different version. The gruesome rituals of heteromatriarchy make the violent reinforcement of heteropatriarchy visible for what they are: power, expressed through rigid rituals of heterosexual interaction, reinforced by sexually charged violence (corrective rape, castration and murder).

Be Gay, Do Witchcraft

In contrast to the urbanoid is the small town as the enclave of resistance to the mainstream, safe from the dangers of the city and closer to nature. Given the history of rural oppression, these same isolated communities can be seen as a 'resistance and opposition after decades of poverty, social, cultural, and political marginality'.[23] Demonising rural populations as loci of evil or bastions of racist, patriarchal heteronormativity ignores the individuality of community members and the reality that these oppressive social structures are just as present in an urban context. Removing the false equivalence of urban/modern and rural/outdated, rural isolation represents freedom from the pressures of mainstream society. The adherence to seemingly outdated traditions, when reframed outside of urban condescension, suggests the ephemerality of the modern moment. The modern is defamiliarised by contextualising it as the younger of two traditions, and by contextualising the modern as a moment in history its absolute power is undermined. Even monoliths such as Christianity become fragile when compared in age to pagan practices throughout the whole of human history.

The resurgence of folk horror in the 1960s and 1970s, as evidenced by the unholy trinity of British cinema mentioned above, coincided with the growth of paganism in the US and UK.[24] Contemporary paganism is an umbrella term for the various religions that combine reverence for the natural world with folklore and pre-Christian ethnography. While reconstruction of pre-Christian spiritual traditions is central to some pagan practices, there is no centralised authority for pagan worship, nor is there an unbroken history of paganism, because the term itself is one of convenience for distinguishing Christians from non-Christians, flattening the distinction between various religious traditions. The revival of pagan spirituality as a countercultural movement to Christianity shared a strong connection with feminist and queer communities who found that paganism offered 'images and practices that empower women both as individuals and as community leaders'.[25] Paganism allows room for queer identities by challenging the architecture of patriarchal heterosexism. Rather than a monotheistic male God in a religion that distinguishes the body and soul from one another, paganism offers goddess worship and a celebration of the physical world, including the body. Christianity relies on a framework of erotophobia: sex is centred on reproduction, pleasure is temptation, and shame is a powerful social and religious force for controlling errant sexuality. In paganism, eroticism is sacred, not profane. Paganism, for many practitioners, offers a connective framework for understanding their body and spirituality in conjunction with nature, decentralising heterosexuality in their spiritual practice and rejecting the shame that Christianity places on deviant bodies and alternative forms of love and community structure.

The queerness of *The Wicker Man* is in the contrast between the residents of Summerisle and Police Sergeant Neil Howie, the model of a cisgender straight white man in a position of authority. The island residents practise a folkloresque amalgamation of vaguely Celtic paganism that Howie finds repulsive. Summerisle's neo-paganism is presented as openly, shamelessly sexual, much to the dismay of Sgt Howie, who is devoutly Christian. The people of Summerisle have little regard for Christianity and they tempt Sgt Howie to engage in sex out of wedlock. The town's sexual promiscuity still focuses primarily on reproduction, but the explicit connections between nature and sex foster dread in Howie, particularly when he watches the children participate in May Day festivities such as the maypole, which is openly celebrated as a phallic symbol. The sexual terror in *The Wicker Man* is banal; physical violence is not a factor. The threat it poses for Howie is spiritual, a fear that he will succumb to desire and lose his virtue. This low-grade sexual terror combines with the town's deliberate, coordinated interference in the missing child investigation to create a feeling of dis-ease throughout the film. The shock of *The Wicker Man*, however, is in the conclusion, when the people of Summerisle celebrate as they burn Sgt Howie alive as a virgin sacrifice. The townspeople sway and sing a joyful folk song as Howie burns to death, backdropped by an idyllic sunset. Summerisle residents face no consequences for the murder of this symbol of Christian heteropatriarchy, and the only one to suffer in the film is Howie himself. By not allowing the symbol of Christian patriarchy to restore 'proper' hegemonic order, the movie threatens the norm, simply by creating a scenario in which the dominant culture does not prevail in the end.

Queer Negativity and Resistance

Simon Stranzas' 'The King of Stones' tells the story of Judith and Rose, a queer couple taking a road trip. Judith's frustration at highway traffic leads her to drive along side roads, hoping to skip the source of the snarl. They drive, eventually losing sight of the highway and any sign of people nearby. When Rose spots a peach orchard, they stop and get out, hoping to find someone who can point them back to their route. They find a massive, uprooted peach tree with roots that form an optical illusion of an old man. In front of these roots is a pot full of blackened stones that look to Judith like peach pits. As they leave, Rose confronts Judith about her interminable negativity:

> Why do you have to be like that? . . . Always so negative about everything. Don't you care about me? . . . It affects me, you know. I try not to let it. I try to keep us happy. But you make it so hard sometimes. It's like you're trying to ruin things. I feel like . . . like . . . like you're emitting bad vibes or something. All this negative energy radiating from you that I constantly absorb, and I don't know how much longer I can do it. Do you get what I'm saying? I don't know how much more I can take on.[26]

Judith is dismissive of Rose's frustration, causing her to storm off ahead to the car. When Judith gets there, she finds Rose talking to two women who have pulled up behind their car on the road. The narrative abruptly jumps forward to Judith and Rose being held captive by a group led by an older woman. The women bathe Judith and guide her back to the fallen peach tree. There, they bind Judith and force her to watch a ritual in which Rose is crowned with the blackened, burning stones from the pot before being suspended among the tree roots. As she transforms, the tree roots envelop her, and she disappears. Rose is sacrificed to the King of Stones, becoming his queen and the vessel of forgiveness. Judith, overcome with guilt, cuts out her own tongue and throws it into the pot, where it shrivels to stone with the others.

Judith's guilt over Rose's death is a complex thing; Judith bears the burden of having 'primed [Rose] to suffer, to take on what wasn't hers, until it bore her out'.[27] Judith's 'bad vibes' were made Rose's burden, priming her for the supernatural transformation into a pagan goddess of forgiveness. The ritual sacrifice parallels the Christian crucifixion story, with Rose being suspended from the roots of the peach tree with arms outstretched and adorned in a bloody crown. Her crown, though, is made of the severed tongues of the villagers, charred to stone in the pot as an offering of confession, seeking the absolution of the Stone King, god of the harvest.

Judith's self-mutilation is symbolic of her abjection; her narrative, full of all her mistakes and regrets, has become unbearable. She must either offer her own forgiveness or her story, the only thing she has left. Julia Kristeva, in *Powers of Horror*, describes abjection as 'when narrative identity is unbearable, when the boundary between subject and object is shaken and when even the claim between inside and outside is shaken'.[28] Judith, overwhelmed by her narrative identity after having witnessed Rose's torturous death and transformation, cuts out her tongue and offers it to the Stone King, a sense of relief flooding her now that she 'no longer had the words'.[29]

By cutting out her own tongue, Judith symbolically castrates herself, restricting her own narrative power. Even though she feels alone, she is surrounded by likewise tongueless villagers, silent witnesses to her self-mutilation. Judith's silence, and the silence of the townspeople around her, is symbolic of queer victimhood. Derrida's definition of a victim, from the same discussion as his definition of monstrosity, is of a figure whose meaning is erased, 'totally excluded or covered over by language, annihilated by history, a victim one cannot identify'.[30] Victims are those without narratives, excluded from language and meaning, scrubbed from the dominant narrative. In *Harvest Home*, Ned is a victim through his mutilation, and he is left spectral in his own home, blind and silent, as his family continues to thrive without him. His 'unspeakable' tragedy is a double entendre for his removed tongue and the inexpressible trauma of its removal. Judith's decision to remove her own tongue is different from Ned's victimisation because it is an act of self-preservation. Judith feels crushed by the narrative burden, and her anger would corrupt the world 'like a poisonous seed in the soil [. . .] until it was all destroyed'.[31]

The Stone King, god of the harvest, represents the heteronormative goal of reproductive futurity. As Rose is sacrificed to him, the old woman guiding the ceremony tells Judith, 'From their union might sweet fruit spill.'[32] All the sacrifices, personal and communal, are meant to preserve life and tradition in a village that seems to be clinging desperately to hope for the future. Characters such as Judith, who cannot fulfil or outright refuse this goal, are seen as threats because they undermine the future of the community. Olu Jenzen's 'The Queer Uncanny' discusses the uncanniness of the queer body within the heteronormative paradigm, specifically that the queer figure 'functions as a reminder of the "negative," non-procreative or "meaningless" aspects of sexuality haunting the normalising heterosexual narrative'.[33] They will not reproduce, they will not be subjugated in patriarchal heteronormative systems, and in their refusal of the system, they suggest an alternative way of living. Rose's crucifixion transforms her and binds her to the King of Stones as his queen, symbolising the corrective violence enacted against queer bodies to subjugate them to the heterosexual imperative.

Judith's refusal to forgive even herself can be seen as a queer form of resistance, in line with Jack Halberstam's theory of queer failure. Judith, who is a constant force of negativity, anger and vitriol, can be interpreted as an expression of 'queer darkness [. . .] the terrain of the failed and miserable'.[34] Further, by combining Halberstam's queer failure as resistance with Jenzen's queer uncanny, Judith's self-inflicted silence is how she 'declines intelligibility and violates the boundaries that secure the ontological basis of heterosexual normativity'.[35] By intentionally removing herself from the narrative and refusing to forgive, Judith represents a radical rejection of futurity and positive affect. She becomes spectral, surrounded by likewise tongueless villagers. She reclaims the notion of silence: she is not silenced by anyone else, but her silence is 'as a part of language, rendered performative in the same way as speech'.[36] The reclamation of the space of the uncanny as a place of resistance to power is key to queer folk horror, and in the same way Judith's silence challenges the deliberate silencing of queer voices in history, the trope of the undead challenges the distinction of natural and unnatural that dehumanises queer people.

Unburying Your Gays

The monstrous Other is a way of reinforcing our definition of self. What we identify as different and a threat is given physical form, and thus opens to a question: do we identify with the protagonist or the monster? American media has a long history surrounding its treatment of queer bodies and stories. In the 1920s and 1930s, Hollywood had a reputation for being accepting of queer talent and narratives; men and women cross-dressed on screen and inverted gender norms in a way that signalled homosexuality to the audience of the time.[37] In *Morocco*, Marlene Dietrich, clad in a tuxedo, kisses a woman on the lips. The mounting homophobic backlash against such transgressive entertainment was codified in the 1930s as the Hays Code, which censored 'taboo' content in American film and television from 1934 to 1968. Films were not allowed to sympathise with 'amoral' characters, and queer representation was considered an unacceptable threat to the moral character of the audience. Hollywood did not stop making films with queer themes and characters, but they became more subtle. In an interview, screenwriter Jay Presson

Allen once stated, 'the guys who ran that Code weren't rocket scientists. They missed a lot of stuff, and when the director was subtle enough and clever enough, they [sic] got around it.'[38] By the 1960s the restrictions had loosened enough to permit open homosexuality on screen, but their transgression had to be punished by the end of the film to avoid glorifying devious behaviour. Thus, the trope of 'Bury Your Gays' was born: queer characters can be happy on screen, but only if they suffer or die in the end. This trope is not exclusive to cinema and has been used as a critique of queer representation in television and literature as well.

One of the obvious flaws of homophobic censorship is that queer audiences cannot be made to disappear just by stripping them of empowering stories. The subversive inclusion of queer-coded characters gives queer audiences someone to identify with, whether intentionally or not. After being told for decades, both implicitly and explicitly, that queer identity is immoral and unacceptable, it's an easy jump to begin identifying with the monster, especially when the monster is portrayed as sexually transgressive, like many queer-coded villains. Ursula, the antagonist of Disney's 1989 film *The Little Mermaid*, is an homage to Divine, a well-loved drag queen closely associated with John Waters and queer filth cinema.[39] Even in media as seemingly innocuous as Powerpuff Girls, which originally aired on Cartoon Network from 1998 to 2005, one of the villains is HIM, a cross-dressing Satan with lobster claws and a lisp.[40] In the grand tradition of Dante, many young viewers had sympathy with the devil. By empathising with queer-coded characters, those caricatures are reclaimed and given power.

Dark Harvest (2006) is a young adult Gothic novel set in an unnamed small Midwestern town. Every year, a supernatural creature with a pumpkin head (alternately called Sawtooth Jack or the October Boy) is harvested at the edge of town. The October Boy is released on the edge of town with the goal of reaching the church before midnight. At the same time, all the teenage boys in the town must hunt the October Boy. The boy who successfully kills the October Boy wins prestige for his parents and a means of leaving the town, which is otherwise impossible. It is unclear what happens if the October Boy wins, since he has always been killed before reaching the church.

The protagonist, Pete McCormick, is a clever but outcast boy who craves escape from the town and the bleak future it represents. Pete is kind and compassionate, in contrast to the other male characters, who either revel in the cruelty and violence of the game or have had their spirits broken by it. Along the way he teams up with Kelly, a newly arrived girl who is also looking to use the contest as a means of escape. Pete saves Kelly from two other boys who are assaulting her for being a girl trying to participate in the hunt, a strictly boys-only contest. Kelly's disruption of the gendered norm, and Pete's decision to work with her, queer the narrative by deviating both from gendered restrictions and from the gendered expectation of violence from the boys. The Harvester's Guild is the authority that oversees the contest, enforced by a cruel cop named Jerry Ricks, who serves as a constant threat to Pete as he learns the ugly truth about the contest.

It is revealed late in the plot of *Dark Harvest* that the October Boy is recreated annually through the death of the winner of the hunt, whichever teenage boy is able to kill his predecessor. The winner doesn't escape, he is murdered and becomes the next year's October Boy. These victims are kids who may have disrupted the status quo, causing trouble when they 'started to wise up to the way the world spins'.[41] Pete and Kelly realise that the powers that be in the town have kept these secrets intentionally – and crucially, they now know that to win doesn't mean escaping. For Pete and every other boy like him, following the rules and rituals is the key to a cruel death, rebirth as a monster, and a violent hunt.

Pete's willingness to identify with the October Boy, just as he did with Kelly, creates his means of escaping the system and breaking the cycle of violence. Pete rejects his role in the game once he learns the truth, choosing instead to help the October Boy beat the game. The October Boy starts a massive fire that threatens to burn down the whole town, and once he has survived until midnight, he murders Jerry Ricks before walking into the blaze he set. Pete's empathy and willingness to buck the status quo are what allow him, his father, his sister and Kelly to leave the town and its cruel rituals to burn behind them.

While not explicitly queer, the message of tradition and violent enforcement of the status quo aligns with Hughes and Smith's definition of queer as signifying difference and disruption of the norm.[42] The indiscriminate violence of the Harvester's Guild, spearheaded by Jerry Ricks, who represents all the worst stereotypes about the police and small-town bullies, is a reminder of the visible and invisible power structures that are committed to maintaining the status quo. As the plot progresses and Ricks becomes more and more desperate to maintain his power, he becomes more violent, murdering multiple people in pursuit of his goal.

As Mair Rigby posits in 'Uncanny Recognition', 'queer and uncanny is a relationship that is culturally constructed but deeply felt'.[43] In a cultural milieu where queerness is marginalised and stigmatised, representations of monstrosity are familiar to those whose identities are seen as unnatural. Gothic monsters, when sympathetic, interrogate 'the very idea of what is monstrous, opening up spaces where we can read sympathy for others who are queer, who are multiracial, who live outside of the heteronormative paradigm'.[44] Gothic bodies offer an alternative to 'acceptable' bodies, disrupting what it even means to be human. Returning to Olu Jenzen's queer uncanny, 'by considering the queer as a challenge to the borders of life and death, natural and unnatural life [...] we may formulate a critique of the notion of naturalness which works to sustain the heteronormative paradigm'.[45] The October Boy was once human, but has become a mass of vaguely humanoid vines, crowned with a jack-o-lantern head and stuffed full of candy. He is almost human, and his body is the target of the town's revulsion and desire. By identifying with the monster and offering compassion, queer readers claim power within the narrative. The willingness to find commonality with the perverse and outcast militates against the status quo by challenging the limits of normalcy and gradually expanding them.

In this way, despite not being explicitly queer, Pete's actions in *Dark Harvest* queer the novel. By seeing the humanity in the October Boy despite his uncanny appearance, Pete defamiliarises the normal and exposes the fact that the monstrosity is not the October Boy, but the system that creates monsters just to kill them. The narration is sympathetic to the October Boy from the beginning, inviting the reader to witness the tragedy that the October Boy represents: the failure of the community to protect children who are different, and the cycles of violence that wear people such as Pete's father into submission. The October Boy's violence is framed as righteous, suggesting that resistance to the oppressive value system of the town is the only path forward, but kindness and compassion such as Pete exhibits are the only way to survive. There is an implicit threat in the October Boy's victory: the differences that you try to kill will not stay buried.

Conclusion

The folk horror chain that loosely binds these works as a genre contributes to a specific sense of uncanniness that undermines heteronormative social structures. The urban/rural divide explores the feeling of unbelonging and estrangement from social systems that is familiar to queer people. The use of pagan aesthetics works to make the power structure of heteropatriarchal Christianity visible and weaken its absolute power. The undead and spectral are uncanny and queer in that they, like queerness, exist on the edge of acceptable heteronorms. These types of monsters challenge the binaries that constitute what is normal/abnormal and natural/unnatural. Finally, queer silence, violence and compassion are spaces of resistance to the oppressive cultural forces that have marginalised queer voices.

Further research into different cultural traditions of folklore and scary stories would add considerable depth to the discussion. Indigenous traditional folk horror and non-European stories would reflect a different perspective on queerness, particularly in cultures that recognise genders outside of the male/female binary. Furthermore, analysis could be done on the shift in queer representation in horror as queer liberation movements have fought back against oppressive heterosexuality. As queerness becomes more acceptable in the mainstream, representations will change, what is monstrous will become known, and unknown horrors will rise anew.

Notes

1. For the folk horror chain, see Adam Scovell, *Folk Horror: Hours Dreadful and Things Strange* (Leighton Buzzard: Auteur Publishing, 2017), pp. 15–16.
2. Ibid., p. 7.
3. *Witchfinder General*, dir. Michael Reeves (Tigon Pictures, 1968); *The Blood on Satan's Claw*, dir. Piers Haggard (Tigon Pictures, 1971); *The Wicker Man*, dir. Robin Hardy (British Lion Films, 1973).
4. Michael Kearney, 'La Llorona as a Social Symbol', *Western Folklore*, 28 (1969), pp. 199–206 (p. 199).
5. Scovell, *Folk Horror*, pp. 15–16.
6. Ibid., p. 5.
7. Andy Paciorek, 'Folk Horror: From the Forest, Fields, and Furrows: An Introduction', in *Folk Horror Revival: Field Studies*, ed. Andy Paciorek et al., 2nd edn (Middletown, DE: Wyrd Harvest Press, 2018), pp. 12–19 (p. 12).
8. Ardel Haefele-Thomas, 'Queering the Female Gothic', in *Women and the Gothic: An Edinburgh Companion*, ed. Avril Horner and Sue Zlosnik (Edinburgh: Edinburgh University Press, 2016), pp. 169–83 (p. 169).
9. Sigmund Freud, *The Uncanny*, trans. David McClintock (New York: Penguin, 2003), pp. 1–21.
10. George Haggerty, *Queer Gothic* (Urbana, IL: University of Illinois Press, 2011), p. 384.
11. Ibid., p. 396.
12. Jacques Derrida, 'Passages – from Traumatism to Promise', in *Points . . . : Interviews 1974–1994*, ed. Elisabeth Weber (Stanford, CA: Stanford University Press, 1995), pp. 372–95 (p. 386).
13. Ibid., p. 385.
14. Ibid., p. 386.
15. Carol Clover, *Men, Women, and Chain Saws: Gender in the Modern Horror Film* (Princeton, NJ: Princeton University Press, 1992), p. 115.

16. Paul Cowdell, '"Practicing witchcraft myself during the filming": Folk Horror, Folklore, and the Folkloresque', *Western Folklore*, 78 (2019), pp. 295–326 (p. 312).
17. Thomas Tryon, *Harvest Home* (New York: Open Road Integrated Media, 2018), p. 13.
18. Ibid., p. 26.
19. Ibid., p. 33.
20. Ibid., p. 326.
21. Ibid., p. 373.
22. Ibid.
23. Walter S. DeKeseredy, Stephen L. Muzzatti and Joseph F. Donnermeyer, 'Mad Men in Bib Overalls: Media's Horrorfication and Pornification of Rural Culture', *Critical Criminology*, 22 (2013), pp. 179–97 (p. 189).
24. Scovell, *Folk Horror*, p. 27.
25. Christine Hoff Kraemer, 'Gender and Sexuality in Contemporary Paganism', *Religion Compass*, 6 (2012), pp. 390–401 (p. 391).
26. Simon Strantzas, 'The King of Stones', in *The Mammoth Book of Folk Horror: Evil Lives on in the Land!*, ed. Stephen Jones (New York: Skyhorse Publishing, 2021), pp. 233–53 (p. 241).
27. Ibid., p. 251.
28. Julia Kristeva, *Powers of Horror* (New York: Columbia University Press, 1982), p. 141.
29. Strantzas, 'The King of Stones', p. 253.
30. Derrida, 'Passages', p. 389.
31. Strantzas, 'The King of Stones', p. 252.
32. Ibid., p. 251.
33. Olu Jenzen, 'The Queer Uncanny', *eSharp*, 9 (2007), p. 11.
34. Jack Halberstam, *The Queer Art of Failure* (Durham, NC: Duke University Press, 2011), pp. 97–8.
35. Jenzen, 'The Queer Uncanny', p. 12.
36. Ibid., p. 13.
37. *Celluloid Closet*, dir. Rob Epstein and Jeffrey Friedman (Sony Pictures Classics, 1996).
38. Ibid.
39. Nicole Pasulka and Brian Ferree, 'Unearthing the Sea Witch', *Hazlitt*, 14 January 2016, https://hazlitt.net/longreads/unearthing-sea-witch (accessed 22 March 2022).
40. Rebecca Long, 'Lil Nas X's "Montero" is the Latest in Red-Hot, Sexy, Queer Satanic Panic', *Observer*, 4 April 2021, https://observer.com/2021/04/montero-call-my-by-your-name-devil-queerness-pop-culture/ (accessed 22 March 2022).
41. Norman Partridge, *Dark Harvest* (New York: Tor, 2010), p. 84.
42. William Hughes and Andrew Smith, *Queering the Gothic* (Manchester: Manchester University Press, 2011), p. 3.
43. Mair Rigby, 'Uncanny Recognition: Queer Theory's Debt to the Gothic', *Gothic Studies*, 11 (2009), pp. 46–57 (p. 51).
44. Ardel Haefele-Thomas, *Queer Others in Victorian Gothic: Transgressing Monstrosity* (Cardiff: University of Wales Press, 2012), p. 5.
45. Jenzen, 'The Queer Uncanny', p. 9.

Chapter 16

This is What Queer Resistance Looks Like: AIDS Gothic Art
Ardel Haefele-Thomas

Introduction: Objectifying Queer Gothic Disease/ Embracing Queer Gothic Disease

AIDS is a Queer disease.
AIDS is a Gothic disease.
Let me explain what I mean. We need to consider, first, the medical domain, which conflated AIDS and queers (not necessarily consciously in the beginning); and, second, mainstream heteronormative popular culture's interpretation of the medical information that linked the queer body and the AIDS body as Gothic monstrosities. On 5 June 1981, in their *Morbidity and Mortality Weekly* report, the Centers for Disease Control and Prevention (CDC) in the United States published a special report on a Los Angeles doctor's unusual finding: five previously healthy gay men were suffering from Pneumocystis carinii pneumonia (PCP). Their immune systems were failing them for no obvious reason. By the time the report was published, two of the men had already died; the other three died shortly afterwards. That same day, in New York, a dermatologist placed a call to the CDC to report 'a cluster of cases of a rare and unusually aggressive cancer – Kaposi's Sarcoma (KS) – among gay men . . .'[1] On 3 July 1981 the *New York Times* published an article singling out gay men who were suffering with the new disease; at this moment, '"gay cancer" entered the public lexicon'.[2] The stereotype in the American public imagination from 1981 onwards has been that AIDS is a 'queer disease' – AIDS is a queer contagion. Like so many things exported from the US, AIDS as a queer disease gained global purchase.

Laura Westengard notes that 'As knowledge about the virus slowly unfurled, media portrayal of bodies decaying from an unfamiliar and uncontrolled disease became a kind of spectacle of horror.'[3]

While Gothic imagery certainly entered into the early reporting on AIDS both in reliable news sources as well as the tabloids, the coalescence of AIDS and Gothic monstrosity can be found in a plethora of mainstream reactions to and creations of stories about people with AIDS. For example, in 1986, the young brothers Ricky, Robert and Randy Ray – who were under the age of 18 and all suffering from haemophilia and AIDS – had their Florida home burned to the ground for trying to attend school; the message was clear – their 'monstrous' bodies were unwelcome.[4] The burning of the Ray home is reminiscent of the torch-wielding mob scene in James Whale's 1931 film *Frankenstein*, and underscores mob paranoia, irrational fear and the power of rumour regarding the fearfulness of anomalous physicality.[5]

Conversely, in 1993, Hollywood congratulated itself (as it is wont to do) for producing a 'sensitive', award-winning drama about AIDS: Jonathan Demme's *Philadelphia* won two Oscars, two Golden Globes, and a Silver Bear Award at the Berlin International Film Festival, among other accolades.[6] In brief, the story revolves around a young, white, gay, male lawyer, Andrew Beckett (played by Tom Hanks), who lives in Philadelphia and finds himself on the brink of promotion to partner in an elite law firm when he is fired because he has AIDS. Beckett's partner, Miguel Alvarez, is played by the Spanish actor Antonio Banderas in one of his earliest American film roles. Beckett decides to sue his firm for wrongful termination and hires a young Black (and initially homophobic) accident claims lawyer, Joe Miller (played by Denzel Washington), because he is the only one who will take the case. What gets Beckett fired in the first place is the proverbial 'mark of Cain' – a Kaposi sarcoma lesion that becomes visible to the senior partner of the firm, the elder white patriarch Charles Wheeler (Jason Robards).

In his revolutionary essay 'Is the Rectum a Grave?', Leo Bersani writes the following:

> Malignant aversion has recently had an extraordinary opportunity both to express (and expose) itself, and, tragically, to demonstrate its power. I'm thinking of course of responses to AIDS – more specifically, of how a public health crisis has been treated like an unprecedented sexual threat.[7]

This type of 'malignant aversion' is precisely the visceral reaction Wheeler has to Beckett: 'You brought AIDS in here', he says with revulsion.[8] Not only is AIDS horrific to the senior partner, but more to the point, a diseased queerness has winnowed its way into an elite, white, masculine, heteronormative space. In the course of Demme's film, the audience witnesses Beckett's diseased queer body age and disintegrate as his T-cell count plummets and as the stress of sitting in the courtroom day in and day out wears on him. After hearing numerous slanderous and false accounts attributing his firing to his mediocrity as an attorney, Beckett finally takes the stand, and it is this particular scene that, I think, is the most insidious in the film.

The firm has claimed that Beckett purposely hid his 'dangerous' condition – that he was a walking health hazard to everyone who worked there. In order to prove that Andrew Beckett was not purposely hiding his condition, Joe Miller has the weak and pale protagonist rise up on the stand and shakily unfasten his shirt buttons to show the courtroom his KS lesion-ridden torso. The audience in the courtroom gasps. The audience in the cinema gasps. *This* is AIDS as a Gothic disease; *this* is AIDS as a queer disease. Hanks's character stands there – a messianic messenger – simultaneously beatific and horrific. He is a spectacle of the AIDS body for the horror and the empathy of the heteronormative viewer – a cautionary tale to those 'bad' queers who are not monogamous and who do not adhere to some sort of normative plan. In the course of the film, we find out that Andy had *one* anonymous sexual encounter at a gay porn theatre, which is how he contracted the disease. *Philadelphia* becomes AIDS porn (not unlike the 'Inspiration porn' roundly criticised in Disability Studies) for the self-righteous. Tempered for a Hollywood audience, horror and pity co-mingle to ensure that the queer AIDS body is read as a gothically diseased body. *Philadelphia* is not a Gothic film; however, this revelatory moment is imbued with Gothic imagery.

I am certainly not the only queer theorist who finds *Philadelphia* to be a sanitised and homophobic depiction of queer lives. As Douglas Crimp writes in his collection of AIDS essays, *Melancholia and Moralism*, he feels betrayed by the scene in which Andy dances to Maria Callas's operatic voice as he glides around the room with his IV pole. Miller has just left Andy and Miguel's home to drive across town and crawl into bed with his wife – and the audience sees this entire sequence. We do not, however, see Andy and Miguel in bed *ever*. The two men barely touch one another. The queer sex in Demme's film is literally relegated to the back row of the seamy movie theatre. Crimp rhetorically asks, 'So whose subjectivity is represented here, anyway? The answer, of course, is that it's the subjectivity of the spectator, constructed by Demme's film as straight and unaffected by AIDS.'[9] Beckett's literal last standing moment in the film is the revelation of his diseased body – his Gothic body. It is important to remember this mainstream Hollywood image for what it is: a judgmental anecdote about what happens if one is a 'bad' queer. That is the overt message. *Philadelphia*'s targeted straight audience, however, was not the sole audience. For many young (and many closeted) queer people, this Oscar-winning film was the first queer movie they had seen – sometimes sitting uncomfortably with family members. So, on a covert level, another message was clear: to be a 'good' queer, one needed to embrace monogamy, normativity, and to police and sanitise one's actions. If you did not, you, too, could become a shameful and horrific queer embodiment like Andrew Beckett.

Deborah B. Gould discusses queer theorist Michael Warner's observation about gay shame.[10] Gould writes that 'gay shame – specifically shame about gay sexual difference – has encouraged the mainstream lesbian and gay movement to repudiate gay sexual difference, and indeed, sex itself, and to embrace a "normalizing" political agenda'; she further notes that marriage equality, specifically, acted to eclipse 'all struggles that require an acknowledgement of gay sexuality'.[11] Shame functions to 'normalise' queer sex to the point that, well, there is no sex. Gould explores the effect that societal 'nonrecognition' has on queers: 'a desire for relief from the painful condition of nonrecognition owing to sexual difference [which] can create a pull toward social conformity, and specifically toward adoption of mainstream political norms'.[12]

But what happens to queers who do not feel shame? What happens to sick queers who, instead, embrace this non-recognition and create an empowering space by giving voice to the silences? This chapter focuses on five visual artists (three living with AIDS and two deceased from AIDS) who employ Gothic imagery and Gothic modes to explore themes of sex positivity, AIDS, queer filth, BDSM, contagion, ostracism, rebellion and empowerment in the face of continued societal pressures (from both the straight and queer communities) to normativise and sanitise their lives amid a pandemic that *still has no vaccine and no cure*. The artists explored in this chapter embrace their own diseased bodies in defiance as they confront the AIDS crisis on personal, cultural and political levels. Collectively, these artists tell us 'here is my unsanitised, beautiful, sexual, ill, and furious queer Gothic body – deal with it!'

Their Words to Jesse Helms Across the Senate Floor: Performing Sick Queer Rage[13]

When David Wojnarowicz died of AIDS-related complications in 1992 he was only 37 years old, yet he left behind an amazing legacy of outraged queer AIDS art. At one point in his career, Wojnarowicz wrote, 'To make the private into something public is an action that has terrific ramifications.'[14] The lasting effects of Wojnarowicz's 'terrific' (read also his pun – terrifying) art continue into the twenty-first century. The late 1980s and early 1990s in the US saw the rise of the 'culture wars' between Evangelical political leaders such as North Carolina's Senator Jesse Helms and radical political artists – many of whom were queer people with AIDS such as Black filmmaker and artist Marlon Riggs and his lover, Black poet Essex Hemphill, white photographer Robert Mapplethorpe, and, as explored here, white multi-media artist Wojnarowicz. At the centre of the fight for 'American morality' was a right-wing attack on the National Endowment for the Arts (NEA) – a government-funded institution that grants artists money to support their craft.

Like the work of Mapplethorpe, Hemphill and Riggs – all artists who lived with and died from AIDS – Wojnarowicz's works were often initially accepted and then ultimately banned from museums as a result of conservative religious and political pressure. The funding agency was forced to cut funds to 'subversive' artists, regardless of how minuscule the grant was. At the time of his death in 1992, Wojnarowicz was living in poverty in a cramped studio in the East Village in New York City – so clearly any conservative claims that he became wealthy from NEA funding were erroneous. One of his enduring works is his video *Fire In My Belly*, which employs numerous Gothic tropes: dripping blood, vampiric imagery, Día de los Muertos skulls, and the twisted bodies of petrified corpses in a mass grave. Wojnarowicz's original nightmarish video lasted over twenty minutes, but has been edited into shorter portions since his death. The inspiration for his video (which originally did not have any sound) came from Goth avant-garde composer Diamanda Galás's 'This is the Law of the Plague', which she originally composed in 1986 and then later utilised as part of a political Catholic Mass for People with AIDS (PWAs) in 1991 at St John the Divine's, 'against the wishes of John Cardinal O'Connor, who tried to prevent its performance'.[15] Galás was raised in a strict Greek Orthodox home, and much of her work underscores what she experienced as the hypocritical and abusive nature of not only the Greek Orthodox Church, but strict religious practices in general.[16] In the 1980s the archdiocese in New York, specifically, which was known for spewing anti-AIDS and anti-queer sentiment, became a target for queer artists with AIDS as well as the radical political activist group AIDS Coalition to Unleash Power (ACT UP).

The specific edition of *Fire In My Belly* that I am focusing on is the four-minute video edited after Wojnarowicz's death, which is a collaboration (in a very Gothic sense) between the living Galás and the deceased Wojnarowicz.[17] Galás contributes her uncanny and haunting composition 'This is the Law of the Plague' in which she recites Leviticus as the unsettling Goth music grinds in the background:

> And the priest shall look upon the plague
> For a rising, and for a scab, and for a bright spot
> And the priest shall shut up he that hath the plague
> He shall carry them forth to a place unclean
> He shall separate them in their uncleanness
> This is the law of the plague:
> To teach when it is clean and when it is unclean[18]

In this excerpt, the priest takes agency in judging those with the plague (read as people with AIDS) as unclean and in need of being transported to an unclean space. 'Clean' in this context can be read as heteronormative, healthy and productive, while 'unclean' reads as queer, sick and decadent. As Ian Gittins writes of Galás in his 2009 article for the *Guardian*, 'Her most high-profile and notorious venture to date was her late-1980s Masque of the Red Death trilogy of albums, which customised biblical language to lambast the Catholic church for its early bigotry towards Aids sufferers.'[19] 'This is the Law of the Plague' is a part of this controversial trilogy and has continued, into the twenty-first century, coupled with Wojnarowicz's Gothic video, to be one of the most powerful and eerie pieces of queer AIDS Gothic art activism.

As Galás's voice screams out these laws of Leviticus about bodily uncleanliness, Wojnarowicz's video flashes between frenetic images of him sewing together a torn loaf of bread with a large fabric needle and thread, a wooden icon of Christ on the cross on the ground with blood dripping from above and ants crawling over the figure, a man (presumably Wojnarowicz) masturbating with blue and black flashing lights reminiscent of a dark and throbbing corner of a gay sex club (but not depicted in a shameful light like the gay porn theatre in *Philadelphia*), Wojnarowicz's lips sewn together like the loaf of bread with blood dripping down his chin, and a saucer collecting drops of blood.[20] With his lips sewn together, Wojnarowicz cannot speak to affirm the sacrament, much less ingest it. And yet he is partaking of it in a sense by turning his body literally into the bread, which is of course, in Catholicism, literally the Body of Christ. Clearly, the body and blood of Christ are depicted in numerous ways and this hearkens back (as does Ron Athey's work discussed later) to the profusion of Italian Renaissance art that is obsessed with images of numerous saints and Christ's graphic physical suffering. The loaf of bread being sewn back into a whole signifies the body of Christ and communion. Wojnarowicz's lips, sewn together like the bread, conflates vampiric imagery as the blood drips down his face with the images of a saviour. His queer body becomes the body of Christ; and the body of Christ has AIDS. Neither Wojnarowicz masturbating and sewing his lips together, nor the horrific images of mummified corpses in a mass grave were the reason this piece was banned. Rather, it was the small statue of Christ on the cross with blood gently dripping on to it as ants crawl over the figure that was the centre of conservative wrath and caused Wojanrowicz's art to be removed from various exhibitions.

In 2010, eighteen years after Wojnarowicz's death, his art was still provocative enough to be banned from museums. The Smithsonian's National Portrait Gallery opened a major exhibition exploring queer and trans desire in portraiture, and *Fire In My Belly* was part of the exhibition. Shortly after the opening, however, Wojnarowicz's piece was removed after the Catholic League in Washington DC claimed that the depiction of Christ with AIDS was hate speech.[21] In her fiery defence of Wojnarowicz's Gothic depictions, Diamanda Galás wrote the following:

> FIRE IN THE BELLY is a HOLY film. IT MUST be. And why is this?
>
> The text that I chose in 1986 in London was from LEVITICUS, chapter 15, THE BOOK OF LAWS, from the OLD TESTAMENT – whose treatment of the **unclean** is proscribed therein by any church that employs this text and by the many legislators who for years have wanted to separate the **infected** from the **uninfected**. My liturgical treatment of LEVITICUS is a march of the priests and lawmakers forcing the unclean from the gates of the City into warehouses out of town, and is very **gently** illustrated by David's depiction of the crucified Christ covered with ants. Ants are only **one** of the many insects and animals that would cover a man removed from his village and deposited in a leper asylum. There would also be maggots and rats and crows. David was **gentle**, I must insist.[22]

When the Smithsonian refused to reinstate *Fire In My Belly*, over a hundred protestors marched through the museum holding iPads and playing the video so that visitors could still experience the impact of this political Gothic AIDS piece. Many of the protestors were detained by the police.

Ron Athey is no stranger to controversy and NEA squabbles surrounding outrageously subversive performance art. Athey is a white queer man living with HIV who has, for four decades now, utilised his own body as his canvas to explore religious themes surrounding the beauty and abjection of the diseased queer body. He has injected his genitals with fluid so they resemble balloons, cut himself, and has had members of his troupe pierce his body with surgical needles made to look like arrows while performing in various underground venues throughout the world. For Athey, the audience is crucial: 'I have a churchy outlook on the role of audience: they serve as witnesses, and this is what is needed to make the experience possible.'[23] In the prologue to her interview with Ron Athey, white trans media artist and activist Zackary Drucker writes that

> Athey's proverbial brand as a performance artist includes bleeding, speaking in tongues, and blasting his audience into the stratosphere with visceral, fantastical visions, hypnotic voices, and wild laughter. People often faint, vomit, and hallucinate at his performances. To speak to Ron is to become a completely embodied presence at the intersection of art and language, a liminal space with no name.[24]

It is within the liminality of these spaces that Athey's work epitomises queer AIDS Gothic. Athey's audiences witness him as a person living with HIV who literally anally fists himself, slices open, punctures and prostrates his body, which is, by hegemonic ideals, deemed filthy, diseased and horrific. In his interview with Drucker in 2017, Athey told her that 'AIDS was such a nightmare because those who were sick were judged. And why? Because we came from dysfunctional families who never loved us for whom we were. Then, when we died of the plague, there was a righteousness coming . . .'[25] Given Athey's strict Pentecostal upbringing – one that rejects queer and trans children as demonic – it is no surprise that in performances Athey reclaims religious icons in a queer light as he reclaims his own body via figures such as St Sebastian and Christ – both tortured and left to bleed to death in front of a hungry audience.

His performance as St Sebastian, which Athey continues to revisit four decades into his work as an artist, is particularly stunning in terms of depicting queer AIDS Gothic symbolism. As theatre scholar Mary Richards writes, 'Saint Sebastian's suffering is given meaning because it represents his resistance to relinquishing his faith. St. Sebastian is also the saint prayed to in times of plague because the arrow marks are seen as analogous to the pock marks of disease.'[26] On Athey's stage, the arrow marks symbolise KS lesions and the blood oozing from his wounds reads as contaminated: here is a literal and metaphorical diseased and contagious body; this is the Gothic AIDS body. Ron Athey's HIV+ body is presented as a dangerous social contagion. Athey's embodiment of St Sebastian also calls upon a rich history of controversial and confrontational queer masculinity. Italian Renaissance painter Giovanni Antonio Bazzi, aka Il Sodoma (yes, the sodomite), painted the martyrdom of St Sebastian in 1525.[27] In this rendering, arrows piercing his body, the saint's muscular torso is eroticised and the beautiful saintly face looks heavenward; there is a femininity in his masculinity, which was often incorporated by queer Renaissance painters as a sign of their own homosexuality. Guido Reni's 1615 oil painting of

St Sebastian influenced the famous twentieth-century queer Japanese author Yukio Mishima. In his coming-of-age novel *Confessions of a Mask* (1949), the autobiographical protagonist, Kochan, masturbates for the first time while gazing upon Reni's painting; Mishima, himself, was photographed as St Sebastian, complete with arrows.[28] British New Queer Cinema filmmaker and activist Derek Jarman (who died from AIDS-related complications in 1994) also utilised the figure of St Sebastian in his 1976 queer thriller *Sebastiane*, in which the martyr takes pleasure in the torture.[29] This is a common theme in Catholic hagiographies, where the pain signifies the holy sacrifice and is, therefore, simultaneously a source of pleasure.

Laura Westengard argues that 'Athey's performing body – both monstrous and queer –provides an interrogation of corporeal integrity that raises questions about what it means to be human . . .'[30] Through his staging of St Sebastian, Athey performs his rage against an overarching system that not only wanted to censor his art, but that would have been relieved by his death – a system that sees queer people as less than human. Athey's art reclaims the Gothic beauty of a body with HIV. As Westengard locates Athey's performances within discourses of trauma (which they are), I argue that his work is also healing as a reclaiming of religious experience from a queer Gothic perspective. As Athey says in an interview, 'For me it was activism to be who I am, and to represent it in a performance . . . lots of the symbols were didactic around HIV iconography.'[31] Taking his own body back, Athey has agency over how his HIV+ body is displayed (unlike Beckett's in *Philadelphia*); the spectacle is his to manage and it was intended for an audience who would be open to his message – as he said that he wanted the audience to be witnesses. Also, it is important to note that through these performances in the 1990s, Athey was physically reclaiming images of the Gothic diseased body for audiences that were receptive to his subversive performance art, which focused on taking back the power of an AIDS Gothic body. Via Gothic horror modes, Athey reclaims his body. His bloated, saline-filled testicles, surgical needles that become arrows, and blood seeping down his head serve to show a reality – to reclaim or maybe just to claim the humanity of a queer person living with HIV.

Gould posits the following:

> When sexual outlaws openly engage in oppositional and disruptive protest politics, their actions potentially provoke anxiety – among observers, gay and straight . . . their visibility as sexual outsiders who, as such, are making demands on state and society raises the specter of sexual disorder. Their very existence, in public, suggests the unraveling of the prevailing sex/gender/sexuality system and a system of compulsory heterosexuality that privileges

heterosexual monogamy over all other forms of intimacy; even more, the actions of sexual outlaws create a sense of the world put at risk by the potential triumph of hedonistic and irresponsible pleasure seeking over practical, rational, tempered living.[32]

In an AIDS Gothic world Athey and Wojnarowicz are sexual outlaws, and they may very well, in their righteous anger, look as though they are 'irresponsible' and not 'practical', 'rational' or adhering to 'tempered living'. However, their art illuminates the exact hypocrisy of this so-called normativity – who really puts the world at risk? In 1990 at a reading at the Drawing Center, David Wojnarowicz recalled a governor of Texas speaking on national television: 'If you want to stop AIDS, shoot the queers.'[33] The implication is that the governor was just voicing what mainstream Americans were truly feeling. What is more outrageous – the art of Wojnarowicz and Athey or the governor's statement? Who is the true outlaw? And yet there is that internal part of gay shame where queers hear the governor's message and think we *deserve* this hate. Wojnarowicz and Athey are screaming out against such abuse. They both reject what has been put upon queers – they reject the notion that having HIV or AIDS proves that the queer body is a morally diseased body. Rather, the work of Wojnarowicz and Athey shows that the AIDS body is a sick body that needs to be taken care of. Wojnarowicz and Athey will not let us forget – their work will not let us sanitise the thousands of lives lost. Their art is meant to haunt us so that we do not forget, so that we do not lose the fire in the belly of our collective righteous anger.

Bloody Sick and Beautiful, Darling!

Prior to her HIV diagnosis, Valerie Caris Blitz, a radical white heterosexual artist, actor and activist, lived in New York and was a part of the Lower East Side ABC No Rio art space; she also lived in Berlin and appeared in over forty avant-garde films.[34] In 1989 she was diagnosed with HIV, and from then until her death from AIDS-related complications in 2009 her art focused on sex positivity and AIDS activism. Caris Blitz epitomises heterosexual queerness because she rejected 'good girl' heteronormativity as evidenced through her entire body of art. Not only is she queer by way of her art, but also by way of her activism as a feminist and ally in the queer community – and more specifically the AIDS community. Like Wojnarowicz and Athey, Caris Blitz did not shy away from images of BDSM, blood play and representing her own body with AIDS in a queer Gothic vein. In his essay 'Portrait of the Artist as a Sex

Bomb', Jack Waters notes that 'Caris has straddled high, low and gutter culture throughout her career.'[35] For example, Nan Goldin photographed Caris Blitz for a display at the Whitney Museum in New York around the same time that Caris Blitz also appeared in the short film *Can I Be Your Bratwurst, Please?* which features queer porn legend Jeff Stryker.[36]

In the early 1990s Caris Blitz began utilising lab reports from her own blood work to create mixed media art that toured with Penny Arcade's *Bitch! Dyke! Faghag! Whore* show, 'an in-your-face tirade against puritanical views of sex and AIDS hypocrisy'.[37] Caris Blitz was not only open about being HIV+ but also about her sex work. As a sex-positive radical artist, she also employed Gothic modes as part of her message of taking back her own body:

> Since being diagnosed with HIV . . . she says that she has come to view her body 'as both fragile and deadly. I'm trying to deal with having a sexually transmittable illness – and a lethal one at that – and somehow reconcile all of the lab tests and viral loads with the part of me that's an erotic being – that's juicy, passionate, completely different from the clinical.'[38]

Caris Blitz's 1993 instalment, *Vestment*, was part of the show *A Living Testament of the Blood Fairies*, which curator Frank Moore explained was 'about magic and alchemy – using art as a medium for transformation – and that's very much the spirit of Valerie's work'.[39] *Vestment* is a hospital gown that, on the outside, is made entirely of printouts of the artist's actual blood lab work. The papers sewn together appear like retrieved notices from a garbage bin – crumpled, black-typed letters on white paper. The inside of the gown, which peeks out at the neck and sleeves, is satin and blood red. There is a tear on the front that reveals a photo of Caris Blitz's thigh with a tiger tattoo. Moore notes that 'The lab reports are very official and dry, black and white, but she rips them just enough to let you know there's someone quite different underneath.'[40] *Vestment* asks the viewer to consider what is more frightening – the crumpled sterile test results that confirm contagion or the actual blood underneath? Vestments also have an association with religious clergy, so it is clear that in her title, Caris Blitz is playing with the idea of a hospital gown and a religious gown. The tiger tattoo and exposed thigh remind the viewer of the ' bad girl' depicted as sanitised (the lab tests) and diseased (the HIV+ blood underneath) *and* perhaps most importantly, still sexual.

With a similar blood red colour to her 1993 *Vestment*, Caris Blitz's *Queen Sex Positive* (1995) is a corset made out of mixed media materials. On the front of the black corset is an overlay of red material and beads that make up a fleur-de-lys, which is the royal emblem of Mary's lily, an icon of the message that the angel gave her at the

Visitation – especially in French Catholicism.[41] Within the vulval imagery of the fleur-de-lys, Caris Blitz has hand-written white cursive statements such as 'Her majesty enjoys your visitations.'[42] The viewer cannot help but think of the two Mary's; it becomes clear that Caris Blitz is playing with the virgin/whore dichotomy. While the viewer begins to visualise various penetrative and caressing visitations, the eye moves to other words such as 'death', 'lethal' and 'Holocaust'. Clearly, pleasure and death co-mingle, and the artist's own words about her embodiment as an erotic and lethal being concurrently are realised in this piece. Like Athey's blood art, in particular, Caris Blitz invites the viewer to enter into her HIV+ body, which evokes simultaneous feelings of danger and desire. The black material of the back and ties on the corset recall notions of titillating risk in underground BDSM dungeons. In both pieces, the vibrancy of HIV+ blood and Caris Blitz's sex positivity hum with anticipation laced with apprehension.

Maxime Angel Starling is a British trans woman, former sex worker (like Valerie Caris Blitz) and HIV+ artist. She is politically active in the fight for AIDS rights and LGBTQ+ rights. Starling is also a survivor of childhood sexual abuse and, for the past few years, has embraced asexuality. As she explained in a 2011 interview:

> My dad raped me when I was little, and then, later, I was infected with HIV. Because of that I have a weird relationship with sex. I carry myself as this overtly sexual being on a day-to-day basis, but when it comes to the nitty gritty I pull away, probably because I'm worried I might be abused again. Ultimately I've become asexual, and I've stopped having sex.[43]

Starling utilises Gothic modes in order to explore what she refers to as a dualism – 'I want everything to be attractive and repulsive at the same time.'[44] And this statement is an excellent summation of Gothic – the conflation of the beautiful and the horrific. Her choice of artistic tools also represents this dualism, since she tends to use cardboard boxes she finds in recycling bins – and other bits of refuse that people throw away – to create beautiful and political art.

In her 2009 graphite on cardboard piece entitled *Bestiality*, Starling has drawn two erect penises flanking an eerie smiling skull. In keeping with her interest in displaying dualisms, the penises signify pleasure, beauty and the possibility of an erotic encounter. However, the skull is a reminder that this pleasure could kill. The Gothic symbolism is placed front and centre here so that the viewer must contemplate the threat of death while simultaneously anticipating an erotic encounter.

Starling's title recalls a historical time when Church law often conflated sodomy and bestiality – further enforcing the stereotype that sex acts between men were not human. When the first cases of AIDS were reported in 1981, the anti-sodomy laws in Britain had only been struck off of the statute books for fourteen years; and, in the United States, the anti-sodomy laws would not all fall until a 2003 Supreme Court ruling.[45] These legal changes were part of a measure to help humanise queer people and queer sexuality in the eyes of religious, criminal and legal institutions as well as in the perspective of the general public. However, queerness and bestiality are *still* conflated in the public imagination – and the AIDS pandemic and AIDS phobia often fuelled these ideas.[46]

In her 2009 double exposure colour photograph entitled *Vampire Slut*, Starling embraces her identities as a former sex worker and a trans woman living with HIV. The focal point is the bright red flowing from Starling's mouth. Vampirism can be read both as erotic enticement and as plague in this image. Starling works specifically with Gothic imagery to depict 'things that might look beautiful, but are infected'.[47] Part of the erotic allure of the vampire is, of course, eternal life or, rather, eternal undeath. And yet to engage with the vampire, no matter how beautiful, is to become infected. The vibrancy of the blood red lips dripping on to her tanned chest highlights her deathly pale face and wild dark hair. In this image, she simultaneously invites the viewer in with the erotic posture and yet repels with a sense of illness. Her identification with vampirism, again, equates living with AIDS to embodying being undead. As a former sex worker and a person living with AIDS, *Vampire Slut* epitomises Starling's lived reality.

The final artist I would like to examine is Luna Luis Ortiz, a queer Puertorriqueño artist based in New York. In 1986, at the age of 14, Ortiz contracted HIV.[48] He initially started taking self-portraits with his father's camera because 'I just wanted to take pictures of myself before I died of AIDS. I want people to remember me.'[49] Ortiz's entire life has been dedicated to HIV awareness, art and activism. In 2019 the New York Historical Society Museum and Library spotlighted Ortiz as part of their 50th anniversary commemoration of the Stonewall Rebellion.[50] Ortiz has been part of the queer and trans Black and Latinx ball culture made famous to general audiences by Jennie Livingston's controversial 1990 documentary, *Paris is Burning*. When he was only 16, Ortiz began to talk about being HIV+ within this community, where he initially faced resistance: 'People were really shocked. They were, like, "why is this kid doing that?" You could see HIV destroying their body.'[51] Ortiz organised the annual Latex Ball in collaboration with the Gay Men's Health Crisis in order to address the huge disparities of HIV/AIDS awareness, prevention and care within the Black and Brown ballroom community. His photography embraces Gothic symbolism and campy satire, and, at the end of the day, it is full of fabulous survivor attitude – he is yet another artist who refuses to 'normalise' his work in the face of a pandemic that still kills poor Black and Brown people at a much higher rate than their white counterparts.

Ortiz's 1990 classic noir black and white photo entitled *Self Portrait: HIV Glamour Puss* shows the 18-year-old gazing into a mirror as he exhales smoke from the long cigarette he is holding. His stance is reminiscent of Marlene Dietrich in her tux and top hat. Ortiz plays with gender (he has been a part of the New York drag ball culture for years) in this image, as he is a gay man posing as a transgressively 'butchy femme' cis woman cinema icon. While the actual photo may not be Gothic per se, it does rely on certain Gothic lighting, melodrama and effects that recall 1930s queer horror films such as *Dracula's Daughter* (1936). The title of the piece is both tongue-in-cheek and radical. To make a disease glamorous and erotic recalls what other artists explored in this chapter have also done in their work – especially Valerie Caris Blitz. At the same time, an air of melancholy also pervades the image as we consider that this is an 18-year-old staring at what, he fears, will soon be a corpse.

In his 1995 colour photo *UNTITLED Chleo*, and his 1996 *Bloody chleo*, respectively, Ortiz contemplates his model, Chleo, who is trans, in two different scenes covered in blood. In the 1995 image, Chleo's neck is nicked and blood drips down while she holds her head back in an erotic pose as if inviting someone to come lick (or perhaps further bite) her neck. This scene is more overtly vampiric than the 1996 piece. In *Bloody chleo*, her entire face is covered in blood as she stares pleadingly and/or seductively at the camera. Her palms, which are bloody have clearly touched her nipples, so that her torso resembles an image (again) of Christ (or St Sebastian). Chleo is erotically (especially autoerotically) and vampirically martyred.

Finally, *NY Awards Ball klub kid face* (2006) is a colour photograph depicting a young Black drag queen walking the Ball floor. With pink and orange fishnet full-length gloves and a pink and black partially laced corset, the Ball klub kid looks down towards the floor in a voguing pose – caught midstep and full of fabulous attitude. Her face, hair and chest reflect glitter. What makes this scene jarringly Gothic is the large skull she is holding in her left hand up by her face as she walks the Ball floor. This skull is there haunting us next to the klub kid's fabulous living face depicted with vibrant make-up. This image tells the viewer: Still sick. Death is still there on my shoulder. But my make-up is fabulous. I am fabulous. I am a queer sick man of colour but here I am in your face. Or, as the octogenarian Black trans activist Miss Major Griffin-Gracy loves to tell the world, 'I'm still fucking here!'[52]

Conclusion: 'Lover of Blood'[53]

In their poem, 'Eulogy for the 40th', Two-Spirit author Qwo-Li Driskill contemplates the death of former US President Ronald Reagan, who was touted as an American hero. For queer people like me living through the nightmare of Reagan's AIDS inaction, we visualise the blood of the thousands he had on his hands. As they kiss their lover, Driskill considers the following about Reagan's actual actions:

> Murdered nuns flashed in his eyes. Granada, Nicaragua, El Salvador, AIDS flashed in his eyes.
> King of Lies. Composer of Invasion. Leader of Genocide. Lover of Blood.
> Say it: we're not sad to see him go. No one I know shed a single
> Tear for his passing.
> When I kiss my lover, a generation of ghosts arises.[54]

The ghosts between Driskill and their lover is what the queer and trans dance performance group Sean Dorsey Dance refer to as the Missing Generation: a generation of queers needlessly murdered by governmental, medical and societal inaction.[55] The AIDS body is a Gothic body. The AIDS body is a site of queer contagion. The artists covered in this essay leave us in all of their uncensored, filthy, beautiful and bloody glory. We know their work must be something fearsome and glorious – something not contained within sanitised and normativised conversations. We need to see it, listen to it deeply, and shout it loud. **Silence *does* equal death.**

Notes

1. https://www.hiv.gov/hiv-basics/overview/history/hiv-and-aids-timeline (accessed 1 April 2022).
2. Ibid.
3. Laura Westengard, *Gothic Queer Culture: Marginalized Communities and the Ghosts of Insidious Trauma* (Lincoln, NE: University of Nebraska Press, 2019), p. 99.
4. Shawn Decker, '25 Years Ago Yesterday: The Ray Brothers' Home Burned Down', *POZ*, 29 August 2012, https://www.poz.com/blog/25-years-ago-yesterd (accessed 1 April 2022).
5. *Frankenstein*, dir. James Whale (Universal Pictures, 1931).

6. See IMDb website: https://www.imdb.com/title/tt0107818/awards/?ref_=tt_awd (accessed 1 April 2022).
7. Leo Bersani, *Is the Rectum a Grave? And Other Essays* (Chicago: University of Chicago Press, 2010), p. 4.
8. *Philadelphia*, dir. Jonathan Demme (TriStar, 1993).
9. Douglas Crimp, *Melancholia and Moralism: Essays on AIDS and Queer Politics* (Cambridge, MA: MIT Press, 2002), p. 255.
10. Here, the term 'gay' is being utilised as an umbrella term for LGBTQ+ people. I would also argue, though, that part of the function of the word 'queer' is to signal a departure from the 'norms' that specifically 'gay' and 'lesbian' signal to many people.
11. Deborah B. Gould, 'The Shame of Gay Pride in Early AIDS Activism', in *Gay Shame*, ed. David M. Halperin and Valerie Traub (Chicago: University of Chicago Press, 2009), pp. 221–55 (p. 221).
12. Gould, 'The Shame of Gay Pride', p. 224.
13. The title for this section is a tip of the hat to Susan Stryker's phenomenal and classic essay 'My Words to Victor Frankenstein above the Village of Chamounix: Performing Transgender Rage', which originally appeared in *GLQ*, 1.3 (1994), pp. 237–54. Jesse Helms was an Evangelical (religious right) US senator who worked tirelessly to block any forms of socially radical art – especially art by people of colour, queer people and queer people of colour. He was a major figure in the 'culture wars' of the 1980s and 1990s.
14. *David Wojnarowicz: History Keeps Me Awake at Night* at the Whitney Museum of American Art, 13 July–30 September 2018, https://whitney.org/exhibitions/david-wojnarowicz (accessed 13 February 2021).
15. Jonathan L. Fischer, 'Diamanda Galás Responds to the Smithsonian's Removal of David Wojnarowicz's Work', *Washington City Paper*, 3 December 2010, https://washingtoncitypaper.com/article/429164/diamanda-galas-responds-to-the-smithsonians-removal-of-david-wojnarowiczs-work/ (accessed 13 February 2021).
16. Jason Ankeny, 'Artist Biography', *ALLMUSIC*, https://www.allmusic.com/artist/diamanda-gal%C3%A1s-mn0000253098/biography (accessed 2 April 2022).
17. David Wojnarowicz and Diamanda Galás, *Fire In My Belly*, https://www.youtube.com/watch?v=0fC3sUDtR7U (accessed 20 March 2023).
18. Diamanda Galás, 'This is the Law of the Plague', track 2 on *Plague Mass*, https://genius.com/Diamanda-galas-this-is-the-law-of-the-plague-lyrics (accessed 2 April 2022).
19. Ian Gittins, 'My Performance is Catharsis', *The Guardian*, 9 April 2009, https://www.theguardian.com/music/2009/apr/10/diamanda-galas-exile (accessed 13 February 2021).
20. David Wojnarowicz and Diamanda Galás, *Fire In My Belly*, 1986–87 [original silent 20-minute mixed video] and 1990 for the collaboration and the addition of Galás's music, 'This is the Law of the Plague', https://www.dailymotion.com/video/x3uf7x (accessed 2 April 2022).
21. 'David Wojnarowicz Video Pulled from National Portrait Gallery Exhibition', *Artforum International*, 1 December 2010, https://www.artforum.com/news/david-wojnarowicz-video-pulled-from-national-portrait-gallery-exhibition-26941 (accessed 3 April 2022).

22. Fischer, 'Diamanda Galás Responds'.
23. Ron Athey, 'Getting It Right ... Zooming Closer', *Art Journal*, 70.3 (2011), pp. 38–40 (p. 40).
24. Zackary Drucker and Ron Athey, 'Ron Athey', *BOMB*, 139 (Spring 2017), pp. 49–56 (p. 50).
25. Ibid., p. 51.
26. Mary Richards, 'Ron Athey, A.I.D.S. and the Politics of Pain', *Body, Space & Technology*, 3.2 (2003), DOI: http://doi.org/10.16995/bst.224 (accessed 3 April 2022).
27. Giovanni Antonio Bazzi [Il Sodoma], *Martyrdom of St. Sebastian*, oil on canvas, 1525, The Uffizi, Florence, Italy, https://www.uffizi.it/en/artworks/sodoma-st-sebastian (accessed 3 April 2022).
28. V. M. Simandan, '"Confessions of a Mask" – Yukio Mishima's Finest Novel', 26 October 2010, https://www.simandan.com/confessions-of-a-mask-yukio-mishimas-finest-novel/ (accessed 3 April 2022).
29. Flora Doble, 'Saint Sebastian as a gay icon', *ART UK*, 20 January 2020, https://artuk.org/discover/stories/saint-sebastian-as-a-gay-icon (accessed 3 April 2022).
30. Westengard, *Gothic Queer Culture*, p. 123.
31. Amelia Abraham, 'Ron Athey Literally Bleeds For His Art', *VICE*, 24 September 2014, https://www.vice.com/en/article/vdpx8y/ron-athey-performance-art-amelia-abraham-121 (accessed 31 March 2022).
32. Gould, 'The Shame of Gay Pride', p. 226.
33. Jesse Firestone, 'David Wojnarowicz', *Sculpture: A Publication of the International Sculpture Center*, 11 April 2019, https://sculpturemagazine.art/david-wojnarowicz/#:~:text=In%20a%20recording%20of%20a,%2C%20but%20raturous%2C%20sex%2Dcrazed (accessed 3 April 2022).
34. 'Valerie Caris Blitz 1957–2009', *VisualAIDS* artist description, https://visualaids.org/artists/valerie-caris-blitz (accessed 4 April 2022).
35. Jack Waters, 'Portrait of the Artist as a Sex Bomb', *POZ*, 1 January 2000, https://www.poz.com/article/Portrait-of-the-Artist-as-a-Sex-Bomb-10617-2086 (accessed 30 March 2022).
36. Ibid., p. 2.
37. Ibid., pp. 8–9.
38. Ibid., p. 3.
39. Ibid., p. 9.
40. Ibid., p. 3.
41. *Queen Sex Positive*, 1995, Archivo Arte y Enfermedades, Valencia, Spain, http://www.archivoarteyenfermedades.com/valerie-caris-queen-sex-positive/ (accessed 4 April 2022).
42. For a closer view of the front of the corset, the website at VisualAIDS is more clear: https://visualaids.org/artists/valerie-caris-blitz (accessed 4 April 2022).
43. Elektra Kotsoni, 'It's Not Easy Being Maxime Angel', *Vice: In Your Inbox*, 10 May 2011, https://www.vice.com/en/article/dp4z3q/its-not-easy-being-maxime-angel (accessed 13 February 2021).
44. Ibid.
45. The Texas case of *Lawrence* v. *Texas* which was heard by the US Supreme Court in 2003 finally struck down all of the sodomy laws in each

US state – with 'state's rights', US states up to that point could choose to keep the sodomy laws (however each state defined sodomy) on the statute. A previous case, the 1986 Georgia sodomy case of *Bowers* v. *Hardwick* heard by the Supreme Court, upheld the sodomy laws – and many people think this was particularly in light of the fact that we were in the middle of the first stage of the AIDS pandemic. In England, 1967 saw the laws criminalising men who had sex with men struck from the statute.
46. Writing this in the autumn of 2022, I would be remiss if I did not note the Monkeypox (or MPox) outbreak that occurred this year. Yet again, a virus that carries the moniker of an animal is being related to men who have sex with men. The connections between queerness and bestiality have produced more homophobic perceptions.
47. Kotsoni, 'It's Not Easy Being Maxime Angel'.
48. Luna Luis Ortiz, https://visualaids.org/artists/luna-luis-ortiz (accessed 4 April 2022).
49. Ibid.
50. Staff, 'Stonewall 50: Meet Luna Luis Ortiz, One of New York Historical's Experts on House and Ballroom Culture', *Behind the Scenes: New-York Historical Society Museum and Library*, 24 June 2019, https://behindthescenes.nyhistory.org/meet-luna-luis-ortiz-one-of-new-york-historicals-experts-on-house-and-ballroom-culture/ (accessed 4 April 2022).
51. Luna Luis Ortiz, https://www.youtube.com/watch?v=afVTz8EK3bA (accessed 4 April 2022).
52. *Major!*, dir. Annalise Ophelian (Floating Ophelia Productions, 2015).
53. Qwo-Li Driskill, 'Eulogy for the 40th', in *Walking With Ghosts* (Cambridge: Salt, 2005), pp. 40–1 (p. 41).
54. Ibid., pp. 40, 41.
55. See Sean Dorsey Dance, https://seandorseydance.com/ (accessed 14 April 2022).

Bibliography

Primary Works

AIDS timeline, https://www.hiv.gov/hiv-basics/overview/history/hiv-and-aids-timeline (accessed 1 April 2022).
Ainsworth, William Harrison, *The Lancashire Witches: A Romance of Pendle Forest* (London: Henry Colburn, 1849).
Allard, Jeannine, *Légende: The Story of Philippa and Aurélie* (Boston, MA: Alyson Publications, 1984).
'Amendment 2', *Colorado Springs Pioneer Museum*, https://www.cspm.org/cos-150-story/amendment-2/ (accessed 26 January 2022).
Anthropy, Anna, *Dys4ria* [videogame] (Newgrounds, 2012).
Armitage, Simon, *The Pendle Witch Child*, BBC 4 (August 2012).
Austen, Jane, *Northanger Abbey*, ed. Claire Grogan (Peterborough, Ont.: Broadview, 2002).
Beauvoir, Simone de, 'Must We Burn Sade?', trans. Annette Michelson, in Marquis de Sade, *The 120 Days of Sodom*, trans. Austryn Wainhouse and Richard Seaver (New York: Grove Press, 1966), pp. 3–64.
Bernhardi, Wilhelm, *Der Uranismus: Lösung eines mehrtausendjährigen Räthsels* (Berlin: Verlag der Volksbuchhandlung, 1882).
The_Bistander_Ben, '"Horny Harry and Life before Hogwarts": Part I of the *Harry Potter and a Life of Lust* series', Harry Potter slash fan fiction, *Archive of Our Own*, 16 May 2021, https://archiveofourown.org/works/31321055 (accessed 11 May 2021).
Blisterdude, 'Ginger Snaps: The Last Straw', Ginger Snaps slash fan fiction, *Archive of Our Own*, 3 February 2017, https://archiveofourown.org/works/9397847/chapters/21422711 (accessed 26 May 2021).
Brontë, Charlotte, *Jane Eyre* (New York: W. W. Norton, 2001).
Brooks, Max, *World War Z: An Oral History of the Zombie War* (New York: Broadway Books, 2007)
Browne, S. G., *Breathers: A Zombie's Lament* (London: Pitkus, 2011 [2009]).
Browning, Robert, 'Childe Roland to the Dark Tower Came', in *The Penguin Book of Victorian Verse*, ed. Daniel Karlin (London: Penguin, 1998), pp. 234–41.

—— 'My Last Duchess', in *The Penguin Book of Victorian Verse*, ed. Daniel Karlin (London: Penguin, 1998), pp. 207–8.

Buck, Rebecca S., *Ghosts of Winter* (Valley Falls, NY: Bold Stroke, 2011).

Carey, M. R., *The Girl with All the Gifts* (London: Orbit, 2015).

CharityDingle, 'I said I would die for you!', digital meme, *Tumblr*, 4 October 2020 https://filmreel.tumblr.com/post/631068395428839424/ginger-snaps-2000-dir-john-fawcett (accessed 26 May 2021).

Cline, Ernest, *Ready Player One* (New York: Crown, 2011).

Coleridge, Samuel Taylor, *Biographia Literaria*, in *The Major Works*, ed. H. J. Jackson (Oxford: Oxford University Press, 2000), pp. 155–482.

—— *Christabel*, in *The Major Works*, ed. H. J. Jackson (Oxford: Oxford University Press, 2000), pp. 69–87.

—— 'Kubla Khan', in *The Major Works*, ed. H. J. Jackson (Oxford: Oxford University Press, 2000), pp. 102–4.

Collins, Wilkie, *The Law and the Lady* (New York: Penguin, 1998).

—— *The Woman in White* (Oxford: Oxford University Press, 1973).

copperbadge. 'Stealing Harry', Harry Potter slash fan fiction, *Archive of Our Own*, 1 May 2004, https://archiveofourown.org/works/987408 (accessed 10 May 2021).

Culpeper, Nicholas, *A Directory for Midwives, or, a guide for women, in their conception, bearing, and suckling their children* (London: Printed for J. and A. Churchill, 1701).

Currier, Jameson, 'The Country House', in *The Haunted Heart and Other Tales* (Maple Shade, NJ: Lethe Press, 2009), pp. 63–92.

Cuvier, Georges, *Cuvier's Animal Kingdom* (London: W. M. S. Orr, 1840).

Dacre, Charlotte, *Zofloya, or, The Moor* (Oxford: Oxford University Press, 1997).

Dana, James Dwight, *Coral Reefs and Islands* (New York: G. P. Putnam, 1853).

Dickens, Charles, *Our Mutual Friend* (New York: Penguin, 1971).

Donoghue, Emma, *Kissing the Witch: Old Tales in New Skins* (Harmondsworth: Penguin, 1997).

Dontnod Entertainment, *Tell Me Why* [videogame] (Xbox Game Studio, 2020).

Driskill, Qwo-Li, 'Eulogy for the 40th', in *Walking With Ghosts* (Cambridge: Salt, 2005), pp. 40–1.

Duffy, Carol Ann, 'The Lancashire Witches' (2012), https://literarylancasterpoems2.weebly.com/the-lancaster-witches-carol-ann-duffy.html (accessed 25 June 2021).

Ellis, Havelock, *Sexual Inversion* (Honolulu, HI: University Press of the Pacific, 2001).

Frame, Jenny, *Hunger for You* (Valley Falls, NY: Bold Strokes, 2018).

Freud, Sigmund, 'Civilisation and its Discontents', in *Civilisation, Society and Religion*, ed. Angela Richards, Penguin Freud Library, vol. 12 (London: Penguin, 1991 [1930/31]).

—— 'The History of an Infantile Neurosis', in *The 'Wolfman' and Other Cases* (London: Penguin, 2002 [1918]).

—— 'The Uncanny', in *The Pelican Freud Library*, vol. 14, ed. Angela Richards and James Strachey (London: Penguin, 1973), pp. 339–76.

—— *The Uncanny*, trans. David McClintock (New York: Penguin, 2003).

Fullbright, *Gone Home* [videogame] (Fullbright, 2013).

Galás, Diamanda, 'This is the Law of the Plague', track 2 on *Plague Mass*, https://genius.com/Diamanda-galas-this-is-the-law-of-the-plague-lyrics [accessed 2 April 2022).
Game Grumps, *Dream Daddy: A Dad Dating Simulator* [videogame] (Game Grumps, 2017).
Garland, Rosie, *The Night Brother* (London: Borough Press, 2017).
Gaskell, Elizabeth, 'The Grey Woman' [1861], *Project Gutenberg*, 29 April 2007, https://www.gutenberg.org/files/28636/28636-h/28636-h.htm (accessed 26 January 2022).
Ginsberg, Allen, 'Howl', in *Howl and Other Poems* (San Francisco: City Lights, 1956).
Gomez, Jewell, *The Gilda Stories* (San Francisco: City Lights, 2016).
Hirschfeld, Magnus, *Die Homosexualität des Mannes und des Weibes* (Berlin: Louis Marcus Verlagsbuchhandlung, 1914).
—— *Die Transvestiten. eine Untersuchung über den erotischen Verkleidungstrieb* (Berlin: Pulvermacher, 1910).
—— (ed.), *Jahrbuch für sexuelle Zwischenstufen unter besonderer Berücksichtigung der Homosexualität* (Leipzig: Max Spohr, 1902).
Human Dignity Trust, https://www.humandignitytrust.org/lgbt-the-law/map-of-criminalisation/ (accessed 6 April 2022).
Isherwood, Christopher, *Christopher and His Kind, 1929–1939* (New York: Avon Books, 1977).
Johnson, Samuel, *A Dictionary of the English Language*, https://johnsonsdictionaryonline.com/ (accessed 1 February 2021).
Keats, John, *Lamia*, in *Keats's Poetry and Prose*, ed. Jeffrey N. Cox (New York: W. W. Norton, 2009).
Krafft-Ebing, Richard von, *Psychopathia Sexualis: The Classic Study of Deviant Sex*, trans. Franklin S. Klaf (New York: Arcade Publishing, 1965).
Kramer, Heinrich, and James Sprenger, *Malleus Maleficarum*, trans. Montague Summers (New York: Dover Press, 1971).
LeFanu, J. Sheridan, 'Carmilla', in *In a Glass Darkly* [1872] (Bath: Cedric Chivers, 1971).
—— *Carmilla* (Cabin John, MD: Wildside Press, 2005).
Lewis, Matthew Gregory, *The Monk*, ed. Howard Anderson (Oxford: Oxford World's Classics, 2006).
—— *The Monk: A Romance* (London: Penguin, 1998).
'Lili Elbe Digital Archive', http://lilielbe.org/narrative/publicationHistory.html (accessed 7 July 2021).
Lyssandra_Med, 'Bonds', Ginger Snaps femslash fiction, *Archive of Our Own*, 17 March 2021, https://archiveofourown.org/works/30107151 (accessed 26 May 2021).
Machen, Arthur, *The Great God Pan and Other Horror Stories*, ed. Aaron Worth (Oxford: Oxford University Press, 2018).
madman fred, 'Ginger Snaps: The Feral Bond', Ginger Snaps femslash fiction, *FanFiction*, 1 February 2010, https://m.fanfiction.net/s/5709622/1 (accessed 26 May 2021).
Malfoy, Ophiuchus, 'Excerpts from On the Plethora of Uses for Zingiber officinale by S. Snape, PM; with notations by D. Malfoy, App', Harry Potter slash fanfiction, *Adult-FanFiction*, n.d., http://hp.adult-fanfiction.org/story.php?no=600007817 (accessed 10 May 2021).

Marryat, Florence, *The Blood of the Vampire* (Kansas City, KS: Valencourt Books, 2009).
Milton, John, *Paradise Lost*, ed. Gordon Teskey (New York: W. W. Norton, 2005).
Morrison, Blake, *Pendle Witches* (London: Enitharmon, 1996).
Naughty Dog, *The Last of Us Part II* [videogame] (Sony Interactive Entertainment, 2020).
Neill, Robert, *Mist over Pendle* (London: Arrow, 1951).
netrixie, 'Come Kid With Me', Harry Potter Mpreg slash fiction, *FanFiction*, 25 March 2008, <https://www.fanfiction.net/s/4154664/1/Come-Kid-With-Me (accessed 10 May 2021).
Neumann, Caryn E., 'The Labouchère Amendment (1885–1967)', *glbtq* (2004), http://www.glbtqarchive.com/ssh/labouchere_amendment_S.pdf (accessed 16 February 2023).
Obscurasoft, *Coming Out on Top* [videogame] (Obscurasoft, 2014).
Partridge, Norman, *Dark Harvest* (New York: Tor, 2010).
pklovesdw, 'Drarry masterlist', fanfic blog featuring Drarry Veela animae fanart and fanfic synopses, *Tumblr*, n.d., https://pklovesdw.tumblr.com/post/36687401572/drarry-masterlist (accessed 27 May 2021).
Polidori, John, *The Vampyre; A Tale* (London: Sherwood, Neely, and Jones, 1819; repr. Project Gutenberg, 2009, https://www.gutenberg.org/files/6087/6087-h/6087-h.htm).
Potts, Thomas, *The Wonderfull Discoverie of Witches in the Countie of Lancaster* (1612), ed. Robert Poole (Lancaster: Palatine Books, 2011).
Redekop, Corey, *Husk: A Novel* (Toronto: ECW Press, 2012).
Rice, Anne, *Interview with the Vampire* (New York: Ballantyne, 1997).
Rossetti, Christina, *Goblin Market*, in *The Penguin Book of Victorian Verse*, ed. Daniel Karlin (London: Penguin, 1998), pp. 473–88.
Rossetti, William Michael, *The Poetical Works of Christina Georgina Rossetti* (London: Macmillan, 1904).
Rowling, J. K., 'J. K. Rowling Writes about Her Reasons for Speaking out on Sex and Gender Issues', *In My Own Words*, 10 July 2020, https://www.jkrowling.com/opinions/j-k-rowling-writes-about-her-reasons-for-speaking-out-on-sex-and-gender-issues/ (accessed 16 December 2021).
Sade, Marquis de, *The 120 Days of Sodom*, trans. Austryn Wainhouse and Richard Seaver (New York: Grove Press, 1966).
SciFiNerd92, *Choke*, online video recording, YouTube, 19 February 2011, https://www.youtube.com/watch?v=f3p8wO_FIr4 (accessed 10 May 2021).
—— *Late At Night*, online video recording, YouTube, 11 October 2009, https://youtu.be/Htwc_8njQh0 (accessed 10 May 2021).
Shan, Darren, *Zom-B*, in *The Zom-B Chronicles* (New York: Little, Brown, 2014 [2012]), pp. 1–184.
Shelley, Mary, *Frankenstein; or, The Modern Prometheus* (New York: W. W. Norton, 1996).
—— *Frankenstein; or, The Modern Prometheus* (London: Penguin, 1992).
Shelley, Percy Bysshe, 'Mont Blanc', in *Shelley's Poetry and Prose*, ed. Donald H. Reiman and Neil Fraistat (New York: W. W. Norton, 2002), pp. 97–101.
Stevenson, Robert Louis, *Strange Case of Dr Jekyll and Mr Hyde*, ed. Martin A. Danahay, 3rd edn (Peterborough, Ont.: Broadview, 2015).

Stoker, Bram, *Dracula*, ed. Glennis Byron (Peterborough, Ont.: Broadview, 1998).
—— *Dracula* (New York: W. W. Norton, 1997).
Strantzas, Simon, 'The King of Stones', in *The Mammoth Book of Folk Horror: Evil Lives on in the Land!*, ed. Stephen Jones (New York: Skyhorse Publishing, 2021), pp. 233–53.
Swinburne, Algernon Charles, 'Anactoria', in *Poems and Ballads & Atalanta in Calydon*, ed. Kenneth Haynes (London: Penguin, 2000), pp. 47–54.
—— 'Sappho', *Saturday Review*, 117 (1914), p. 228.
Tamàs, Rebecca, *Witch* (London: Penned in the Margins, 2019).
Tennyson, Alfred Lord, 'The Lady of Shalott', in *Tennyson's Poetry*, ed. Robert W. Hill Jr (New York: W. W. Norton, 1999), pp. 41–5.
The Transgender Oral History Project at the Tretter Collection, University of Minnesota Libraries, https://www.lib.umn.edu/collections/special/tretter/transgender-oral-history-project (accessed 15 April 2022).
Tryon, Thomas, *Harvest Home* (New York: Open Road Integrated Media, 2018).
volchiha, 'My Sweet Prince', online video recording, YouTube, 17 January 2011, https://www.youtube.com/watch?v=y5eE0SLZBW0 (accessed 10 May 2021).
Walpole, Horace, *The Castle of Otranto*, ed. W. S. Lewis (Oxford: Oxford World's Classics, 2008).
Waters, Daniel, *Generation Dead* (London: Simon and Schuster, 2008).
Waters, Sarah, *Tipping the Velvet* (London: Virago, 1998).
Weatherspoon, Rebekah, *A Soul to Keep* (Valley Falls, NY: Bold Strokes, 2016).
Whitehead, Colson, *Zone One* (New York: Anchor, 2012).
Wilde, Oscar, *The Ballad of Reading Gaol* (New York: Brentanos, 1898 [1906]).
Winterson, Jeanette, *The Daylight Gate* (London: Hammer, 2012).
Wojnarowicz, David, and Diamanda Galás, *Fire In My Belly*, 1986–1987, silent 20-minute mixed video; 1990 collaboration Diamanda Galás, 'This is the Law of the Plague', https://www.dailymotion.com/video/x3uf7x (accessed 2 April 2022).
Wordsworth, William, 'The Thorn', in *The Major Works*, ed. Stephen Gill (Oxford: Oxford University Press, 2008), pp. 59–66.
WOWPresents, 'UNHhhh Ep. 131: Straight People', YouTube, 14 October 2020, https://youtu.be/rXSKCE4-BEI?list=PLhgFEi9aNUb2BNrIEecCGXApgeX7Yjwz8 (accessed 15 February 2021).
Yeats, William Butler, 'Leda and the Swan', in *The Collected Poems of W. B. Yeats*, ed. Richard J. Finneran (New York: Scribner, 1996), pp. 214–15.

Secondary Works

Abraham, Amelia, 'Ron Athey Literally Bleeds for His Art', *VICE*, 24 September 2014, https://www.vice.com/en/article/vdpx8y/ron-athey-performance-art-amelia-abraham-121 (accessed 31 March 2022).
Aldana Reyes, Xavier, 'Beyond the Metaphor: Gay Zombies and the Challenge to Homonormativity', *Journal for Cultural and Religious Theory*, 13.2 (2014), pp. 1–12.

Allen, Emily, 'Gender and Sensation', in *The Companion to Sensation Fiction*, ed. Pamela K. Gilbert (Hoboken, NJ: John Wiley & Sons, 2011), pp. 401–13.

Altman, Dennis, Carole Vance, Martha Vicinus and Jeffrey Weeks (eds), *Homosexuality, Which Homosexuality?* (London: GMP, 1989).

Amin, Kadji, 'Haunted by the 1990s: Queer Theory's Affective Histories', *Women's Studies Quarterly*, 44.3/4 (2016), pp. 173–89.

Andeweg, Agnes, and Sue Zlosnik, 'Introduction', in *Gothic Kinship* (Manchester: Manchester University Press, 2013), pp. 1–11.

Andrews, Jennifer, 'Native Canadian Gothic Refigured: Reading Eden Robinson's *Monkey Beach*', *Essays on Canadian Writing*, 73 (2001), pp. 1–24.

Ankeny, Jason, 'Artist Biography', *ALLMUSIC*, https://www.allmusic.com/artist/diamanda-gal%C3%A1s-mn0000253098/biography (accessed 2 April 2022).

Antosa, Silvia, 'In a Queer Gothic Space and Time: Love Triangles in Jeanette Winterson's *The Daylight Gate*', *Altre Modernità/Other Modernities*, 13 (May 2015), pp. 152–67.

Armstrong, Isobel, *Victorian Poetry: Poetry, Poetics and Politics* (London: Routledge, 2002).

Athey, Ron, 'Getting It Right . . . Zooming Closer', *Art Journal*, 70.3 (2011), pp. 38–40.

Auerbach, Nina, *Our Vampires, Ourselves* (Chicago: University of Chicago Press, 1995).

Augustine, Afiya, 'Five Reason Gomez and Morticia Addams are Relationship Goals', *Syfy Wire*, 11 November 2020, https://www.syfy.com/syfywire/five-reasons-gomez-and-morticia-addams-are-relationship-goals (accessed 4 March 2021).

Ayers, Mary A., *Masculine Shame: From Succubus to the Eternal Feminine* (Abingdon: Routledge, 2011).

Babuscio, Jack, 'The Cinema of Camp (aka Camp and the Gay Sensibility)', in *Camp: Queer Aesthetics and the Performing Subject: A Reader*, ed. Fabio Cleto (Edinburgh: Edinburgh University Press, 1999), pp. 117–35.

Barnes, Sequoia, '"If You Don't Bring No Grits, Don't Come": Critiquing a Critique of Patrick Kelly, Golliwogs, and Camp as a Technique of Black Queer Expression', *Open Cultural Studies*, 1 (2017), pp. 678–89, doi: https://doi.org/10.1515/culture-2017-0062.

Batchelor, James, 'Dontnod's *Tell Me Why* Aims for a Transgender Story not "Rooted in Pain or Trauma"' (2020), https://www.gamesindustry.biz/articles/2020-07-24-dontnods-tell-me-why-aims-for-a-transgender-story-not-rooted-in-pain-or-trauma (accessed 30 March 2021).

Bauer, Heike, *English Literary Sexology: Translations of Inversion, 1860–1930* (Basingstoke: Palgrave Macmillan, 2009).

Beachy, Robert, *Gay Berlin: Birthplace of a Modern Identity* (New York: Vintage, 2014).

Benshoff, Harry M., *Monsters in the Closet: Homosexuality and the Horror Film* (Manchester: Manchester University Press, 1997).

Bergstrom, Janet, 'Sexuality at a Loss: The Films of F.W. Murnau', *Poetics Today*, 6.1/2 (1985), pp. 185–203, https://doi.org/10.2307/1772129.

Bernhardt-House, Phillip A., 'The Werewolf as Queer, the Queer as Werewolf, and Queer Werewolves', in *Queering the Non/Human*, ed. Noreen Giffney and Myra J. Hird (Abingdon: Routledge, 2008), pp. 187–212.

Bernini, Lorenzo, *Queer Apocalypses: Elements of Antisocial Theory*, trans. Julia Heim (Basingstoke: Palgrave Macmillan, 2017 [2013]).
—— *Queer Theories: An Introduction*, trans. Michela Baldo and Elena Basile (Abingdon: Routledge, 2021 [2017]).
Bersani, Leo, *Homos* (Cambridge, MA: Harvard University Press, 1995).
—— 'Is the Rectum a Grave?', *October*, 43 (1987), pp. 197–222.
—— *Is the Rectum a Grave? And Other Essays* (Chicago: University of Chicago Press, 2010).
Bilson, Anne, 'The Werewolf Howls Again', *The Guardian*, 5 February 2020, https://www.theguardian.com/film/2010/feb/04/werewolves-cinema (accessed 24 March 2022).
Boellstorff, Tom, *Coming of Age in Second Life* (Princeton, NJ: Princeton University Press, 2008).
Bolton, Andrew, Karen van Godtsenhoven and Amanda Garfinkel, *Camp: Notes on Fashion*, vol. II (New Haven, CT: Yale University Press, 2019).
Bourgault du Coudray, Chantal, *The Curse of the Werewolf: Fantasy, Horror and the Beast Within* (London: Bloomsbury, 2006).
Bowers, Katherine, 'Haunted Ice, Fearful Sounds, and the Arctic Sublime: Exploring Nineteenth Century Polar Gothic Space', *Gothic Studies*, 9.2 (2017), pp. 71–84, https://euppublishing.com/toc/gothic/19/2 (accessed 29 December 2021).
Bowles, Emily, 'Maternal Culpability in Fetal Defects: Aphra Behn's Satiric Interrogations of Medical Models', in *Recovering Disability in Early Modern England*, ed. Allison Hobgood and David Houston Wood (Columbus, OH: Ohio State University Press, 2013), pp. 43–56.
Braidotti, Rosi, *The Posthuman* (Malden, MA: Polity, 2013).
Brennan, Summer, *High Heel* (London: Bloomsbury, 2019).
Briggs, Robin, *Witches and Neighbours: The Social and Cultural Context of European Witchcraft*, 2nd edn (London: Blackwell, 2002).
Bristow, Joseph, '"No Friend Like a Sister"? Christina Rossetti's Female Kin', *Victorian Poetry*, 33.2 (1995), pp. 257–81.
Brockmann, Stephen, *A Critical History of German Film, Second Edition* (Melton: Boydell & Brewer, 2020).
Broedel, Hans Peter, *The* Malleus Maleficarum *and the Construction of Witchcraft: Theology and Popular Belief* (Manchester: Manchester University Press, 2003).
Bronski, Michael, *A Queer History of the United States* (Boston, MA: Beacon Press, 2015).
Bruder, Helen P., and Tristanne Connolly, 'Introduction: What is now proved, was once only imagin'd', in *Queer Blake*, ed. Helen P. Bruder and Tristanne Connolly (Basingstoke: Palgrave Macmillan, 2010), pp. 1–20.
Bruhm, Steven, 'Gothic Sexualities', in *Teaching the Gothic*, ed. Anna Powell and Andrew Smith (Basingstoke: Palgrave Macmillan, 2006), pp. 93–106.
Bruin-Molé, Megen de, *Gothic Remixed: Monster Mashups and Frankenfictions in 21st-Century Culture* (London: Bloomsbury, 2020).
Buckley, Jenifer, *Gender, Pregnancy and Power in Eighteenth-Century Literature: The Maternal Imagination* (London: Palgrave Macmillan, 2017).
Bury, Louis, 'Kiyan Williams Digs Into the Meaning of Soil', *Hyperallergic*,

7 November 2020, https://hyperallergic.com/586039/kiyan-williams-digs-into-the-meaning-of-soil/ (accessed 4 February 2021].

Busse, Kristina, *Framing Fan Fiction* (Iowa City: University of Iowa Press, 2017).

Butler, Judith, *Bodies That Matter: On the Discursive Limits of Sex* (New York: Routledge, 1993).

—— 'Frames of War: When Is Life Grievable?', https://www.versobooks.com/blogs/2339-judith-butler-precariousness-and-grievability-when-is-life-grievable (accessed 14 July 2021).

—— 'Melancholy Gender – Refused Identification', *Psychoanalytic Dialogues*, 5.2 (1995), pp. 165–80.

—— *Precarious Life. The Powers of Mourning and Violence* (London: Verso, 2006).

—— *The Psychic Life of Power: Theories in Subjection* (Stanford, CA: Stanford University Press, 1997).

—— *Undoing Gender* (London: Routledge, 2004).

Carr, Diane, et al., *Computer Games, Text, Narrative, Play* (Malden, MA: Polity, 2006).

Castle, Terry, *The Apparitional Lesbian: Female Homosexuality and Modern Culture* (New York: Columbia University Press, 1993).

—— *The Literature of Lesbianism: A Historical Anthology from Ariosto to Stonewall* (New York: Columbia University Press, 2003).

Chow, Jeremy, 'Go to Hell: William Beckford's Skewed Heaven and Hell', in *Transgothic in Literature and Culture*, ed. Jolene Zigarovich (New York: Routledge, 2018), pp. 53–76.

—— 'Mellifluent Sexuality: Female Intimacy in Ann Radcliffe's *The Romance of the Forest*', *Eighteenth-Century Fiction*, 30.2 (2018), pp. 125–221.

—— 'Showing the Eunuch: Disability, Sexuality, and Dryden's *All for Love*', in *Castration, Impotence, and Emasculation in the Long Eighteenth Century*, ed. Anne Greenfield (New York: Routledge, 2020), pp. 105–24.

Clare, Eli, *Exile and Pride: Disability, Queerness, and Liberation* (Durham, NC: Duke University Press, 2015).

Clarke, Bruce, 'Fabulous Monsters of Conscience: Anthropomorphosis in Keats's *Lamia*', *Studies in Romanticism*, 23.4 (1984), pp. 555–79.

Clayton, John A., *The Lancashire Witch Conspiracy* (Pendle: Barrowford Press, 2007).

Cleto, Fabio, 'Introduction: Queering the Camp', in *Camp: Queer Aesthetics and the Performing Subject: A Reader*, ed. Fabio Cleto (Edinburgh: Edinburgh University Press, 1999), pp. 1–42.

Clover, Carol J., *Men, Women, and Chain Saws: Gender in the Modern Horror Film* (Princeton, NJ: Princeton University Press, 1992).

Cloud, Dana L., 'The Rhetoric of "Family Values": Scapegoating, Utopia and the Privatization of Social Responsibility', *Western Journal of Communication*, 62.4 (1998), pp. 387–419, doi: https://doi.org/10.1080/10570319809374617.

Cocks, H. G., *Nameless Offences: Homosexual Desire in the Nineteenth Century* (London: I.B. Tauris, 2003).

Cohen, Jeffrey Jerome, 'Monster Culture (Seven Theses)', in *Monster Theory: Reading Culture*, ed. Jeffrey Jerome Cohen (Minneapolis, MN: University of Minnesota Press, 1996), pp. 3–25.

Cole, Alayna, and Dakoda Barker, *Games as Texts* (London: CRC Press, 2021).

Coleman, Robin R. Means, *Horror Noire: Blacks in American Horror Films from the 1890s to Present* (Abingdon: Routledge, 2011).

Conlin, Edward, 'The Drag Queen and the Mummy', *Transition*, 65 (1995), pp. 4–24, https://www.jstor.org/stable/2935316n (accessed 11 February 2021).

Cook, Matt, *London and the Culture of Homosexuality, 1885–1914* (Cambridge: Cambridge University Press, 2003).

Costantini, Mariaconcetta, 'Polar Contagion: Ecogothic Anxiety across Media in the Twenty-First Century', *Lingue e Linguaggi*, 44 (2021), pp. 67–80, http://siba-ese.unisalento.it/index.php/linguelinguaggi/issue/current (accessed 29 December 2021).

Cowdell, Paul, '"Practicing Witchcraft Myself during the Filming": Folk Horror, Folklore, and the Folkloresque', *Western Folklore*, 78 (2019), pp. 295–326, https://www.jstor.org/stable/26864166 (accessed 15 June 2020).

Craft, Christopher, '"Kiss Me with Those Red Lips": Gender and Inversion in Bram Stoker's *Dracula*', *Representations*, 8 (1984), pp. 107–33.

Craske, Matthew, *Art in Europe 1700–1830* (Oxford: Oxford University Press, 1997).

Creed, Barbara, 'Ginger Snaps: The Monstrous Feminine as *femme animale*', in *She-Wolf: A Cultural History of Female Werewolves*, ed. Hannah Priest (Manchester: Manchester University Press, 2015), pp. 180–95.

—— *Phallic Panic: Film, Horror and the Primal Uncanny* (Melbourne: Melbourne University Press, 2005).

Crimp, Douglas, *Melancholia and Moralism: Essays on AIDS and Queer Politics* (Cambridge, MA: MIT Press, 2002).

Curran, Andrew, *Sublime Disorder: Physical Monstrosity in Diderot's Universe* (Oxford: Voltaire Foundation, 2001).

'David Wojnarowicz Video Pulled From National Portrait Gallery Exhibition', *Artforum International*, 1 December 2010, https://www.artforum.com/news/david-wojnarowicz-video-pulled-from-national-portrait-gallery-exhibition-26941 (accessed 3 April 2022).

Day Lewis, C., 'A Hope for Poetry', in *Gerard Manley Hopkins: The Critical Heritage*, ed. Gerald Roberts (London: Routledge, 1934), pp. 276–83.

Dean, Tim, 'No Sex Please, We're American', *American Literary History*, 27.3 (2015), pp. 614–24.

Decker, Shawn, '25 Years Ago Yesterday: The Ray Brothers' Home Burned Down', *POZ*, 29 August 2012, https://www.poz.com/blog/25-years-ago-yesterd (accessed 1 April 2022).

DeKeseredy, Walter S., Stephen L. Muzzatti and Joseph F. Donnermeyer, 'Mad Men in Bib Overalls: Media's Horrification and Pornification of Rural Culture', *Critical Criminology*, 22 (2013), pp. 179–97, http://dx.doi.org/10.1007/s10612-013-9190-7.

Deleuze, Gilles, and Félix Guattari, *A Thousand Plateaus: Capitalism and Schizophrenia*, trans. Brian Massumi (London: Bloomsbury, 1980).

Dellamora, Richard, *Masculine Desire: The Sexual Politics of Victorian Aestheticism* (Chapel Hill, NC: University of North Carolina Press, 1990).

D'Emilio, John, 'Capitalism and Gay Identity', in *The Lesbian and Gay Studies Reader*, ed. Henry Abelove, Michèle Aina Barale and David M. Halperin (London: Routledge, 1993), pp. 467–76.

Derrida, Jacques, 'Passages – from Traumatism to Promise', in *Points ...: Interviews 1974–1994*, ed. Elisabeth Weber (Stanford, CA: Stanford University Press, 1995), pp. 372–95.

Deutsche, Helen, 'Deformity', in *Keywords for Disability Studies*, ed. Rachel Adams, Benjamin Reiss and David Serlin (New York: NYU Press, 2015), pp. 52–4.

Dickie, Simon, *Cruelty and Laughter: Forgotten Comic Literature and the Unsentimental Eighteenth Century* (Chicago: University of Chicago Press, 2011).

Dinshaw, Carolyn, *Getting Medieval: Sexualities and Communities, Pre and Postmodern* (Durham, NC: Duke University Press, 1999).

Doble, Flora, 'Saint Sebastian as a Gay Icon', *ART UK*, 20 January 2020, https://artuk.org/discover/stories/saint-sebastian-as-a-gay-icon (accessed 3 April 2022).

Dose, Ralf, *Magnus Hirschfeld: The Origins of the Gay Liberation Movement* (New York: Monthly Review Press, 2014).

Dowson, Thomas A., 'Queer Theory Meets Archaeology: Disrupting Epistemological Privilege and Heteronormativity in Constructing the Past', in *The Ashgate Companion to Queer Theory*, ed. Noreen Giffney and Michael O'Rourke (Farnham: Ashgate, 2009), pp. 277–94.

Dreger, Alice D., and April M. Herndon, 'Progress and Politics in the Intersex Rights Movement: Feminist Theory in Action', *A Journal of Lesbian and Gay Studies*, 15.2 (2009), pp. 199–224.

Drucker, Zackary, and Ron Athey, 'Ron Athey', *BOMB*, 139 (spring 2017), pp. 49–56.

Dubois, Martin, *Gerard Manley Hopkins and the Poetry of Religious Experience* (Cambridge: Cambridge University Press, 2017).

Duggan, Lisa, *The Twilight of Equality? Neoliberalism, Cultural Politics, and the Attack on Democracy* (Boston, MA: Beacon Press, 2003).

Dunham, Cyrus Grace, 'The "Terrorist Drag" of Vaginal Davis', *New Yorker*, 12 December 2015, https://www.newyorker.com/culture/culture-desk/terrorist-drag-vaginal-davis (accessed 2 February 2021).

Dyer, Richard, 'Less and More than Women and Men: Lesbian and Gay Cinema in Weimar Germany', *New German Critique*, 51 (1990), 5–60, https://doi.org/10.2307/488171.

Eagles, Jordan, 'About', jordaneagles.com, https://jordaneagles.com/about (accessed 21 January 2021).

Edelman, Lee, *No Future: Queer Theory and the Death Drive* (Durham, NC: Duke University Press, 2004).

Edwards, Natalie, 'From Minority to Mainstream: Channel 4's Queer Television', *e-Media Studies*, 2.1 (2009), https://journals.dartmouth.edu/cgi-bin/WebObjects/Journals.woa/1/xmlpage/4/article/325 (accessed 30 March 2021).

Egan, Timothy, 'Oregon Measure Asks State to Repress Homosexuality', *New York Times*, 16 August 1992, https://www.nytimes.com/1992/08/16/us/oregon-measure-asks-state-to-repress-homosexuality.html (accessed 26 January 2022).

Eisner, Lotte H., *The Haunted Screen: Expressionism in the German Cinema and the Influence of Max Reinhardt* (Berkeley, CA: University of California Press, 1969).

Elfenbein, Andrew, *Romantic Genius: The Prehistory of a Homosexual Role* (New York: Columbia University Press, 1999).

Elliott-Smith, Darren, '"Death is the New Pornography!": Gay Zombies, Homonormativity and Consuming Masculinity in Queer Horror', in *Screening the Undead: Vampires and Zombies in Film and Television*, ed. Leon Hunt, Sharon Lockyer and Milly Williamson (London: I.B. Tauris, 2014), pp. 148–70.

—— 'Gay Zombies: Consuming Masculinity and Community in Bruce LaBruce's *Otto; or Up with Dead People* and *L.A. Zombie*', in *Zombies and Sexuality: Essays on Desire and the Living Dead*, ed. Shaka McGlotten and Steven Jones (Jefferson, NC: McFarland, 2014), pp. 140–58.

—— *Queer Horror Film and Television: Sexuality and Masculinity at the Margins* (London: I.B. Tauris, 2016).

—— 'Revolting Queers: The Southern Gothic in Queer Horror Film and Television', in *Queering the South on Screen*, ed. Tison Pugh (Athens, GA: University of Georgia Press, 2020), pp. 88–112.

Elsaesser, Thomas, *Weimar Cinema and After: Germany's Historical Imaginary* (London: Routledge, 2000).

Elsam, Sara, 'Trans Games Professionals Explore *Tell Me Why*'s Landmark Depiction of Trans Identity' (2020), https://www.gamesindustry.biz/articles/2020-09-15-trans-games-professionals-explore-tell-me-whys-landmark-depiction-of-trans-identity (accessed 30 March 2021).

Endo, Paul, 'Seeing Romantically in *Lamia*', *ELH*, 66.1 (1999), pp. 111–28.

Fanlore, 'Harry/Draco', *Fanlore*, 2021, https://fanlore.org/wiki/Harry/Draco (accessed 1 May 2021).

—— 'Harry Potter Art', *Fanlore*, 2020, https://fanlore.org/wiki/Harry_Potter_Art (accessed 1 May 2021).

—— 'History of Slash Fandom', *Fanlore*, 9 September 2019, https://fanlore.org/wiki/History_of_Slash_Fandom (accessed 26 May 2021).

—— 'Veelafic', *Fanlore*, n.d., https://fanlore.org/wiki/Veelafic (accessed 27 May 2021).

Farr, Jason, *Novel Bodies: Disability and Sexuality in Eighteenth-Century British Literature* (Lewisburg, PA: Bucknell University Press, 2019).

Ferber, Sarah, *Demonic Possession and Exorcism in Early Modern France* (London: Routledge, 2004).

Fetner, Tina, *How the Religious Right Shaped Lesbian and Gay Activism* (Minneapolis, MN: University of Minnesota Press, 2008).

Fincher, Max, *Queering Gothic in the Romantic Age: The Penetrating Eye* (London: Palgrave Macmillan, 2007).

Firestone, Jess, 'David Wojnarowicz', *Sculpture: A Publication of the International Sculpture Center*, 11 April 2019, https://sculpturemagazine.art/david-wojnarowicz/#:~:text=In%20a%20recording%20of%20a,%2C%20but%20rapturous%2C%20sex%2Dcrazed (accessed 3 April 2022).

Fischer, Jonathan L., 'Diamanda Galás Responds to the Smithsonian's Removal of David Wojnarowicz's Work', *Washington City Paper*, 3 December 2010, https://washingtoncitypaper.com/article/429164/diamanda-galas-responds-to-the-smithsonians-removal-of-david-wojnarowiczs-work/ (accessed 13 February 2021).

Fisher, Mark, *Capitalist Realism: Is There No Alternative?* (Alresford: Zero Books, 2009).

Fleming, Kaleigh, 'Queering Brigitte Fitzgerald', *An Injustice: Voices, Values, and Identities*, 17 June 2020, https://aninjusticemag.com/queering-brigitte-fitzgerald-98738f7b6628 (accessed 25 May 2021).

Fletcher, Harriet, '"Gothic" TV: High-quality Modern Horror Series Providing Powerful Roles for Hollywood's Older Women', *The Conversation*, 27 October 2020, https://theconversation.com/gothic-tv-high-quality-modern-horror-series-providing-powerful-roles-for-hollywoods-older-women-148870 (accessed 10 February 2021).

Flinn, Caryl, 'The Deaths of Camp', in *Camp: Queer Aesthetics and the Performing Subject: A Reader*, ed. Fabio Cleto (Edinburgh: Edinburgh University Press, 1999), pp. 433–57.

Forman, Ross G., 'Queer Sensation', in *The Companion to Sensation Fiction* (Hoboken, NJ: John Wiley & Sons, 2011), pp. 414–29.

Foster, Jeanette Howard, *Sex Variant Women in Literature* (Baltimore, MD: Diana Press, 1975).

Foucault, Michel, *The History of Sexuality: An Introduction*, vol. 1 (New York: Vintage, 1990).

Francus, Marilyn, *Monstrous Motherhood: Eighteenth-Century Culture and the Ideology of Domesticity* (Baltimore, MD: Johns Hopkins University Press, 2013).

Frayling, Christopher, 'Fuseli's *The Nightmare*: Somewhere between the Sublime and the Ridiculous', in *Gothic Nightmares: Fuseli, Blake, and the Romantic Imagination*, ed. Martin Myrone (London: Tate, 2006), pp. 9–20.

Freccero, Carla, *Queer/Early/Modern* (Durham, NC: Duke University Press, 2006).

Freeman, Elizabeth, *Time Binds: Queer Temporalities* (Durham, NC: Duke University Press, 2010).

Friedmann, Walther, 'Homosexuality and Jewishness: The Latest Method of Agitation against "Aufklärungsfilme"', in *The Promise of Cinema: German Film Theory, 1907–1933*, ed. Anton Kaes, Nicholas Baer and Michael J. Cowan (Oakland, CA: University of California Press, 2016), pp. 240–2.

Fron, Janine, et al., *The Hegemony of Play*, proceedings of DiGRA Situated Play (2007), https://ict.usc.edu/pubs/The%20Hegemony%20of%20Play.pdf (accessed 30 March 2021).

Fuss, Diana, 'Introduction', in *Inside/Out: Lesbian Theories, Gay Theories*, ed. Diana Fuss (New York: Routledge, 1991), pp. 1–10.

Gabbard, D. Christopher, and Susannah Mintz (eds), *A Cultural History of Disability in the Long Eighteenth Century* (New York: Bloomsbury, 2020).

Gallop, Jane, *Sexuality, Disability, and Aging: Queer Temporalities of the Phallus* (Durham, NC: Duke University Press, 2019).

Gan, Jessi, '"Still at the Back of the Bus": Sylvia Rivera's Struggle', in *The Transgender Studies Reader 2*, ed. Susan Stryker and Aren Z. Aizura (New York: Routledge, 2013), pp. 291–301.

Gardner, Abby, 'A Complete Breakdown of the J.K. Rowling Transgender-Comments Controversy', *Glamour*, 20 July 2021, https://www.glamour.com/story/a-complete-breakdown-of-the-jk-rowling-transgender-comments-controversy (accessed 16 December 2021).

Gaskill, Malcolm, *Witchcraft: A Very Short Introduction* (Abingdon: Routledge, 2010).

Giacopasi, Caitlin B., 'The Werewolf Pride Movement: A Step Back from Queer Medieval Tradition', *Theses*, paper 4 (2011), http://scholarship.shu.edu/theses/4 (accessed 8 February 2022).

Gigante, Denise, *Life: Organic Form and Romanticism* (New Haven, CT: Yale University Press, 2009).

Gilbert, Sandra M., and Susan Gubar, *The Madwoman in the Attic: The Woman Writer and the Nineteenth-Century Literary Imagination* (New Haven, CT: Yale University Press, 1979).

Gittins, Ian, 'My Performance is Catharsis', *The Guardian*, 9 April 2009, https://www.theguardian.com/music/2009/apr/10/diamanda-galas-exile (accessed 13 February 2021).

Gonzales, Erica, 'Lena Waithe's Met Gala Suit Says "Black Drag Queens Invented Camp"', *Harper's Bazaar*, 7 May 2019, https://www.harpersbazaar.com/celebrity/red-carpet-dresses/a27382445/lena-waithe-met-gala-2019/ (accessed 10 February 2021).

Gould, Deborah B., 'The Shame of Gay Pride in Early AIDS Activism', in *Gay Shame*, ed. David M. Halperin and Valerie Traub (Chicago: University of Chicago Press, 2009), pp. 221–55.

Griffin, Gabriele, *Heavenly Love? Lesbian Images in Twentieth Century Women's Writing* (Manchester: Manchester University Press, 1993).

Gumbs, Alexis Pauline, 'Afterword', in Jewell Gomez, *The Gilda Stories* (San Francisco: City Lights, 2016), pp. 253–9.

Gunning, Tom, 'The Cinema of Attraction[s]: Early Film, Its Spectator and the Avant-Garde', in *The Cinema of Attractions Reloaded*, ed. Wanda Strauven (Amsterdam: Amsterdam University Press, 2006), pp. 381–8, https://doi.org/10.5040/9781838710170.

Guo, Jeff, 'Why the Age of 40 is so Important in Hollywood', *Washington Post*, 19 September 2016, https://www.washingtonpost.com/news/wonk/wp/2016/09/19/these-charts-reveal-how-bad-the-film-industrys-sexism-is/ (accessed 10 February 2021).

Haefele-Thomas, Ardel, *Introduction to Transgender Studies* (New York: Columbia University Press, 2019).

—— *Queer Others in Victorian Gothic: Transgressing Monstrosity* (Cardiff: University of Wales Press, 2012).

—— 'Queer Victorian Gothic', in *Victorian Gothic: An Edinburgh Companion*, ed. Andrew Smith (Edinburgh: Edinburgh University Press, 2012), pp. 142–55.

—— 'Queering the Female Gothic', in *Women and the Gothic: An Edinburgh Companion*, ed. Avril Horner and Sue Zlosnick (Edinburgh: Edinburgh University Press, 2016), pp. 169–83.

—— '"That Dreadful Thing That Looked Like a Beautiful Girl": Trans Anxiety/Trans Possibility in Three Late Victorian Werewolf Tales', in *Transgothic in Literature and Culture*, ed. Jolene Zigarovich (New York: Routledge, 2018), pp. 97–115.

Haggerty, George E., *Gothic Fiction/Gothic Form* (University Park, PA: Pennsylvania State University Press, 1989).

—— 'Gothic Fiction and Queer Theory', in *The Gothic and Theory: An Edinburgh Companion*, ed. Jerrold E. Hogle and Robert Miles (Edinburgh: Edinburgh University Press, 2019), pp. 147–62, http://dx.doi.org/10.3366/edinburgh/9781474427777.003.0008.

—— 'The History of Homosexuality Reconsidered', in *Developments in the Histories of Homosexuality*, ed. Chris Mounsey (Lewisburg, PA: Bucknell University Press, 2013), pp. 1–11.

—— 'Literature and Homosexuality in the Late Eighteenth Century: Walpole, Beckford, and Lewis', *Studies in the Novel*, 18.4 (1986), pp. 341–52.

—— *Queer Gothic* (Urbana, IL: University of Illinois Press, 2006).

—— 'What is Queer about *Frankenstein*?', in *The Cambridge Companion to Frankenstein*, ed. Andrew Smith (Cambridge: Cambridge University Press, 2016), pp. 116–27.

Halberstam, Jack, *In a Queer Time and Place: Transgender Bodies, Subcultural Lives* (New York: NYU Press, 2005).

—— *The Queer Art of Failure* (Durham, NC: Duke University Press, 2011).

—— *Skin Shows: Gothic Horror and the Technology of Monsters* (Durham, NC: Duke University Press, 2006 [1995]).

—— *Trans*: A Quick and Quirky Account of Gender Variability* (Oakland, CA: University of California Press, 2018).

Hale, C. Jacob, 'Consuming the Living, Dis(re)membering the Dead', *GLQ, A Journal of Lesbian and Gay Studies: Transgender*, 4 (1998), pp. 311–49.

Halperin, David M., 'Why Gay Shame Now?', in *Gay Shame*, ed. David M. Halperin and Valerie Traub (Chicago: University of Chicago Press, 2009), pp. 41–6.

Hancock, Michael, 'Doppelgamers: Video Games and Gothic Choice', in *American Gothic Culture: An Edinburgh Companion*, ed. Joel Faflak and Jason Haslam (Edinburgh: Edinburgh University Press 2016), pp. 166–85.

Hanson, Ellis, 'Queer Gothic', in *The Routledge Companion to Gothic*, ed. Catherine Spooner and Emma McEvoy (Abingdon: Routledge, 2007), pp. 174–82.

—— 'Undead', in *Inside/Out: Lesbian Theories, Gay Theories*, ed. Diana Fuss (London: Routledge, 1991), pp. 324–40.

Harrison, Antony, 'Swinburne's Losses: The Poetics of Passion', *ELH*, 49.3 (1982), pp. 689–706.

Hasted, Rachel A. C., *The Pendle Witch Trial 1612* (Lancaster: Lancashire County Books, 1993).

Heath, Stephen, 'Psychopathia Sexualis: Stevenson's Strange Case', *Critical Quarterly*, 28.1 (1986), pp. 93–108.

Heilmann, Ann, and Mark Llewellyn, 'The Victorians, Sex, and Gender', in *The Oxford Handbook of Victorian Literary Culture*, ed. Juliet John (Oxford: Oxford University Press, 2016), pp. 161–77.

Hill, John Spencer, *A Coleridge Companion: An Introduction to the Major Poems and the Biographia Literaria* (London: Palgrave Macmillan, 1983).

Hiller, Alice, '"I wanted to think about the possibility of a revolution based on female principles": Rebecca Tamàs Speaks with Alice Hiller' (2019), https://alicehiller.info/2019/03/26/i-wanted-to-think-about-the-possibility-of-a-revolution-based-on-female-principles-rebecca-tamas-speaks-with-alice-hiller/ (accessed 31 July 2021).

Hobson, Christopher Z., *Blake and Homosexuality* (Basingstoke: Palgrave Macmillan, 2000).

Hoff Kraemer, Christine, 'Gender and Sexuality in Contemporary Paganism', *Religion Compass*, 6 (2012), pp. 390–401.

Hoffer, Lauren N., and Sarah J. Kersh, 'The Victorian Family in Queer Time: Secrets, Sisters, and Lovers in *The Woman in White* and *Fingersmith*', in *Queer Victorian Families: Curious Relations in Literature*, ed. Duc Dau and Shale Preston (Abingdon: Routledge, 2015), pp. 207–22.

Hogg, Makhesha, 'Stonewall: 50 Years of Throwing Shoes!', *The Gayly*, 25 June 2019, https://www.gayly.com/stonewall-50-years-throwing-shoes (accessed 29 July 2021).

Hollinger, Veronica, 'Fantasies of Absence: The Postmodern Vampire', in *Blood Read: The Vampire as Metaphor in Contemporary Culture*, ed. Joan Gordon and Veronica Hollinger (Philadelphia, PA: University of Pennsylvania Press, 1997), pp. 199–212.

Holmes, Clive, 'Women, Witches and Witnesses', *Past and Present*, 140 (1993), pp. 44–64.

Holmes, Martha Stoddard, 'Queering the Marriage Plot: Wilkie Collins's *The Law and the Lady*', in *Victorian Freaks: The Social Context of Freakery in Britain*, ed. Marlene Tromp (Columbus, OH: Ohio State University Press, 2008), pp. 237–58.

Horner, Avril, and Sue Zlosnik, *Gothic and the Comic Turn* (Basingstoke: Palgrave Macmillan, 2005).

—— 'No Country for Old Women: Gender, Age and the Gothic', in *Women and the Gothic: An Edinburgh Companion*, ed. Avril Horner and Sue Zlosnik (Edinburgh: Edinburgh University Press, 2016), pp. 184–98.

Hughes, William, *Key Concepts in the Gothic* (Edinburgh: Edinburgh University Press, 2018).

Hughes, William, and Andrew Smith, 'Introduction: Queering the Gothic', in *Queering the Gothic*, ed. William Hughes and Andrew Smith (Manchester: Manchester University Press, 2009), pp. 1–10.

—— (eds), *Queering the Gothic* (Manchester: Manchester University Press, 2011).

Humphries, Reynold, *The American Horror Film: An Introduction* (Edinburgh: Edinburgh University Press, 2002).

Hurley, Kelly, *The Gothic Body: Sexuality, Materialism, and Degeneration at the Fin de Siècle* (Cambridge: Cambridge University Press, 1996).

Hutcheon, Linda, *A Poetics of Postmodernism: History, Theory, Fiction* (London: Routledge, 1988).

Jackson, Rosemary, *Fantasy: The Literature of Subversion* (London: Routledge, 1981).

Jagose, Annamarie, *Queer Theory: An Introduction* (New York: NYU Press, 1996).

Jeffreys, Sheila, *The Spinster and Her Enemies: Feminism and Sexuality 1880–1930* (London: Pandora, 1985).

Jenkins, Henry, 'Game Design as Narrative Architecture' (2002), http://web.mit.edu/~21fms/People/henry3/games&narrative.html (accessed 30 March 2021).

Jenzen, Olu, 'The Queer Uncanny', *eSharp*, 9 (2007), pp. 1–14, https://www.academia.edu/17415419/_2007_The_Queer_Uncanny_eSharp_issue_9 (accessed 6 October 2021).

Johnson, Dominic, 'Vaginal Davis Biography', vaginaldavis.com, http://www.vaginaldavis.com/bio.shtml (accessed 28 January 2021).

Jones, Jamie, 'PSA: Morticia and Gomez Addams are Literally the Perfect Couple', *Buzzfeed*, 27 April 2018, https://www.buzzfeed.com/jamiejones/morticia-and-gomez-addams-are-the-perfect-couple (accessed 4 March 2021).

Kafer, Alison, *Feminist, Queer, Crip* (Bloomington, IN: Indiana University Press, 2013).

Kaylor, Michael M., *Secreted Desires: The Major Uranians: Hopkins, Pater and Wilde* (Brno, CZ: Masaryk University Press, 2006).

Keach, William, 'Rhyme and the Arbitrariness of Language', in *English Romantic Poetry*, ed. Harold Bloom (New York: Chelsea House, 2004), pp. 129–48.

Kearney, Michael, 'La Llorona as a Social Symbol', *Western Folklore*, 28 (1969), pp. 199–206, https://doi.org/10.2307/1499265.

Kent, Elizabeth, 'Masculinity and Male Witches in Old and New England', *History Workshop Journal*, 60.1 (2005), pp. 69–92.

Kilgour, Maggie, *The Rise of the Gothic Novel* (London: Routledge, 1995).

Kinnard, Roy, *Horror in Silent Films: A Filmography, 1896–1929* (Jefferson, NC: McFarland, 1995).

Klimmt, Christoph, Dorothée Hefner, Peter Vorderer, Christian Roth and Christopher Blake, 'Identification with Video Game Characters as Automatic Shifts of Self-Perceptions', *Media Psychology*, 13.4 (2010), https://www.tandfonline.com/doi/abs/10.1080/15213269.2010.524911 (accessed 30 March 2021).

Koestenbaum, Wayne, *Double Talk: The Erotics of Male Literary Collaboration* (New York: Routledge, 1990).

Kotsoni, Elektra, 'It's Not Easy Being Maxime Angel', *Vice: In Your Inbox*, 10 May 2011, https://www.vice.com/en/article/dp4z3q/its-not-easy-being-maxime-angel (accessed 8 April 2022).

Kracauer, Siegfried, *From Caligari to Hitler: A Psychological History of the German Film* (Princeton, NJ: Princeton University Press, 1947).

Krobová, Tereza, Ondrej Moravec and Jaroslav Švelch, 'Dressing Commander Shepard in Pink: Queer Playing in a Heteronormative Game Culture', *Cyberpsychology: Journal of Psychosocial Research on Cyberspace*, 9.3 (2015), https://doi.org/10.5817/CP2015-3-3.

Kuzniar, Alice A., *The Queer German Cinema* (Stanford, CA: Stanford University Press, 2000).

Lady Saika, 'Sexualized Saturdays: The Everyone is Gay Trope in Fanfiction', *Lady Geek Girl and friends*, 20 April 2013, https://ladygeekgirl.wordpress.com/2013/04/20/sexualized-saturdays-the-everyone-is-gay-trope-in-fanfiction/ (accessed 1 May 2021).

LaFleur, Greta, '"Defective in One of the Principal Parts of Virility": Impotence, Generation, and Defining Disability in Early North America', *Early American Literature*, 52.1 (2017), pp. 79–107.

Lamar, M., 'Biography', mlamar.com, https://www.mlamar.com/biography/ (accessed 26 January 2021).

Larner, Christina, *Witchcraft and Religion: The Politics of Popular Belief* (London: Blackwell, 1984).

Leck, Ralph Matthew, *Vita Sexualis: Karl Ulrichs and the Origins of Sexual Science* (Urbana, IL: University of Illinois Press, 2016).

Lehrer, Riva, 'Golem Girl Gets Lucky', in *Sex and Disability*, ed. Robert McCruer and Anna Mollow (Durham, NC: Duke University Press, 2012), pp. 231–55.

Linge, Ina, 'Sexology, Popular Science and Queer History in *Anders als die Andern (Different from the Others)*', *Gender & History*, 30.3 (2018), pp. 595–610, https://doi.org/10.1111/1468-0424.12381.

Long, Rebecca, 'Lil Nas X's "Montero" Is the Latest in Red-Hot, Sexy, Queer Satanic Panic', *Observer*, 4 April 2021, https://observer.com/2021/04/montero-call-my-by-your-name-devil-queerness-pop-culture/ (accessed 22 March 2022).

Lorenz, Renate, *Queer Art: A Freak Theory* (New Brunswick, NJ: Transaction Publishers, 2012).

Love, Heather, *Feeling Backward: Loss and the Politics of Queer History* (Cambridge, MA: Harvard University Press, 2007).

Luna Luis Ortiz, https://visualaids.org/artists/luna-luis-ortiz (accessed 4 April 2022).

—— https://www.youtube.com/watch?v=afVTz8EK3bA (accessed 4 April 2022].

Macdonald, D. L., and Kathleen Scherf, 'Introduction', in *The Vampyre and Ernest Brechtold; or, The Modern Oedipus* (Peterborough, Ont.: Broadview, 2008), pp. 9–31.

MacDonald, Tanis, '"Out by Sixteen": Queer(ed) Girls in *Ginger Snaps*', *Jeunesse: Young People, Texts, Cultures*, 3.1 (2011), pp. 58–79, doi.org/10.1353/jeu.2011.0001.

Mahon, Alyce, *The Marquis de Sade and the Avant-Garde* (Princeton, NJ: Princeton University Press, 2020).

Malakaj, Ervin, 'Richard Oswald, Magnus Hirschfeld, and the Possible Impossibility of Hygienic Melodrama', *Studies in European Cinema*, 14.3 (2017), pp. 216–30, https://doi.org/10.1080/17411548.2017.1376857.

Marcus, Sharon, *Between Women: Friendship, Desire, and Marriage in Victorian England* (Princeton, NJ: Princeton University Press, 2007).

Marshall, Bridget M., *The Transatlantic Gothic Novel and the Law, 1790–1860* (Farnham: Ashgate, 2011; repr. Abingdon: Routledge, 2016).

Marshall, Nowell, 'Transtextuality in the Male Gothic: Beckford, Lewis, Byron', in *TransGothic in Literature and Culture*, ed. Jolene Zigarovich (Abingdon: Routledge, 2018), pp. 25–52.

Mbembe, Achille, 'Necropolitics', *Public Culture*, 15 (2003), pp. 11–40.

McCallum, E. L., 'The "Queer Limits" in the Modern Gothic', in *The Cambridge Companion to the Modern Gothic*, ed. Jerrold E. Hogle (Cambridge: Cambridge University Press, 2014), pp. 71–86.

McCobb, Anthony, *George Eliot's Knowledge of German Life and Letters* (Salzburg: Institut für Anglistik und Amerikanistik, Universität Salzburg, 1982).

McConnaughy, James, 'What Led to Lexa: A Look at the History of Media Burying its Gays', *The Mary Sue*, 26 March 2016, https://www.themarysue.com/lexa-bury-your-gays/ (accessed 16 May 2017).

McGavran, James Holt, '"Insurmountable barriers to our union": Homosocial Male Bonding, Homosexual Panic, and Death on Ice in Frankenstein', *European Romantic Review*, 11.1 (2000), pp. 46–67, doi.org/10.1080/10509580008570098.

McGlotten, Shaka, 'Dead and Live Life: Zombies, Queers and Online Sociality', in *Generation Zombies: Essays on the Living Dead in Modern Culture*, ed. Stephanie Boluk and Wylie Lenz (Jefferson, NC: McFarland, 2011), pp. 182–93.

McKenna, Neil, *The Secret Life of Oscar Wilde* (New York: Basic Books, 2005).

McLaren, Angus, *Sexual Blackmail: A Modern History* (Cambridge, MA: Harvard University Press, 2002).

McRuer, Robert, *Crip Theory: Cultural Signs of Queerness and Disability* (New York: NYU Press, 2006).

McRuer, Robert, and Anna Mollow, *Sex and Disability* (Durham, NC: Duke University Press, 2012).

Mellor, Anne, *Romanticism and Feminism* (Bloomington, IN: Indiana University Press, 1988).

Mendik, Xavier, 'Menstrual Meanings: Brett Sullivan Discusses Werewolves, Hormonal Horror and the *Ginger Snaps* Audience Research Project', *Film International*, 4.21 (2006), pp. 78–83.

Mercurio, Marisa, 'Queer Moon Rising: Introducing the Werewolf Reread', *Ancillary Review of Books*, https://ancillaryreviewofbooks.org/2020/10/31/queer-moon-rising-introducing-the-werewolf-reread/ (accessed 8 February 2022).

Michie, Helena, '"There is no Friend Like a Sister": Sisterhood as Sexual Difference', *ELH*, 56.2 (1989), pp. 401–21.

Mighall, Robert, 'Diagnosing Jekyll: The Scientific Context to Dr Jekyll's Experiment and Mr Hyde's Embodiment', in Robert Louis Stevenson, *The Strange Case of Dr Jekyll and Mr Hyde and Other Tales of Terror* (London: Penguin, 2002), pp. 206–26.

Miles, Robert, *Gothic Writing, 1750–1820*, 2nd edn (Manchester: Manchester University Press, 2007).

Miller, April, '"The Hair that Wasn't There Before": Demystifying Monstrosity and Menstruation in *Ginger Snaps* and *Ginger Snaps Unleashed*', *Western Folklore*, 6.3–4 (2005), pp. 281–303, https://www.jstor.org/stable/25474753 (accessed 26 May 2021).

Miller, D. A., *The Novel and the Police* (Berkeley, CA: University of California Press, 1988).

Milligan, Barry, *Pleasures and Pains: Opium and the Orient in 19th-Century British Culture* (Charlottesville, VA: University of Virginia Press, 1995).

Moers, Ellen, 'Female Gothic: The Monster's Mother', in *Frankenstein*, ed. J. Paul Hunter (New York: W. W. Norton, 1996).

Moran, Leslie J., 'Law and the Gothic Imagination', in *The Gothic*, ed. Fred Botting (Woodbridge: D. S. Brewer, 2001), pp. 87–109.

Morgan, Thäis, 'Male Lesbian Bodies: The Construction of Alternative Masculinities in Courbet, Baudelaire, and Swinburne', *Genders*, 15 (1992), pp. 37–57.

Morowitz, Laura, 'The Monster Within: *The Munsters*, *The Addams Family* and the American Family in the 1960s', *Critical Studies in Television: The International Journal of Television Studies*, 3.1 (2007), pp. 35–56.

Muñoz, José Esteban, *Cruising Utopia: The Then and There of Queer Futurity* (New York: NYU Press, 2019 [2009]).

—— '"The White to Be Angry": Vaginal Davis's Terrorist Drag', *Social Text*, 52/53 (1997), pp. 80–103.

Murray, Janet, *Hamlet on the Holodeck* (Cambridge, MA: MIT Press, 1997).
Nathan, Emily, 'Southern Gothic and Goth-Kid Makeup: M. Lamar on Racialized Art and Black Leather', *Observer*, 16 February 2015, https://observer.com/2015/02/southern-gothic-and-goth-kid-makeup-m-lamar-on-racialized-art-and-black-leather/ (accessed 25 January 2021).
Neibaur, James L., 'Gothic Cinema during the Silent Era', in *Gothic Film: An Edinburgh Companion*, ed. Richard J. Hand and McRoy Jay (Edinburgh: Edinburgh University Press, 2020), pp. 11–20.
Nemesvari, Richard, 'The Mark of the Brotherhood: The Foreign Other and Homosexual Panic in *The Woman in White*', *ESC: English Studies in Canada*, 28.4 (2002), pp. 603–27; reprinted in *Straight Writ Queer: Non-Normative Expression of Heterosexuality in Literature*, ed. Richard Fantina and Calvin Thomas (Jefferson, NC: McFarland, 2006), pp. 95–108.
Nussbaum, Felicity, *The Brink of All We Hate: English Satires of Women, 1660–1750* (Lexington, KY: University of Kentucky Press, 1984).
—— '"Savage Mothers": Narratives of Maternity in the Mid-Eighteenth Century', *Cultural Critique*, 20 (1991–92), pp. 123–51.
Oldridge, Darren, 'Witchcraft and Gender', in *The Witchcraft Reader. Second Edition*, ed. Darren Oldridge (Abingdon: Routledge, 2008), pp. 248–53.
Orme, Jennifer, 'Mouth to Mouth: Queer Desires in Emma Donoghue's *Kissing the Witch*', *Marvels & Tales*, 24.1 (2010), special issue, 'The Fairy Tale after Angela Carter', pp. 116–30.
O'Rourke, Michael, and David Collings, 'Queer Romanticisms: Past, Present, and Future', *Romanticism on the Net*, 36–37 (2004–05), para. 1–42.
Ortiz-Ospina, Esteban, 'The Rise of Social Media' (2019), https://ourworldindata.org/rise-of-social-media (accessed 30 March 2021).
Otto, Elizabeth, 'Schaulust: Sexuality and Trauma in Conrad Veidt's Masculine Masquerades', in *The Many Faces of Weimar Cinema: Rediscovering Germany's Filmic Legacy*, ed. Christian Rogowski (New York: Camden House, 2010), pp. 134–52.
Paciorek, Andy, 'Folk Horror: From the Forest, Fields, and Furrows: An Introduction', in *Folk Horror Revival: Field Studies*, ed. Andy Paciorek et al., 2nd edn (Middletown, DE: Wyrd Harvest Press, 2018), pp. 12–19.
Paglia, Camille, 'The Stiletto Heel', *Design and Violence*, 25 October 2019, https://www.moma.org/interactives/exhibitions/2013/designandviolence/the-stiletto-heel/ (accessed 23 March 2021).
Palmer, Paulina, 'Lesbian Gothic: Genre, Transformation, Transgression', *Gothic Studies*, 6.1 (2004), pp. 118–30.
—— *The Queer Uncanny: New Perspective on the Gothic* (Cardiff: University of Wales Press, 2012).
Parkin-Gounelas, Ruth, *Literature and Psychoanalysis: Intertextual Readings* (Basingstoke: Palgrave, 2001).
Pasulka, Nicole, and Brian Ferree, 'Unearthing the Sea Witch', *Hazlitt*, 14 January 2016, https://hazlitt.net/longreads/unearthing-sea-witch (accessed 22 March 2022).
Peirse, Alison, *After Dracula: The 1930s Horror Film* (London: I.B. Tauris, 2013).
Poole, Robert, *The Lancashire Witches: Histories and Stories* (Manchester: Manchester University Press, 2002).

Port, Cynthia, 'No Future? Aging, Temporality, History, and Reverse Chronologies', *Occasion*, 4 (2012), pp. 1–19.
Price, Theodore, *Hitchcock and Homosexuality: His 50-Year Obsession with Jack the Ripper and the Superbitch Prostitute: A Psychoanalytic View* (Metuchen, NJ: Scarecrow Press, 1992).
Prins, Yopie, *Victorian Sappho* (Princeton, NJ: Princeton University Press, 1999).
'The Production Code', in *Movies and Mass Culture*, ed. John Belton (New Brunswick, NJ: Rutgers University Press, 1996), pp. 135–49.
Prosser, Jay, *Second Skins: The Body Narratives of Transsexuality* (New York: Columbia University Press, 1998).
Punter, David, 'Introduction', in *The Edinburgh Companion to Gothic and the Arts*, ed. David Punter (Edinburgh: Edinburgh University Press, 2019), pp. 1–11.
—— *The Literature of Terror: A History of Gothic Fiction from 1765 to the Present Day, vol. 1: The Gothic Tradition*, 2nd edn (London: Longman, 1996).
Purkiss, Diane, *The Witch in History. Early Modern and Twentieth-century Representations* (London: Routledge 1996).
Reid, Robin Anne, 'Lost in Space between "Center" and "Margin"', in *Feminist Nightmares: Women at Odds: Feminism and the Problem of Sisterhood*, ed. Susan Ostrov Weisser and Jennifer Fleischner (New York: NYU Press, 1994), pp. 343–57.
Reis, Elizabeth, *Damned Women: Sinners and Witches in Puritan New England* (New York: Cornell University Press, 1997).
Reynolds, Daniel, 'How *What We Do in the Shadows* Became Cable's Queerest Comedy', *The Advocate*, 15 April 2020, https://www.advocate.com/television/2020/4/15/how-what-we-do-shadows-became-cables-queerest-comedy (accessed 5 February 2021).
Rich, Adrienne, 'Compulsory Heterosexuality and Lesbian Existence', *Signs*, 5.4 (1980), pp. 631–60.
Richards, Mary, 'Ron Athey, A.I.D.S. and the Politics of Pain', *Body, Space & Technology*, 3.2 (2003), http://doi.org/10.16995/bst.224.
Rigby, Mair, '"Prey to some cureless disquiet": Polidori's Queer Vampyre at the Margins of Romanticism', *Romanticism on the Net*, 36–37 (2004), https://www.erudit.org/fr/revues/ron/2004-n36-37-ron947/011135ar/ (accessed 16 February 2021).
—— 'Uncanny Recognition: Queer Theory's Debt to the Gothic', *Gothic Studies*, 11 (2009), pp. 46–57, https://link.gale.com/apps/doc/A381057953/LitRC?u=viva_odu& sid=bookmark-LitRC&xid=4043c982 (accessed 10 June 2020).
Robertson, Pamela, *Guilty Pleasures: Feminist Camp from Mae West to Madonna* (London: I.B. Tauris, 1996).
Romano, Aja, 'Canon, Fanon, Shipping and More: A Glossary of the Tricky Terminology that Makes up Fan Culture', *Vox*, 7 June 2016, https://www.vox.com/2016/6/7/11858680/fandom-glossary-fanfiction-explained (accessed 1 May 2021).
Roper, Lyndal, *The Witch in the Western Imagination* (Charlottesville, VA: University of Virginia Press, 2012).

Ross, Andrew, 'Uses of Camp', in *Camp: Queer Aesthetics and the Performing Subject: A Reader*, ed. Fabio Cleto (Edinburgh: Edinburgh University Press, 1999), pp. 308–29.
Royle, Nicholas, *The Uncanny* (Manchester: Manchester University Press, 2003).
Saul, Jack, *The Sins of the Cities of the Plain*, ed. Wolfram Setz (Richmond, VA: Valancourt, 2012).
Scarre, Geoffrey, *Witchcraft and Magic in Sixteenth and Seventeenth-century Europe* (London: Macmillan, 1987).
Schaffer, Talia, '"A Wilde Desire Took Me": The Homoerotic History of *Dracula*', in Bram Stoker, *Dracula*, ed. Nina Auerbach and David J. Skal (New York: W. W. Norton, 1997), pp. 470–82.
Scheunemann, Dietrich, 'The Double, the Décor, and the Framing Device: Once More on Robert Wiene's "The Cabinet of Dr. Caligari"', in *Expressionist Film – New Perspectives*, ed. Dietrich Scheunemann (Rochester, NY: Camden House, 2003), pp. 125–56.
Schmid, David, 'The Devil You Know: *Dexter* and the "Goodness" of American Serial Killing', in *Dexter: Investigating Cutting Edge Television*, ed. Douglas Howard (London: I.B. Tauris, 2010), pp. 132–42.
Scovell, Adam, *Folk Horror: Hours Dreadful and Things Strange* (Leighton Buzzard: Auteur Publishing, 2017).
Sedgwick, Eve Kosofsky, *Between Men: English Literature and Male Homosocial Desire* (New York: Columbia University Press, 1992).
—— *The Coherence of Gothic Conventions* (New York: Arno, 1980).
—— *Tendencies* (London: Routledge, 1994).
Senf, Carol A., *The Vampire in 19th-Century English Literature* (Madison, WI: University of Wisconsin Press, 1988).
Sha, Richard, 'Romanticism and Sexuality – A Special Issue of Romanticism on the Net', *Romanticism on the Net*, 23 (2001), para. 1–12.
Sharpe, Cristina, *In the Wake: On Blackness and Being* (Durham, NC: Duke University Press, 2016).
Showalter, Elaine, *Sexual Anarchy: Gender and Culture at the Fin de Siècle* (New York: Viking, 1990).
Silva, Cynthia, '"Tell me Why": Video Game Features Transgender Lead Character' (2020), https://www.nbcnews.com/feature/nbc-out/tell-me-why-video-game-features-transgender-lead-character-n1239123 (accessed 30 March 2021).
Simandan, V. M., '"Confessions of a Mask" – Yukio Mishima's Finest Novel', 26 October 2010, https://www.simandan.com/confessions-of-a-mask-yukio-mishimas-finest-novel/ (accessed 3 April 2022).
Smith, Andrew, *Victorian Demons: Medicine, Masculinity and the Gothic at the Fin-de-Siècle* (Manchester: Manchester University Press, 2004).
Smith, F. B., 'Labouchere's Amendment to the Criminal Law Amendment Bill', *Historical Studies*, 17.67 (1976), pp. 165–75.
Smith, Jill Suzanne, 'Richard Oswald and the Social Hygiene Film: Promoting Public Health or Promiscuity?', in *The Many Faces of Weimar Cinema: Rediscovering Germany's Filmic Legacy*, ed. Christian Rogowski (New York: Camden House, 2010), pp. 13–30.
Snorton, C. Riley, *Black on Both Sides: A Racial History of Trans Identity* (Minneapolis, MN: University of Minnesota Press, 2017).

Sontag, Susan, 'Notes on "Camp"', in *Camp: Queer Aesthetics and the Performing Subject: A Reader*, ed. Fabio Cleto (Edinburgh: Edinburgh University Press, 1999), pp. 53–65.

Sparks, Tabitha, *The Doctor in the Victorian Novel: Family Practices* (Abingdon: Routledge, 2009).

Spooner, Catherine, *Fashioning Gothic Bodies* (Manchester: Manchester University Press, 2004).

—— *Post-Millennial Gothic: Comedy, Romance and the Rise of Happy Gothic* (London: Bloomsbury, 2017).

Spooner, Catherine, and Emma McEvoy (eds), *The Routledge Companion to Gothic* (New York: Routledge, 2007).

Staff, 'Stonewall 50: Meet Luna Luis Ortiz, One of New York Historical's Experts on House and Ballroom Culture', *Behind the Scenes: New-York Historical Society Museum and Library*, 24 June 2019, https://behindthescenes.nyhistory.org/meet-luna-luis-ortiz-one-of-new-york-historicals-experts-on-house-and-ballroom-culture/ (accessed 4 April 2022).

Stafford, Tim, 'Like and Lycanthropy: The New Pack Werewolf according to Tyler, Tyler and Taylor', in *New Queer Horror Film and Television*, ed. Darren Elliott-Smith and John Edgar Browning (Cardiff: University of Wales Press, 2020), pp. 169–88.

Steakley, James D., *The Writings of Dr. Magnus Hirschfeld: A Bibliography* (Toronto: Canadian Gay Archives, 1985).

Stewart, Garrett, '*Lamia* and the Language of Metamorphosis', *Studies in Romanticism*, 15.1 (1976), pp. 3–41.

Stobbart, Dawn, 'Playing the Future History of Humanity: Situating *Fallout 3* as a Narratological Artefact', in *On the Fringes of Literature and Digital Media*, ed. Irena Kalla et al. (Leiden: Brill, 2018), pp. 123–34.

—— *Videogames and Horror: From Amnesia to Zombies, Run!* (Cardiff: University of Wales Press, 2019).

Stryker, Susan, '(De)Subjugated Knowledges: An Introduction to Transgender Studies', in *The Transgender Studies Reader*, vol. I, ed. Susan Stryker and Stephen Whittle (New York: Routledge, 2006), pp. 1–17.

—— 'My Words to Victor Frankenstein above the Village of Chamounix: Performing Transgender Rage', *GLQ: A Journal of Lesbian and Gay Studies*, 1.3 (1994), pp. 237–54.

—— 'My Words to Victor Frankenstein above the Village of Chamounix: Performing Transgender Rage', in *The Transgender Studies Reader*, vol. II, ed. Susan Stryker and Stephen Whittle (New York: Routledge, 2006), pp. 244–56.

Sutton, Katie, *Sex between Body and Mind: Psychoanalysis and Sexology in the German-Speaking World, 1890s–1930s* (Ann Arbor, MI: University of Michigan Press, 2019).

—— '"We Too Deserve a Place in the Sun": The Politics of Transvestite Identity in Weimar Germany', *German Studies Review*, 35.2 (2012), pp. 335–54.

'Terrorist Novel Writing', *Spirit of the Public Journals for 1797*, vol. 1 (London: James Ridgeway, 1802), pp. 227–9.

Thompson, Kristin, and David Bordwell, *Film History: An Introduction*, 3rd edn (New York: McGraw-Hill Higher Education, 2010).

Thornham, Helen, *Ethnographies of the Videogame* (Farnham: Ashgate, 2011).

Tosenberger, Catherine, 'Homosexuality at the Online Hogwarts: *Harry Potter* Slash Fanfiction', *Children's Literature*, 36.1 (2008), pp. 185–207, doi.org/10.1353/chl.0.0017.

Townshend, Dale, 'Doubles', in *The Encyclopedia of the Gothic* (John Wiley & Sons, 2012), https://doi.org/10.1002/9781118398500.wbeotgd007.

—— *The Orders of Gothic: Foucault, Lacan, and the Subject of Gothic Writing, 1764–1820* (New York: AMS Press, 2007).

Traub, Valerie, *The Renaissance of Lesbianism in Early Modern England* (Cambridge: Cambridge University Press, 2002).

Trimm, Ryan, 'Witching Welcome: Haunting and Post-Imperial Landscape in Hilary Mantel and Helen Oyeyemi', in *Haunted Landscapes: Super-Nature and the Environment*, ed. Ruth Heholt and Niamh Downing (Lanham, MD: Rowman and Littlefield, 2016), pp. 59–74.

Tucker, Herbert, 'Rossetti's Goblin Marketing: Sweet to Tongue and Sound to Eye', *Representations*, 82 (2003), pp. 117–33.

'Valerie Caris Blitz 1957–2009', *VisualAIDS*, https://visualaids.org/artists/valerie-caris-blitz (accessed 4 April 2022).

Veeder, William, 'Children of the Night: Stevenson and Patriarchy', in *Dr Jekyll and Mr Hyde after One Hundred Years*, ed. William Veeder and Gordon Hirsch (Chicago: University of Chicago Press, 1988), pp. 107–60.

Vicinus, Martha, 'They Wonder to Which Sex I Belong: The Historical Roots of Lesbian Identity', in *Homosexuality, Which Homosexuality?*, ed. Dennis Altman, Carole Vance, Martha Vicinus and Jeffrey Weeks (London: GMP, 1989), pp. 171–98.

Wakefield, Lily, 'Activists Reclaim Pride in Manchester, Hold Protest on Same Day as Official Festival', *Pink News*, 28 August 2021, https://www.pinknews.co.uk/2021/08/28/manchester-pride-protest/ (accessed 15 November 2021).

Warner, Marina, *Fantastic Metamorphoses, Other Worlds: Ways of Telling the Self* (Oxford: Oxford University Press, 2002).

Waters, Jack, 'Portrait of the Artist as a Sex Bomb', *POZ*, 1 January 2000, https://www.poz.com/article/Portrait-of-the-Artist-as-a-Sex-Bomb-10617-2086 (accessed 30 March 2022).

Webber, Andrew, *The Doppelgänger: Double Visions in German Literature* (Oxford: Clarendon Press, 1996).

Weeks, Jeffrey, *Against Nature: Essays on History, Sexuality, and Identity* (London: Rivers Oram Press, 1991).

Weiss, Andrea, *Vampires and Violets: Lesbians in Film* (Harmondsworth: Penguin, 1993).

Westengard, Laura, *Gothic Queer Culture: Marginalized Communities and the Ghosts of Insidious Trauma* (Lincoln, NE: University of Nebraska Press, 2019).

Whisnant, Clayton J., *Queer Identities and Politics in Germany: A History 1880–1945* (New York: Harrington Park Press, 2016).

White, John, 'Das Kabinett des Dr. Caligari / The Cabinet of Dr. Caligari (1919)', in *The Routledge Encyclopedia of Films*, ed. John White, Sarah Barrow and Sabine Haenni (Abingdon: Routledge, 2015), pp. 287–9.

Williams, Anne, 'Wicked Women', in *Women and the Gothic: An Edinburgh Companion*, ed. Avril Horner and Sue Zlosnik (Edinburgh: Edinburgh University Press), pp. 91–105.

Williams, Kiyan, 'Bio', kiyanwilliams.com, http://www.kiyanwilliams.com/bio (accessed 2 February 2021).
Williams, Linda, 'Film Bodies: Gender, Genre, and Excess', *Film Quarterly*, 44.4 (1991), pp. 2–13.
Wood, Robin, 'Murnau', *Film Comment*, 12.3 (1976), pp. 4–19.
Worthen, Meredith, 'Tarana Burke', The Biography.com, 1 March 2018, https://www.biography.com/activist/tarana-burke (accessed 14 November 2021).
Zigarovich, Jolene, 'Gothic and the History of Sexuality', in *The Cambridge History of the Gothic, Vol. I: Gothic in the Long Eighteenth Century*, ed. Dale Townshend, Angela Wright and Catherine Spooner (Cambridge: Cambridge University Press, 2020), pp. 382–405.
—— 'Introduction: Transing the Gothic', in *TransGothic in Literature and Culture*, ed. Jolene Zigarovich (New York: Routledge, 2018), pp. 1–22.
—— '"A Strange and Startling Creature": Transgender Possibilities in Wilkie Collins's *The Law and the Lady*', *Victorian Review: An Interdisciplinary Journal of Victorian Studies* 44.1 (2019), special issue, 'Trans Victorians', ed. Ardel Haefele-Thomas, pp. 95–108.
—— 'The Trans Legacy of *Frankenstein*', *Science Fiction Studies*, 45 (2018), special issue, 'Mary Shelley's *Frankenstein* at 200', ed. Nicole Lobdell and Michael Griffin, pp. 260–72.
—— 'Transgothic Desire in Charlotte Dacre's *Zofloya*', in *TransGothic in Literature and Culture*, ed. Jolene Zigarovich (New York: Routledge, 2018), pp. 77–96.
Zorrilla, Michelle, *Video Games and Gender*, thesis, https://www.academia.edu/5594515/Video_Games_and_Gender_Game_Representation_Gender_Effect.s_Differences_in_Play_and_Player_Representation (accessed 30 March 2021).

Filmography

The Addams Family Values, dir. Barry Sonnenfeld (Paramount, 1993)
An American Werewolf in London, dir. John Landis (Polygram, 1981)
Anders als die Andern, dir. Oswald Richard (Richard-Oswald-Produktion, Filmmuseum München, 1919)
Arrival of a Train at La Ciotat, dir. Lumière Brothers (Société Lumière, 1896)
Babylon Berlin, X Filme Creative Pool, 2017–present
Blacula, dir. William Crain (American International Pictures, 1972)
Blood and Roses, dir. Roger Vadim (Paramount Pictures, 1960)
The Blood on Satan's Claw, dir. Piers Haggard (Tigon Pictures, 1971)
Bloodthirsty, dir. Michio Yamamoto (Toho Studio, 2020)
'Butterfly/Cocoon', *Pose*, FX, 25 June 2019
Cabaret, dir. Bob Fosse (ABC Pictures, 1972)
Das Cabinet des Dr. Caligari, dir. Robert Wiene (Decla-Bioscop AG, 1920)
The Celluloid Closet, dir. Rob Epstein and Jeffrey Friedman (Sony Pictures Classics, 1996)
The Company of Wolves, dir. Neil Jordan (Palace Pictures, 1984)
Creatures from the Pink Lagoon, dir. Chris Diani (Ariztical, 1967)
The Curse of the Queerwolf, dir. Mark Pirro (Pirromount Pictures, 1988)
The Curse of the Werewolf, dir. Terence Fisher (Universal, 1961)
The Danish Girl, dir. Tim Hooper (Focus Features, 2015)
Daughters of Darkness, dir. Harry Kümel (Ciné Vog, 1971)
Dracula, dir. Tod Browning (Universal Pictures, 1931)
Dracula's Daughter, dir. Lambert Hiller (Universal Pictures, 1936)
Elvira, Mistress of the Dark, dir. James Signorelli (New World Pictures, 1988)
Escamotage d'une dame Chez Robert Houdin (*Conjuring A Lady at Robert Houdin's*), dir. Georges Mélière (Star Film, 1896)
Faux Paws, dir. Doug Bari (Doug and Judy Productions, 2013)
Fire In My Belly, video by David Wojnarowicz and Diamanda Galás (independent short film, 1990)
Frankenstein, dir. James Whale (Universal Pictures, 1931)
Ginger Snaps, dir. John Fawcett (20th Century–Fox, 2000)
Ginger Snaps Back: The Beginning, dir. Grant Harvey (Nice Doggle, 2004)
Ginger Snaps II: Unleashed, dir. Brent Sullivan (Lion's Gate, 2004)
Un Homme de Têtes, dir. Georges Méliès (Star-Film, 1898)
The Howling, dir. Joe Dante (Embassy, 1981)

The Hunger, dir. Tony Scott (MGM/UA Entertainment, 1983)
I Was A Teenage Werebear, dir. Tim Sullivan (ArieScope Pictures, 2011)
Ich möchte kein Mann sein (*I Don't Want to be a Man*), dir. Ernst Lubitsch (Projektions-AG Union (PAGU), 1918)
Interview with the Vampire, dir. Neil Jordan (The Geffen Film Company, 1994)
Jennifer's Body, dir. Karyn Kusama (20th Century–Fox, 2009)
L.A. Zombie, dir. Bruce LaBruce (Wurst Film, 2010)
The Lair, Here! Network, 2007–2009
Legacies, dir. M. Lamar (2017)
Mädchen in Uniform, dir. Leontine Sagan and Carl Froelich (Deutsche Film-Gemeinschaft, 1931)
Major!, dir. Annalise Ophelian (Floating Ophelia Productions, 2015)
Mobilier Fidèle, dir. Émile Cohl (Société des Etablissements L. Gaumont, Pathé Frères, 1910)
Et Mourir de Plaisir (*Blood and Roses*), dir. Roger Vadim (Paramount, 1960)
The Munsters, Universal Television, 1964–1966
Negro Antichrist, dir. M. Lamar and Taylor Clark (2012)
Nosferatu, dir. F. W Murnau (Prana Film, 1922)
Otto; Or, Up with Dead People, dir. Bruce LaBruce (Bruce LaBruce, 2008)
Paris is Burning, dir. Jennie Livingston (Academy Entertainment, 1991)
The Pendle Witch Child, dir. Simon Armitage (BBC 4, August 2012)
Philadelphia, dir. Jonathan Demme (TriStar Pictures, 1993)
Rebecca, dir. Alfred Hitchcock (United Artists, 1940)
The Rocky Horror Picture Show, dir. Jim Sharman (20th Century–Fox, 1975)
Screaming Queens: The Riot at Compton's Cafeteria, dir. Susan Stryker and Victor Silverman (Frameline, 2005)
She Wolf of London, dir. Jean Yarbrough (Universal, 1946)
Silver Bullet, dir. Daniel Attias (Paramount, 1985)
Der Student von Prag (*The Student of Prague*), dir. Stellan Rye (Grapevine, 1913)
That Certain Summer, dir. Lamont Johnson (Universal Television, 1972)
True Blood, HBO, 2008–2014
Twilight, dir. Catherine Hardwick (Aura Films, 2008)
The Vampire Lovers, dir. Roy Ward Baker (Hammer Film Productions, 1970)
Vampyros Lesbos, dir. Jesús Francos (Fénix Films, 1971)
The Wailing, dir. Na Hong-jin (20th Century–Fox, 2016)
Werewolf Woman, dir. Rino Di Silvestro (Agora, 1976)
What We Do in the Shadows, creator Jermaine Clement (FX, 2019–)
Whatever Happened to Baby Jane?, dir. Robert Aldrich (Warner Bros., 1962)
The Wicker Man, dir. Robin Hardy (British Lion Films, 1973)
Witchfinder General, dir. Michael Reeves (Tigon Pictures, 1968)
The Wolves of Wall Street, dir. David DeCoteau (DEJ Productions, 2002)

Notes on Contributors

Xavier Aldana Reyes is Reader in English Literature and Film at Manchester Metropolitan University and co-lead of the Manchester Centre for Gothic Studies. He is author of *Gothic Cinema* (2020), *Horror Film and Affect* (2016) and *Body Gothic* (2014), and editor of *Twenty-First Century Gothic* (with Maisha Wester, 2019) and *Horror: A Literary History* (2016). He is chief editor of the Horror Studies academic book series.

Silvia Antosa is Associate Professor of English at the University for Foreigners of Siena (Italy). She has published extensively on nineteenth-century fiction and travel accounts and contemporary British novels. She is the author of *Frances Elliot and Italy: Writing Travel, Writing the Self* (2018), *Richard Francis Burton: Victorian Explorer and Translator* (2012) and *Crossing Boundaries: Bodily Paradigms in Jeanette Winterson's Fiction 1985–2000* (2008). Antosa is the editor of several interdisciplinary volumes on queer theories and practices. She is a member of the Board of the Italian Association of English Studies (AIA), the co-editor of the Series AngloSophia. Studi di Letteratura e Cultura Inglese (Mimesis) and a member of the editorial board of Textus, English Studies in Italy. She is currently working on a project with the University of Birmingham (UK) entitled 'Cultural Discourses on Desire between Women: A Queer Comparative Analysis', supported by the British Academy/Leverhulme Trust.

Tom Brassington has authored a chapter in *Nosferatu in the 21st Century* (2022), and two articles which appear in the 2022 special issue of *Queer Studies in Media and Popular Culture* 'Rethinking Marginality in New Queer Television', which Tom guest edited with Danielle Girard and Debra Ferreday.

Brooke Cameron is Associate Professor of English at Queen's University in Kingston, Ontario. She is the author of *Critical Alliances: Economics* *and Feminism in English Women's Writing, 1880–1914* (2020), as well as multiple peer-reviewed articles and book chapters on gender and economic themes in Victorian literature. She has published peer-reviewed articles on *Dracula* and Count Stenbock's *A True Story of a Vampire*, and is currently co-editing, with Lara Karpenko, *The Vampire in 19th-Century Literature: A Feast of Blood* (2022).

Jeremy Chow is Assistant Professor of English at Bucknell University, which occupies the unceded and ancestral territories of the Susquehannock peoples. His research enfolds eighteenth-century literature and culture, queer studies, and the environmental humanities. His first book, *The Queerness of Water: Troubled Ecologies in the Eighteenth Century*, is forthcoming.

Gregory Luke Chwala is Graduate Professor of Humanities and Culture at Union Institute & University. He specialises in nineteenth-century British literature, as well as postcolonial and transatlantic queer studies from the nineteenth to the twenty-first century; his most recent work proposes what he has coined as decolonial queer ecologies as a reparative reading strategy of colonial-themed transatlantic Gothic and speculative fiction. He has published work in queer, postcolonial, race and Gothic studies, including *eTropic* and the *Victorian Review*. He is also co-editor (with Ardel Haefele-Thomas) on the new series, *Queer and Trans Intersections*.

Amanda Cruz is an independent Gothic, horror, and queer studies scholar. Her work focuses on queer themes in horror and queer reclamations of monstrosity. She currently lives in southern California with her husband, close friend, and several cats.

Darren Elliott-Smith is Senior Lecturer in Film and Gender at the University of Stirling, Scotland, and is currently the programme director for Gender Studies MSc/MLitt programme. His research and publications extend to considerations of gender and sexuality in the horror genre, queerness in film and television and videographic film studies. He has published extensively on masculinity in queer horror and is known online as the Queer Horror Doctor.

Ardel Haefele-Thomas is the Chair of LGBTQ+ Studies at City College of San Francisco. Their book publications include *Queer Others in Victorian Gothic: Transgressing Monstrosity* (2012) and *Introduction to Transgender Studies* (2019). They also served as a guest editor for *Victorian Review*'s special edition entitled *Trans Victorians* (2019). They have published numerous essays on various queer and trans Gothic themes and are currently working on two major forthcoming projects: a monograph, *AIDS Gothic: Intersections of Gothic Modes and Disease*, and a four-volume edited set of rare and hard to find archival materials on LGBTQ+ nineteenth-century British history. Along with Luke Chwala, they are thrilled to co-edit an exciting new series, *Queer and Trans Intersections*. Ardel also serves as the global non-binary trans and intersex ambassador for the LGBTQ+ International Powerlifting Congress.

Jamil Mustafa is a Professor of English studies at Lewis University, where he hosted the 2019 meeting of the International Gothic Association. He is the author of *The Blaxploitation Horror Film: Adaptation, Appropriation and the Gothic* (2023). He has published in books including *Neo-Gothic Narratives* (2020), *Gothic Britain: Dark Places in the Provinces and Margins of the British Isles* (2018), *Wilde's Other Worlds* (2018) and *The Gothic Tradition in* Supernatural (2016), and in journals such as *Neo-Victorian Studies, Humanities, The New Ray Bradbury Review* and *American Imago*. He is the co-editor of 'Gothic Adaptation: Intermedial and Intercultural Shape-Shifting', a special issue of *Humanities* (2023).

Paulina Palmer retired from a senior lectureship in the Department of English at Warwick University where she helped establish the MA in Women's Studies. After her retirement, Palmer taught for the MA in Gender and Sexuality at Birkbeck College, London University. She also taught classes on feminist and queer fiction at City Lit College, London. Her publications include *Contemporary Women's Fiction: Narrative Practice and Feminist Theory* (1989), *Contemporary Lesbian Writing: Dreams, Desire, Difference* (1993), *Lesbian Gothic: Transgressive Fictions* (1999), *The Queer Uncanny: New Perspectives on the Gothic* (2012) and *Queering Contemporary Gothic Narrative 1970–2012* (2016). She is a trustee of Encompass, the Cambridge-based organisation that aims to improve the life of LGBTQ people in the Cams area by means of networking and capacity building.
paulinapalmer@aol.com; http:paulinapalmer.org.uk

Dawn Stobbart completed her doctorate at Lancaster University and is currently focusing on how videogames function in a trans and intermediary capacity for her second monograph. She has fingers in many pies, including queer studies, cultural studies and media studies, as well as a focus on horror and the Gothic that bleeds into everything she does. She has an interest in contemporary media, and especially in looking at how narrative translates to videogames.

Clayton Carlyle Tarr is an Assistant Teaching Professor at the University of North Carolina at Charlotte, where he specialises in nineteenth-century literature. He is the author of *Personation Plots: Identity Fraud in Victorian Sensation Fiction* (2022), and he has published essays on subjects ranging from the plague and bog bodies to teeth and stillbirth. His current book project examines representations of legs in Victorian literature and culture.

Dennis Wegner is a PhD candidate in German Studies at Cornell University where he is currently working on a dissertation project on literary cultures associated with migration between Germany and Russia/post-Soviet countries from the early twentieth century to the present. He is a co-editor for the online comics studies journal *Closure*. His research interests include queer cinema, Gothic in the German context, and transnational approaches to literature and film.

Laura Westengard is an Associate Professor of English at New York City College of Technology, City University of New York. She serves as Board Co-Chair of CLAGS: Center for LGBTQ Studies and sits on the Editorial Board for the journal *WSQ: Women's Studies Quarterly*. She co-edited *The 25 Sitcoms that Changed Television: Turning Points in American Culture* (2017) and has published in journals such as *JNT: Journal of Narrative Theory* and *Steinbeck Review*. Her book, *Gothic Queer Culture: Marginalized Communities and the Ghosts of Insidious Trauma*, was released in 2019.

Jolene Zigarovich is Associate Professor of English in the Department of Languages & Literatures at the University of Northern Iowa. She is the author of *Writing Death and Absence in the Victorian Novel: Engraved Narratives* (2012), and editor of *Sex and Death in Eighteenth-Century Literature* (2013) as well as *TransGothic in Literature and Culture* (2018). Her recently published monograph *Death and the Body in the Eighteenth-Century Novel* had the support of the National Endowment for the Humanities. In spring 2021 she was a visiting research fellow at the Institute for Advanced Studies in the Humanities, University of Edinburgh and in 2021–2022 was a fellow at the Netherlands Institute for Advanced Study, Amsterdam. These fellowships are in support of her book project, *Victorian Necropolitics: Legislating the Dead Body and the Novel, 1847–1874*, which considers the posthumous life of characters uncannily bound by regulation.

Index

Abraham, Amelia, 'Ron Athey Literally Bleeds For His Art', 311n
Abraham, Nicholas, 'Notes on the Phantom: A Complement to Freud's Metapsychology', 185
AIDS
  AIDS Coalition to Unleash Power (ACT-UP), 299
  archdiocese in New York and AIDS protest, 299
  Athey, Ron, 13, 301–4
  Blitz, Valerie Caris, 13, 304–6
  Centers for Disease Control and Prevention (CDC USA), 127, 295
  Crimp, Douglas, *Melancholia and Moralism: Essays on AIDS and Queer Politics*, 297
  Eagles, Jordan, 12, 230–3
  Galás, Diamanda, 13, 299–301
  gay men's health crisis (NYC), 307
  Kaposi's Sarcoma (KS), 231, 295–7, 302
  Latex Ball (NYC), 307
  Ortiz, Luna Luis, 307–9
  Philadelphia, 13, 296–8
  Ray, Ricky, Robert and Randy (haemophilia and AIDS panic), 296
  Reagan administration, 127, 129
  Reagan, Ronald, 129, 309
  Starling, Maxime Angel, 13, 306–7
  Tryon, Thomas, 13, 283–5, 288
  in werewolf narratives, 158
  Wojnarowicz, David, 13, 298–301
AIDS art
  A Living Testament to the Blood Fairies, 305
  Bestiality (Starling), 306
  Bloody chleo (Ortiz), 308
  Bloody Nick (Eagles), F4, 230–3
  Fire in My Belly (Wojnarowicz), 299–301
  Illuminations (Eagles), F3, 230–3
  The Missing Generation (Sean Dorsey Dance), 309
  NY Awards Ball klub kid face (Ortiz), 308
  Queen Sex Positive (Blitz), 305–6
  relative to Zombie narratives, 140
  Self Portrait: HIV Glamour Puss (Ortiz), 308
  'This is the Law of the Plague' (Galás), 299–301
  Vampire Slut (Starling), 307
  UNTITLED Chleo (Ortiz), 308
  Vestment (Blitz), 305
Allard, Jeannine, *Légende: The Story of Philippa and Aurelie*, 10, 176–9, 186
American folk horror
  The Blood on Satan's Claw, 279–80
  Dark Harvest (Partridge), 13, 290–2
  Harvest Home (Tryon), 1, 283–5, 288
  'The King of Stones' (Strantzas), 13, 287–9
  paganism and neo-paganism, 281, 283–8, 292
  The Wicker Man, 279–80, 286
  Witchfinder General, 279–80
Amin, Kadij, 'Haunted by the 1990s: Queer Theory's Affective Histories', 1,2
Andeweg, Agnes, and Sue Zlosnik, *Gothic Kinship*, 100–1

Andrews, Jennifer, 'Native Canadian Gothic Refigured: Reading Eden Robinson's *Monkey Beach*', 272
Anonymous, 'Terrorist Novel Writing', 209
Armstrong, Isobel, *Victorian Poetry: Poetry, Poetics and Politics*, 217
Athey, Ron, 13, 301–4
Auerbach, Nina, *Our Vampires, Ourselves*, 119–120
Ayers, Mary A., *Masculine Shame: From Succubus to the Eternal Feminine*, 110

ball culture
  gay men's health crisis (NYC), 307
  NY Awards Ball klub kid face (Ortiz), 308
  Paris is Burning, 307
  Self Portrait: HIV Glamour Puss (Ortiz), 308
Barnes, Sequoia, '"If You Don't Bring No Grits, Don't Come": Critiquing a Critique of Patrick Kelly, Golliwogs, and Camp as a Technique of Black Queer Expression', 104
Batchelor, James, 'Dontnod's *Tell Me Why* Aims for a Transgender Story not "Rooted in Pain or Trauma"', 270
BDSM
  Les 120 Journées de Sodome (*The 120 Days of Sodom*) (Sade), 17, 29–34
  in AIDS art, 298, 304, 306
  in *The Curse of the Queerwolf*, 160
  Dracula (Stoker), 70–2
  Jane Eyre (Brontë), 44–6
  in *The Lair*, 166
  in Lamar, M.'s art, 238–9
  in lesbian vampire films, 9, 125
  in *The Monk* (Lewis), 238
  in slash fiction, 247, 249
  in Swinburne's 'Anactoria', 220
Beachy, Robert, *Gay Berlin: Birthplace of a Modern Identity*, 79–82
Bear culture in werewolf narratives, 10, 163–4
Beauvoir, Simone de, 'Must We Burn Sade?', 19, 30, 32–3

Beckford, William
  The Episodes of Vathek, 39
  Vathek, 39, 40
Benshoff, Harry M., *Monsters in the Closet: Homosexuality and the Horror Film*, 136, 154, 158
Bergstrom, Janet, 'Sexuality at a Loss: The Films of F. W. Murnau', 83
Bernhardt-House, Phillip A., 'The Werewolf as Queer, the Queer as Werewolf, and Queer Werewolves', 156
Bernini, Lorenzo, *Queer Theories: An Introduction*, 147
Bersani, Leo
  Homos, 141, 165
  'Is the Rectum a Grave?', 149, 161, 296
Bilson, Anne, 'The Werewolf Howls Again', 155
Black Lives Matter, 239
Blake, William, *The Ghost of a Flea*, F2, 11, 229, 231
Blaxploitation, 9, 103–5
Blisterdude, 'Ginger Snaps: The Last Straw', 256
Blitz, Valerie Caris, 13, 304–6
Boellstorff, Tom, *Coming of Age in Second Life*, 264–5
Bowers, Katherine, 'Haunted Ice, Fearful Sounds, and the Arctic Sublime: Exploring Nineteenth Century Polar Gothic Space', 272
Bowles, Emily, 'Maternal Culpability in Fetal Defects: Aphra Behn's Satiric Interrogations of Medical Models', 22
Braidotti, Rosi, *The Posthuman*, 168
Brennan, Summer, *High Heel*, 108
Briggs, Robin, *Witches and Neighbours: The Social and Cultural Context of European Witchcraft*, 189
Broedel, Hans Peter, *The Malleus Maleficarum and the Construction of Witchcraft: Theology and Popular Belief*, 189–90
Brontë, Charlotte, *Jane Eyre*, 7, 34, 44–6, 275
Brooks, Max, *World War Z: An Oral History of the Zombie War*, 148

Browne, S. G., *Breathers: A Zombie's Lament*, 137
Browning, Robert
  'Childe Roland to the Dark Tower Came', 216–17
  'My Last Duchess', 216
  'Porphyria's Lover', 212
Bruhm, Steven, 'Gothic Sexualities', 40
Bruin-Molé, Megen de, *Remixed*, 98, 110
Bubuscio, Jack, 'The Cinema of Camp (aka Camp and the Gay Sensibility)', 97
Buck, Rebecca S., *Ghosts of Winter*, 10, 176, 179–82, 186
Buckley, Jennifer, *Gender, Pregnancy and Power in Eighteenth-Century Literature: The Maternal Imagination*, 214
Busse, Kristina, *Framing Fan Fiction*, 248
Butler, Judith
  Bodies that Matter: On the Discursive Limits of Sex, 117
  'Frames of War: When Is Life Grievable?', 198
  'Melancholy Gender – Refused Identification', 26
  The Psychic Life of Power: Theories in Subjection, 194
  Undoing Gender, 142–3
Byron, Lord George Gordon, 118–19, 131, 229
Byron, Lord George Gordon, *The Deformed Transformed*, 34

camp
  The Addams Family, 101
  The Addams Family Values, 98, 102–3
  Blacula, 9, 98, 103–5
  Can I Be Your Bratwurst, Please?, 305
  Creatures from the Pink Lagoon, 136
  Elvira, Mistress of the Dark, 98, 106–9
  feminist camp, 107–9
  Jennifer's Body, 98, 109–10
  The Munsters, 101
  Pose, 9, 98, 103–5
  The Rocky Horror Picture Show, 1
  I Was A Teenage Werebear!, 163
  Whatever Happened to Baby Jane?, 98–100

Carr, Diane, *Computer Games, Text Narrative, Play*, 264–5
Carr, Helen, 'Introduction' *From My Guy to Sci-Fi: Genre and Women's Writing in the Postmodern World*, 176
Castle, Terry
  The Apparitional Lesbian: Female Homosexuality and Modern Culture, 175, 178–9, 194
  The Literature of Lesbianism, 217, 219
Centers for Disease Control and Prevention (CDC USA), 295
CharityDingle, 'I said I would die for you!', 257
Chow, Jeremy, 'Go to Hell: William Beckford's Skewed Heaven and Hell', 40
Cinema of Attraction, 85, 95
Clare, Eli, *Exile and pride: Disability, Queerness, and Liberation*, 21
Clark, Bruce, 'Fabulous Monsters of Conscience: Anthropomorphosis in Keats's *Lamia*, 215
Cleto, Fabio, *Camp: Queer Aesthetics and the Performing Subject*, 97
Cline, Ernest, *Ready Player One*, 262, 276
Clover, Carol, *Men, Women, and Chain Saws: Gender in the Modern Horror Film*, 282
Cocks, H. G., *Nameless Offences: Homosexual Desire in the Nineteenth Century*, 118
Cohen, Jeffrey Jerome, 'Monster Culture (Seven Theses)', 233
Cole, Alayna and Dakoda Barker, *Games as Texts*, 266–7
Coleman, Robin R. Means, *Horror Noire: Blacks in American Horror Films from the 1890's to Present*, 104
Coleridge, Samuel Taylor
  Christabel, 11, 217–19
  'Kubla Kahn', 11, 213–14, 217
  Lyrical Ballads, 212, 217
Collins, William Wilkie
  Armadale, 47
  The Dead Secret, 47
  The Law and the Lady, 7, 47, 50–2

Collins, William Wilkie (*cont.*)
 No Name, 47
 The Woman in White, 7, 34, 47–52
Cook, Matt, *London and the Culture of Homosexuality, 1885–1914*, 75n
copperbadge, 'Stealing Harry', 250
Costantini, Mariaconcetta, 'Polar Contagion: Ecogothic Anxiety across Media in the Twenty-First Century', 272
Cote, Rachel Vorona, *Too Much: How Victorian Constraints Still Bind women Today*, 53
Coudray, Chantal Bourgault du, 154, 156
Cowdell, Paul, '"Practicing witchcraft myself during the filming": Folk Horror, Folklore, and the Folkloresque', 282
Craft, Christopher, '"Kiss Me with Those Red Lips": Gender and Inversion in Bram Stoker's *Dracula*, 77n
Creed, Barbara
 'Ginger Snaps: The Monstrous Feminine as *femme animale*', 156
 Phallic Panic: Film, Horror and the Primal Uncanny, 156
Crimp, Douglas, *Melancholia and Moralism: Essays on AIDS and Queer Politics*, 297
Culpepper, Nicholas, *A Directory for Midwives, or, a guide for women, in their conception, bearing, and suckling their children*, 24
Curran, Andrew, *Sublime Disorder: Physical Monstrosity in Diderot's Universe*, 31
Currier, Jameson, 'The Country House', 10, 176, 181–4, 186

Dacre, Charlotte, *Zafloya, or, The Moor*, 7, 38, 40–1, 44, 52
daddies in gay culture, 164–6
Davis, Vaginal
 Come On Daughter Save Me, 234
 Fountain of Salmacis, F5, 12, 234–6
Dean, Tim, 'No Sex Please, We're American', 19
DeCouteau, David, *The Wolves of Wall Street*, 160–1

deformity
 Les 120 Journées de Sodome (*120 Days of Sodom*) (Sade), 17–21, 29–34
 The Castle of Otranto (Walpole), 21–6
 The Deformed Transformed (Byron), 34
 Frankenstein: Or, the Modern Prometheus (Shelley), 34, 234
 Frankenstein, 296
 Jane Eyre (Brontë), 34
 The Law and the Lady (Collins), 47, 50–2
 The Monk (Lewis), 28–9
 Our Mutual Friend (Dickens), 7, 34, 53
 Strange Case of Dr Jekyll and Mr Hyde (Stevenson), 34
 The Woman in White (Collins), 34
DeKeseredy, Walter S. and Stephen L. Muzzatti and Joseph F. Donnermeyer, 'Mad Men in Bib Overalls: Media's Horrorfication and Pornification of Rural Culture', 285
Dellamora, Richard, *Masculine Desire: The Sexual Politics of Victorian Aestheticism*, 58, 121
Derrida, Jacques, 'Passages – from Traumatism to Promise', 281–2
Deutsch, Helen, 'Deformity' in *Keywords for Disability Studies*, 18
Dickens, Charles
 Great Expectations, 52
 Little Dorrit, 44
 The Mystery of Edwin Drood, 52
 Our Mutual Friend, 7, 34, 52–3
Dickie, Simon, *Cruelty and Laughter: Forgotten Comic Literature and the Unsentimental Eighteenth Century*, 18
Dickinson, Emily, 'Because I could not stop for death', 211
Dinshaw, Carolyn, *Getting Medieval: Sexualities and Communities, Pre and Postmodern*, 179
disability
 Les 120 Journées de Sodome (*120 Days of Sodom*) (Sade), 17–21, 29–34
 The Castle of Otranto (Walpole), 21–6
 Frankenstein: Or, the Modern Prometheus (Shelley), 34
 Generation Dead (Waters), 137

Jane Eyre (Brontë), 34
The Law and the Lady (Collins), 47, 50–2
The Monk (Lewis), 26–9
Our Mutual Friend (Dickens), 7, 34
Strange Case of Dr Jekyll and Mr Hyde (Stevenson), 34
The Woman in White (Collins), 34
Donoghue, Emma, *Kissing the Witch: Old Tales in New Skins*, 11, 191, 198–200, 203
doppelgänger
  in *Anders als die Andern* (*Different from the Others*), 84, 86, 89–93
  in *Nosferatu*, 84
  in *The Student of Prague*, 8, 86
  in *Strange Case of Dr Jekyll and Mr Hyde*, 59–67
  trope, 84, 86
  in video games, 265
Doty, Alexander, *Flaming Classics: Queering the Film Canon*, 87–9
Dreger, Alice D. and April M. Herndon, Progress and Politics in the Intersex Rights Movement: Feminist Theory in Action', 190
Driskill, Qwo-Li, 'Eulogy for the 40th, 309
Drucker, Zackary, 'Ron Athey', 302
Dubois, Martin, *Gerard Manley Hopkins and the Poetry of Religious Experience*, 211
Duggan, Lisa, *The Twilight of Equality: Neoliberalism, Cultural Politics, and the Attack on Democracy*, 144
Duffy, Carol Ann, 'The Lancashire Witches', 11, 191, 196–8, 203
Dyer, Richard, 'Less and More than Women and Men: Lesbian and Gay Cinema in Weimar Germany', 82, 84

Eagles, Jordan
  as artist, 12
  Bloody Nick, F4, 230–3
  Illuminations, F3, 230–3
early Gothic cinema
  Arrival of a Train at La Ciotat, 85
  Das Cabinet des Dr. Caligari (*The Cabinet of Dr. Caligari*), 87–9, 93
  Cleopatra, 85
  Escamotage d'une dame Chez Robert-Houdin (*Conjuring a Lady at Robert Houdin's*), 85
  Un homme de têtes (*The Four Troublesome Heads*), 85
  Maschinenmensch in Metropolis (*Machine-Human in the Metropolis*), 86
  Le Mobilier fidèle (*The Automatic Moving Company*), 86
  Nosferatu: A Symphony of Horror, 8, 83–4, 86, 89, 123
  Der Student von Prag (*The Student of Prague*), 8, 86
Edelman, Lee, *No Future: Queer Theory and the Death Drive*, 26, 127, 149
effeminaphobia, 10, 157, 161
Eisner, Lotte H., *The Haunted Screen: Expressionism in the German Cinema and the Influence of Max Reinhardt*, 86–7
Elbe, Lili (early gender affirmation surgery at Institut für Sexualwissenschaft), 82
Elfenbein, Andrew, *Romantic Genius: The Prehistory of a Homosexual Role*, 217
Elliott-Smith, Darren
  '"Death is the New Pornography!": Gay Zombies, Homonormativity and Consuming Masculinity in Queer Horror', 143–4, 158
  'Gay Zombies: Consuming Masculinity and Community in Bruce LaBruce's *Otto; or Up with Dead People* and *L.A. Zombie*', 146
  Queer Horror Film and Television: Sexuality and Masculinity in the Margins, 154
  'Revolting Queers: The Southern Gothic in Gothic Horror Film and Television', 155
Ellis, Havelock
  Sexual Inversion, 71
  Studies in the Psychology of Sex, Volume 2, 43–4
Endo, Paul, 'Seeing Romantically in *Lamia*', 215–16
Erickson, Laurel, '"In Short, She is an Angel, and I am—": Odd Women and Same-Sex Desire in Wilkie Collins's *Woman in White*', 49–50

Farr, Jason, *Novel Bodies: Disability and Sexuality in Eighteenth-Century British Literature*, 19, 21, 25
Fetner, Tina, *How the Religious Right Shaped Lesbian and Gay Activism*, 142
Fincher, Max, *Queering Gothic in the Romantic Age: The Penetrating Eye*, 226
Fisher, Mark, *Capitalist Realism: Is There No Alternative?*, 148
Fleming, Kaleigh, 'Queering Brigitte Fitzgerald', 255–6
Fletcher, Harriet, '"Gothic" TV: High-quality Modern Horror Series Providing Powerful Roles for Hollywood's Older Women', 99
Flinn, Caryl, 'The Deaths of Camp', 99
Foster, Jeanette Howard, *Sex Variant Women in Literature*, 219
Foucault, Michel
  The History of Sexuality: An Introduction, 39
  The History of Sexuality: Volume 1, 17
Frame, Jenny, *Hunger for You*, 130–2
Francus, Marilyn, *Mostrous Motherhood: Eighteenth-Century Culture and the Ideology of Domesticity*, 22
Frecerro, Carla, *Queer/Early/Modern*, 10, 174–6, 179–80, 182–6, 233
Freeman, Elizabeth, *Time Binds: Queer Temporalities, Queer Histories*, 101–2
Freud, Sigmund
  'Civilisation and its Discontents', 165
  'The Uncanny', 180, 275
  The Uncanny, 281
  The 'Wolfman' and Other Cases, 165
Fuseli, Henry, *The Nightmare*, F1, 11, 226–7, 229

Gabbard, D. Christopher and Susannah Mintz, *A Cultural History of Disability in the Long Eighteenth Century*, 22–3
Galás, Diamanda
  archdiocese in New York and AIDS protest, 299
  defense of *Fire in My Belly* at Smithsonian National Portrait Gallery's removal of art, 301
  Fire in My Belly, 13
  'This is the Law of the Plague', 299–301
  Masque of the Red Death Trilogy, 300
  'This is the Law of the Plague', 13, 299–301
Gallop, Jane, *Sexuality, Disability, and Aging: Queer Temporalities of the Phallus*, 20–1, 26
Gan, Jessi, '"Still at the Back of the Bus": Sylvia Rivera's Struggle', 13n
Gardner, Abby, 'A Complete Breakdown of the J. K. Rowling Transgender Comments Controversy', 244
Garland, Rosie, *The Night Brother*, 10, 176, 184–6
Gaskell, Elizabeth, *The Grey Woman*, 5, 6
Gaskill, Malcolm, *Witchcraft: A Very Short Introduction*, 189, 192, 197
Gay and Lesbian Alliance Against Defamation (GLAAD), 132, 269–70
Gay Liberation Movement, 1, 2, 174, 307, 14n; *see also* Stonewall Rebellion
genderqueer in Wilkie Collins, 47, 50, 53–4; *see also* non-binary
Giacopasi, Caitlin B., 'The Werewolf Pride Movement: A Step Back from Queer Medieval Tradition', 168
Gigante, Denise, *Life: Organic Form and Romanticism*, 215
Gilbert, Sandra M. and Susan Gubar, *The Madwoman in the Attic: The Woman Writer and the Nineteenth-Century Literary Imagination*, 219
Ginger Snaps, slash fiction, 12
Ginsberg, Allen, 'Howl', 154
Gittins, Ian, 'My Performance is Catharsis', 300
Goldin, Nan, 305
Gomez, Jewelle, *The Gilda Stories*, 128–30
Gonzales, Erica, 'Lena Waithe's Met Gala Suit Says, "Black Drag Queens Invented Camp"', 103
Gothic poetry
  'Anactoria' (Swinburne), 11
  Christabel (Coleridge), 11

Goblin Market (Rosetti), 11
'Kubla Kahn'(Coleridge), 11
'The Lancashire Witches'(Duffy), 11
Witch (Tamàs), 11
Gould, Deborah B, 'The Shame of Gay Pride in Early AIDS Activism', 298, 303–4
Griffin, Gabrielle, *Heavenly Love? Lesbian Images in Twentieth Century Women's Writing*, 174
Griffin-Gracy, Miss Major, 13n
Gumbs, Alexis Pauline, 'Afterword to *The Gilda Stories*', 129
Gunning, Tom, 'The Cinema of Attraction[s]: Early Film, Its Spectator and the Avant-Garde', 85

Haefele-Thomas, Ardel
 Introduction to Transgender Studies, 14n
 'Queering the Female Gothic', 281
 Queer Others in Victorian Gothic: Transgressing Monstrosity, 5, 6, 38–9, 47–9, 210, 291–2
 'Queer Victorian Gothic', 53, 210
 '"That Dreadful Thing That Looked Like a Beautiful Girl": Trans Anxiety/Trans Possibility in Three Late Victorian Werewolf Tales', 168
Haggerty, George
 Gothic Fiction/Gothic Form, 227
 'Gothic Fiction and Queer Theory', 41–2
 'The History of Homosexuality Reconsidered', 174–5
 'Literature and Homosexuality in the Late Eighteenth Century: Walpole, Beckford, and Lewis', 245
 Queer Gothic, 5, 6, 20–1, 23, 28, 40, 100, 127, 191, 227, 245–6, 209–10, 281
Halberstam, Jack
 In a Queer Time and Place: Transgender Bodies, Subcultural Lives, 7, 9, 148–9, 196, 198
 The Queer Art of Failure, 176, 289
 Skin Shows: Gothic Horror and the Technology of Monsters, 41–2, 136, 240, 246
 'Telling Tales: Brandon Teena, Billy Tipton, and Transgender Biography', 174
Trans*" A Quick and Quirky Account of Gender Variability, 151
Hale, C. Jacob, 'Consuming the Living, Dismembering the Dead', 178
Halperin, David M., 'Why Gay Shame Now?', 142
Hancock, Michael, 'Doppelgamers: Video Games and Gothic Choice', 265
Hanson, Ellis
 'Queer Gothic', 210
 'Undead', 158
Harry Potter slash fiction, 12
Hasted, Rachel A. C., *The Pendle Witch Trial 1612*, 192
Hays Code (Motion Picture Production Code US), 9, 124, 289
hermaphrodite and hermaphroditic *see* intersex
hillbilly horror/hillbilly slashers, 282
Hirschfeld, Magnus
 Anders als die Andern (*Different From the Others*), 8, 82, 89–93
 Die Homosexualität des Mannes und Weibes (*Homosexuality of Men and Women*), 80
 Institut für Sexualwissenschaft (Institute for Sexual Studies, Berlin), 8, 81–2
 Jahrbuch für sexualle Zwischenstufen (*Yearbook for Sexual Intermediates*), 80–1
 Scientific-Humanitarian Committee (SHC), 80
 Transvestites, 81
Hollinger, Veronica, 'Fantasies of Absence: The Postmodern Vampire', 117
Holmes, Clive, 'Women, Witches and Witnesses', 190
Horner, Avril and Sue Zlosnik
 Gothic and the Comic Turn, 111n
 'No Country for Old Women: Gender, Age, and the Gothic', 98
Hughes, William, *Key Concepts in the Gothic*, 4
Hughes, William and Andrew Smith, *Queering the Gothic*, 5,6, 191, 210, 269, 291

Hurley, Kelly, *The Gothic Body: Sexuality, Materialism, and Degeneration at the 'Fin de Siècle*, 56–7n
Hutcheon, Linda, *A Poetics of Postmodernism: History, Theory, Fiction*, 197

incest
  The Castle of Otranto (Walpole), 20, 23–4, 26, 40
  Ginger Snaps, 157
  in Halberstam's theory of *Frankenstein*, 41
  The Mystery of Edwin Drood (Dickens), 52
  in slash fiction, 248
intersex
  in Arthur Machen, 68–9
  definition of *baeddel* in Old English, 190
  in *Harry Potter* slash fiction, 250
  in *Jahrbuch für sexualle Zwischenstufen* (*Yearbook for Sexual Intermediates*), 80–1
  regarding Rowling controversy, 244
  in Vaginal Davis's art, F5, 234–6
  in Wilkie Collins, 47–8, 50
Isherwood, Christopher
  Christopher and His Kind, 79
  Goodbye to Berlin, 79

Jackson, Rosemary, *Fantasy: The Literature of Subversion*, 191
Jenkins, Henry, 'Game Design as Narrative Architecture', 273
Jenzen, Olu, 'The Queer Uncanny', 288–9, 292
Johnson, Samuel, *A Dictionary of the English Language*, 23–4

Kafer, Alison, *Feminist, Queer, Crip*, 35n
Kaposi's Sarcoma (KS), 295–97, 231, 302
Kearney, Michael, 'La Llorona as a Social Symbol', 279
Keats, John, *Lamia*, 215–16, 218
Kent, Elizabeth, 'Masculinity and Male Witches in Old and New England', 190

Kilgour, Maggie, *The Rise of the Gothic Novel*, 227–8, 235
Kinnard, Roy, *Horror in Silent Films: A Filmography, 1896–1929*, 85
Koestenbaum, Wayne, *Double Talk: The Erotics of Male Literary Collaboration*, 212
Krafft-Ebing, Richard von, *Psychopathia Sexualis with Especial Reference to Contrary Sexual Instinct: A Medico-Legal Study*, 8, 43–4, 50, 58–60, 63–73, 79–80
Kristeva, Julia, *Powers of Horror*, 288
Krobová, Tereza, et al, 'Dressing Commander Shepard in Pink: Queer Playing in a Heteronormative Game Culture', 262–3, 265
Kuzniar, Alice, *The Queer German Cinema*, 82–3

Lady Saika, 'Sexualized Satrudays: The Everyone is Gay Trope in Fanfiction', 251
Lafleur, Greta, '"Defective in One of the Principal Parts of Virility": Impotence, Generation, and Defining Disability in Early North America', 23
Lamar, M.
  Black queer artist, 12
  Legacies, F8, 239–40
  Mapplethorpe's Whip, F7, 238–9
  'Negrogothic', 238
  Negro Antichrist, F9, 239–40
Le Fanu, Josheph Sheridan, *Carmilla*, 9, 119–20, 125–6, 128–9
Lehrer, Riva, 'Golem Girl Gets Lucky', 26–7
Lewis, C. Day, 'A Hope for Poetry', 211
Lewis, M. G., *The Monk*, 7, 20, 26–9, 33, 38–40, 109, 237–8
Lindqvist, John Ajvide, *Hanteringen av odöda* (*Handling the Undead*), 140
Love, Heather, *Feeling Backward: Loss and the Politics of Queer History*, 177

Macdonald, D. L. and Kathleen Scherf, 133n

MacDonald, Tanis, '"Out by Sixteen": Queer(ed) Girls in *Ginger Snaps*', 254
McGavran, James Holt, '"Insurmountable barriers to our union": Homosocial Male Bondin, Homosexual Panic, and Death on Ice in Frankenstein', 245
Machen, Arthur, *The Great God Pan*, 8, 66–70, 73
McKenna, Neil, *The Secret Life of Oscar Wilde*, 245
McLaren, Angus, *Sexual Blackmail: A Modern History*, 118
McRuer, Robert, *Crip Theory: Cultural Signs of Queerness and Disability*, 35n
McRuer, Robert and Anna Mollow, *Sex and Disability*, 35n
Mattel, Trixie, 'UNHhhh Ep. 131: Straight People', 100
Mahon, Alyce, *The Marquis de Sade and the Avant-Garde*, 20
Major!, 312n
Malakaj, Ervin, 'Richard Oswald, Magnus Hirschfeld, and the Possible Impossibility of Hygienic Melodrama', 90–1
Mann, Craig Ian, *Phases of the Moon: A Cultural History of the Werewolf Film*, 154–6, 170
Marryat, Florence, *The Blood of the Vampire*, 121–3
Marsh, Richard, *The Beetle*, 5
Marshall, Bridget M., *The Transatlantic Gothic Novel and the Law, 1790–1860*, 59
Marshall, Nowell, 'Beyond Queer Gothic: Charting the Gothic History of the Trans Subject in Beckford, Lewis, Byron', 40
Mbembe, Achille, 'Necropolitics', 237
Meerscheidt-Hüllessem, Leopold von, 79–81
Méliès, George
  Cleopatra, 85
  Escamotage d'une dame Chez Robert-Houdin (*Conjuring a Lady at Robert Houdin's*), 85
  Un homme de têtes (*The Four Troublesome Heads*), 85

Mellor, Anne K.
  Romanticism and Feminism, 213
  Romanticism and Gender, 42
Mendik, Xavier, 'Menstrual Meanings: Brett Sullivan Discusses Werewolves Hormonal Horror and the Ginger Snaps Audience Research Project', 255
Mercurio, Marisa, 155–6
Meyers, Moe, *The Politics and Poetics of Camp*, 97
Michie, Helena, '"There is no Friend Like a Sister": Sisterhood as Sexual Difference', 219
Mighall, Robert, 'Diagnosing Jekyll: The Scientific Context to Dr Jekyll's Experiment and Mr Hyde's Embodiment', 74n
Miles, Robert, *Gothic Writing, 1750–1820*, 102
Miller, D. A., *The Novel and the Police*, 47–8
Milton, John, *Paradise Lost*, 209
Miss Major Griffin-Gracy, 309
Moers, Ellen, 'Female Gothic: The Monster's Mother', 273
Moore, Frank, curator of *A Living Testament of the Blood Fairies*, 305
Moran, Leslie J., 'Law and the Gothic Imagination', 59
Morgan, Thäis, 'Male Lesbian Bodies: The Construction of Alternative Masculinities in Courbet, Baudelaire, and Swinburne', 220
Morowitz, Laura, 'The Monster Within: *The Munsters*, *The Addams Family* and the American Family in the 1960's', 101
Motion Picture Production Code (Hays Code US), 124–6
Muñoz, Jose Esteban
  Cruising Utopia: The Then and There of Queer Futurity, 1, 3, 6, 26, 149–50
  '"The White to Be Angry": Vaginal Davis's Terrorist Drag', 235

Nathan, Emily, 'Southern Gothic and Goth-Kid Makeup: M. Lamar on Racialized Art and Black Leather', 238

National Endowment for the Arts (NEA)
censored queer artists with AIDS, 299
culture wars and controversial funding, 299
Ron Athey and controversy, 301
Senator Jesse Helms and Evangelical outcry against the NEA, 299
Wojnarowicz and controversy, 300–1
non-binary
in Allard, 176–9, 186
in Garland,
in Wilkie Collins, 47, 50, 53–4
Nussbaum, Felicity, '"Savage Mothers": Narratives of Maternity in the Mid-Eighteenth Century', 22, 26

older women
Les 120 Journées de Sodome (*The 120 Days of Sodom*) (Sade), 17–19, 29–33
as camp artifacts, 99
The Castle of Otranto (Walpole), 20–6
The Monk (Lewis), 20, 26–9
'No Country for Old Women: Gender, Age and the Gothic' (Horner and Zlosnik), 98
Rebecca, 9, 124
Oldridge, Darren, 'Witchcraft and Gender', 190
Orme, Jennifer, 'Mouth to Mouth: Queer Desires in Emma Donoghue's "Kissing the Witch"', 199
O'Rourke, Michael and David Collings, 'Queer Romanticism: Past, Present, and Future', 210
Ortiz, Luna Luis, 307–9

Paciorek, Andy, 'Folk Horror: From the Forest, Fields, and Furrows: An Introduction', 280–1
paganism and neo-paganism, 281, 283–8, 292
Paglia, Camille, 'The Stiletto Heel', 108
Palmer, Paulina
'Lesbian Gothic: Genre, Transformation, Transgression', 194–5

The Queer Uncanny: New Perspectives on the Gothic, 210
Parkin-Gounelas, Ruth, *Literature and Psychoanalysis: Intertextual Readings*, 194
Partridge, Norman, *Dark Harvest*, 13, 290–2
Penny Arcade, *Bitch! Dyke! Faghag! Whore*, 305
Pierse, Alison, *After Dracula: The 1930s Horror Film*, 158
Poe, Edgar Allan, *The Fall of the House of* Usher, 275
Polar Gothic, 271–2
Polidori, John William, *The Vampyre*, 9, 117–20, 131, 133, 229–30
Poole, Robert, *The Lancashire Witches: Histories and Stories*, 193
Port, Cynthia, 'No Future? Aging, Temporality, History, and Reverse Chronologies', 20, 26
Prins, Yopie, *Victorian Sappho*, 220
Prosser, Jay, *Second Skins: The Body Narratives of Transsexuality*, 185
Punter, David, *Edinburgh Companion to Gothic and the Arts*, 4
Purkiss, Diane, *The Witch in History: Early Modern and Twentieth-Century Representations*, 190

queer crip
Les 120 Journées de Sodome (*The 120 Days of Sodom*) (Sade), 17–20, 29–34
The Castle of Otranto (Lewis), 20–6, 34
The Deformed Transformed (Byron), 34
Frankenstein (Shelley), 34
Jane Eyre (Brontë), 34
The Monk (Lewis), 20, 26–9, 34
Our Mutual Friend (Dickens), 34
Strange Case of Dr Jekyll and Mr Hyde (Stevenson), 34
The Woman in White (Collins), 34
Queer Nation, 1

Radcliffe, Ann
The Mysteries of Udolpho, 39, 40
The Romance of the Forest, 39

Ray, Ricky, Robert and Randy (haemophilia and AIDS panic), 296
Reagan, Ronald (US President 1980–1988), 309
Redekop, Corey, *Husk: A Novel*, 138–9
Renate, Lorenz, *Queer Art: A Freak Theory*, 240
Reynolds, Daniel, 'How *What We Do in the Shadows* Became Cable's Queerest Comedy', 135n
Rice, Anne, *Interview with the Vampire*, 126–8, 230
Richards, Mary, 'Ron Athey, A.I.D.S. and the Politics of Pain', 302
Rich, Adrienne, 'Compulsory Heterosexuality and Lesbian Existence', 217
Rigby, Mair, 'Uncanny Recognition: Queer Theory's Debt to the Gothic', 191, 291
Robertson, Pamela, *Guilty Pleasures: Feminist Camp from Mae West to Madonna*, 106
Romantic Age literature
  Les 120 Journées de Sodome (The 120 Days of Sodom) (Donatien Alphonse François, Marquis de Sade), 7, 17–21, 29–34
  The Castle of Otranto (Walpole), 7, 11, 18–26, 39, 40, 210, 226–7, 245
  'Childe Roland to the Dark Tower Came'(Browning), 216–17
  Christabel (Coleridge), 11, 217–19
  The Deformed Transformed (Byron), 34
  The Episodes of Vathek, 39
  Frankenstein: or, The Modern Prometheus (Shelley), 7, 11, 34, 41–2, 209, 229, 233–4
  The Ghost of a Flea (Blake), F2, 11, 229, 231
  'Kubla Kahn'(Coleridge), 11, 213–14, 217
  Lyrical Ballads (Coleridge and Wordsworth), 212, 217
  'The Lady of Shalott' (Tennyson), 212, 216
  The Monk (Lewis), 7, 20, 26–9, 33, 38–40, 109, 237–8, 245
  'My Last Duchess'(Browning), 216
  The Mysteries of Udolpho (Radcliffe), 39–40
  The Nightmare (Fuseli), F1, 11, 226–7, 229
  Northanger Abbey (Austen), 210
  'Porphyria's Lover' (Browning), 212
  The Romance of the Forest (Radcliffe), 39
  'The Thorn'(Wordsworth), 213–14
  The Vampyre (Polidori), 9, 11, 117–20, 131, 133, 229–30
  Vathek (Beckford), 39, 40
  Zafloya, or, The Moor (Dacre), 7, 38, 40–1, 44, 52
Roper, Lyndal, *The Witch in the Western Imagination*, 191
Rossetti, Christina, 'Goblin Market', 11, 53, 219–20
Rossetti, Dante Gabriel, illustrations for *Goblin Market and Other Poems*, 219
Rossetti, William Michael, *The Poetical Works of Christina Georgina Rossetti*, 220
Ross, Andrew, 'Uses of Camp', 102
Rowland, Diana, 'White Trash Zombie' series, 137
Rowling, J. K., *Harry Potter Wizarding World* franchise, 244

Sade, Donatien Alphonse François, Marquis de, *Les 120 Journées de Sodome (The 120 Days of Sodom)*, 7, 17–21, 29–34
Saint Sebastian
  depictions in Derek Jarman's *Sebastiane*, 303
  depictions in Giovanni Antonio Bazzi's (Il Sodoma) painting, 302
  depictions in Guido Reni's painting, 302
  depictions in Yukio Mishima's *Confessions of a Mask*, 303
  staging in Ron Athey's performance art, 303
Scarre, Geoffrey, *Witchcraft and Magic in Sixteenth and Seventeenth-Century Europe*, 190
Schaffer, Talia, '"A Wilde Desire Took Me": The Homoerotic History of *Dracula*', 245

Scheunemann, Dietrich, 'The Double, the Décor, and the Framing Device: Once More on Robert Wiene's *The Cabinet of Dr. Caligari*', 86
Scovell, Adam, *Folk Horror: Hours, Dreadful and Things Strange*, 279–81, 285
Sean Dorsey Dance, 309
Sedgwick, Eve Kosofsky
  Between Men: English Literature and Male Homosocial Desire, 52, 84, 119, 195
  The Coherence of Gothic Conventions, 191, 209, 227
  Tendencies, 212, 230
Senf, Carol A., *The Vampire in 19th-Century Literature*, 133n
sex work
  in *Elvira, Mistress of the Dark*, 106–7, 109
  in *Screaming Queens: The Riot at Compton's*, 114n
sexology
  Anders als die Andern (*Different From the Others*), 8, 82,89–93
  Hirschfeld, Magnus, 8, 80–2, 89–93
  Die Homosexualität des Mannes und Weibes (*Homosexuality of Men and Women*) (Hirschfeld), 80
  Institut für Sexualwissenschaft (Institute for Sexual Studies, Berlin), 8, 81–2
  Jahrbuch für sexuelle Zwischenstufen (*Yearbook for Sexual Intermediates*) (Hirschfeld), 80–1
  Krafft-Ebing, Richard von, 8, 43–4, 50, 58–60, 63–73, 79–80
  Lombroso, Cesare, 48
  Psychopathia Sexualis (Krafft-Ebing), 8, 43–4, 50, 58–60, 63–73
  Scientific-Humanitarian Committee (SHC), 80
  Sexual Inversion (Ellis), 71
  sexual taxonomies in the Victorian Age, 42–4, 48, 50
  Studies in the Psychology of Sex, Volume 2 (Ellis), 43–4
  Studies on the Riddle of Male–Male Love (Ulrichs), 79
  Transvestites (Hirschfeld), 81
Sha, Richard, 'Romanticism and Sexuality – A Special Issue of Romanticism on the Net', 210, 212
Shan, Darren, *Zom-B* series, 137
Sharpe, Cristina, *In the Wake: On Blackness and Being*, 236
Shelley, Mary *Frankenstein: or, The Modern Prometheus*, 7, 34, 41–2, 229, 233–4, 245, 272
Shelley, Percy Bysshe, 'Mont Blanc', 214–15
Showalter, Elaine, *Sexual Anarchy: Gender and Culture at the Fin de Siècle*, 60
Silva, Cynthia, '"Tell me Why": Video Game Features Transgender Lead Character', 269
slash fandom websites
  Adult FanFiction.org, 256
  Archive of Our Own, 248
  ArtisticAlley, 252
  Fanfiction.net, 256
  Fanlore, 247, 251–2
  LiveJournal, 247–9, 252
  Potter Puppet Pals, 252
  Veritaserum, 252
slash fiction
  The Adventures of Sherlock Holmes, 245
  Buffy the Vampire Slayer, 245, 253
  Ginger Snaps, 245–8, 253–8
  Ginger Snaps Back: The Beginning, 254
  Ginger Snaps 2: Unleashed, 254
  Harry Potter, 245–53, 256–8
  Star Trek, 246
  Stealing Harry Verse Collection, 247
  Supernatural, 245, 248
  Twilight, 245
slash fiction modes
  Drarry erotica in *Harry Potter*, 249–50, 253
  fanvids, 252
  femslash, 247
  genderswap, 248
  incest, 248
  manips, 249, 256
  M/M, 247–9, 253, 256
  Mpreg, 248–50
  online video recording (*Harry Potter*), 252–3
  OT3, 249
  OT4, 249

smut vids, 256
Veelafic, 251
Smith, Andrew, *Victorian Demons: Medicine, Masculinity and the Gothic at the Fin-de-Siècle*, 59
Snorton, C. Riley, *Black on Both Sides: A Racial History of Trans Identity*, 236
sodomy
　Les 120 Journées de Sodome (*The 120 Days of Sodom*) (Sade), 30, 32–3
　in Oscar Wilde's trials, 118, 121
sodomy laws
　Bowers v Hardwick (US), 312n
　CLA Bill, sexual acts between women (UK), 122
　Cocks, H. G., *Nameless Offences: Homosexual Desire in the Nineteenth Century*, 118
　Department of Homosexuality and Blackmail, Weimar Berlin, Leopold von Meerscheidt-Hüllessem and Hans von Tresckow, 79–81
　Lawrence v Texas (US), 311–12n
　McLaren, Angus, *Sexual Blackmail: A Modern History*, 118
　Paragraph 175 of the German Penal Code, 79–80, 90, 92–3
　Section 11 Criminal Law Amendment Act (Labouchère Amendment) (England), 58–61, 69, 118, 121
Sontag, Susan, 'Notes on "Camp"', 97, 106–7
Sparks, Tabitha, *The Doctor in the Victorian Novel: Family Practices*, 59
spectres
　in *Anders als die Andern* (*Different from the Others*), 91
　gay male in 'The Country House' (Currier), 10, 176, 181–4, 186
　lesbian in *Ghosts of Winter* (Buck), 10, 176, 179–82, 186
　of suicide in *Anders als die Andern* (*Different from the Others*), 92
　trans and gender non-conforming in *Légende: The Story of Philippa and Aurelie* (Allard), 10, 176–9, 186
　trans and gender non-conforming in *The Night Brother* (Garland), 10, 176, 184–6
Spooner, Catherine
　Fashioning Gothic Bodies, 108
　Post-Millennial Gothic: Comedy, Romance and the Rise of Happy Gothic, 111n
Spooner, Catherine and Emma McEvoy, *The Routledge Companion to Gothic*, 19–20
Stafford, Tim, 'Lie and Lycanthropy: The New Pack Werewolf According to Tyler, Tyler and Taylor', 168–9
Starbuck, Sam, *The Stealing Harry Verse Collection*, 247, 249
sterility, 20–6
Stevenson, Robert Louis, *Strange Case of Dr Jekyll and Mr Hyde*, 8, 34, 59–64, 67, 71, 73
Stewart, Garrett, '*Lamia* and the Language of Metamorphosis', 215
Stobbart, Dawn
　'Playing the Future History of Humanity: Situating *Fallout 3* as a Narratological Artefact', 273
　Videogames and Horror: From Amnesia to Zombies, Run!, 273
Stoker, Bram, *Dracula*, 8, 70–3, 120–1, 123, 126, 133, 229–30, 232–3, 239, 245
Stonewall Rebellion, 1, 2, 79, 174, 307, 14n; *see also* Gay Liberation Movement
Strantzas, Simon, 'The King of Stones', 13, 287–9
Stryker, Jeff, 305
Stryker, Susan
　'(De) Subjugated Knowledges: An Introduction to Transgender Studies', 43
　'My Words to Victor Frankenstein above the Village of Chamounix: Performing Transgender Rage', 42, 234
　Screaming Queens: The Riot at Compton's (with Victor Silverman), 114n
Swinburne, Algernon Charles, 'Anactoria', 11, 220

Tamàs, Rebecca, *Witch*, 11, 191, 200–3
Tarr, Clayton Carlyle, 'Pleasurable Suspension: Erotic Asphyxiation in the Nineteenth Century', 212
Tennyson, Lord Alfred, 'The Lady of Shalott', 212, 216

Thompson, Kristin and David Bordwell, *Film History: An Introduction*, 87
Thornam, Helen, *Ethnographies of the Videogame*, 265
transphobia in J. K. Rowling's commentary, 244, 266
Traub, Valerie, *The Renaissance of Lesbianism in Early Modern England*, 175
Trimm, Ryan, 'Witching Welcome', 177
Tryon, Thomas, *Harvest Home*, 1, 283–5, 288
Tucker, Herbert, "Rossetti's Goblin Marketing: Sweet to Tongue and Sound to Eye', 219
twentieth-century literature
  Christopher and His Kind (Isherwood), 79
  The Gilda Stories (Gomez), 128–130
  Goodbye to Berlin (Isherwood), 79
  Harvest Home (Tryon), 1, 283–5, 288
  'Howl' (Ginsberg), 154
  Hunger for You (Frame), 130–2
  Interview with the Vampire (Rice), 126
  Kissing the Witch: Old Tales in New Skins (Donoghue), 11
  Légende: The Story of Philippa and Aurelie (Allard), 10, 176–9, 186
twenty-first-century literature
  'The Country House' (Currier), 10, 176, 181–4, 186
  Dark Harvest (Partridge), 13, 290–2
  The Daylight Gate (Winterson), 10–11, 191–6, 203
  'Eulogy for the 40th (Driskill), 309
  Generation Dead (Waters), 137
  The Ghosts of Winter (Buck), 10, 176, 179–82, 186
  Husk: A Novel (Redekop), 138–9
  'The Lancashire Witches'(Duffy), 11, 191, 196–8, 203
  The Night Brother (Garland), 10, 176, 184–6
  A Soul to Keep (Weatherspoon), 130–2

Ulrichs, Karl Heinrich, *Studies on the Riddle of Male–Male Love*, 79

vampires
  Blacula, 9, 98, 103–5
  Bloodthirsty, 157
  The Blood of the Vampire (Marryat), 121–3
  Buffy the Vampire Slayer, slash fiction, 12
  Byron, Lord George Gordon, 118–19, 131
  Carmilla (Le Fanu), 9, 119–20, 125–6, 128–9
  Daughters of Darkness, 230
  Dracula (Stoker), 8, 70–3, 84, 120–1, 123, 126, 133, 229–30, 232–3, 239
  Dracula, 123
  Dracula's Daughter, 9, 123–4
  Et Mourir de Plaisir (*Blood and Roses*), 125
  The Gilda Stories (Gomez), 128–30
  The Hunger, 124, 230
  Hunger for You (Frame), 130–2
  Interview with the Vampire (Rice), 126–8, 230
  Interview with the Vampire, 126–8, 230
  Nosferatu: A Symphony of Horror, 8, 83–4, 86, 89, 123 123
  Rebecca, 9, 124
  A Soul to Keep (Weatherspoon), 130–2
  True Blood, 230
  Twilight, 230
  The Vampire Lovers, 9, 125
  Vampire Slut (Starling), 307
  The Vampyre (Polidori), 9, 117–20, 131, 133
  Vampyros Lesbos, 9, 125
  What We Do in the Shadows, 132–3
Vicinus, Martha, 'They Wonder to Which Sex I Belong: The Historical Roots of the Modern Lesbian Identity', 174–5
Victorian Age literature
  'Anactoria' (Swinburne), 11, 220
  Armadale (Collins), 47
  The Beetle (Marsh), 5
  The Blood of the Vampire (Marryat), 121–3
  Carmilla (Le Fanu), 9, 119–20, 125–6, 128–9
  The Dead Secret (Collins), 47
  Dracula (Stoker), 8, 70–3, 84, 120–1, 123, 126, 133, 209, 229–30, 232–3, 239

The Fall of the House of Usher (Poe), 275
'Goblin Market' (Rossetti), 53
Great Expectations (Dickens), 52
The Great God Pan (Machen), 8, 66–70, 73
The Grey Woman (Gaskell), 5–6
Jane Eyre (Brontë), 7, 34, 44–6
The Law and the Lady (Collins), 7, 47, 50–2
Little Dorrit (Dickens), 44
The Mystery of Edwin Drood (Dickens), 52
Our Mutual Friend (Dickens), 7, 34, 52–3
No Name (Collins), 47
The Picture of Dorian Gray (Wilde), 210, 245
Psychopathia Sexualis with Especial Reference to Contrary Sexual Instinct: A Medico-Legal Study (Krafft-Ebing), 8, 43–4
Strange Case of Dr Jekyll and Mr Hyde (Stevenson), 8, 34, 59–64, 67, 71, 73
The Woman in White (Collins), 7, 34, 47–52
video games
  Amnesia: The Dark Descent, 274
  Coming Out on Top, 266
  Dream Daddy: A Dad Dating Simulator, 266
  Dys4ia, 266
  Gone Home, 273–5
  The Last of Us, 266
  The Last of Us2, 267–8, 270, 276
  Resident Evil, 273
  Second Life, 267
  Silent Hill, 273
  Tell Me Why, 263, 267, 270–2, 275
video game modes, BBS, 263–4

Walpole, Horace, *The Castle of Otranto*, 7, 18–26, 39, 40, 210, 226–7, 245
Warner, Marina, *Fantastic Metamorphoses, Other Worlds: Ways of Telling the Self*, 192
Waters, Daniel, *Generation Dead*, 137
Waters, Jack, 'Portrait of the Artist as a Sex Bomb', 304–5
Waters, John, queer filth cinema, 290
Weatherspoon, Rebekah, *A Soul to Keep*, 130–2
Webber, Andrew, *The Doppelgänger: Double Visions in German Literature*, 84
Weimar Republic
  Anders als die Andern (Different From the Others), 8, 82, 89–93
  Arrival of a Train at La Ciotat, 85
  in *Babylon Berlin*, 78
  Berlin's cabaret culture and nightlife, 78–9
  Cabaret, 78–9
  Das Cabinet des Dr. Caligari (The Cabinet of Dr. Caligari), 87–9, 92–3
  Christopher and His Kind (Isherwood), 79
  The Danish Girl, 82
  Department of Homosexuality and Blackmail, Weimar Berlin, Leopold von Meerscheidt-Hüllessem and Hans von Tresckow, 79–81
  doppelgänger as trope, 84, 86, 89–93
  Elbe, Lili (early gender affirmation surgery at Institut für Sexualwissenschaft, 82
  first known gay magazine *Die Freundschaft (Friendship)*, 82
  Goodbye to Berlin (Isherwood), 79
  Hirschfeld, Magnus, 8, 80–2, 89–93
  Ich möchte kein Mann sein (I Don't Want to Be a Man), 83
  Mädchen in Uniform (Girls in Uniform), 82
  Maschinenmensch in Metropolis *(Machine-Human in the Metropolis)*, 86
  Le Mobilier fidèle (The Automatic Moving Company), 86
  Nosferatu: A Symphony of Horror, 8, 83–4, 86, 89, 123
  Paragraph 175 of the German Penal Code, 79–80, 90, 92–3
  queer activism, 78
  Der Student von Prag (The Student of Prague), 8, 86
Weiss, Andrea, *Vampires and Violets: Lesbians in Film* 134n

werewolves
  An American Werewolf in London, 169
  Bloodthirsty, 157
  The Company of Wolves, 157, 169
  The Curse of the Queerwolf, 159–60
  The Curse of the Werewolf, 171n
  Cursed, 161
  Dirty Paws, 167
  Faux Paws, 166
  Ginger Snaps, 157, 245–8, 253–8
  Good Manners, 157
  The Howling, 171n
  I Was A Teenage Werebear!, 163–4
  I Was A Teenage Werewolf, 163
  Penny Dreadful, 161
  psychosis of lycanthropy, 156
  Der Samurai (The Samurai), 163
  She Wolf of London, 156–7
  Silver Bullet, 171n
  Swallow, 167
  Teen Wolf, 161
  werebear, 165
  were-daddy, 165
  Werewolf of London, 158–9
  Werewolf of Washington, 171n
  Werewolf Woman, 157
  Wolfwalkers, 157
  The Wolves of Kromer, 162–3
  The Wolves of Wall Street, 160–1
Westengard, Laura, Gothic Queer Culture: Marginalized Communities and the Ghosts of Insidious Trauma, 111, 210, 233, 295, 303
Whitehead, Colson, Zone One, 148
Wilde, Oscar
  The Picture of Dorian Gray, 210, 245
  trials of 118, 121
Williams, Anne, 'Wicked Women', 202
Williams, Kiyan
  Dirt Eater, F6, 12, 236–8
  Reaching Towards Warmer Suns, 236
Williams, Linda, "Film Bodies: Gender, Genre, and Excess', 169
Winterson, Jeanette, The Daylight Gate, 10–11, 191–6, 203
witches
  case of the Lancashire witches (Pendle witches 1612), 190
  Daemonologie (James I, 1597), 192
  The Daylight Gate (Winterson), 10–11
  Kissing the Witch: Old Tales in New Skins (Donoghue), 11
  'The Lancashire Witches' (Duffy), 11
  The Monk (Lewis),
  Pendle Witch Trials, 197
  Witch (Tamàs), 11
Wojnarowicz, David
  Fire in My Belly, 13, 299–301, 304
  politics of art, 298
Wood, Robin, 'Murnau', 84
Wordsworth, William
  Lyrical Ballads, 212, 217
  'The Thorn', 213–14

Yeats, William Butler, 211
Yuri-World-Ruler, 'G and B' Ginger Snaps fanart, 256

Zigarovich, Jolene
  'Introduction: Transing the Gothic', 20
  'Transgothic Desire in Charlotte Dacre's Zafloya', 40
Zlosnik, Sue and Avril Horner, 'No Country for Old Women: Gender, Age, and the Gothic', 8
zombies
  Breathers: A Zombie's Lament (Browne), 137
  Creatures from the Pink Lagoon, 136
  The Cured, 10, 139–43, 148
  Husk: A Novel (Redekop), 138–9
  In the Flesh, 10, 139–43, 148
  iZombie, 137–8
  L.A. Zombie, 10, 139, 144–6, 150–1
  Otto; Or, Up with Dead People, 10, 139, 144–7, 150–1
  PDS (Partially Deceased Syndrome), 141–3
  Les Revenants (The Returned), 140
  The Walking Dead, 148
  World War Z: An Oral History of the Zombie War (Brooks), 148
  Zone One (Whitehead), 148
Zorilla, Michelle, Video Games and Gender, 265, 267

EU representative:
Easy Access System Europe
Mustamäe tee 50, 10621 Tallinn, Estonia
Gpsr.requests@easproject.com

www.ingramcontent.com/pod-product-compliance
Lightning Source LLC
Chambersburg PA
CBHW050200240426
43671CB00013B/2188